Movers
and Shakers

Movers
and Shakers

The 100 Most Influential Figures in Modern Business

BASIC
BOOKS

A MEMBER OF THE PERSEUS BOOKS GROUP

Cataloging-in-Publication Data is available from the Library of Congress

ISBN 0-7382-0914-7

Basic Books is a member of the Perseus Books Group
Find us on the World Wide Web at **www.basicbooks.com**

Basic Books publications are available at special discounts for bulk purchases in the U.S. by corporations, institutions, and other organizations. For more information, please contact the Special Markets Department at the Perseus Books Group, 11 Cambridge Center, Cambridge, MA 02142, or call (800) 255-1514 or (617) 252-5298, or e-mail j.mccrary@perseusbooks.com.

Text design by Fiona Pike, Pike Design, Winchester, U.K.
Typeset by RefineCatch Limited, Bungay, Suffolk, U.K.

First printing, December 2003
1 2 3 4 5 6 7 8 9 10-

Contents

Contents

A Note to the User

Drawing on the lives and impact of the 100 most influential figures in modern business, **Movers and Shakers** offers concise and colorful overviews of the theories behind, and the practice of, successful international business.

The **management thinkers** section (pp. 1–111) contains over 45 summaries of the lives, careers, and impact of the most world's most influential management gurus and writers, ranging from Peter Drucker to Tom Peters, Sun Tzu to Machiavelli.

The profiles of the **business giants** (pp. 113–358) make up a highly selective gallery of some of the world's most effective leaders and entrepreneurs. As with any list, it is as much distinguished by whom it omits as who is included. Our aim has been to identify the key figures in a range of industries who by their efforts have transformed the way a business is conducted. Being nice is not one of the main criteria; being effective is.

For more information about *Business: The Ultimate Resource*™ and related titles, and to register for your free electronic upgrades, please visit: **www.ultimatebusinessresource.com**.

At the subscriber registration page enter your name, e-mail address, and your password: **mybiz**

Management
Thinkers

R. Meredith Belbin

1926	Born.
1981	Publication of *Management Teams: Why They Succeed or Fail*.
1987	Founds Belbin Associates.
1990	Publication of *The Job Promoters: A Journey to a New Profession*
1993	Publication of *The Coming Shape of Organization* and *Team Roles at Work*.
1997	Publication of *Changing the Way We Work*.
2000	Publication of *Beyond the Team*.
2001	Publication of *Managing without Power*.
	Visiting Professor of Leadership at the University of Exeter, United Kingdom.

Summary

R. Meredith Belbin is acknowledged as the father of team-role theory. As a result of research conducted in the 1970s, he identified eight (later extended to nine) useful roles that are necessary for a successful team. His contribution has gained in significance because of the widespread adoption of teamworking in the late 1980s and 1990s.

Life and Career

Belbin, who was born in 1926, is an academic who has also spent periods working in industry and who now has his own consulting company. It was while working at the Industrial Training Research Unit in Cambridge that he was asked by Henley Management College to conduct some research into the operation of management teams. The college's approach to management education was based on group work, and researchers there had noticed that some teams of individually able executives performed poorly and others well. This impression was reinforced when a business game was introduced to one of the courses. Belbin discovered that it was the contribution of particular personality types, rather than the merits of the individuals themselves, that was important to the success and failure of such teams.

Contribution

There has been a continuing interest in Belbin's work because teamworking is an increasingly important strategy for organizations. There are many reasons for this. Teamworking is variously seen as a means of:
- providing greater worker flexibility and cooperation;
- helping to achieve cultural shifts within an organization;
- improving problem-solving and project management;
- tapping the talents of everyone in the organization.

There are also different types of teams involved in working together, for example, temporary teams, cross-functional teams, top management teams, and self-directed teams. Because of this interest in teams, the issue of team building, including team selection, group dynamics, and team performance, has become particularly vital. Although there are many models of team relationships, such as the Team Management Systems (TMS) developed by Margerison and McCann, Belbin's model is probably the best known.

Team Role Theory

It is important to remember that Belbin's findings relate to teams of managers rather than other types of teams. They were first published in *Management Teams: Why They Succeed or Fail* and later refined in *Team Roles at Work*. In Belbin's own words, a team role "describes a pattern of behavior characteristic of the way in which one team member interacts with another where his performance serves to facilitate the progress of the team as a whole."

The essence of his theory is that, given knowledge of the abilities and characteristics of individual team members, success or failure can be predicted within certain limits. As a result, unsuccessful teams can be improved by analyzing their shortcomings and making changes. But it is also important for individuals within the team to understand the roles that others play, when and how to let another team member take over, and how to compensate for shortcomings. Although each of the eight roles has to be filled for a team to work effectively, the eight roles are not needed in equal measure, nor are they needed at the same time. There can be fewer than eight people in a team, since people are capable of taking on back-up roles where there is less need for them to fulfill a primary team role.

The roles themselves are determined largely by the psychological makeup of the individuals who instinctively adopt them. Four principal factors are involved: intelligence, dominance, extroversion/introversion, and stability/anxiety. Each role demands a particular combination of the four. Any individual can be rated in terms of them. In the list of team role contributions, the ratings for each particular trait are shown.

The Self-Perception Inventory and the *Interplace* System

Belbin devised a self-perception inventory, which has been through several revisions, as a quick and easy way for individual managers to work out what their own team roles should be. It was taken up by organizations and used to determine employees' team types, and it has been questioned whether it is psychometrically acceptable for this purpose. Academics were concerned that it was too subjective and recommended that feedback should come instead from a variety of sources. Belbin answered this criticism by reiterating that the inventory was never designed for this purpose and by developing a computerized system called *Interplace* to cater to the wider needs of organizations.

Interplace is a more sophisticated approach to role analysis than the self-perception inventory because it incorporates feedback from other people, not just the individual concerned. The main inputs to the *Interplace* system use data from self-perception exercises, observer assignments, and job requirement evaluations. *Interplace* filters, scores, stores, converts, and interprets the data gathered. It offers advice based on the three inputs with respect to counseling, team role chemistry, career development, and the behaviors needed in certain jobs and team positions. The system works as a diagnostic and development tool for organizations.

Later Theories

In the 1990s Belbin extended his work on teams to explore the link between teams and the organizational environment in which they operate. He suggested that an effective model for the new flatter organization might be a spiral or helix in which individuals and teams move forward on the basis of excellence rather than of function.

He has also very recently devised a system for defining jobs which he calls "Workset." The aim of the concept is to define the boundaries and content of a job through an interactive communication process between the manager and the jobholder. The system uses color to denote different aspects of the job. There should be five key outcomes:

- the facilitation of empowerment;
- the encouragement of greater job flexibility;
- the promotion of teamworking;
- the support of cultural change;
- a continuous improvement process for jobs and job holders.

It is too early to say what impact the Progression Helix theory or Workset system will have. They are undoubtedly a contribution, however, to management in today's delayered organizations and flexible working environments, with their associated need to involve and communicate with staff.

Context and Conclusions

Although independent recent research has thrown doubt on the existence of eight separate team roles, Belbin's broad findings have not been questioned, nor has the popularity of his theories been disputed. There has been an enduring interest in team role categories on the part of practicing managers in a wide variety of organizations. This is because:

- there is an increasing interest in teamworking;
- Belbin made his ideas accessible to the lay person;
- Belbin is recognized as the first to develop our understanding of the dynamics of teams.

For More Information

Books:
Belbin, R. Meredith. *Management Teams: Why They Succeed or Fail*. Woburn, MA: Heinemann, 1981.
Belbin, R. Meredith. *Team Roles at Work*. Woburn, MA: Butterworth-Heinemann, 1993.
Belbin, R. Meredith. *The Coming Shape of Organization*. Woburn, MA: Butterworth-Heinemann, 1996.
Belbin, R. Meredith. *Changing the Way We Work*. Woburn, MA: Heinemann, 1997.

Journal Articles:
Belbin, R. Meredith, Barrie Watson, and Cindy West. "True Colours." *People Management*, 6 March 1997, pp. 36–38, 41.
Furnham, Adrian, Howard Steele and David Pendleton. "A Psychometric Assessment of the Belbin Team Role Self-perception Inventory." *Journal of Occupational and Organizational Psychology*, vol. 66 no 3, 1993, pp. 245–261 (This article includes Belbin's criticism of the research and the response of the authors).

Senior, Barbara. "An Empirically-based Assessment of Belbin's Team Roles." *Human Resource Management Journal*, vol. 8 no 3, 1998, pp. 54–60.

Web site:
www.belbin.com contains a useful list of answers to frequently asked questions about team role theory, as well as an online team analysis and reports service. It also contains helpful information on Belbin's latest work on Work Roles.

Warren Bennis

1925	Born.
1959	Sets up department for organizational studies at MIT.
1967	Appointed Provost of State University of New York (SUNY).
1971	President of the University of Cincinnati.
1979	Professor of Management at the University of Southern California.
1985	Publication of *Leaders: The Strategies for Taking Charge*.
1989	Publication of *On Becoming a Leader*.
1997	Publication of *Organizing Genius*.

Summary

Warren Bennis has worked as an educator, writer, administrator, and consultant, besides authoring or coauthoring many books on different topics. He has performed highly respected work in the areas of small group dynamics, change in social systems, T-groups, and sensitivity training, and during the 1960s became a recognized futurologist. Bennis wrote his first article on leadership in 1959, and he has become a widely accepted authority on the subject since 1985, when *Leaders* was published.

Life and Career

Bennis was born in New York in 1925 and educated at Antioch College, Ohio, and the Massachusetts Institute of Technology (MIT). Later, he studied group dynamics, and during the 1950s was involved in the U.S. National Training Laboratories teamworking experiments. His early field of work was organizational development. Bennis was a great admirer of Douglas McGregor and his "Theory Y" approach to motivation. In fact, Bennis became very close to McGregor and was strongly influenced by him. His career path even followed McGregor's to some extent. First, he was an undergraduate student at Antioch College while McGregor was President there, and later, in 1959, he was recruited by McGregor to establish a new department for organization studies at MIT. From the late 1960s, Bennis's career moved for a time from academic research and teaching to administration. He became Provost at the State University of New York (SUNY), Buffalo, in 1967, staying there until 1971, when he moved to take on the post of President of the University of Cincinnati.

As an administrative leader from 1967 to 1978, Bennis attempted to put McGregor's motivation theories into practice, and found them unworkable without some adaptation in the form of strengthened structure and direction.

During the 1960s, Bennis became known as a student of the future, and predicted (with coauthor Philip Slater in a March 1964 article for the *Harvard Business Review* called "Democracy Is Inevitable") the downfall of communism in the face of inevitable democracy. By the mid-1960s, he was predicting the demise of bureaucratic organization. His 1968 book, *The Temporary Society*, explored new forms of organization, advocating an "adhocracy" of free-moving project teams as a necessity for the future. This idea has since been taken up by other writers, such as Alvin Toffler and Henry Mintzberg.

In an adhocracy, responsibility and leadership are distributed to groups or task forces on the basis of the relevance of members' qualifications or abilities for the specific task or purpose of the group. For Bennis, adhocracy was an important concept as a counter to hierarchy, centralized control, and bureaucratic organization.

Contribution

In his early book on leadership, *The Unconscious Conspiracy* (1976), Bennis highlights how leaders can positively influence others to bring about change. His most distinctive ideas on the subject, however, partly grew out of the broad, general response to a landmark *Harvard Business Review* article of 1977 by Abraham Zaleznik (then Professor of Social Psychology of Management at Harvard).

The Zaleznik article was entitled "Managers and Leaders—Are They Different?" Bennis's research and writing were extreme in emphasizing a complete, qualitative difference between management and leadership, and he drew up a list of sharp distinctions that ended with the now familiar aphorism: "Managers do things right, leaders do the right thing." While Bennis considers that managers can become leaders through learning and development, he is firm about the functional differences between the roles and the approaches involved, and the distinctions he draws echo throughout most of his writings on leadership.

The Leaders Study

In 1979, on his return to research and teaching as Professor of Management at the University of Southern California, Bennis sought to unravel the lessons of his practical experience of leadership. He explored the subject through a 1985 serial study that was published as a book coauthored with Burt Nanus, called *Leaders: The Strategies for Taking Charge* (1985). While Bennis has written or cowritten many other books relating to leadership, these largely expand on the ideas developed in *Leaders*.

Leaders aimed to identify common characteristics among 90 successful American leaders who had all, the authors considered, demonstrated "mastery over present confusion" in their careers. The leaders ranged from an orchestra conductor to Ray Kroc, the founder of McDonalds, and included a baseball player and a tightrope walker, as well as the astronaut Neil Armstrong. It was Bennis's second book on leadership, selling over 300,000 copies, and is still considered an important text on the subject.

In *Leaders*, Bennis and Nanus identify four common factors amongst the subjects, and these form the core of their ideas about leadership.

- Attention through vision—all had an agenda, an intense vision and commitment that drew others in. The leaders also gave much attention to other people.
- Meaning through communication—all had an ability to communicate their vision and bring it to life for others, sometimes using drawings or models as well as metaphor and analogy.
- Trust through positioning—through establishing a position with a set of actions to implement their vision, and staying the course, the leaders established trust.
- The deployment of self through positive self-regard—the creative deployment of self is essential to leadership, involving an honest appreciation of oneself and one's own worth, and instilling confidence in others.

Positive self-regard is related to "emotional wisdom," and five key skills in emotional wisdom are given as the abilities to:

- accept others as they are;
- approach things in terms of only the present;
- treat others, even familiar contacts, with courteous attention;
- trust others, even where the risk seems high;
- do without constant approval and recognition.

One quality common to these leaders that Bennis and Nanus particularly distinguished was their way of responding to failure as a learning experience. Karl Wallenda, the great tightrope aerialist, was taken as a main example. The authors illustrate his manner of putting his energies completely into his task, thinking of failure as a mistake from which he could learn, and viewing this experience (of learning based on failure) as a new beginning, rather than the end, for a project or idea.

"Transformative" Leadership

The style of leadership discussed by Bennis and Nanus is termed "transformative," in that it is said to have an empowering effect on others, enabling them to translate intentions into reality. A transformative leadership style is described as one that motivates through identification with the leader's vision, pulling rather than pushing others on.

Four elements of empowerment are distinguished as:

- significance—a feeling of making a difference;
- competence—development and learning "on the job";
- community—a sense of interreliance and involvement in a common cause;
- enjoyment—capacity to have fun at work because it is enjoyable and involving.

The four major characteristics of transformative leaders identified earlier are linked to strategic approaches through which a leader leads.

- The creation of a compelling vision: a leader must develop and communicate an image, or vision, of a credible and attractive future for the organization.
- The translation of meaning into social architecture: social architecture is the intangible variable that translates the buzz and confusion of organizational life into meaning. While similar to culture, social architecture is more precise in meaning, in that it can be defined, assessed, and, to some extent, managed. Three styles of social architecture are distinguished as formalistic, collegial, and personalistic.
- The position of the organization in the outside world: positioning of an organization is described as the process by which it establishes a viable niche in its environment. It encompasses all that must be done to align the internal and external environments of the organization.
- The development of organizational learning: good leaders are experts at learning within an organizational context, and their behavior can help to direct and energize innovative learning within the organization as a whole.

The end result of transformative leadership is, Bennis and Nanus consider, an empowering environment and accompanying culture, enabling employees to generate a sense of meaning in their work. Higher profits and wages, the authors suggest, inevitably accompany this sort of culture, if it is genuinely established.

At the end of the book, five myths about leadership are identified and contradicted.

- That leadership is a rare skill—it is not.

- That leaders are born—they are not.
- That leaders are charismatic—most are ordinary.
- That leadership can exist only at the "top"—it is relevant at all levels.
- That leaders control, direct, and manipulate—they do not. Transformative leaders align the energies of others behind an attractive goal.

Later Work

A later, prominent book by Bennis, *On Becoming a Leader* (1989), looks at learning to lead and how leadership can be taught. It uses 29 well-known Americans as case studies to illustrate leadership qualities. Its main message suggests that leadership involves continual learning, development, and the reinvention of the self. Bennis has since written or cowritten many books and articles that develop his ideas on leadership. His more recent works focus on the important roles of followers and groups. In *Organizing Genius* (1997), a collaborative work with Patricia Ward Biederman, Bennis almost returns to his roots in group work. The book looks at the history of seven well-known groups in action, including President Clinton's 1992 election campaign and Lockheed's "skunk works." Common features of these successful groups are highlighted, and the mutually interdependent relationship between great leaders and great groups is stressed.

Context and Conclusions

The importance of Bennis's work in the field of leadership is indisputable, and his informal style of writing and use of illustrations make his books very approachable. Bennis views leadership as a skill that can be developed by ordinary people and that centers on empowering others rather than on control and direction. Sometimes criticized as a romantic, he has himself affirmed (in *The Director* of October 1988) that he is indeed a romantic, if that term accurately describes someone who believes in possibilities and is optimistic.

For More Information

Books:

Bennis, Warren. *The Unconscious Conspiracy: Why Leaders Can't Lead*. New York: AMACOM Press, 1976.

Bennis, Warren, and Burt Nanus. *Leaders: The Strategies for Taking Charge*. New York: Harper & Row, 1985.

Bennis, Warren. *On Becoming a Leader*. Cambridge, MA: Perseus, 1989.

Bennis, Warren. *Why Leaders Can't Lead: The Unconscious Conspiracy Continues*. San Francisco: Jossey-Bass, 1989.

Bennis, Warren, and Patricia Ward Biederman. *Organizing Genius: The Secrets of Creative Collaboration*. Cambridge, MA: Perseus, 1997.

Bennis, Warren. *Managing People is like Herding Cats*. Provo, VT: Executive Excellence Publishing, 1998.

Bennis, Warren. *Managing the Dream: Reflections on Leadership and Change*. Cambridge, MA: Perseus, 2000.

Kenneth Blanchard

1939	Born.
1982	Publication of *The One Minute Manager*.
1984	Publication of *Putting the One Minute Manager to Work*.

Summary

The One Minute Manager was first published in in 1982. Lambasted as trite and shallow by academics, it has since sold over 7 million copies, been translated into over 25 languages, and is frequently found on managers' bookshelves. It launched a new genre of management publishing, providing the model for a host of imitations.

Life and Career

Kenneth Blanchard graduated from Cornell University in Government and Philosophy and went on to complete his Ph.D. in Administration and Management. In the early 1980s he was Professor of Leadership and Organizational Behavior at the University of Massachusetts, Amherst. He wrote and researched extensively in the fields of leadership, motivation, and the management of change, and his *Management of Organizational Behavior: Utilizing Human Resources* (coauthored with Paul Hersey) is now in its 8th edition and has become a classic text. In the introduction to *The One Minute Manager* (OMM), Blanchard and his coauthor, Spencer Johnson, MD, describe the book as an allegory, a simple compilation of what "many wise people have taught us and what we have learned ourselves."

Contribution

One-minute Management

The framework story of *The One Minute Manager* imagines a young manager going off in search of that holy grail of the aspiring newcomer—an effective manager on whom to model his own thinking and actions. The novice—a cross between *Le Petit Prince* and *Candide*—is caught between the two extremes of the scientific and human relations schools: some managers get good results (but at a price that few colleagues and subordinates seem willing to support), while others (whose people really like them) have results which leave much to be desired. Our hero, however, soon comes across a manager who gets excellent results as a result of—apparently—very little effort on his part—the One Minute Manager. The OMM has three simple secrets that bring about increases in productivity, profits, and satisfaction—one-minute goal-setting, one-minute praising, and one-minute reprimanding.

One-minute Goal-setting

Although staff cannot know how well they are doing without clear goals, claims the OMM, many are not clear on priorities, and many are spoken to only when they make a mistake. The OMM requires managers to make it clear what tasks people are to do and what sort of behavior or performance is expected of them, and to get staff to write down their most important goals on a single sheet of paper for continued clarification.

One-minute Praising

The second secret—one-minute praising—is the key to improved performance and increased productivity. Instead of criticizing people for doing something wrong, the opposite is recommended: "the key to developing people is to catch them doing something right." There are three steps in one-minute praising.

- Praise someone as close in time to the good behavior as possible. If you can't find someone to praise every day, then you should wonder why.
- Be specific. Make it clear what it was that was performed well.
- Share feelings—tell them how you feel about what they did, not what you think about what they did.

One-minute Reprimanding

The third secret of the One Minute Manager is the key to changing the attitude of the poor performer and there are four aspects to it.

- Immediacy—when a reprimand is necessary, it is best to deliver it as soon as possible after the instance of poor performance that led to it.
- Be specific—don't tell people about your reactions or give vent to your feelings, tell them what they did wrong; admonish the action, not the person.
- Share feelings—once you have established what was wrong, share your feelings.
- Tell them how good they are—the last step in the reprimand. If you finish on negative feedback, they will reflect on your style of behavior, not on their own performance.

The Development of One-minute Management

Putting the One Minute Manager to Work was a follow-up in 1984 by Blanchard and coauthor Richard Lorber (an expert in performance improvement) to flesh out some of the basic ideas which had met initial success in *The One Minute Manager*. Subtitled *How to Turn the Three Secrets into Skills*, the 1984 follow-up focuses on the "ABCs" of management, "effective reprimanding," and the "PRICE" system.

The ABCs

- Activators—those things that a manager has to do before anyone else can be expected to achieve anything, such as goal-setting, laying down areas of accountability, issuing instructions, and setting performance standards.
- Behavior—or performance—what a person says or does, such as filing, writing, selling, ordering, buying, etc.
- Consequence—what a manager does after performance, such as sharing feelings, praising, reprimanding, supporting, etc.

Effective Reprimanding

A manager has to distinguish between a situation where an employee can't do something—which implies a need for training and signals a return to the activator of goal-setting—and one where an employee won't do something—which implies an attitude problem and a case for a reprimand. Reprimands do not teach skills, they can only change attitudes. Positive consequences on the other hand can influence future performance to the good, so it is important, as *The One Minute Manager* had already suggested, to end a reprimand with praise, making the employee think about his or her own behavior, not that of the reprimander.

The PRICE System
PRICE takes the three basic secrets of one-minute management and turns them into five steps.

- **Pinpointing**—defining key performance areas in measurable terms – part of one-minute goal-setting;
- **Recording**—gathering data to measure actual performance and keep track of progress;
- **Involving**—sharing the information recorded with whomsoever is responsible;
- **Coaching**—providing constructive feedback on improving performance;
- **Evaluating**—part of coaching, also part of reprimanding or praising.

Later Works
Leadership and the One Minute Manager stresses that there is no single, best method of leadership, but that there are in fact four styles: directing, delegating, coaching, and support. Whichever style is employed depends on the situation to be managed. "Situational leadership is not something you do to people, but something you do with people." Blanchard turns conventional leadership thinking on its head, using the analogy of turning the organizational pyramid upside down; instead of staff working for their boss, the boss should work for the staff.

The One Minute Manager Builds High-Performing Teams can be seen as a companion to *Leadership* and concentrates on integrating the simplicity of the one-minute techniques into understanding group dynamics and adjusting leadership style to meet developing circumstances.

The One Minute Manager Meets the Monkey deals with the problems of time management and overload. Paying tribute to Bill Oncken, Blanchard's coauthor who created the monkey analogy, Blanchard points the finger at the concept of the manager as the "hero with all the answers," stressing that bosses are not there to try and tackle every problem themselves, rather to get others to come up with solutions. The monkey is the problem being passed from subordinate to superior, making the superior rapidly ineffective; the one-minute manager is not a collector of monkeys, rather a facilitator and coach helping others to solve their own problems.

Context and Conclusions
So where does Blanchard sit in the Hall of Fame of management thinkers?

In the early years of the 21st century, much of what Blanchard et al. have to say in *The One Minute Manager* series no longer seems earth-shattering. Countless publications and endless seminars on leadership, change, delegation, and time management have, unsurprisingly, rendered a glance back to Blanchard an entertaining experience, yes, and a comforting one in its confirmation of what one has learned elsewhere, but—like the key message of a contemporaneous publication, *In Search of Excellence* (Peters and Waterman, 1982)—one-minute management is no longer the inspiration it was.

When asked why *In Search of Excellence* did so well, critics and commentators argued that its timing was impeccable: it was published at a time when Western business concepts were being trashed in favor of analyses of the Japanese business boom. If Peters and Waterman were largely about reinvigorating pride in successful American organizations, Blanchard's book was excellently timed for its impact on individual skills and techniques.

It is important to remember that before Blanchard, Peters, and the host of others following in their wake, management—as far as the hard-nosed manager was concerned—was a stuffy, dry subject reserved for lengthy academic treatises and exposés. Most books—not that there were many of them—focused on building the arguments of the human relations school and tackling the monstrous scientific/bureaucratic establishment so convincingly constructed by Taylor, Ford, and Weber. Books on management were not popular, not widely read, and certainly not best-sellers. It is often claimed that Peters and Waterman changed all that. But Ken Blanchard's contribution was also hugely influential. *The One Minute Manager* may have been panned by the academics, but it did more to make management digestible, readable, and accessible to a wide audience than any of its predecessors. By means of allegory, anecdotes, and allusions, it brought management to a level where many believed they could do it and do it well. Others have followed the story-telling format of OMM, *One Page Management* (Khadem) and *Zapp! The Lightning of Empowerment* (Byham) to name but two.

So what is the appeal of *The One Minute Manager*, rejected (like Maslow) by academia, but wholeheartedly adopted (as was Maslow) by practicing managers around the world? Blanchard's book was, first and foremost, short and to the point. Moreover, it was written in readable, everyday language, offering practical, everyday solutions to practical, everyday problems. This was no dry, stuffy theory, but a collection of honest sensible techniques to try out straight away. This is where Blanchard scored a first.

Any author who sells over 7 million copies deserves a place in the Management Hall of Fame. For Blanchard, that place has to be broadly in the human relations school alongside the great popularizers of empowerment on the one hand and the self-help school, stretching from Samuel Smiles and Dale Carnegie to present-day figures like Stephen Covey and, recently, Tom Peters, on the other. Blanchard's message may not be original but few have spread the simple message more effectively, or to such a wide audience.

For More Information
Books:

Blanchard, Kenneth, and Spencer Johnson. *The One Minute Manager*. New York: Berkley Publishing Group, 1983.

Blanchard, Kenneth, Robert Lorber. *Putting the One Minute Manager to Work*. New York: William Morrow & Co., 1984.

Blanchard, Kenneth, Patricia Zigarmi, and Drea Zigarmi. *Leadership and the One Minute Manager*. New York: William Morrow & Co., 1985.

Blanchard, Kenneth, William Oncken, and Hal Burrows. *The One Minute Manager Meets the Monkey*. New York: William Morrow & Co. 1990.

Blanchard, Kenneth, Donald Carew, and Eunice Parisi-Carew. *The One Minute Manager Builds High-performing Teams*. New York: William Morrow & Co., 1980.

Blanchard, Kenneth, and Terry Waghorn. *Mission Possible*. New York: McGraw-Hill, 1997.

Blanchard, Kenneth, and Sheldon Bowles. *Gung Ho*. New York: William Morrow & Co., 1998.

Dale Carnegie

1888	Born.
1908	Graduates from State Teachers College, Warrensburg, Missouri.
1912	Teaches first public speaking class at YMCA in upper Manhattan.
1912–1920	Formalizes course in public speaking.
1926	Publication of textbook *Public Speaking: A Practical Course for Businessmen*.
1936	Publication of *How to Win Friends and Influence People*.
1939	Introduces sales course.
1955	Dies.

Summary

Dale Carnegie's main focus is on dealing with people successfully. His best-known work, *How to Win Friends and Influence People* (1936), puts forward the essential principles for doing this in the form of commonsense advice, such as that you should never criticize, complain about, or condemn another person, that you should give sincere appreciation to others, and that, in order to motivate people, you need to stimulate a specific desire in them.

Life and Career

Dale Carnegie (1888–1955) came from a poor, farming background and had to struggle through college. Looking for a way to distinguish himself, he began to enter speaking contests and, despite a shaky start, was soon winning every contest he entered. On leaving college he worked for some time as a salesman, making his territory the most successful one in the company, before deciding to train and work as an actor. This was another false start, however. He gave up the stage to run his own business, and then eventually decided to write novels and support himself by teaching at night.

Carnegie's first courses on public speaking for businessmen at the YMCA schools in New York were run purely on a commission basis, as he was initially refused any pay. The courses did well, however, and their popularity made him a great success. They were so successful, in fact, that he was able to turn them into a series of popular books that extended beyond his initial sphere of public speaking into the realm of human relations in general. Providing simple rules on how to achieve success with people and illustrated from his own and others' experiences and with stories about historical figures such as Roosevelt and Lincoln, the books became runaway successes in their turn. Carnegie went on to found the Dale Carnegie Institute of Effective Speaking and Human Relations to spread his ideas yet further. In 1997, over 40 years after his death, *How to Win Friends and Influence People*, the book that made him internationally famous, was still on the bestseller list in Germany.

Contribution

Carnegie believed that criticism was counterproductive and should never be used to try to change or motivate people. In his view, people who are criticized tend to respond by justifying themselves and condemning the critical person in return. Great leaders such as

Abraham Lincoln achieved their success partly because they never criticized others. Carnegie recommended instead the practice of self-control, understanding, and forgiveness. Most importantly, he advised that you should always try to see the other person's point of view.

In order to influence people and achieve your aims, Carnegie suggests, it is necessary to understand individual motivation. You need to ask yourself what will motivate a person to want to do a task for you, before you attempt to persuade them to do it. He considers most people to be interested only in their own desires, but suggests that, if they are given what they want, they can help the giver to achieve great success in business.

People may simply want to drive a better car or buy a bigger house. For most people, however, the desire to be important is a main, if not the main motivator. It can inspire them to do great things, such as become important leaders or make their fortune in business. It can also take morbid forms. Sometimes individuals become invalids to gain attention or become insane so that they can live in a dream world where their importance is exaggerated by imagination. In any event the urge to be important should not be ignored. Using very human, anecdotal evidence, Carnegie illustrates how nourishing a person's self-esteem can achieve far better results than criticism.

The Rules

How to Win Friends and Influence People has "in a nutshell" conclusions at the end of each section. In them Carnegie summarizes the main messages each section offers in terms of behavior. Some of these are paraphrased below.

Six ways to make people like you:

1. Show a genuine interest in other people.
2. Be happy and positive.
3. Remember that people love hearing the sound of their own name.
4. Listen to other people and develop good listening skills.
5. Talk about others' interests rather than your own.
6. Give others a sincere sense of their importance.

Twelve ways to win people to your way of thinking:

1. To get the best of a situation, avoid arguments.
2. Always listen to others' opinions and never tell anyone they are wrong.
3. Admit it if you are wrong.
4. Show friendliness.
5. Make statements that the other person can agree with.
6. Let the other person talk more than you.
7. Make the other person feel that an idea is their own.
8. See the other person's point of view.
9. Show empathy with others' ideas and desires.
10. Infuse some drama into your ideas.
11. Appeal to the better nature of others.
12. Finish with a challenge.

Nine ways to change people without arousing resentment:

1. Start with genuine praise and appreciation.
2. Draw attention to people's mistakes gradually.

3. Admit that you have made mistakes and then talk to other people about theirs.
4. Don't give direct orders but ask questions.
5. Never humiliate anyone, and let people keep their pride intact.
6. Use plenty of genuine praise and encouragement when there is the slightest improvement.
7. Give people a reputation to maintain.
8. Encourage people. Show them that their task is easy to accomplish.
9. Suggest what you want them to do and make them happy about it.

Becoming a Good Public Speaker

Some of the advice given by Dale Carnegie at the start of his career, when he trained and wrote to help people to make speeches in public, is summarized below.

Preparation

From the beginning, Carnegie suggested, you should generate an enthusiasm within yourself for public speaking, whether you have a financial or a social goal in view. Prepare as much as possible for the speech and have it ready well in advance. Begin planning as soon as you can and look for a topic that you know a lot about. Always try to use your own ideas, but bring the topic of your talk into conversation, so that you can explore any interesting stories on the subject that others may be able to tell you. Think about your talk at every possible opportunity and research it thoroughly, using libraries and other sources and collecting more material than you will need.

Do not memorize the talk word for word, as you will then be more likely to forget it. It may also lose much of its effectiveness if it seems too studied. While having plenty of material prepared, you should not try to say too much in the talk itself. Your material needs to be structured simply, so that you can talk as if you were in ordinary conversation.

Most people are nervous about talking in public. If you try to act bravely and pretend that you feel more confident than you really do, you will often actually gain in confidence. Practice will help you to feel more certain of yourself, and it is a good idea to rehearse your speech as much as possible, maybe in front of the mirror, or with family and friends as an audience.

Delivery

Dress the part for your speech. Smile, and make sure you are clearly visible to your audience. Show respect and affection for the audience, and let the first sentence capture their attention. Examples of techniques to help you to achieve this are:

- start with a striking incident or example;
- state an arresting fact;
- ask for a show of hands;
- use an exhibit;
- do or say something to arouse suspense;
- promise to tell the audience how they can get something they want.

You should not, however, open a talk with either an apology or a funny story. Humorous stories often fail to work, and this is particularly likely to be the case when you are nervous.

Use statistics or the testimony of experts to support your main ideas, but know your audience and do not use technical terms if you are addressing a lay audience. Be eager to share your talk with your listeners, putting passion into your way of speaking and using your emotions without fear. Represent things visually when possible, turning a fact into a picture to help your audience to understand what you are talking about and using specific instances and concrete cases.

Stress important words and avoid any hackneyed expressions or clichés. Once your talk is launched, you may feel freer to be humorous when appropriate, but take care to target any fun at yourself rather than others.

Your talk should have some marked form of closure. Summarize what you have said, then use a finalizing climax or close of some sort that is appropriate within the context, for example:

- make an appeal for action;
- pay the audience a sincere compliment;
- raise a final laugh;
- use a fitting verse of poetry or a quotation.

Carnegie's Concluding Advice

- Remember that many famous speakers were originally terrified of speaking in public and that a certain amount of stage fright is useful.
- Predetermine your mind to success and seize every opportunity to practice.
- Remember that as you increase your experience your fear will lessen, so seek opportunities to speak in public, and believe in yourself.

Context and Conclusions

Carnegie claimed that his theories do really work and that he had seen them transform the lives of many people. Some management writers have, however, dismissed Carnegie's ideas as being simple wisdom dressed up in a commercial coating.

Certainly, Carnegie's ideas are based on common sense and are hardly revolutionary. All his self-help books are based on down-to-earth and simply illustrated basic principles. Despite this simplicity, Carnegie has expressed many general truths which people acknowledge and, whatever his critics may say, the books he wrote are still popular.

In fact, Carnegie created a highly successful business out of his ideas, and his books have sold millions. Even today, much money is still being made from his work, which suggests that people still find him very relevant. Certainly, it is possible to see Carnegie's influence in some of today's ideas about management, particularly in discussions on the treatment of customers, and in approaches to interpersonal skills development.

For More Information
Books:
Carnegie, Dale. *How to Win Friends and Influence People*. New York: Pocket Books, 1984 (reissue).
Carnegie, Dale. *How to Enjoy Your Life and Your Job*. New York: Pocket Books, 1986.
Carnegie, Dale. *How to Stop Worrying and Start Living*. New York: Pocket Books, 1985.

Alfred D. Chandler, Jr.

1918	Born.
1952	Completes Ph.D. at Harvard.
1962	Publication of *Strategy and Structure*.
1970	Appointed Isidor Strauss Professor of Business History, Harvard Business School.
1977	Publication of *The Visible Hand: The Managerial Revolution in American Business*

Summary

The U.S. academic Alfred D. Chandler, Jr. is the first historian in the modern era to both forge his own subject area and dominate it for almost half a century. When he stumbled on the genre after World War II, business history was just a virgin cousin of the emerging and wider-based topic called economic history, a largely theoretical discipline that deals with macrofiscal issues as they affect national and international economies.

Life and Career

Chandler was born in 1918 and acquired his first interest in history from Wilbur Fiske Gordy's *Elementary History of the United States*, which his father gave him at the age of seven. He was educated at Phillips Exeter Academy, Harvard College, the University of North Carolina, where he received his MA, and Harvard University, where he completed his Ph.D. in history in 1952. His wartime experience was with a unit responsible for analyzing photographs of gunnery exercises by the Atlantic Fleet and bombing raids in the Pacific.

He acquired an interest in sociology and saw the value of explicit concepts, generalizations, and theories in analyzing human behavior, but it was when he came to choose his dissertation topic that his interest in business history was initially sparked. His great-aunt died suddenly, and Chandler and his family moved into her house, in which were stored the personal papers of his grandfather, Henry Varnum Poor. Poor, whose name survives as one half of the business information company Standard and Poor's Corporation, had been one of the people most knowledgeable about American railroads, having edited the *American Railway Journal* for nearly 20 years. Using Poor's personal papers, together with the extensive backfiles of his newspapers and related publications in the Baker Library at Harvard, Chandler produced a classic series of articles, his dissertation, and a book entitled *Henry Varnum Poor: Business Editor, Analyst, and Reformer*. This treatise, a seminal work on American railroad companies during their formative years, enabled him to develop—through his genius at widespread comparative analysis—what became his characteristic way of extracting clear historical patterns that tended toward inductively derived theory.

Chandler's career as a working business historian was spent at the Massachusetts Institute of Technology, where he had the opportunity of working on the individual histories of Du Pont, General Motors, Standard Oil (now Exxon), and Sears, Roebuck & Co., a course of study that culminated in *Strategy and Structure*; at the Johns Hopkins University, where he wrote the biography of Pierre du Pont; and later at the Harvard Business School, where in 1970 he was appointed the Isidor Strauss Professor of Business History, the world's only endowed chair in the field at the time. Since then he has led a growing field of teachers and studies; about 200 American academics now work on the subject.

Contribution

Until Chandler turned to business history as his principal interest, mainstream economic history predominated as the subject matter of business education. There was, admittedly, a detour, the result of imported Western European attitudes, when both popular journalism and academia started to take an interest in the corrupt practices of businessmen. The perception emerged that they were "robber barons," a viewpoint that only started to change when Joseph Schumpeter's *The Theory of Economic Development*, which depicted the busi-nessman as a force for positive advancement, was translated from German into English in 1934. Several notable academics started to reevaluate the same robber barons as construct-ive, daring, and far-seeing "industrial statesmen," who deserved credit for making the United States a predominant economic power able to defend itself and its allies from the totalitarian assaults on freedom of the 20th century. Nevertheless, it was Chandler who made business history a linchpin of the curriculum.

His work has been pioneering in several other respects. It has been conducted in front of a largely unreceptive audience: The majority of management educators long resisted the concept of using the real example of corporate and business history as a teaching tool. With an attachment to the more empirical methodologies dominated by macroeconomics and quantitative analysis, they believed that business historians painted with too broad a brush on too wide a canvas and lacked a solid or explicitly stated methodology. They also accused the genre of being largely irrelevant given the perceived pace of change. Chandler's work has done much to change these attitudes, although it is instructive to note that business and management teachers—unlike educators in disciplines such as the military, politics, music, architecture, sociology, and so on—still widely resist both the concept and the development of history-based experiential learning in their own discipline. Chandler has also spent his life challenging economic thinking, in particular the static equilibrium theory. Although he used the results of quantitative research, he did not employ mathematical notation, remain-ing skeptical of highly theorized arithmetical manipulations that, he says, while elegantly logical, distort intelligible generalizations about the past.

In shifting the focus of business history, Chandler's work, which in fact specifically addresses the process of evolution and change, uses a systematic and analytical approach that has evolved from an intellectual outlook, which he labeled "managerial enterprise." As he explains it, this concept moves in two directions—forward from the past to the present and backward from the present to the past. Using the former perspective, for example, he examined why early 19th-century industry did not employ any managers, a phenomenon which changed decisively and for ever in the second half of the 19th century. Using the latter perspective, he questioned the 1950s moves by industry toward decentralization of their functionally-specialized and multidepartmentalized organizations. His answers—in a landmark book entitled *Strategy and Structure*, published in 1962—took business history into a new dimension by establishing a fresh framework and rationale for the subject. He intro-duced the feature of making comparisons within and between industries and over time, and enabled business history to acquire relevance in a wide variety of related fields.

In *The Visible Hand*, another milestone book, Chandler used the concept of managerial enterprise to illustrate how Germany became the most powerful industrial nation in Europe before World War II, the United States became the most productive country in the world for 40 years until the 1960s, and Japan became its most successful competitor there-after. For this book he won the Pulitzer Prize. These and other works—including, with Richard Tedlow, *The Coming of Managerial Capitalism*—are routinely used in at least 30 higher educational establishments in the United States and many more abroad.

Business history's role at the operational level, Chandler explains, is not about teaching specific management techniques. It has a more strategic function. Any meaningful analysis of an organization today, he says, must be based on an accurate understanding of its past. "Such data has to come from business history based on company records or from historic-ally based case studies. Certainly a restructuring of enterprises to meet changing conditions requires an understanding of both why and how the existing organization evolved and how and why competitive conditions changed. Managers facing such problems can get insights by observing the working out of such processes in other enterprises." Companies such as McKinsey & Co and AT&T have applied *Strategy and Structure* to this end. The former, for example, has used it to teach its clients about the timing of strategic change and how to adjust their organizational structures, while the latter put it to use in one of its reorganizations.

At the wider education level, Chandler believes that business history can provide insights into the processes of businesses such as the development of competitive strategy, the restructuring of organizational forms, and the effectiveness of investment and monitoring techniques. His view is that the value of teaching business histories in universities is to make MBA students and those in more advanced management courses aware of recent as well as long-term changes in functional activities such as production, marketing, research and development, finance, labor relations, and the like; also in monitoring and coordinating the activities of the current operations of an enterprise as well as in locating resources for future production and distribution. "Not only can the students learn something about the nature of the functions but also the complexities of carrying out change," he says.

Context and Conclusions

For students and practitioners alike, Chandler's name may be remembered principally as the pioneer who placed strategy before structure in his seminal work published in 1962. Not only has he championed the systematic study of modern bureaucratic administration in an original way, he has also turned what is often dismissed as an artless medium into a valid and powerful educational tool. Using the conglomerate history of individual companies to arrive at a historical theory of big business instead of the mainstream—economic—discipline of the day, he revolutionized the fledgling discipline by refocusing attention away from individual entrepreneurs and seeking patterns in the rise of large-scale modern busi-ness. Almost uniquely, his work—which has given rise to the term "Chandlerianism"—has had a profound effect on historians and business thinking all over the world, particularly in Japan and Germany. Some of his books have been translated into Chinese and Russian.

Following his lead, U.S. business historians have moved to more thematic areas: for example, how companies formulate and implement policy, how industries evolve, the impact of administrative hierarchies on the modern economy, industrial evolution across national boundaries, the interaction of business with governmental institutions and regula-tory bodies, and organized labor and the consumer.

History will no doubt endow him with the distinction of giving modern management educators a less theoretical way of teaching the business of business. In essence, he has skillfully recycled the tried and tested past to provide both practicing and aspiring managers with an inheritance that has practical corporate application in today's highly competitive world. In truth, history is the only way individuals and companies can learn from experience. And learning from experience is the only way to increase productivity and competitiveness.

For More Information

Books:

Chandler, Alfred. *Strategy and Structure*. Cambridge, MA: MIT Press, 1962.

Chandler, Alfred. *The Visible Hand: The Managerial Revolution in American Business*. Cambridge, MA: Harvard University Press, 1977.

Chandler, Alfred. *Managerial Hierarchies*. Cambridge, MA: Harvard University Press, 1980.

Chandler, Alfred, and Richard Tedlow. *The Coming of Managerial Capitalism*. Homewood, IL: Richard D. Irwin, 1985.

Chandler, Alfred. *Scale and Scope; The Dynamics of Industrialized Capitalism*. Cambridge, MA: Harvard University Press, 1994.

Chandler, Alfred. *Big Business and the Wealth of Nations*. New York: Cambridge University Press, 1997.

Chandler, Alfred. *The Dynamic Firm*. New York: Oxford University Press, 1998.

REFERENCES: Both quotations are extracts from private correspondence with Chandler.

Stephen R. Covey

1932	Born.
1985	Founds Covey Leadership Center.
1989	Publication of *The Seven Habits of Highly Effective People*.
1997	Covey Leadership Center merges with Franklin Quest.

Summary

In *The Seven Habits of Highly Effective People*, Stephen Covey offers a holistic approach to life and work that has struck a significant chord with the perplexed manager working in turbulent times. The recurring themes in his various works are the transforming power of principles rooted in unchanging natural laws that govern human and organizational effectiveness; the necessity of adapting every aspect of one's life to accord with these principles; effective leadership; and empowerment.

Life and Career

Stephen Covey is founder and Chairman of the Covey Leadership Center—now part of Franklin Covey—and the Institute for Principle-Centered Leadership in Utah. Born in 1932, he received an MBA from Harvard Business School and a doctorate from Brigham Young University, where he was subsequently Professor of Organizational Behavior and Business Management. Through his writing—chiefly *The Seven Habits of Highly Effective People* (which has sold over five million copies)—and through consulting, his message has reached millions of individuals in business, government, and education.

Contribution

The Seven Habits of Highly Effective People

The Seven Habits is addressed to readers not only in their capacity as managers but also as members of a family, and as social, spiritual, sporting, and thinking individuals. It offers a "life-transforming prescription," which calls for a reappraisal of many fundamental assumptions and attitudes (paradigms), and builds on the fundamental concept of interdependence. Covey traces a personal development outline from:

- dependence in childhood (many people never grow out of a dependency culture), through...
- independence in adolescence—selfassurance, a developing personality, and a positive mental attitude, to...
- interdependence—recognition that the optimum outcome results from everyone giving of their best, each aiming for a common goal, sharing the same mission and vision, but having the freedom to use their best judgment to achieve that common goal.

Habit 1

Be proactive.

Covey distinguishes between proactive people—those who focus their efforts on things which they can do something about—and reactive people, who blame, accuse, behave like victims, pick on other people's weaknesses, and complain about external factors over which they have no control (for example, the weather).

Proactive people are responsible for their own lives and recognize their responsibility to make things happen. Those who allow their feelings to control their actions have abdicated responsibility. When proactive people make a mistake, they not only acknowledge it, they also correct it if possible and, most importantly, learn from it.

Habit 2

Begin with the end in mind.

Leadership is about effectiveness—the vision of what is to be accomplished. It calls for direction (in every sense of the word), purpose, and sensitivity. Management, on the other hand, is about efficiency—how best to accomplish the vision. It depends on control, guidance, and rules.

To identify the end, and to formulate one's route or strategy to achieving that end, Covey maintains the need for a "principle-centered" basis to all aspects of life. Most people adopt something as the basis (or pivotal point) of their life—spouse, family, money, church, pleasure, friends, sports, etc. Of course all of these have some influence over the life of every individual. However, only by clearly establishing one's own principles, in the form of a personal mission, does one have a solid foundation.

Habit 3

Put first things first.

Covey's first major work, *First Things First*, sets out his views on time management. The important thing is not managing time, but managing oneself, focusing on results rather than on methods when prioritizing within each compartment of work and life.

He breaks down life's activities into four quadrants:

Quadrant 1: Urgent and important—for example, crises, deadlines, opportunities.

Quadrant 2: Not urgent, but important—for example, planning, recreation, relationship-building, doing, learning.

Quadrant 3: Urgent, but not important—for example, interruptions, meetings.

Quadrant 4: Not urgent and not important—for example, trivia, time-wasters, gossip.

Essentially all activity of effective people should focus on the second quadrant, apart from the genuinely unpredictable quadrant 1 events. However, effective planning and doing in Quadrant 2 should minimize the number of occasions on which crises occur.

The outcomes of a Quadrant 2 focus include: vision, perspective, balance, discipline, and control, while the results of placing one's main focus on the other quadrants are:

Quadrant 1: stress, burnout, inability to manage time (and thus loss of control of one's own life).

Quadrant 3: short-termism, loss of control, shallowness, feelings of being a victim of circumstances.

Quadrant 4: irresponsibility, dependency, unsuitability for employment.

Habit 3 is therefore about managing oneself effectively, by prioritizing according to the principles adopted in Habit 2. This approach transcends the office diary or day-planner, embracing all roles in life—as manager, mentor, administrator, strategist, and also as parent, spouse, member of social groups, and as an individual with needs and aspirations.

Habits 1–3 are about the development of the personal attributes that provide the foundations for independence. Habits 4–6 are the basic paradigms of interdependence.

Habit 4

Think win/win.

Interdependence occurs when there is cooperation, not competition, in the workplace (or the home). Covey holds that competition belongs in the marketplace.

Covey points out that, from childhood, many people are conditioned to a win/lose mentality by school examinations, by parental approval being related to "success," by external comparisons and league standings. This results in a "scarcity mentality," a belief that there is only a finite cake to be shared. A "scarcity mentality" is evident in people who have difficulty in sharing credit, power or profit. It restricts their ability to celebrate other people's success, and even brings about a perverse satisfaction at others' misfortune.

By contrast Covey advocates an "abundance mentality" that:

- recognizes unlimited possibilities for positive growth and development;
- celebrates success, recognizing that one person's success is not achieved at the expense, or to the exclusion, of others;
- understands and seeks a win/win solution.

Covey argues that it is sometimes necessary to walk away if the other party is interested only in a win/lose outcome: Covey describes this as "win/win or no deal."

Habit 5

Seek first to understand, then to be understood.

"I just can't understand my son ... he won't listen to me." The absurdity of this statement is highlighted by Covey in emphasizing the importance of listening in order to understand. The parent needs to stop and listen to the son if he or she truly wants to understand him.

However, most people want to make their point first, or are so busy looking for their opportunity to butt into the conversation that they fail to hear and understand the other party. Covey defines the different levels of listening as:

- hearing but ignoring;
- pretending to listen ("Yes," "Oh," "I see...");
- selective listening (choosing to hear only what we want to hear);
- attentive listening, without evaluation (e.g., taking notes at a lecture);
- empathic listening (with intent to understand the other party).

Empathic listening requires a great deal of personal security, as one is vulnerable to having one's opinions changed. "The more deeply you understand other people," Covey says, "the more you appreciate them, the more reverent you feel about them." Likewise, when you feel that someone is genuinely seeking to understand your point of view, you recognize and share their openness and willingness to negotiate and to reach a win/win situation.

Habit 6

Synergize.

The essence of synergy is where two parties, each with a different agenda, value each other's differences. Everything in nature is synergistic, with every creature and plant being interdependent with others.

We also have personal effectiveness where there is synergy at an individual level—where both sides of the brain are working on a problem, the intuitive, creative, visual right side and the analytical, logical, verbal left side combining to achieve the optimum outcome. Synergy is lacking in insecure people, and of such insecurity is born prejudice—racism, bigotry, nationalism, and any other form of prejudging others.

Habit 7
Sharpen the saw.

The seventh and final habit relates to renewal. Covey uses the metaphor of a woodcutter who is laboring painfully to saw down a tree. The saw is obviously in need of sharpening, but when asked why he doesn't stop and sharpen the saw, the woodcutter replies, "I can't stop—I'm too busy sawing down this tree."

The warning is quite clear. Everyone can become so engrossed in the task in hand that the basic tools are neglected:

- "the physical self"—which requires exercise, a sensible and balanced diet, and management of stress;
- "the social/emotional self"—which connects with others through service, empathy, and synergy, and which is the source of intrinsic security;
- "the spiritual self"—which through meditation, reflection, prayer, and study helps to clarify and refine our own values and strengths, and our commitment to them;
- "the mental self"—building on to our formal education through reading, visualizing, planning, writing, and maintaining a coherent program of continuing personal development.

Context and Conclusions

Commentators have both attacked and applauded Covey's approach for mixing the self-help message, which can be traced back to Samuel Smiles, with current management theories and religious fervor.

In times of change and confusion, however, when failure, redundancy, and unemployment dominate individual thinking and lead to stress, Covey's message offers the individual something to hang on to. *First Things First*, coauthored with Roger and Rebecca Merrill, has achieved twice the sales of *The Seven Habits* over the same period.

He is undoubtedly a philosopher for our times, highlighting the significance of changing industrial and human relations in this postconfrontational era, and recognizing the potential of the untapped resources within each individual.

For More Information

Books:

Covey, Stephen. *The Seven Habits of Highly Effective People*. New York: Simon & Schuster, 1989.

Covey, Stephen. *Principle-centered Leadership*. New York: Summit Books, 1991.

Covey, Stephen, A. Roger Merrill, and Rebecca R. Merrill., *First Things First*. New York: Simon & Schuster, 1996.

Covey, Stephen. *The Seven Habits of Highly Effective Families*. New York: Golden Books, 1997.

W. Edwards Deming

1900	Born.
1928	Completes Ph.D. at Yale.
1950	Begins teaching management quality in Japan.
1986	Publication of *Out of the Crisis*.
1987	Receives National Medal of Technology.
1993	Founds W. Edwards Deming Institute.
1993	Dies.

Summary

W. Edwards Deming is widely acknowledged as the leading management thinker in the field of quality. He is credited with being the most influential catalyst of Japan's postwar economic transformation, although it wasn't until much later that the value of his ideas and practices began to be recognized by the U.S. manufacturing and service industries.

Life and Career

Deming obtained a Ph.D. in mathematical physics from Yale University in 1928 and concentrated on lecturing and writing on mathematics, physics, and statistics for the next ten years. It was only in the late 1930s that he became familiar with the work of Walter Shewhart, who was experimenting with the application of statistical techniques to manufacturing processes. Deming became interested in applying Shewhart's techniques to non-manufacturing processes, particularly clerical, administrative, and management activities. After joining the U.S. Census Bureau in 1939, he applied statistical process control to their techniques, which contributed to a sixfold improvement in productivity. Around this time he also started to run courses for engineers and designers on his—and Shewhart's—evolving methods of statistical process control.

Deming's expertise as a statistician was instrumental in his posting to Japan after World War II as an adviser to the Japanese Census. At this time, the United States was the leading economic power, with products much envied by the rest of the world; it saw no need for Deming's new ideas. The Japanese, on the other hand, recognized that their own goods were shoddy by international standards. Moreover, after the war, they could not afford the wastage of raw materials that postproduction inspection processes brought about, and were consequently looking for techniques to help them address these problems. While in Japan, Deming became involved with the Union of Japanese Scientists and Engineers (JUSE) and his career of lecturing to the Japanese on statistical methods and company-wide quality, a combination of techniques now known as Total Quality Management (TQM), had begun.

It was only in the late 1970s that the United States became aware of his achievements in Japan. The 1980s saw a spate of publications explaining his work and influence. In his American seminars during 1980, Deming talked of the need for the total transformation of Western-style management. In 1986 he published *Out of the Crisis*, which documented the thinking and practice that had led to the transformation of Japanese manufacturing industry. His ideas gained acceptance in the United Kingdom following the foundation of the British Deming Association in 1987. Deming died in 1993.

Contribution

Deming's work and writing constitute not so much a technique as a philosophy of management, one that focuses on quality and continuous improvement, but that has also—justifiably—had a much wider influence.

Below we consider Deming's interest in variation and his approach to systematic problem-solving, which led on to his development of the 14 points that have gained widespread recognition and are central to the quality movement.

Variation and Problem Solving

The key to Deming's ideas on quality lies in his recognition of the importance of variation. In *Out of the Crisis* he states that "the central problem in management and in leadership...is failure to understand the information in variation."

Deming was preoccupied with why things do not behave as predicted. All systems (be they the equipment, the process, or the people) have variation, but, he argued, it is essential for managers to be able to distinguish between special and common causes of variation. He developed a theory of variation: that special causes of variation are usually attributable to easily recognizable factors such as a change of procedure, change of shift or operator, and so on, but that common causes will remain when special causes have been eliminated and are normally inherent in the design, process, or system. These common causes often are recognized by workers, but only managers have the authority to change them to avoid repeated occurrence of the problem. Deming estimated that management was responsible for more than 85% of the causes of variation. This formed his central message to the Japanese.

Deming's 14 Points for Management

Deming created 14 points that provided a framework for developing knowledge in the workplace and guiding long-term business plans and aims. The points constitute not so much an action plan as a philosophical code for management. They have been extensively interpreted, both by commentators on quality control and by experts on other management disciplines.

- Create constancy of purpose toward the improvement of products and services, with the aim of becoming competitive, staying in business, and providing jobs.
- Adopt the new philosophy. Western management must awaken to the challenge, learn its responsibilities, and take on leadership for change.
- Cease dependence on mass inspection. Build quality into the product from the start.
- End the practice of awarding business on the basis of price tag alone. Instead, minimize total cost. Move toward a single supplier for any item, based on a long-term relationship of loyalty and trust.
- Improve constantly and forever the system of production and service to improve quality and reduce waste.
- Institute training and retraining.
- Institute leadership. The aim of supervision should be to lead and help people to do a better job.
- Drive out fear so that everyone may work effectively for the company.

- Break down barriers between departments. People in research, design, sales, and production must work as a team to foresee and solve problems of production.
- Eliminate slogans, exhortations, and targets for the workforce, as they do not necessarily achieve their aims.
- Eliminate numerical quotas in order to take account of quality and methods, rather than just numbers.
- Remove barriers to pride in workmanship.
- Institute a vigorous program of education and retraining for both the management and the workforce.
- Take action to accomplish the transformation. Management and workforce must work together.

These principles are relevant to management in general, not simply to quality and process control. They contributed to Deming's status as a founder of the quality management movement, and attracted an audience much wider than the quality lobby.

Context and Conclusions

Naturally enough, no one as universally acclaimed as Deming escapes without criticism. Some have criticized his approach as being good for improvement but uninspiring for creativity and innovation. Others say his approach is not effective in generating new products or penetrating new markets.

Others—particularly Juran, another quality guru—accuse him of overreliance on statistical methods. Deming's American lectures in the 1980s, however, point time and time again to a mistaken preoccupation with the wrong type of statistics. He argued against figures that focused purely on productivity and control and argued for more evidence of quality, a message that Tom Peters adopted in the 1980s and 1990s.

Deming also stirred up wide interest with his rejection of management by objectives and performance appraisals. Similarly, his attitude toward integrating the workforce led TQM to be perceived as a caring philosophy. Paradoxically, however, his focus on cost-reduction has been pointed to as a cause of downsizing.

Although in the 1980s America paid tribute to Deming—not only for what he did in Japan, but also for his thinking and approach to quality management—few American companies use his methods today. One reason for this is perhaps that, by the 1980s, Deming was selling a system that worked, thereby implying that he had discovered the only way to achieve quality; thus he was no longer alert to changes in the problems. In Japan, in the beginning, he had listened to Japanese needs and requirements, showed them respect, and developed his thinking with them. In the United States of the 1980s, he appeared to try to dispense his philosophy rather than readapt it to a different culture.

In 1951, in early recognition of their debt to Deming, the JUSE awarded the Deming prize to Japanese organizations that excelled in company-wide quality. It was not until the 1980s that the United States recognized Deming's achievements in Japan and elevated him to guru status. In 1987 the British Deming Association was founded to disseminate his ideas in the United Kingdom. From the 1990s it seemed as if Deming's legacy was likely to have both a lasting and significant impact on management theory. Why is this?

The first reason must lie in the nature of his achievement. Deming has been universally acclaimed as one of the founding fathers of Total Quality Management, if not the founding father. The revolution in Japanese manufacturing management that led to the economic miracle of the 1970s and 1980s has been attributed largely to him.

Second, if the 14 points make less of an impact today than they did just after World War II in Japan, it is probably because many aspects of those points were adopted, assimilated, and integrated into management practice in the 1990s and have been continuously debated and taught in business schools around the world.

The third reason is more complex and lies in the scope of his legacy. Deming's 14 points add up to a code of management philosophy that spans the two major schools of managerial thought that have predominated since the early 20th century: scientific (hard) management, on the one hand, and human relations (soft) management, on the other. Deming succeeds—despite criticisms of his overuse of statistical techniques—in marrying them together. Over half of his 14 points focus on people as opposed to systems. Many management thinkers veer towards one school or the other. Deming, like Drucker, melds them together.

The originality and freshness of Deming is that he took his philosophy not from the world of management, but from the world of mathematics, and wedded it with a human relations approach that did not come from management theory but from observation and from seeing what people needed from their working environment in order to contribute of their best.

For More Information

Book:

Deming, W. Edwards. *Out of the Crisis: Quality, Productivity, and Competitive Position.* Cambridge, MA: MIT Press, 2000.

Peter Drucker

1909	Born.
1927	Commences study at University of Hamburg.
1931	Doctorate in Public and International Law, University of Frankfurt, Germany.
1933	Moves to London to work as an investment banker.
1937	Leaves for United States to become investment adviser and correspondent for *Financial News*.
1939	Publication of *The End of Economic Man*.
1940	Private consultant to business and on government policy; teacher at Sarah Lawrence College; Professor at Bennington College, Vermont.
1943	Spends 18 months interviewing senior management at General Motors, which results in the bestselling *The Concept of the Corporation*.
1950	Professor of Management at New York University Graduate School of Business.
1969	Publication of *The Age of Discontinuity*.
1971	Marie Rankin Clarke Professor of Management, Graduate School, Claremont.
1974	Publication of *Management: Tasks, Responsibilities, Practices*.
1975	Columnist for *Wall Street Journal*.
1990	Founding of The Peter F. Drucker Foundation for Non-Profit Management.
1999	Publication of *Management Challenges for the 21st Century*.

Summary

Peter Drucker is accepted by both practicing managers and writers throughout the world as *the* management guru. He himself prefers to be known as a writer. He does not claim to have invented management—but does concede that he discovered it as a way of life central to the well-being of society and the economy.

He has shown interests as diverse as journalism, art appreciation, mountaineering, and reading. With more than 33 books published over seven decades Drucker is, by common consent, the founding father of modern management studies.

Life and Career

Peter Ferdinand Drucker was born in Vienna in 1909 into a high-achieving, intellectual family and was surrounded in his early years by members of the prewar Viennese cultural elite. He began his studies at the University of Hamburg, but transferred to the University of Frankfurt, where he obtained a Doctorate in Public and International Law in 1931.

While still a student in Frankfurt, he worked on the city's *General Anzeiger* newspaper and rose to the posts of foreign and financial editor. Recognized as a talented writer, he was offered a job in the Ministry of Information. Observing the Nazis' rise to power with abhorrence, he wrote a philosophical essay condemning Nazism; this was probably instrumental in hastening his departure to England in 1933. It was in 1937 that he left for the United States to become an investment adviser to British industry and correspondent for several British newspapers, including the *Financial Times*, then called the *Financial News*.

His first book, *The End of Economic Man*, appeared in 1939. In 1940 he began work as as a private consultant to business and government policy-makers, specializing in the German economy and external politics. From 1940 to 1942 he was a teacher at Sarah Lawrence College, and this was followed by the post of Professor of Philosophy, Politics, History, and Religion at Bennington College, Vermont.

It was in the early stages of this appointment that he was invited by the vice President of General Motors (GM) to investigate what constitutes a modern organization, and to examine what the managers running it actually do. Although Drucker was relatively inexperienced in business at the time, his analysis led to the publication, in 1946, of *The Concept of the Corporation*, which had a mixed reception but nonetheless confirmed Drucker's future as a management writer.

The period 1950–1972 was a time of prolific writing, teaching, and consulting while he was Professor of Management at New York University Graduate School of Business. In 1971 he was appointed the Marie Rankin Clarke Professor of Social Science and Management at the Graduate School in Claremont, a school that was subsequently named after him. In 1994 he was appointed Godkin Lecturer at Harvard University.

Drucker holds decorations from the governments of Austria and Japan as well as 22 honorary doctorates from universities in Belgium, Japan, Spain, Switzerland, the United Kingdom, and the United States. He is also a Fellow of the American Association of Science, an Honorary Member of the National Academy of Public Administration, a Fellow of the American Academy of Arts and Sciences, and a Fellow of the American, British, Irish, and International Academies of Management. He lives in Claremont, 40 miles east of Los Angeles, and has four children and six grandchildren.

Contribution

Drucker's management writings are phenomenal in their coverage and impressive in their clarity. With over 33 books to his credit, we can provide only a snapshot of his thinking here. His earlier works made a significant contribution to establishing what constitutes management practice; his later works tackle the complexities—and the management implications—of the postindustrial 1980s and beyond. It is that range and development that we have tried to represent in our comments on the books covered here.

The End of Economic Man—1939

The End of Economic Man concentrates on the politics and economics of the 1930s in general and the rise of Nazism in particular; Drucker signaled a warning about the Holocaust and predicted that Hitler would forge an alliance with Stalin. This was his first book in English as sole author; J.B. Priestley said of it: "At once the most penetrating and the most stimulating book I have read on the world crisis. At last there is a ray of light in the dark chaos."

This was followed by *The Future of Industrial Man* (1942), which assumed Hitler's defeat and started to look ahead to peacetime, warning of the dangers of an approach to planning founded on the denial of freedom. It attracted the interest of critics, who argued that it mixed economics with social sciences; it was, in fact, the first book to argue that any organization is both an economic and social organ. As such, it laid the foundations for Drucker's interest in management in general and, as it turned out, General Motors in particular.

The Concept of the Corporation—1946

When General Motors invited Drucker to write about the company, it was expected that the invitation would result in a glowing description of GM's success. What in fact emerged was something different, something that recognized success but also looked to the future.

General Motors provided Drucker with the opportunity to test in practice the theory he had propounded in *The Future of Industrial Man*, that is, that an organization was essentially a social system as well as an economic one. *The Concept of the Corporation* questioned whether what had worked in the past—a foolproof system of objective policies and procedures throughout every layer of the organization—would continue to work in a future of global competition, changing social values, and automation, and with the drive for quality and the growth of the knowledge worker.

The assembly line, he argued, actually created inefficiency because activity took place at the pace of the slowest. Demotivation was rife because no one saw the end result, and initiative was stifled by the minutiae of checks, rules, and controls. The layers of bureaucracy slowed down decision making, created adversarial labor relations, and did nothing to create a "self-governing plant community" (the phrase Drucker used for an empowered workforce). Drucker reported the benefits of decentralized operations—an issue that critics were quick to praise and organizations quick to mimic—but suggested that the GM hierarchy of commands and controls would be slow to respond in a rapidly changing future.

The fundamental difference between Drucker and GM was that GM saw the workforce as a cost in the quest for profits, whereas Drucker saw people as a resource who would be better able to satisfy customers if they had more involvement in their jobs and gained some satisfaction from doing them. *The Concept of the Corporation*, consequently, was decades ahead of its time in terms of its espousal of empowerment and self-management. Although Alfred Sloan—the chief executive and powerhouse behind General Motors' success—had no time for Drucker's book, Drucker was, in the early 1950s, to advise Sloan on setting up a School of Administration at MIT. His criticism of Sloan was implicit rather than explicit, saying he had vision rather than perspective, and implying that leadership had been sacrificed to the rulebook. Sloan was measured in his reply—after all, at the time, General Motors was the largest and arguably one of the most successful companies in the world. His response came in 1963 with the publication of *My Years with General Motors*, which sets out the scientific credo of GM's philosophy, yet talks little of people, transparently because they had little importance relative to the systems they were following.

Another effect of *The Concept of the Corporation* was the establishment of management as a discipline, bringing to the fore the notions of:

- the social and environmental responsibility of the organization;
- the relationship between the individual and the organization;
- the role of top management and the decision-making process;
- the need for continual training and retraining of managers with the focus on their own responsibility for self-development;
- the nature of labor relations;
- the imperatives of community and customer relations.

It is interesting that Japanese industry listened to these messages and U.S. industry did not.

The Practice of Management—1954

The Practice of Management was Drucker's second book on management, and it established him as a leader in his field. It set trends in management for decades, and reputations were built by adopting and expanding on the ideas that he set out in it. It is still regarded by many as the definitive management text.

Drucker states that there is only one valid purpose for the existence of a business, that is, to create a customer. It is not, he argues, the internal structure, controls, organization, and procedures that keep a business afloat; rather, it is the customer—who pays, and decides what is important—who fills this role. He sets out eight areas in which objectives should be set and performance should be measured:

- market standing
- innovation
- productivity
- physical and financial resources
- profitability
- managers' performance and development
- workers' performance and attitude
- public responsibility

The Practice of Management is probably best remembered for setting out the principles of Management by Objectives and Self Control (Drucker's term, although he didn't coin it)—a management process that has become the accepted basis for management theory and practice.

The book also identified the seven tasks of the manager of tomorrow. He or she must:

- manage by objectives;
- take risks and allow risk-taking decisions to take place at lower levels in the organization;
- be able to make strategic decisions;
- be able to build an integrated team whose members are capable of managing and measuring their own performance and results in relation to overall objectives;
- be able to communicate information quickly and clearly, and motivate employees so as to gain commitment and participation;
- be able to see the business as a whole and to integrate his or her function within it;
- be able to relate the product and industry to the total environment, to find out what is important and what needs to be taken into account. This perspective must embrace developments outside the company's particular market or country and the manager must begin to see economic, political, and social developments on a worldwide scale.

Management: Tasks, Responsibilities, Practices—1974

Much of the work in *The Practice of Management* is updated, expanded, and revised in *Management: Tasks, Responsibilities, Practices*, which establishes where management has come from, where it is now, and where it needs to go. It draws upon a wide variety of international examples and sets out principles for managers and management. Effectively, it is a complete management handbook.

Moving on from his earlier work, Drucker defines the manager's work in terms of five basic operations. He or she:

- sets objectives;
- organizes;
- motivates and communicates;
- measures;
- develops people, including him/herself.

Top management's tasks are to:

- define the business mission;
- set standards;
- build and maintain the human organization;
- develop and maintain external relationships;
- perform social and civic functions;
- know how to get on with the task in hand if and when necessary.

Management: Tasks, Responsibilities, Practice is regarded by many as Drucker's finest book.

The Age of Discontinuity—1969 (reissued 1992)

It is in *The Age of Discontinuity* that Drucker describes the very changes that he had signaled to General Motors 23 years earlier. He writes in the preface: "This book does not project trends; it examines discontinuities. It does not forecast tomorrow; it looks at today. It does not ask: 'What will tomorrow look like?' It asks instead: 'What do we have to tackle today to make tomorrow?'"

The book deals with the forces changing society as new technology impacts on old industries, changing social values impact on consumer behavior, and markets become international. Drucker advocates privatization, pointing out the ineffectiveness of government in leading and stimulating change; he examines the role of organizations in society in an age of discontinuity and looks at different ways of managing the knowledge worker.

Managing in Turbulent Times—1980

The issues raised in *The Age of Discontinuity* were revisited a decade later in *Managing in Turbulent Times*. Change, uncertainty, and turbulence are the underpinning themes as Drucker highlights the new realities of changing population demographics, global markets, and a "bisexual" workforce.

Drucker issues challenges to junior, middle, and senior management.

- In the knowledge organization, the "supervisor" has to become an "assistant," a "resource," a "teacher."
- The very term "middle management" is becoming meaningless [as some] will have to learn how to work with people over whom they have no direct line control, to work transnationally, and to create, maintain, and run systems—none of which is a traditionally middle management task.
- It is top management that faces the challenge of setting directions for the enterprise, of managing the fundamentals. It is top management that will have to restructure itself to meet the challenges of the "sea-change," the changes in population structure and population dynamics.

- It is top management that will have to concern itself with the turbulences of the environment, the emergence of the world economy, the emergence of the employee society, and the need for the enterprises in its care to take the lead in respect to political process, political concepts, and social policies.

Drucker Said It First

Part of Drucker's success and longevity as a management expert was that he had a remarkable knack of spotting trends that were later picked up and made fashionable by others. Invariably, research will trace the origin back to something Drucker wrote ten years— sometimes 20 years—ago. It is interesting that Drucker noted that one of the key aspects of leadership is timing; he, in fact, upbraided himself for being ten years ahead with his forecasts.

The following section is adapted from work by Clutterbuck and Crainer, who summarized the work of James O'Toole, Professor of Management at the University of Southern California. O'Toole said that Drucker was the first to:

- define the role of top managers as the keepers of corporate culture;
- advocate mentoring, career planning, and executive development as top management tasks;
- say that success hinges on the vision expressed by the C.E.O.;
- show that structure follows strategy;
- suggest a reduction of management layers between the top and the bottom;
- argue that success comes from sticking to the basics;
- state that the primary purpose of the organization is to create a customer;
- say that success boils down to sensitivity to the consumer and the marketing of innovative products;
- suggest that quality is a measure of productivity;
- describe the coming knowledge worker;
- state that new approaches to management would be needed in the postindustrial age.

It must be said, however, that Drucker also prophesied the continuing growth of the middle manager as he or she evolved into the knowledge worker of postindustrial society. It has not quite happened like that and the massive delayerings of the early 1990s suggest that Drucker may well have got it wrong...so far.

"Druckerisms"

On business:

A business is not defined by the company's name, statutes, or articles of incorporation. It is defined by the want the customer satisfies when he buys a product or service. (*Management: Tasks, Responsibilities, Practices*)

On leadership:

There is no substitute for leadership. But management cannot create leaders. It can only create the conditions under which potential leadership qualities become effective; or it can stifle potential leadership. (*The Practice of Management*)

On management:

The function which distinguishes the manager above all others is his educational one.

The one contribution he is uniquely expected to make is to give others vision and ability to perform. It is vision and moral responsibility that, in the last analysis, define the manager. (*The Practice of Management*)

On decision making:

[In] these specifically managerial decisions, the important and difficult job is never to find the right answer, it is hard to find the right question. For there are few things as useless—if not as dangerous—as the right answer to the wrong question. (*The Practice of Management*)

On the knowledge worker:

Increasingly, the knowledge workers of tomorrow will have to know and accept the values, the goals, and the policies of the organization—to use current buzzwords, they must be willing—nay, eager—to buy into the company's mission. ("Drucker speaks his mind," *Management Review*)

[The knowledge worker]...may realize that he depends on the organization for access to income and opportunity, and that without the investment the organization has made—and a high investment at that—there would be no opportunity for him. But he also realizes, and rightly so, that the organization equally depends on him. (*The Age of Discontinuity*)

Context and Conclusions

Critical of the business school system in general, Drucker always set himself apart from mainstream management education. He said of himself: "I have always been a loner. I work best outside. That's where I'm most effective. I would be a very poor manager. Hopeless. And a company job would bore me to death. I enjoy being an outsider."

An outsider maybe, but commentators point consistently to his gentlemanly old-world charm, his humility, and the fact that he has never criticized negatively, always politely and constructively.

Drucker's earlier works no longer strike the reader with the same force that they did in the 1950s, 1960s, and 1970s. But this is entirely to his credit. His thinking has become absorbed and adopted as the prevailing wisdom behind the philosophy and practice of modern management.

What does strike the modern reader, however, is the sheer force of his writing, his clear mastery of the subject matter, and the clarity of his expression. It is as well to remember that readable books on management were very few and far between when Drucker wrote *The Concept of the Corporation* and *The Practice of Management*. Texts for managers concentrated usually on technical and industrial engineering and were too complex to have either a wide readership or the impact or influence that Drucker has had.

"For many business leaders across the world...he remains the doyen of modern management theory, not so much because he can lay claim to being the founder of any particular concept such as business re-engineering, or total quality management, rather because he has demonstrated a rare ability to apply common sense understanding to the analysis of management challenges and their solutions." ("Interview with Peter Drucker," the *Financial Times*)

One of Drucker's achievements lies in the fact that he, a devotee of the human relations school, recognized the value of Taylor's scientific, work-study approach, and succeeded in striking a balance between the two approaches. Management by Objectives, when performed properly, is an effective marriage of both schools, which attaches significance to culture and to the fact that organizations are held together not just by a dictated vision but by a shared vision of the future.

So, although Drucker awards the accolade of "guru's guru" to F. W. Taylor, the world of management will always attribute it to Drucker himself. His ability to see management with a long historical perspective and in a broad social and political context is very rare in management writers. With his capacity for demystifying the apparent complexities of management for millions worldwide, he stands, as he said of himself, quite alone.

For More Information

Books:

Drucker, Peter F. *The Future of Industrial Man: A Conservative Approach*. London: Heinemann, 1943.

Drucker, Peter F. *The Practice of Management*. London: Heinemann, 1955.

Drucker, Peter F.*Managing for Results: Economic Tasks and Risk-taking Decisions*. London: Heinemann, 1964.

Drucker, Peter F. *The Concept of the Corporation*. New York: New American Library, 1964.

Drucker, Peter F. *The Effective Executive*. London: Heinemann, 1967.

Drucker, Peter F. *The End of Economic Man*. New York: Harper & Row, 1969.

Drucker, Peter F. *Technology, Management, and Society*. New York: Harper & Row, 1970.

Drucker, Peter F. *Management: Tasks, Responsibilities, Practices*. New York: Harper & Row, 1973.

Drucker, Peter F. *Managing in Turbulent Times*. New York: Harper & Row, 1980.

Drucker, Peter F. *The Changing World of the Executive*. New York: Times Books, 1982.

Drucker, Peter F. *Innovation and Entrepreneurship: Practice and Principles*. New York: Harper & Row, 1985.

Drucker, Peter F. *The Frontiers of Management: Where Tomorrow's Decisions Are Being Made Today*. New York: Truman Talley Books/Dutten, 1986.

Drucker, Peter F. *Managing the Non-profit Organization: Practices and Principles*. New York: HarperCollins Publishers, 1990.

Drucker, Peter F. *Managing for the Future: The 1990s and Beyond*. New York: Truman Talley Books/Dutten, 1992.

Drucker, Peter F. *Managing in a Time of Great Change*. New York: Truman Talley Books/Dutten, 1995.

Journal Articles:

Donkin, Richard. "Interview with Peter Drucker." *Financial Times*, 14 June 1996, p.13.

Johnson, Mike. "Drucker Speaks His Mind." *Management Review*, October 1995, pp.10–14.

Mary Parker Follett

1868	Born.
1888	Attends Society for Collegiate Instruction of Women, Harvard.
1890	Spends a year at Newnham College, Cambridge University.
1896	Publication of *The House of Representatives*.
1918	Begins writing *The New State*.
1933	Gives inaugural series of lectures for Department of Business Administration (now Department of Industrial Relations) at the London School of Economics.
1933	Dies.

Summary

Mary Parker Follett was one of the first people to apply psychological insight and social science findings to the study of industrial organization.

Her work focused on human relations within industrial groups. She viewed business as a pioneering field within which solutions to human relations problems were being tested out.

After World War II her ideas were largely neglected, except in Japan. Yet her work foreshadowed current Western approaches emphasizing involvement and cross-functional communications.

Life and Career

Born in Massachusetts to a well-off Boston family, Follett was a brilliant scholar who graduated from high school at the age of 12. She was educated at the Thayer Academy, Boston, and Radcliffe College, Massachusetts. At 20 she attended an annex of Harvard University called the Society for Collegiate Instruction of Women. In 1890, as a student of 22, she spent a year at Newnham College in Cambridge, England, and went on to Paris as a postgraduate student. Pauline Graham describes Follett as a polymath, and records that she studied law, economics, government, and philosophy at Harvard, and history and political science at Newnham. While at Cambridge, Follett gave a paper that she later developed into her first book, *The House of Representatives*. This was taken seriously enough to be reviewed by Theodore Roosevelt in the *American Historical Review* of October 1896.

Follett's family life was difficult. Her father, to whom she was close, died when she was in her early teens. Her mother was an invalid with whom Follett did not get along very well. From an early age Follett ran the household and later she also ran the family housing business.

Eventually, Follett broke all family ties and went to share a home with her friend, Isobella Briggs. Over the next 30 years, Isobella provided a stable domestic background, while her social connections were helpful to Follett's work. When Isobella died in 1926, Follett lost her home life as well as her closest friend. Later that year she met Dame Katherine Furse, an Englishwoman who was strongly involved with the Girl Guide scouting movement. Follett later moved to England to share a house in Chelsea with Furse.

Follett the Social Worker

Follett was expected to become an academic, but instead she went into voluntary social work in Boston, where her energy and practicality (as well as her financial support on occasions) achieved much in terms of community-building initiatives. For over 30 years, she was immersed in this work, and proved to be an innovative, hands-on manager whose practical achievements included the original use of schools as centers for community education and recreation after the normal school day. This was Follett's own idea, and the resulting community centers became models for other cities throughout the United States.

Follett established vocational placement centers in Boston schools, and represented the public on the Massachusetts Minimum Wage Board. From 1924 she began to give regular papers relating to industrial organization, especially at conferences of the Bureau of Personnel Administration in New York. She became, in effect, an early management consultant, as businessmen began to seek her advice about their organizational and human relations problems.

In 1926 and 1928, Follett gave papers for the Rowntree Lecture Conference and to the National Institute of Industrial Psychology. In 1933, she gave an inaugural series of lectures for the newly founded Department of Business Administration (now the Department of Industrial Relations) at the London School of Economics (LSE). Later in 1933, Follett returned to America, where she died on December 18 of that year at the age of 65.

Contribution

The New State was written during 1918, and argues for group-based democracy as a process of government. Through this book, Follett became widely recognized as a political philosopher. It was based on her social work experience rather than on business organizations, but the ideas it contains were later applied in the business context.

The New State presented an often visionary interpretation of what Follett viewed as the progress of social evolution, and the tone is occasionally infused with poetical religious feeling. The text argues that democracy "by numbers" should give way to a more valid process of group-based democracy. This form of democracy is described as a dynamic process through which individual conflicts and differences become integrated in the search for overall group agreement. Through it, people will grow and learn as they adapt to one another's views, while seeking a common, long-term good.

The group process works through the relating of individuals' different ideas to each other and to the common interests of the group as a whole. Appropriate action would, Follett held, become self-evident during the consultation process. This would eventually reveal a "law of the situation," representing an objective that all could see would be the best course for the group as a whole to pursue. Conflict and disagreement were viewed as positive forces, and Follett considered social evolution to progress through the ever-continuous integration of diverse viewpoints and opinions in pursuit of the common good.

The New State envisions the basic group democratic process following right through to the international level, feeding up from neighborhoods via municipal and state government into the League of Nations. Sometimes, Follett refers to an almost autonomous group spirit, which develops from the community between people.

The Creative Experience was also written during 1918, and again focused on democratic governance, using examples from business to illustrate ideas. *Dynamic Management—The Collected Papers of Mary Parker Follett* and *Freedom and Coordination* were both published posthumously and edited by L. Urwick. *Freedom and Coordination* collects together six papers given by Follett at the LSE in 1933, and these represent the most developed and concise distillation of her thoughts on business organization.

Follett's business writings extended her social ideas into the industrial sphere. Industrial managers, she saw, confronted the same difficulties as public administrators as regards control, power, participation, and conflict. Her later writings focused on management from a human perspective, using the new approach of psychology to deal with problems between individuals and within groups. She encouraged businessmen to look at how groups formed and how employee commitment and motivation could be encouraged. The participation of everyone involved in decisions affecting their activities is seen as fundamental, in that Follett viewed group power and management through cooperation as the obvious route to achievements that would benefit all.

Views on Power, Leadership, Authority, and Control

Follett envisioned management responsibility as being diffused throughout a business rather than wholly concentrated at the hierarchical apex. Degrees of authority and responsibility are seen as spread all along the line. For example, a truck driver can act with more authority than the business owner in terms of knowing most about the best order in which to make his drops. Leadership skills are required of many people rather than just one person, and final authority, while it does exist, should not be overemphasized. The chief executive's role lies in coordinating the scattered authorities and varied responsibilities that make up the organization into group action and ideas, and also in foreseeing and meeting the next situation.

Follett's concept of leadership as the ability to develop and integrate group ideas, using "power with" rather than "power over" people, is very modern. She understood that the crude exercise of authority based on subordination is hurtful to people, and cannot be the basis of effective, motivational management control. Partnership and cooperation, she sought to persuade people, were of far more ultimate benefit to everyone than hierarchical control and competition.

Follett viewed the group process as a form of collective control, with the experience of all who perform a functional part in an activity feeding into decision making. Control is thus realized through the coordination of all functions rather than imposed from the outside.

Follett's Four Fundamental Principles of Organization

Follett identified four principles of coordination that she considered basic to effective management.

- Coordination consists in the "reciprocal relating" of all the factors in a situation.
- Coordination should be by direct contact, operating by means of direct communication between all responsible people involved, whatever their hierarchical or departmental positions.
- Coordination should begin in the early stages. It should involve all the people directly concerned, right from the initial stages of designing a project or forming a policy.
- Coordination should be a continuing process, based on the recognition that there is no such thing as unity, but only the continuous process of unifying.

Context and Conclusions

The Context of Evolutionary Progress

Follett's thinking was ahead of her time, yet was founded on a conviction of social, evolutionary progress, which the course of subsequent history has shown to be flawed. She lived through momentous times, when social and technological change seemed to make a new order inevitable. The destruction caused by World War I also seemed to dictate the clear need for a determined effort to create a social order that would not break down so disastrously. Simultaneously, the war created pressures in both England and America for labor participation in management, and led to a growth in internationalist ideas and to the birth of the League of Nations. Like other writers of the time, Follett made leaps of the imagination that grew out of the factual changes that were actually taking place. Her view was rational and progressive, and she could not know the degree to which some things would remain constant, undermining the apparently inevitable dynamic of social "progress."

Looking back on the whole of the 20th century, of which Follett saw only the beginning, we have only too full a knowledge of World War II and countless other conflicts, of the discrediting of Russian Communism, and of worsening ethnic divisions and continuing human barbarities. The progressive, internationalist vision seems to be, from our contemporary perspective, a fast-receding dream.

Yet, while Follett's optimistic expectations of radical social change were largely mistaken, she drew from it the imaginative vision to transform at least some of her convictions into ideas about ways of living and working that have contributed much to both social and management practice. In fact, it is almost disheartening to read Follett and realize that she clearly and strongly stated, so many years ago, ideas that are being proffered as "new" today and that are still rarely practiced in any sustained way.

For More Information

Books:

Graham, Pauline, ed. *Mary Parker Follett: Prophet of Management—A Celebration of Writings from the 1920s.* Boston: Harvard Business School Press. 1995

Parker Follett, Mary. *The Speaker of the House of Representatives.* New York: Longmans, Green & Co., 1896.

Parker Follett, Mary. *The New State: Group Organization—the Solution for Popular Government.* New York: Longmans, Green & Co., 1920.

Parker Follett, Mary. *Creative Experience.* New York: Longmans, Green & Co., 1924.

Ghoshal and Bartlett

Summary

Pioneering research with collaborator Christopher Bartlett into what makes large global organizations tick, and an enquiring mind committed to management as the wealth creator, have contributed to the emergence of Sumantra Ghoshal as one of the most respected management thinkers of his generation.

Already a sought-after consultant, teacher, speaker, and prolific writer, his research will continue to play an important role during this era of globalization.

Life and Career

Born in India in 1946, Sumantra Ghoshal studied physics before spending 12 years (1969–81) at the Indian Oil Corporation. He demonstrated his appetite for understanding what makes organizations work by obtaining two doctorates, one from MIT, champion of the rigorous scientific method, the other from more pragmatic Harvard, whose approach is based on case studies, observation, and practice.

After lecturing at MIT and INSEAD, Ghoshal became Professor of Business Policy at INSEAD in 1992, and Professor of Strategic Leadership at the London Business School in 1994. He first came to international prominence with the publication in 1989 of *Managing Across Borders*, coauthored with Christopher Bartlett.

Life and Career

Christopher Bartlett is Thomas D. Casserly, Jr. Professor of Business Administration at Harvard Business School. Before joining the faculty of Harvard, he was a marketing manager with Alcoa in Australia, a management consultant in McKinsey and Company's London office, and general manager at Baxter Laboratories' subsidiary company in France.

His research interests have focused on the strategic and organizational challenges which managers face in running multinational corporations, and these interests have been reflected in his most successful books.

Managing Across Borders was cited by the *Financial Times* as one of the 50 most influential business books of the century.

Contribution
Managing Across Borders
Ghoshal and Bartlett's thinking begins with two fundamental questions:
- What does strategy mean?
- Why do the time-honored business models—exemplified by Alfred Sloan's General Motors—no longer work?

Their initial research involved asking over 250 managers in nine multinational companies how their companies were facing up to the complexities of international competition and the growing global marketplace. They identified a pervasive organizational inability to cope, survive, and succeed in the face of growing diversity and accelerating change.

They found three types of organizational model in operation:

- the multinational model, exemplified by Philips or Unilever—a decentralized federation of local firms held together by posting key people from the center;
- the global model, exemplified by Ford and Matsushita—benefiting from large-scale economies and conduits into new market opportunities;
- a more widespread international model—focusing on technology and the transfer of knowledge to less advanced environments.

They concluded that a fourth model was necessary—the transnational—which would combine all the elements of the other three and, in addition, exploit local know-how as the key weapon in identifying opportunities, and not operate overseas sites as outposts of the center.

Efficiency versus Economic Progress

To understand why the old models no longer worked, Ghoshal examined Alfred Sloan's General Motors, the pioneer of the three Ss (Strategy—Structure—Systems), emulated by other companies for decades.

The three Ss were designed to make the management of complex organizations systematic and predictable. The top people in the organization crafted the strategy, then designed the structure that enabled it to unfold and the systems that made it operational. The information systems they relied on dealt with facts and reduced the human element to a minimum. Employees on Ford's assembly lines, for example, were viewed as replaceable parts; ITT, under Harold Geneen, abolished the possibility of surprise by constantly establishing "unshakeable facts."

For years, this systematic approach worked. It started to break down only in the 1980s, when converging technologies, fluctuating markets, overnight competition, and technological innovation combined to make its control systems cumbersome, unresponsive, and ultimately a risk to the survival of the organization itself. An article by Ghoshal, Christopher A. Bartlett, and Peter Moran in the *Sloan Management Review*, Spring 1999 ("A New Manifesto for Management," pp. 9–20) pointed out that criticisms of these systems for stifling initiative, creativity, and diversity were valid: "They were designed for an organization man who has turned out to be an evolutionary dead end." (p. 11)

In the same article, the authors implicitly attacked Michael Porter's work. Porter had influenced strategic thinking for over a decade by arguing that organizations must beat the competition by gaining a stranglehold on value, that is, by either reducing competitors' value (perhaps through competitive incremental cost or quality improvements) or buying them out. Ghoshal wrote: "Porter's theory is static in that it focuses strategic thinking on getting the largest possible share of a fixed economic pie." (p. 12) For Ghoshal, companies exist not to appropriate value, but to create it—and they get themselves into a position to be able to create value by "changing the smell of the place."

Fontainebleau and Calcutta: The "Springtime Theory"

Ghoshal developed his "springtime theory" while teaching business policy at INSEAD in the forest of Fontainebleau, south of Paris. During a summer visit to his home city of Calcutta, he found the humidity oppressive and draining, and likened this to the stultifying atmosphere in control- and system-oriented corporate climates. Later, walking in the woods at

Fontainebleau, he realized that the fresh, energizing forest reminded him of the cultural atmosphere of more open and dynamic organizations. From this, he went on to propound his "springtime theory," arguing that managers and approaches to management strongly affect cultures and can create or change the organizational context, "the smell of the place." But how?

The Three Ps

Ghoshal considers that today's leading companies are built around the "three Ps": Purpose, Process, and People. In an interview in *Management Skills and Development*, he claimed that, as shapers of purpose, senior managers need "to create a shared ambition among their staff, instil organizational values, and provide personal meaning for the work their staff do." Creating that shared ambition is an active management process that challenges poor performance, establishes a common goal, demonstrates managers' commitment and self-discipline, and provides "meaning for everyone's efforts." (p. 40)

In the same interview, Ghoshal also stresses the need for organizations to:

- start thinking outside the "strategic planning" box and examining how they actually learn;
- complement vertical information flows with horizontal personal relationships;
- build a trust-based culture by spreading a message of genuine openness;
- share all the information that has traditionally been a source of power.

He says: "You cannot have faith in people unless you take action to improve and develop them. The success of businesses depends now more than ever on the talent of people working for them." (p. 39) In short, organizations need to forge a "new moral contract" with their people.

The New Moral Contract

In the past, the contract between organizations and employees promised relative security in return for conformity. In the 1980s and 1990s, however, this changed: job security was undermined by downsizing and reengineering, while managerial approaches such as Total Quality Management and Customer Focus demanded more involvement and initiative from employees. The new contract Ghoshal proposes is based on developing employability, and providing challenging jobs rather than functional boxes. It should be viewed neither as altruism on the company's part nor as something imposed on employees. It is, rather, a new management philosophy that recognizes that personal development both improves employees' performance and makes them more employable in their future working lives, and that market performance stems from the initiative, creativity, and skills of all employees, and not just the wisdom of senior management.

Such a contract involves a great leap for both organizations and employees. Employers must create a working environment with opportunities for personal and professional growth, within a management environment in which it is understood that talented, growing people mean talented, growing organizations. Employees must make greater commitment to continuous learning and development, and accept that, in a climate of constant change and uncertainty, the will to develop is the only hedge against a changing job market.

Companies As Value Creators

Ghoshal feels strongly that organizations must stop focusing on squeezing out every last cost saving, waste reduction, or improvement in quality or efficiency. That may seem like the ultimate goal of TQM and continuous improvement, but organizations with that sole aim are only good at improving existing activities. Their emphasis is wholly on conservation, which, as Ghoshal points out, Jack Welch of GE described as a "ticket to the boneyard."

The main message of Ghoshal and Bartlett's more recent book, *The Individualized Corporation* (1998), is that the key to competitive advantage in a turbulent economy is a company's ability to innovate its way out of relentless market pressures. As companies shift emphasis from acquiring value to creating it, managers should shift their focus away from obedience, control, and conformity to initiative, relationship building, and continuous challenge of the status quo. Instead of being cogs in a system, they should become facilitators and people developers, drawing creativity from others.

Context and Conclusions

Since Ghoshal first came to prominence, his focus has shifted from international strategy to the importance of putting people, creativity, and innovation at the top of the agenda and of emphasizing high-quality management as a social and moral value-creating force. It will be interesting to see where the "smell in the air" takes him next, especially in the light of a 1999 article in the *Financial Times* ("Guru with a Teaching Mission for His Country," 12 April, p.14) in which he describes his plans to open a new business school for India.

For More Information

Books:

Bartlett, Christopher A., and Sumantra Ghoshal. *Managing Across Borders: The Transnational Solution*. 2nd ed. Boston, MA: Harvard Business School Press, 1998.

Bartlett, Christopher A., and Sumantra Ghoshal. *The Individualized Corporation: A Fundamentally New Approach to Management*. Collingdale, PA: DIANE Publishing Co. 1997

Journal Articles:

Bartlett, Christopher A., and Sumantra Ghoshal. "Changing the Role of Top Management: Beyond Strategy to Purpose."*Harvard Business Review*, Nov/Dec, 1994, pp.79–88.

Bartlett, Christopher A., and Sumantra Ghoshal. "Changing the Role of Top Management: Beyond Structure to Processes."*Harvard Business Review*, Jan/Feb, 1995, pp. 86–96.

Bartlett, Christopher A., and Sumantra Ghoshal. "Changing the Role of Top Management: Beyond Systems to People."*Harvard Business Review*, May/June, 1995, pp.132–142.

Frank and Lillian Gilbreth

1868	Frank born.
1878	Lillian born.
1885	Frank develops theory of work simplification.
1890s	Frank founds Society to Promote the Science of Management, in conjunction with F. W. Taylor.
1895	Frank founds engineering consulting company, Gilbreth Inc.
1904	Frank and Lillian marry; go on to produce 12 children.
1912–1913	Lillian's book, *Psychology in the Workplace*, published in installments by the Society of Industrial Engineers.
1915	Lillian awarded a Ph.D. in applied management by Brown University.
1921	Lillian becomes first woman member of the Society of Industrial Engineers; later becomes first woman member of the American Society of Mechanical Engineers.
1924	Frank dies. Lillian presents a paper of his at the International Management Conference in Prague.
1925	Lillian continues the work of Gilbreth Inc., conducting seminars on motion study and accepting consulting jobs.
1972	Lillian dies, having been the first and, to date, only female recipient of the Gilbreth Medal, the Gantt Gold Medal, and the CIOS Gold Medal.
1995	Lillian included in the National Women's Hall of Fame in the United States.

Summary

Management practitioners today largely ignore the Gilbreths, possibly because the principles pioneered by them are now unfashionable. Motion study entailed the detailed examination of the movements individual workers made in their work. However through Frank's concerns that the efficiency of employees should be balanced by economy of effort and minimization of stress, and Lillian's interest in the psychology of management, they laid the foundations for the modern concepts of job simplification, meaningful work standards, and incentive wage plans.

Life and Career

Frank B. Gilbreth (1868–1924) began his career as a bricklayer and, by the age of 27, had worked his way up through the profession to found his own engineering consulting company, Gilbreth Inc. He had a particular interest in the development of people to their fullest potential through training, work methods, and improving the working environment and tools, as well as through the creation of healthier working conditions. An adherent to the principles of scientific management, Frank was one of the first to find practical applications for it. Although he had disagreements with F. W. Taylor (mostly through Taylor's claiming Frank's work as his own, and then implying that it was nothing new), Frank was an advocate of Taylor's methods and founded the Society to Promote the Science of Management (renamed the Taylor Society after Taylor's death).

Frank and Lillian married in 1904, and were the parents of 12 children (one daughter died of diphtheria at the age of five). Frank apparently informed Lillian that he wanted six sons and six daughters. In an interview with the *New York Post* in 1941, Lillian was quoted as having once asked him, "How on earth could anybody have 12 children and continue a career?" To which Frank had replied, "We teach management, so we'll have to practice it."

Lillian Moller Gilbreth (1878–1972) was an inspirational woman. In what was very much a man's world at the time—particularly in the area of engineering consulting work, which she entered with Frank—Lillian achieved an astounding amount. When she completed a thesis on the psychology of management, the University of California refused to award her a doctorate unless she returned to campus for a year's residency. This was impractical, so the family moved to the East Coast, where Lillian undertook a Ph.D. in applied management at Brown University, writing a new thesis, entitled "Some aspects of eliminating waste in teaching." Her Ph.D. was finally awarded in 1915.

Lillian worked closely with Frank in Gilbreth Inc., as well as running their household and bringing up their children. Within a few days of Frank's death in 1924, she traveled to Europe to present a paper that he had intended to give at the International Management Conference in Prague. As Frank's widow, Lillian continued the work of Gilbreth Inc. by conducting seminars on motion study and accepting any consulting jobs that she was not barred from taking simply because she was female.

Often called "the first lady of management," Lillian became the first woman member of both the Society of Industrial Engineers (1921) and the American Society of Mechanical Engineers. She was also the first and, to date, the only female recipient of the Gilbreth Medal, the Gantt Gold Medal, and the CIOS Gold Medal. In 1995, Lillian Gilbreth was included in the National Women's Hall of Fame in the United States.

Contribution
Work Simplification
Work simplification was based on respect for the dignity of people and work, and was developed by Frank Gilbreth from the age of 17, when he began work as a bricklayer. He documented the different ways that individuals laid bricks and from these observations determined the most efficient way to perform this task. For Frank, efficiency was of benefit both to the employer, through an increase in the number of bricks laid, and to the employee, through minimizing the levels of exertion required, and so reducing tiredness and the risk of injury. Through his extensive analysis, Frank pioneered a new system of laying bricks that increased output per worker from 1,000 to 2,700 bricks per day.

Another application of Frank's efficiency studies can be seen in operating rooms in hospitals around the world today. Prior to the efficiency study he conducted, surgeons would find all the instruments they needed for operations for themselves, wasting precious minutes as the patient lay on the table. Frank introduced the procedure of having a nurse assist the surgeon by passing instruments into an open hand, as they were required.

Frank took his efficiency systems very seriously, even at home. In *Cheaper by the Dozen*, it is stated that he used two shaving brushes to lather his face in order to save 17 seconds on his shaving time. He abandoned attempts to shave with two razors however: While it saved 44 seconds in shaving time, he also had to spend an extra two minutes bandaging his cuts.

Neither were the Gilbreths' children exempt from their parents' efficiency methods.

They were all given their own tasks and became individually responsible for duties such as buying the family's birthday presents, or being chairperson of the house budget committee.

Therbligs
In their study of hand movements, the Gilbreths found that terms such as "move hand" were too general to allow detailed analysis. They split hand movements into 17 basic units of motion that could then, through various combinations, form the hand movements being monitored. These units were known collectively as "therbligs"—Gilbreth spelled backwards, with the "th" transposed.

Microchronometer
In the course of their motion study work, the Gilbreths used photographs to record and then analyze workers' movements. To aid in the clear analysis of their films, they developed the microchronometer—a clock that could record time to 1/2000 of a second—which was placed in the area being photographed. This device is still sometimes used today.

Process and Flow Charts
Around the time that the Gilbreths began working, Henry Gantt developed the ideas that grew into what came to be known as the "Gantt chart"—a system of recording the planning and controlling of work in progress. Frank and Lillian used a Gantt chart in their work and, in their turn, added process charts and flow diagrams. These new tools graphically demonstrated the constituent parts that need to be performed to complete a task.

Psychology of Management and Personnel Issues
The importance of employee welfare was reflected throughout the work of both the Gilbreths, ranging from Frank's concern over the minimization of employee fatigue and stress to their mutual interest in incentives, promotion, and employee welfare. Although not the originator of the discipline of industrial psychology, Lillian's research for her doctoral thesis raised awareness of the importance of the human element in industry. Many publishers refused to publish a book by a woman on such a technical subject, but *Psychology in the Workplace* was eventually published in installments by the Society of Industrial Engineers in 1912 and 1913. The Gilbreths' interest in industrial psychology continued throughout their lives and was demonstrated by Lillian's participation in various U.S. government committees, on subjects ranging from unemployment and war production to problems related to aging and disability.

Context and Conclusions
The Gilbreths are largely unknown and uncelebrated in today's modern corporate world, which tends to minimize the importance of measurement minutiae and favors the space and thinking time needed for creativity and innovation. Earlier in the 20th century, however, management writers from the 1940s on, such as Lyndall Urwick and Edward Brech, had lionized the Gilbreths, along with Taylor and Fayol, as scientific management became the popular gospel.

As we move into the 21st century, any glory for original time and motion work is largely assigned to Taylor, and the work of the Gilbreths is often forgotten or ignored. As the human relations school of management gained in momentum, with the Hawthorne studies and the work of motivational theorists such as McGregor, Maslow, Likert, and Herzberg, people rather than processes slowly became the central pivot for many management thinkers.

The overwhelming influence of scientific management faded from the 1960s onward. The work of the Gilbreths, however, combining the disciplines of both motion study and industrial psychology, deserves to be recognized for its lasting contribution to management thought, and to the ways in which we work today.

For More Information
Books:

Gilbreth, Jr., Frank B., and Ernestine Gilbreth Carey. New ed. *Cheaper by the Dozen*. New York: Yearling, 2000.

Spriegel, William R., and Clark E. Myers, eds. *Writings of the Gilbreths* (A compendium of various books and papers by the Gilbreths including: *Field System, Concrete System, Bricklaying System, Primer of Scientific Management, Motion Study, Applied Motion Study, Motion Study for the Handicapped, Fatigue Study, Psychology of Management*). Homewood, IL: Richard D. Irwin, 1953.

Wren, Daniel. *Evolution of Management Thought*. 3rd ed. New York: John Wiley, 1987.

Yost, Edna. *Frank and Lillian Gilbreth: Partners for Life*. New York: American Society of Mechanical Engineers, 1949.

Charles Handy

1932	Born.
1967	Founder of Sloan Program, London Business School.
1972	Professor, London Business School.
1974	Governor, London Business School.
1976	Publication of *Understanding Organizations*.
1977	Warden, St. George's House, Windsor Castle.
1985	Publication of *Gods of Management*.
1989	Publication of *The Age of Unreason*.
1994	Publication of *The Age of Paradox*.

Summary

Charles Handy is well known for his work on organizations. Culminating in the formation of a vision of the future of work and of the implications of change for the ways in which people manage their lives and careers, his observation of work in modern society has identified discontinuous change as the (paradoxically) continuing characteristic of working lives and organizations. He has forecast a future—so far, with a good deal of accuracy— where half of the United Kingdom's workforce will no longer be in permanent full-time jobs.

Life and Career

Born in Ireland, Charles Handy is a self-employed writer, teacher, and broadcaster. He is a visiting professor at the London Business School and consultant to a wide variety of organizations in government, business, and the voluntary and educational sectors.

After he graduated from Oxford, his working life began in the marketing and personnel divisions of Shell International and as an economist with Anglo-American Corporation. He then returned to academia at the Sloan School of Management of the Massachusetts Institute of Technology. In 1967 he was the founder and Director of the Sloan Program at the London Business School, where he also taught managerial psychology and development. Appointments as professor and governor of the School followed in 1972 and 1974 respectively. In 1977 he was appointed Warden of St. George's House in Windsor Castle, a private conference and study center with a strong focus on the discussion of business ethics. As a teacher he later concentrated on the application of behavioral science to management, the management of change, the structure of organizations, and on the theory and practice of individual learning in life.

He is a past Chairman of the Royal Society of Arts; in 1994 he was U.K. Business Columnist of the Year. He has also been a regular contributor to Thought for the Day (a daily brief religious talk) on the *Today* news program on BBC Radio 4.

Contribution

Four of Handy's books in particular consider the structure of organizations in detail, and offer a perspective on the ways in which they work. These are: *Understanding Organizations*

(1976), *Gods of Management* (1985), *The Age of Unreason* (1989), and *The Age of Paradox* (1994).

Understanding Organizations

Handy's *Understanding Organizations*—described by publishers and commentators alike as "a landmark study"—is equally valuable for the student of management and for the practicing manager. Among the subjects with which it deals are motivation, roles and interactions, leadership, power and influence, the workings of groups, and the culture of organizations. They are dealt with both as "concepts" and "concepts in application." A "guide to further study" points the way for further examination of each concept.

Gods of Management

Handy identifies some established structures in organizations and suggests new forms that are emerging. He perceives that, currently, organizations embrace four basic "cultures."

- *Club Culture.* This is represented metaphorically by Zeus, the strong leader who has, likes, and uses power, and graphically by a spider's web. All lines of communication lead, formally or informally, to the leader. Such organizations display strength in the speed of their decision making; their potential weakness lies in the caliber of the "one man bands" running them.
- *Role Culture.* This is personified as Apollo, the god of order and rules, represented by a Greek temple. Such organizations are based on the assumptions that people are rational, and that roles can be defined and discharged with clearly defined procedures. They display stability and certainty, and have great strength in situations marked by continuity; they often display weakness in adapting to, or generating, change.
- *Task Culture.* This is likened to Athena, the goddess of wisdom, and is found in organizations where management is concerned with solving a series of problems. The structure is represented by a net, resources being drawn from all parts of the organization to meet the needs of current problems. Working parties, subcommittees, task forces, and study groups are formed on an ad hoc basis to deal with problems. This type of culture is seen to advantage when flexibility is required.
- *Existential Culture.* This is represented by Dionysus, the god of wine and song. Organizations characterized by a culture of this type are those that exist to serve the individual and in which individuals are not servants of the organization. They consist of groups of professionals, for example, doctors or lawyers, with no "boss." Coordination may be provided by a committee of peers. Such structures are becoming more common as more conventional organizations increasingly contract out work to professionals and specialists whose services are used only as and when required.

The Changing Organization

The link between this analysis of organizational structures and Handy's later work is, in part, provided by the development of "contracting out"—one of a number of changes that he observes in the world of employment. Another major change is the basing of the quest for profit on intelligence and professional skills rather than on manual work and machines. Yet another is that the days of working for one employer and/or in one occupation may be over.

The Shamrock Organization

An example of Handy's changing perception of organizations is provided by his use (in *The Age of Unreason*) of the shamrock. He uses this symbol to demonstrate three bases on which people are often employed by organizations today. The people linked to an organization are beginning to fall into three groups, each with different expectations of it, each managed and rewarded differently.

The first group is a core of qualified professional technicians and managers. They are essential to the continuity of the organization, and have detailed knowledge of it, and of its aims, objectives, and practices. They are rewarded with high salaries and associated benefits, in return for which they must be prepared to give commitment, to work hard, and, if necessary, to work long hours. They must be mobile. They work within a task culture, one within which there is a constant effort to reduce their numbers.

The second group consists of contracted specialists, who may be used, for example, for advertising, R&D, computing, catering, or mailing services. They operate in an existential culture; and are rewarded with fees rather than with salaries or wages. Their contribution to the organization is measured in output rather than in hours, in results rather than in time.

The third group—the third leaf of Handy's shamrock—consists of a flexible labor force, discharging part-time, temporary, and seasonal roles. They operate within a role culture; but, Handy observes, while they may be employed on a casual basis, they must not be managed casually but in a way that recognizes their worth to the organization.

The Federal Organization and the Inverted Doughnut

The concept of the federal organization was first explored in *The Age of Unreason* and expanded in *The Empty Raincoat*. In it, subsidiaries federate to gain benefits of scale. Federal organizations should not be confused with decentralized organizations, in which power lies in the center and is exerted downwards and outwards. In the federal organization, the role of top management is redefined as that of providing vision, motivating, inspiring, and coordinating; initiative comes from the components of the organization. Handy observes and describes the principle of "subsidiarity"—not handing out or delegating power, but ruling and unifying only with the consent and agreement of equal partners.

In *The Empty Raincoat* Handy uses the metaphor of the inverted doughnut to demonstrate how those in the subsidiaries must constantly seek to extend their roles and associated activities. The hole in the conventional doughnut is filled by the core activities of the subsidiary; the substance of the doughnut represents a diminishing vacuum into which the subsidiary can expand its activities given the necessary drive, will, and ability.

Portfolio Working and Downshifting

Following on from his work on organizational change, Handy studied the effects of such change on the individual. He coined the concept "portfolio working," based on the assumption that full-time working for one employer will soon be a thing of the past. Embedded in this is the notion of downshifting—the idea that it is possible to exchange some part of income for a better quality of life.

Although Handy has gone on record as saying that more and more individuals will opt out of formal organizations and sell their services at a pace and at a price to suit themselves, he has also admitted that comparatively few may find themselves in a position to take real advantage of this. He argues, however, that there is much that the organization can do to help the individual to get to grips with the new uncertainty. It was in discussion with the Japanese that Handy coined the "theory of horizontal fast track." In Japan, the most talented people are moved around from experience to experience as quickly as possible, so that their talents can be tested in different situations, with different managers and different cultures. This ensures that they discover what they are really good at and provides a lot of experience.

Context and Conclusions

With his imaginative use of analogy and metaphor, the Handy of the 1990s moved us from the past into the future. He argues that federalist and shamrock organizations can really be successful only if businesses are prepared to invest in their workforces and build relationships of trust.

While he is as much concerned with individuals as organizations, his messages are sometimes disquieting. In *The Hungry Spirit*, he assesses the effects of the competitiveness of capitalism on the individual, suggesting that people can become not only stressed but also selfish and insensitive. But his message is not confined to pessimism about the future. On the contrary, the new capitalism consists of intellectual property—know-how, not merely physical and financial resources; the new knowledge markets enable low-cost entry to those with "a bit of wit and a bit of imagination" and the new products of the knowledge world are not nearly so destructive on the environment as the industrial products of the past.

Handy stands apart from many other management writers by his breadth of vision, his setting of management in a wide social and economic context, and the sheer readability of his writing. He is also ready to modify his views in the light of experience and further thought (he has admitted that some of his expectations have been proved wrong). He is not merely an observer of change but increasingly a catalyst who forces people to stand back from their daily routine, take stock, and view the future through different glasses, acknowledge change, and address its implications.

For More Information

Books:
Handy, Charles. *Understanding Organizations*. New York: Oxford University Press, 1985.
Handy, Charles. *The Gods of Management*. London: Souvenir Press, 1985.
Handy, Charles. *The Age of Unreason*. Boston: Harvard Business School Press, 1989.
Handy, Charles. *The Age of Paradox*. Boston: Harvard Business School Press, 1994.
Handy, Charles. *Beyond Certainty*. Boston: Harvard Business School Press, 1998.
Handy, Charles. *The Hungry Spirit: Beyond Capitalism—A Quest for Purpose in the Modern World*. New York: Broadway Books, 1998.
Handy, Charles. *The Elephant and the Flea.* Boston, MA: Harvard Business School Press, 2002.

Frederick Herzberg

1923	Born.
1945	Enters Dachau concentration camp with U.S. liberating forces.
1946	Graduates from City College of New York.
1951– 1957	Research Director of psychological services in Pittsburgh, Pennsylvania.
1957	Appointed Professor of Management at Case Western Reserve University, Cleveland, Ohio.
1959	*The Motivation to Work* published.
1966	*Work and the Nature of Man* published.
1968	"One more time: how do you motivate employees?" published in the *Harvard Business Review*.
1972	Joins University of Utah's School of Business.
2000	Dies.

Summary

Herzberg is best known for his "hygiene-motivation" or "two factor" theory of what motivates workers. He invented the acronym KITA (Kick In The Ass) to explain why personnel practices such as wage increases, fringe benefits, and job participation often fail to instill motivation and prove to be only short-term solutions. He also coined the term "job enrichment" to describe a process in which positively motivating factors are built into the design of jobs.

Life and Career

Frederick Herzberg (1923–2000) was a U.S. clinical psychologist who became an influential management thinker through his work on the nature of motivation and the most effective ways of motivating people. The "overriding interest in mental health" that led him into a career in psychology stemmed from a belief that "mental health is the core issue of our times," a conviction prompted by his posting, while serving in the American forces during World War II, to the Dachau concentration camp very soon after its liberation. On his return to America, he worked for the U.S. Public Health Service before beginning an academic career. His "hygiene-motivation" theory was first set out in *The Motivation to Work*, published in 1959. From 1972 until his retirement he worked at the University of Utah School of Business.

Contribution

The Hygiene-Motivation Theory

The "hygiene-motivation" or "two factor" theory that made Herzberg's name grew out of research he undertook with two hundred Pittsburgh engineers and accountants in the late 1950s.

He asked his subjects to recall times when they had felt exceptionally good about their jobs, then why they had had these positive feelings, and also what effect those feelings had had both on their performance at work and on their lives outside work. In a second question, he asked them to recall times when their experiences at work had resulted in negative feelings.

Herzberg was struck by the fact that, in the answers to his questionnaire, the positive things that the respondents had to say about their work experiences were not the opposite of the negative ones. From this, he concluded that there were two factors at work.

He postulated first of all that human beings have two sets of needs:

- lower-level needs as an animal to avoid pain and deprivation;
- higher-level needs as a human being to grow psychologically.

These needs have to be satisfied at work as much as in any other sphere of life. He concluded from the results of his survey that some factors in the workplace meet the first set of needs but not the second, and vice versa. The former group of factors he called "hygiene factors" and the latter, "motivators."

"Hygiene factors" have to do with the context or environment in which a person works. They include:

- company policy and administration
- supervision
- working relationships
- working conditions
- status
- security
- pay

The most important thing about these factors is that they do not in themselves promote job satisfaction; they serve primarily to prevent job dissatisfaction, in the same way that good hygiene does not in itself produce good health, but a lack of it will usually cause disease. Herzberg also spoke of them as "dissatisfiers" or "maintenance factors," because their absence or inadequacy causes dissatisfaction at work, while their presence simply keeps workers reasonably happy without motivating them to better themselves or their performance. Some factors are also not to be regarded as true motivators because they need constant reinforcement. Once introduced, they increasingly come to be regarded as rights to be expected, rather than incentives to greater satisfaction and achievement.

"Motivators" (also referred to as "growth factors") relate to what a person does at work, rather than to the context in which it is done. They include:

- achievement
- recognition
- the work itself
- responsibility
- advancement
- growth

Herzberg explains that the two sets of factors are separate and distinct because they are concerned with two different sets of needs. They are not opposites.

Herzberg's hygiene-motivation theory is derived from the outcomes of several investigations into job satisfaction and job dissatisfaction, studies that replicated his original research in Pittsburgh. The theory proposes that most of the factors that contribute to job satisfaction are motivators, while most of the factors that contribute to job dissatisfaction are hygiene factors.

Most of the evidence on which Herzberg based his theory is relatively clear-cut. This is particularly the case with regard to achievement and promotion prospects as potential job satisfiers and with regard to supervision and job insecurity as factors that contribute principally to dissatisfaction.

The element that continues to cause some debate is salary/pay, which seems as if it might belong in either group. Herzberg himself placed salary with the dissatisfiers, although the evidence was not so clear in this instance. This would seem to be the more appropriate classification. Although pay may have some short-term motivational value, it is difficult to conceive of it as a long-term motivator of the same order as responsibility and achievement. Most experience (and the history of industrial relations) would point to pay as a dissatisfier and therefore a hygiene factor along with supervision, status, and security.

KITA

In his extremely influential 1968 article for the *Harvard Business Review*, "One More Time: How Do You Motivate Employees?", Herzberg basically lumped all the hygiene factors together with the less pleasant aspects of work experience under the heading KITA (Kick In The Ass). To explain why managers are unable to motivate employees, he demonstrated again that employees are not motivated by being kicked (figuratively speaking), or by being given more money or benefits, or by a comfortable environment, or by reducing the time they spend at work. These things merely produce movement, the avoidance of pain. What genuinely motivates are things that are intangible, or intrinsic to the work.

Adam and Abraham

Herzberg used biblical allusions to illustrate his theory, especially in his book *Work and the Nature of Man*, first published in 1966 and intended as a psychological underpinning to his workplace-oriented studies. He depicted humanity's basic needs as two parallel arrows pointing in opposite directions. One arrow represents the "Animal-Adam" nature of human beings, concerned with the basic need to avoid physical deprivation (the hygiene factors); the other represents their "Human-Abraham" nature, which is driven by a need to realize their potential for perfection (the motivation factors).

Job Enrichment

Job enrichment was a logical extension of Herzberg's hygiene-motivation theory. Still working on the basic premise that a satisfied workforce is a productive workforce, he proposed that motivators of the type he had always advocated should be built into job design. They included:
- self-scheduling
- control of resources
- accountability
- undertaking specialized tasks in order to become expert in them

He saw it as a continuous function of management to ensure that people were given the opportunity to become more and more responsibly and creatively involved in their jobs.

Context and Conclusions

Herzberg's work—in common with that of Elton Mayo (known for the Hawthorne Experiments), Abraham Maslow (developer of the hierarchy of needs), and Douglas McGregor (creator of Theory X and Theory Y)—can be seen as a reaction to F. W. Taylor's scientific management theories. These last focused on techniques which could be used to maximize the productivity of manual workers and on the division of mental and physical work between management and workers. In contrast, Herzberg and his contemporaries believed that workers wanted the opportunity to feel part of a team and to grow and develop.

Although Herzberg's theory is not highly regarded by psychologists today, managers have found in it useful guidelines for action. Its basic tenets are easy to understand and can be applied to all types of organization. Furthermore, it appears to support the position and influence of management.

More specifically, it has had a considerable impact on reward systems, first, in a move away from payment-by-results systems, and today in the growing proportion of cafeteria benefits schemes, which allow individual employees to choose the fringe benefits which best suit them.

Job enrichment was more theorized about than put into practice. Many schemes that were tried resulted only in cosmetic changes or led to demands for increased worker control and were therefore terminated. Nowadays the concept is more one of people enrichment, although this still owes a great deal to Herzberg's original work. His greatest contribution has been the knowledge that motivation comes mainly from within the individual; it cannot be imposed from the outside by an organization in accordance with some formula. Many of today's trends—career management, self-managed learning, and empowerment—have their basis in Herzberg's insights.

For More Information
Books:
Herzberg, Frederick. *Work and the Nature of Man*. New York: Ty Crowell Co., 1966.
Herzberg, Frederick. *The Managerial Choice: To Be Efficient and To Be Human*. Homewood, IL: Dow Jones-Irwin, 1976.
Herzberg, Frederick, Bernard Mausner, and Barbara Bloch Snyderman. *The Motivation to Work*. 2nd ed. New York: John Wiley, 1959.

Journal Articles:
Cameron, Donald. "Herzberg–Still a Key to Understanding Motivation." *Training Officer*, July/August 1996, pp. 184–186.
Herzberg, Frederick. "One More Time: How Do You Motivate Employees?"*Harvard Business Review*, Jan/Feb 1968, pp. 53–62.
(This article was republished, in *Harvard Business Review*, Sep/Oct 1987, pp.109–120, with a retrospective commentary by the author. By the time of this republication, the article had sold over one million reprints, making it the most requested article in the *Harvard Business Review*'s history)

Joseph M. Juran

1904	Born.
1912	Family joins father in United States.
1920	Enrolls at University of Minnesota.
1924	Goes to work for Western Electric at Hawthorne Works in Chicago.
1926	Chosen for inspection training program by visiting Bell Laboratories team.
1928	Produces first work on quality, the training pamphlet, *Statistical Methods Applied to Manufacturing Problems*.
1937	Head of industrial engineering at Western Electric's corporate headquarters in New York.
1941	Assistant administrator for Lend-Lease program.
1945	Leaves Western Electric for New York University.
1951	Publication of *Quality Control Handbook*.
1954	Invited to lecture in Japan.
1964	*Managerial Breakthrough* first published.
1979	Founds the Juran Institute.

Summary

Joseph M. Juran is a charismatic figure and a legend in his own time, recognized worldwide for his extensive contribution to quality management. He has been instrumental in shaping many of our current ideas about quality. While he is often referred to as one of the leading figures of total quality management, much of his work actually preceded the total quality concept. Regarded as one of the architects of the quality movement in Japan, his influence on manufacturing throughout the world has been substantial.

Life and Career

Juran was born in 1904 in a small village in part of the Austro-Hungarian Empire that is now Romania. He was the third of four children and lived in poverty for much of his childhood. His father left the family in 1909 to find work in America and some three years later there was enough money for the rest of the family to join him in Minnesota.

Juran excelled at school in America and his affinity for mathematics and science meant that he was soon advanced the equivalent of three year-grades. He enrolled at the University of Minnesota in 1920 and became the first member of his family to enter higher education. By 1924 he had earned himself a B.S. in electrical engineering and in 1936 a J.D. in law at Loyola University. During his career Juran has produced many leading international handbooks, training courses, and training books that have all been widely read and have collectively been translated into 16 languages. He has been awarded more than 40 honorary doctorates, honorary memberships, medals, and plaques around the world. For his work on quality in Japan he was awarded the Second Order of the Sacred Treasure for "the development of quality control in Japan and the facilitation of U.S. and Japanese friendship," and in the United States he has been awarded the National Medal of Technology.

Starting out as a professional engineer in 1924, Juran worked in the inspection department of the famous Hawthorne works of Western Electric, and this first job stimulated his interest in quality. The plant was vast, with some 40,000 workers, 5,000 of whom were in inspection. Juran's unfailing memory soon allowed him to develop an encyclopedic knowledge of the place. His intellectual and analytical abilities were recognized early and he quickly progressed through a series of line management and staff jobs.

In 1926 a team of statistical quality-control pioneers from Bell Laboratories came to the Hawthorne plant to apply some of their methods and techniques. Juran was selected as one of twenty trainees to participate in the training program and was later appointed as one of the two engineers in the newly formed inspection statistical department. It was while in this role that he authored his first work, *Statistical Methods Applied to Manufacturing Problems*.

By 1937, Juran was head of industrial engineering at Western Electric's head office in New York. He became the equivalent of an in-house consultant, visiting other companies and discussing ideas about quality and industrial engineering. Indeed, it was on one such visit to General Motors in Detroit that he realized how relevant Pareto's idea of "the vital few and the trivial many" was to quality management. He eventually described this idea as the "Pareto Principle" (see below).

In 1941 Juran was seconded as an assistant administrator to the Lend-Lease Administration in Washington. This assignment was to last for four years, during which he streamlined the shipment process to reduce the number of documents required and to cut costs significantly. Today such an approach might be called business process reengineering; Juran has long claimed that there is nothing new about BPR!

Juran left Washington and Western Electric in 1945 with the aim of writing, lecturing and consulting. In 1951 he published his *Quality Control Handbook*, and this established his reputation as an authority on quality and increased the demand for his lecturing and consulting services. In 1954 he delivered a series of lectures in Japan at the invitation of the Union of Japanese Scientists and Engineers. Though Juran himself plays down their significance, in Japan it is widely held that these lectures formed the basis of the country's shift towards an economy based on quality principles. The ideas from these lectures were published in his book, *Managerial Breakthrough*, in 1964.

In 1979 Juran founded the Juran Institute with the aim of increasing awareness of his ideas. It was through this Institute that the widely acclaimed video series *Juran on Quality Improvement* was produced, and he continued to write and publish into the 1990s. He played a part in setting up the Malcolm Baldrige National Quality Award and only retired from leading the Institute in 1987.

Contribution

Pareto Principle

In his early days as a young engineer Juran noted that when defects were listed in the order of the frequency with which they occurred, a relatively small number of types of defect accounted for the bulk of those found. As his career in management progressed he noted the occurrence of this phenomenon in other areas. The idea of "the vital few and the trivial many" was forming. In the 1930s Juran was introduced to the work of Vilfredo Pareto, an Italian economist, who had produced a mathematical model to explain the unequal distribution of wealth. Pareto had not promoted his model as a universal one and did not talk of an 80:20 split, but in preparing the first edition of the *Quality Control Handbook* Juran needed a form of shorthand to describe his idea. Remembering Pareto's work he captioned his description "Pareto's principle of unequal distribution." Since then the "Pareto Principle" has become a standard term to describe any situation where a relatively small percentage of factors are responsible for the substantial percentage of effect. Juran later published an explanation of his error in attributing more to Pareto than the latter had originally claimed, at the same time recognizing the contribution of another economist, M. O. Lorenz. Juran was, in reality, the first to identify and popularize the 80:20 rule (as it has colloquially become known) as a universal principle.

Breakthrough

In his classic work *Managerial Breakthrough* Juran presents his general theory of quality control. Central to this is the idea of an improvement breakthrough.

Juran defines a breakthrough as "change, a dynamic, decisive movement to new, higher levels of performance" (Juran 1994, p. 3). This he contrasts with control, which means "staying on course, adherence to standard, prevention of change" (Juran 1994, p. 1). Not all control is viewed as negative, and not all breakthroughs are expected to be for the good. Breakthrough and control are seen as part of a continuing cycle of events. Juran highlights the importance of managers' understanding of the attitudes, the organization, and the methodology used to achieve breakthrough, and of how they differ from those used to achieve control.

The Juran Trilogy and Quality Planning Road Map

Juran's message on quality covers a number of different aspects. He focused on the wider issues of planning and organization, managerial responsibility for quality, and the importance of setting targets for improvement. Intrinsic to these, however, was his belief that quality does not happen by accident and needs to be planned. The process of quality improvement is best summarized in his "trilogy" concept, based on the three financial management processes of financial planning, financial control, and financial improvement. Various interpretations of the trilogy have been published, and the following represents one version.

Quality planning
- Identify who the customers are.
- Determine the needs of those customers.
- Translate those needs into our language.

Quality control
- Optimize the product features so as to meet our needs and customer needs.
- Develop a process which is able to produce the product.

Quality improvement
- Optimize the process.
- Prove that the process can produce the product under operating conditions.
- Transfer the process to operations.

Juran's "road map" provides a more detailed approach to the steps within the quality planning element of the trilogy. It is made up of a series of actions with corresponding outputs, and emphasizes the need for measurement throughout. In his book *Juran on Quality by Design*, Juran describes six activities in the road map: establish quality goals; identify the customer; determine customer needs; develop product features; develop process features; establish process controls; and transfer to operations.

Quality Campaigns

Juran has never been a fan of quality campaigns based on slogans and praise. He viewed the Western quality crisis of the early 1980s as being a result of too many quality initiatives based on campaigns with too little planning and substance. In his view, planning and action should make up 90% of an initiative, with the remaining 10% being exhortation.

Juran's formula for success is as follows:

- establish specific goals to be reached;
- establish plans for reaching those goals;
- assign clear responsibility for meeting the goals;
- base the rewards on the results achieved.

Context and Conclusions

Juran's contribution to the revolution in Japanese quality philosophy helped to transform that country into a market leader. Add to this his influence on Western manufacturing and management in general, and you emerge with a guru who has been influential for more than half a century.

Juran has had a varied career in management and, while his fame centers upon his ideas and thinking on quality issues, his influence in the field of management is far wider. He has played a number of roles—writer, teacher, trainer, and consultant—and has contributed a great deal, over many years, to the field of management. Many of the thousands of managers who have learned from him hold him in near reverence, and management today is infused with his techniques and ideas, even though the name of their creator is not always recognized.

For More Information

Books:

Butman, John. *Juran: A Lifetime of Influence*. New York: John Wiley, 1997

Juran, Joseph M. *Managerial Breakthrough*. New York: McGraw-Hill, 1964.

Juran, Joseph M. *Juran's Quality Control Handbook*. New York: McGraw-Hill, 1988.

Juran, Joseph M. *Juran on Planning for Quality*. New York: Free Press, 1988.

Juran, Joseph M. *Juran on Leadership for Quality*. New York: Free Press, 1989.

Juran, Joseph M. *Juran on Quality by Design*. New York: Free Press, 1992.

Juran, Joseph M., and Frank M. Gryna. *Quality Planning and Analysis*. New York: McGraw-Hill, 1993.

Juran, Joseph M. *Managerial Breakthrough*. Revised ed. New York: McGraw-Hill, 1994.

Rosabeth Moss Kanter

1943	Born.
1977	Publication of *Men and Women of the Corporation*.
1983	Publication of *The Change Masters: Corporate Entrepreneurs at Work*.
1986– present	Professor of business administration, Harvard Business School.
1989	Publication of *When Giants Learn to Dance: Master the Challenge of Strategy, Management, and Careers in the 1990s*.
1989– 1992	Editor, *Harvard Business Review*.

Summary

It is difficult to classify Rosabeth Moss Kanter as a specialist in any particular area, as her prolific writings encompass a wide variety of topics. She views herself as a thought leader and developer of ideas, and is best known for her work on change management and innovation. Much of Kanter's success is due to a combination of rigorous research, practical experience, and her ability to write clearly, using many illustrative examples.

Life and Career

Kanter was born in 1943, in Cleveland, Ohio, and attended the top women's academy, Bryn Mawr. She earned her Ph.D. at the University of Michigan and was associate professor of sociology at Brandeis University from 1966 to 1977. Between 1973 and 1974 she was on the Organization Behavior Program at Harvard, and she was a fellow and visiting scholar of Harvard Law School between 1975 and 1976.

From 1977 to 1986 Kanter was Professor of Sociology and Professor of Organizational Management at Yale, and from 1979 to 1986, she was a visiting professor at the Sloan School of Management, Massachusetts Institute of Technology (MIT). In 1986, she returned to Harvard as the "class of 1960" Professor of Entrepreneurship and Innovation, and she still holds the post of Professor of Business Administration at Harvard Business School.

Between 1989 and 1992 Kanter was editor of the *Harvard Business Review*, and she acted as a key economic adviser to Michael Dukakis during his 1988 Presidential campaign. She has traveled widely as a public speaker, lecturer, and international consultant. In 1977, she and her future husband, Barry Stein, established a management consultancy called Goodmeasure, which has some large and well-known multinational companies as clients.

Contribution

Kanter has authored or coauthored several books and well over 150 major articles. Her doctoral thesis was on communes, and her first books, written during the early 1970s, were sociological. The books for which she is best known are *Men and Women of the Corporation*, *The Change Masters* and *When Giants Learn to Dance*. There is a logical progression within them, the first studying the stifling effects of bureaucratic organization on individuals, while the subsequent titles go on to explore ways in which "post-entrepreneurial" organizations release, and make use of, individuals' talents and abilities. Later books include *The*

Challenge of Organizational Change (with Barry A. Stein and Todd D. Jick), *World Class: Thriving Locally in the Global Economy*, and *The Frontiers of Management*.

Men and Women of the Corporation

Men and Women of the Corporation won the C. Wright Mills Award in 1977 as the year's best book on social issues. It is a detailed analysis of the nature and effects of the distribution of power and powerlessness within the headquarters of one large, bureaucratic, multinational corporation (called Industrial Supply Corporation, or Indsco, in the book). The effects of powerlessness on behavior are explored and the detrimental effects of disempowerment, both for the organization and individual employees, are made clear. Women were the most obvious group affected by lack of power, though Kanter emphasizes that other groups outside the white, male norm, such as ethnic minority members, were also affected.

Three main structural variables explained the behaviors observed within Indsco:

- the structure of opportunity;
- the structure of power;
- the proportional distribution of people of different kinds.

Before this book was published, it was generally assumed that behavioral differences underlay women's general lack of career progress. Kanter's findings made structural issues central, however, and the implications for change management were significant. If all employees were to become more empowered, organizations rather than people would need to change. Accordingly, the book ends with practical policy suggestions to create appropriate structural changes.

Kanter identified the need for organizational change to improve working life, create more equal opportunities, and make more use of employees' talents within organizations.

The Change Masters

The Change Masters puts forward various approaches to achieving these ends. Kanter compares four traditional corporations like Indsco with six competitive and successful organizations, described as "change masters." All findings were weighed against the experiences of many other companies and much other material. From the six innovative organizations, Kanter derives a model for encouraging innovation.

Innovative companies were found to have an "integrative" approach to management, while firms unlikely to innovate were described as "segmentalist" compartmentalized by units or departments. The difference begins with a company's approach to problem-solving, and extends through its structure and culture. Entrepreneurial organizations:

- operate at the edge of their competence, focusing on exploring the unknown rather than on controlling the known;
- measure themselves by future-focused visions (how far they have to go) rather than by past standards (how far they have come).

Three clusters of structures and processes are identified as factors that encourage power circulation and access to power: open communication systems, network-forming arrangements, and decentralization of resources. Their practical implementation is discussed.

Individuals can also be change masters. "New entrepreneurs" are people who improve existing businesses rather than start new ones. They can be found in any functional area and are described as, literally, the right people, in the right place, at the right time:

- the right people—those with vision and ideas extending beyond the organization's normal practice;
- the right place—an integrative environment fostering proactive vision, coalitions, and teams;
- the right time—a moment in the historical flow when change becomes most possible.

The ultimate change masters are corporate leaders who translate their vision into a new organizational reality.

The Change Masters advocates "participation management" as the means to greater empowerment. Some major "building blocks" for productive change are identified, and practical measures to remove "road blocks" to innovation are discussed.

When Giants Learn to Dance

When Giants Learn to Dance completes Kanter's trilogy on the need for change which, she considered, U.S. corporations had to confront in order to compete more effectively. The book is based on observation from within various organizations, through consultancy projects. The global economy is likened to a "corporate Olympics" of competing businesses, with results determining which nations, as well as organizations, are winners.

The games differ, but successful teams share some characteristics such as strength, skill, discipline, good organization, and focus on individual excellence. To win, American companies would have to become progressively more entrepreneurial and less bureaucratic. Kanter suggested as a model for the 1990s the "post-entrepreneurial" corporation, in which three shaping forces would play the key roles: the context set at the top; top management values; project ideas and approaches coming up through the organization.

An "athletic" organization of this kind would be lean, flexible, and would seek to create synergies through the use of team and partnership approaches. The organization would be built on empowerment, and employees would be highly valued within team-based or partnership relationships.

Kanter picks out seven skills or sensibilities that characterize individual "business athletes." These are:

- the ability to operate and get results without depending on hierarchical authority, position, or status;
- the ability to compete in a way that enhances cooperation, and aims to achieve high standards rather than destroy competitors;
- the high ethical standards needed to support the trust that is crucial for cooperative approaches when competing in the corporate Olympics;
- a dose of humility, basic self-confidence being tempered by the understanding that new things will always need to be learned;
- process focus, that is, respect for the process of implementation as well as for the substance of what is implemented;
- a multifaceted and ambidextrous approach that makes possible cross-functional or cross-departmental work, the forming of alliances where appropriate, and the cutting of ties where necessary;
- a temperament that derives satisfaction from results, and a willingness to be rewarded according to achievements.

World Class: Thriving Locally in the Global Economy

World Class: Thriving Locally in the Global Economy focuses on world class companies with employees described as "cosmopolitan" in type. These people are rich in the "three Cs"—concepts, competence, and connections—and carry a more universal culture to all the places in which their company operates.

This knowledge-rich breed is compared with "locals," who are set in their ways, and the two groups are viewed as the main classes in modern society. The book is optimistic, in that Kanter believes stakeholders can influence world-class companies to spread best practice around the world. Globalization, it is argued, offers an opportunity to develop businesses and give new life to the regions. From her studies of regenerative areas, Kanter suggests that business and local government can work together to draw companies that will create prosperity.

Later works

The Challenge of Organizational Change: How Companies Experience It and Leaders Guide It, coauthored with Barry A. Stein and Todd D. Jick, draws a distinction between evolutionary and revolutionary change, here described as the "long march" and "bold stroke" approaches.

Rosabeth Moss Kanter on The Frontiers of Management collects Kanter's essays and research articles for the *Harvard Business Review* together into one volume.

Context and Conclusions

Overall, Kanter's books present some fairly complex ideas in a way that many people seem to find approachable. They are well-argued and supported with a wealth of practical research evidence. Some of her central ideas, once viewed by some as unrealistic, have now become absorbed into general management wisdom. These include empowerment, participative management, and employee involvement. In *The Frontiers of Management*, she is presented as a ground-breaking explorer who has initiated a revolution in terms of new ways of working. It is also pointed out, however, that some managers have still not crossed the frontiers, or do so in aspiration rather than actuality.

For More Information

Books:

Moss Kanter, Rosabeth. *Men and Women of the Corporation*. New York: Basic Books Inc., 1977.

Moss Kanter, Rosabeth. *The Change Masters: Corporate Entrepreneurs at Work*. New York: Simon & Schuster, 1983.

Moss Kanter, Rosabeth. *When Giants Learn to Dance: Master the Challenge of Strategy, Management, and Careers in the 1990s*. New York: Simon & Schuster, 1989.

Moss Kanter, Rosabeth, Barry A. Stein, and Todd D. Jick. *The Challenge of Organizational Change: How Companies Experience It and Leaders Guide It*. New York: Free Press, 1992.

Moss Kanter, Rosabeth. *World Class: Thriving Locally in the Global Economy*. New York: Simon & Schuster, 1995.

Moss Kanter, Rosabeth. *Rosabeth Moss Kanter on the Frontiers of Change*. Boston: Harvard Business School Press, 1997.

Moss Kanter, Rosabeth. *Evolve*. Boston: Harvard Business School Press, 2001.

Kaplan and Norton

Summary

The name of Robert S. Kaplan is almost invariably linked with that of his coauthor, David P. Norton, and with the assessment tool they jointly introduced to the business world in the early 1990s—the "balanced scorecard." Kaplan and Norton argued that adherence to quarterly financial returns and the bottom line alone could not provide the organization with an overall strategic view. The balanced scorecard was a breakthrough precisely because it enables the organization to describe its strategy adequately. It shows how nonfinancial factors—intangible assets—tied in with the financial ones.

Life and Career

Robert Kaplan is Marvin Bower Professor of Leadership Development at Harvard Business School in Boston. He was previously based at Carnegie Mellon University, where he was dean of the Graduate School of Industrial Administration, in Pittsburgh. Kaplan's research work has focused on performance measurement systems, in particular activity-based costing and the balanced scorecard.

David P. Norton is a founder and President of the Balanced Scorecard Collaborative, based in Lincoln, Massachusetts. He also founded and was President of Renaissance Solutions, a balanced scorecard consulting firm.

They are jointly recognized as the popularizers of the balanced scorecard concept. Their approach to it was first introduced in a 1992 *Harvard Business Review* article ("The Balanced Scorecard: Measures That Drive Performance"), which began with a variation of the saying "What gets measured gets done"; Kaplan and Norton took as their starting point "What you measure is what you get."

As the story goes, David Norton coined the term "Balanced Scorecard" after a conversation with John Thompson, who was then President of IBM Canada. John Thompson, returning from a round of golf, announced he needed a scorecard just like the one he used during his game to measure the performance of his company. The balanced scorecard grew out of that conversation.

Contribution

Setting up the balanced scorecard, Kaplan and Norton argued that strategies often fail because they are not converted successfully into actions that employees can understand and apply in their everyday work. The problem comes with the search for realistic measures that are meaningful to those doing the work, relate visibly to strategic direction, and provide a balanced picture of what is happening throughout the organization, not just of one facet of it. It is this aspect that the balanced scorecard addresses.

It concentrates on measures in four key strategic areas—finance, customers, internal business processes, and learning and innovation—and requires the implementing organization to identify goals and measures for each of them. Research and experimentation have come up with the following, which seem to be regularly applied in many organizations.

Financial Perspective
- Goals: survival, success/growth, prosperity.
- Measures: return on capital, cash flow, revenue growth, liquidity, cost reduction, project profitability, performance reliability.

Customer Perspective
- Goals: customer acquisition, retention, profitability, and satisfaction.
- Measures: market share, transaction cost ratios, customer loyalty satisfaction surveys/index, supplier relationships, key accounts.

Internal Business Process Perspective
- Goals: core competencies, critical technologies, business processes, key skills.
- Measures: efficiency measures of working practices and production processes, cycle times, unit costs, defect rates, time to market.

Learning and Innovation Perspective
- Goals: continuous improvement, new product development.
- Measures: productivity of intrapreneurship, new ideas and suggestions from employees, employee satisfaction, skill levels, staff attitude, retention, and profitability, rate of improvement.

The scorecard provides a description of the organization's strategy. It will indicate where problems lie because it shows the interrelationships between goals and the activities that are linked to their achievement. It creates an understanding of what is going on elsewhere in the organization and shows all employees how they are contributing. As Kaplan has said: "The business scorecard seeks to empower all levels of the workforce by educating them about their company's strategy and the small steps they can take to achieve their goals." Providing that accurate and timely information is fed into the system, the scorecard also helps to focus attention where change and learning are needed through the cause and effect relationships it can reveal. Examples of the types of insight achieved were detailed in "Linking the balanced scorecard to strategy."

- If we increase employee training about products, then they will become more knowledgeable about the full variety of products they can sell.
- If employees are more knowledgeable about products, then their sales effectiveness will improve.
- If their sales effectiveness improves, then the average margins of products they sell will increase.

Implementing the Balanced Scorecard
In "Putting the balanced scorecard to work" Kaplan and Norton identify eight steps toward building a scorecard:

1. Preparation. Select/define the strategy/business unit to which to apply the scorecard. Think in terms of the appropriateness of the four main perspectives defined above.

2. First interviews. Distribute information about the scorecard to senior managers along with the organization's vision, mission, and strategy. A facilitator will interview each

manager on the organization's strategic objectives and ask for initial thoughts on scorecard measures.

3. First executive workshop. Match measures to strategy. The management team is brought together to develop the scorecard. After agreeing the vision statement, the team debates each of the four key strategic areas, addressing the following questions:

- If my vision succeeds, how will I differ?
- What are the critical success factors?
- What are the critical measurements?

These questions help to focus attention on the impact of turning the vision into reality and what has to be done to make it happen. It is important to represent the views of customers and shareholders, and to gain a number of measures for each critical success factor.

4. Second interviews. The facilitator reviews and consolidates the findings of the workshop and interviews each of the managers individually about the emerging scorecard.

5. Second workshop. Hold a team debate on the proposed scorecard; the participants should discuss the proposed measures, link ongoing change programs to the measures, and set targets or rates of improvement for each of the measures. Start outlining the communication and implementation processes.

6. Third workshop. Final consensus on vision, goals, measures, and targets. The team devises an implementation program to communicate the scorecard to employees, integrate it into management philosophy, and develop an information system to support it.

7. Implementation. The implementation team links the measures to information support systems and databases and communicates the what, why, where, and who of the scorecard throughout the organization. The end product should be a management information system that links strategy to shop-floor activity.

8. Periodic review. Balanced scorecard measures can be prepared for review by senior management at appropriate intervals.

Context and Conclusions

Kaplan and Norton published their first article on the balanced scorecard in early 1992. Since then, elaborating, explaining, and applying the basic concept seems to have become a small industry. The jury is, nevertheless, still out on whether it will be an innovation of lasting importance or merely a passing fad. But an increasing number of organizations are trying it out. David Norton has claimed that 60% of large U.S. companies are now using some sort of scorecard that combines financial with nonfinancial measures.

The balanced scorecard should not be regarded as a panacea. In "The design and implementation of the balanced business scorecard: an analysis of three companies in practice," Stephen Letza states that the balanced scorecard should highlight performance as a dynamic, continuous, and integrated process, act as an integrating tool, function as the pivotal tool determining the organization's direction, and deliver information that forms the backbone of its strategy. He also highlights some of the major drawbacks that may be encountered when using the balanced scorecard and points out the need to:

- avoid being swamped by the minutiae of too many detailed measures and make sure that measures do genuinely relate to the strategic goals of the organization;

- make sure all the organization's activities are included in the assessment—this ensures that everyone is contributing to the organization's strategic goals;
- watch out for conflict as information becomes accessible to those who were not formerly in a position to see it or act on it, and try to harness conflict constructively.

The balanced scorecard can be seen as the latest in a long line of attempts at management control, descending from Taylor through to work measurement systems, quality assurance systems, and performance indicators. Commentators claim that the balanced scorecard could become the management tool of the early 21st century, given that it is flexible and adaptable to each organization's use, and that it is practical, straightforward, and devoid of obscure theory. Most importantly, it responds to many organizations' requirements to expand strategically on traditional financial measures and points to areas for change.

For More Information

Books:

Kaplan, Robert S., and David P. Norton. *The Balanced Scorecard: Translating Strategy into Action*. Boston, MA: Harvard Business School Press, 1996.

Kaplan, Robert S., and David P. Norton. *The Strategy-Focused Organization*. Boston, MA: Harvard Business School Press, 2000.

Journal Articles:

Kaplan, Robert S., and David P. Norton. "The Balanced Scorecard: Measures That Drive Performance." *Harvard Business Review*, Jan./Feb. 1992, pp. 71–79.

Kaplan, Robert S., and David P. Norton. "Putting the Balanced Scorecard to Work."*Harvard Business Review*, Sept./Oct. 1993, pp.134–147.

Kaplan, Robert S., and David P. Norton. "Using the Balanced Scorecard as a Strategic Management System."*Harvard Business Review*, Jan./Feb. 1996, pp. 75–85.

Kaplan, Robert S., and David P. Norton. "Linking the Balanced Scorecard to Strategy."*California Management Review*, Fall 1996, pp. 53–79.

Kaplan, Robert S., and David P. Norton. "Strategic Learning and the Balanced Scorecard."*Strategy and Leadership*, Sept./Oct. 1996, pp. 18–24.

Letza, Stephen. "The Design and Implementation of the Balanced Business Scorecard: An Analysis of Three Companies in Practice." *Business Process Reengineering and Management Journal*, vol. 2 no. 3, 1996, pp. 54–76.

Theodore Levitt

1925	Born.
1935	Leaves Germany for the United States.
1959	Lecturer in business administration at Harvard Business School.
1960	"Marketing Myopia" appears in *Harvard Business Review*.
1965	Edward W. Carter Professor of Business Administration, Harvard Business School.
1990	Resigns post as editor of *Harvard Business Review*.

Summary

Theodore Levitt has made a key contribution to management theory in the marketing field, stimulating debate on the importance of a pervasive marketing mindset within an organization. Having encouraged an awareness of the marketing concept, Levitt proceeded to further analyze the benefits and shortfalls of marketing in a series of journal articles and books over four decades. His talent for expounding his views clearly and for illustrating his arguments with company examples and metaphors makes his work highly accessible.

Life and Career

Born in Volmerz in Germany, Levitt moved with his parents to the United States in 1935, where he later studied economics. In the late 1950s he worked as a consultant in Chicago before being approached by the Harvard Business School. In his very first year there he began to teach marketing, although at the time he had reportedly never read a book on the subject.

Levitt's first article was published in 1956. His tenure at Harvard as an academic lasted for more than 30 years. This period included a spell as a somewhat controversial editor of the *Harvard Business Review*, a post from which he resigned in 1990 following an argument over an article on women in management.

Contribution

Levitt emphasizes the need for a company to achieve a balanced orientation by including marketing in its strategy; he focuses on the need for a marketing outlook to pervade an organization and provide a necessary counterbalance to a preoccupation with production. His landmark article expounding this theory, "Marketing Myopia," appeared in the *Harvard Business Review* in 1960 and is one of the most requested reprints from that journal, having sold over 500,000 copies. Subsequently, Levitt reiterated and expanded his theory in several articles and books. These partly focus on the methodology of implementing the marketing mode, including the proposition of a "marketing matrix" for assessing the degree of marketing orientation existing in a company. They also explore the theory behind the marketing concept and delineate some of its limitations and problems. Other works concentrate on such topics as "the industrialization of service" (examining the potential benefits of applying the production line and quality control methods of industry to service provision), the nature of the product, advertising, and globalization.

"Marketing Myopia" Explored

Levitt himself described his article "Marketing Myopia" as a manifesto. It challenged the conventional thinking of the time by putting forward a persuasive case for the importance of the marketing approach and the shortsightedness of failing to incorporate it into business strategy.

In an era in which post-war shortages contributed to a concentration on production, most companies had developed a product orientation, which, Levitt believed, was too narrow a philosophy to allow continued business success. A drive to increase the efficiency and volume of production took place at the expense of monitoring whether the company was actually producing what the customer wanted. The article stressed that "customer wants and desires should be a central consideration of any business. The organization must learn to think of itself not as producing goods or services but as buying customers, as doing the things that will make people want to do business with it."

In order to achieve this, "the entire corporation must be viewed as a customer-creating and customer-satisfying organism. Management must think of itself not as providing products but as providing customer-creating value satisfactions. It must push this idea (and everything it means and requires) into every nook and cranny of the organization."

Levitt highlighted the need for companies to define what business they are in, as this concentrates attention on customer needs. He used the now famous example of the railroads, which, rather than thinking of themselves as being in the business of running trains, should instead have defined themselves as providing transportation. Self-definition along those lines would have helped the railroad companies to be aware of changing customer demand; if they had had that awareness, they might not have suffered so greatly from the rise of road and air transportation. Focusing on the satisfaction of customer needs, Levitt argues, is a better path to continued business success than concentration on the actual product on offer.

Also presented in "Marketing myopia," as a warning against complacency, is Levitt's belief that "in truth there is no such thing as a growth industry." There are growth opportunities, which can be created or capitalized on, but those companies which believe they are "riding some automatic growth escalator invariably descend into stagnation." The belief that a company is in a growth industry and is therefore secure must never be allowed to overshadow or replace awareness of the need to practice marketing and assert a customer orientation. This is the only route through which a company can hope to achieve sustained expansion.

Of a more practical nature is the "marketing matrix," a device presented by Levitt in *Marketing for Business Growth* to aid the measurement of a company's marketing orientation. A horizontal scale of 1–9 records the degree of customer orientation, and a vertical scale of 1–9 records the degree of company orientation. A score of 9 on both scales is the ideal. Using this method, organizations can assess their incorporation of marketing thinking and determine where steps are needed to improve their strategy and to become more marketing oriented.

Ways of doing this include the "industrialization of service," which involves the measuring and standardizing of customer service to a predetermined quality level, in other words, applying industrial-style quality controls to the service process. For example, a production line can be established for service delivery, and service encounters can be standardized and monitored to ensure that they are of a similar quality. This has been accomplished with great success by the McDonald's fast food chain ("The industrialization of service"). To recognize this concept is, writes Levitt, "...to introduce a potentially emancipating new cognitive mode and operating style into modern enterprise" (*The Marketing Imagination*). Another factor that is important in enhancing a marketing orientation is relationship marketing. (See "After the sale is over.") This revolves around the need not only to acquire customers, but also to keep them and form mutually beneficial long-term relationships with them.

In a 1983 article, "The globalization of markets," Levitt once more produced a forward-looking "manifesto" with a view of the changing nature of the marketplace and the trend, fuelled by technological advances, towards globalization. His thesis is that, in order to survive and prosper, companies must offer standardized products around the world, products that incorporate the best in design, reliability, and price. The efficiency of such an approach will outweigh, in his opinion, the benefits of taking into account varying cultural preferences and tailoring products to different national markets. The reason for this is the overlying trend toward world homogenization. "Two vectors shape the world—technology and globalization. The first helps determine human preferences; the second, economic realities. Regardless of how much preferences evolve and diverge, they also gradually converge and form markets where economies of scale lead to reduction of costs and prices."

Thinking about Management, Levitt's 1991 book, contains a distillation of his thinking on effective management, presented in nuggets in the three categories of thinking, changing, and operating. Many of his theories are here reiterated, and the work forms a useful guide to his collected thought.

Context and Conclusions

A major influence on Levitt's work was the writing of Peter Drucker, who was among the first to see marketing as all-pervasive: "Marketing is not a function, it is the whole business seen from the customer's point of view." (*The Practice of Management*)

However, although influenced by academic thought, Levitt seems to have drawn his greatest inspiration from the real world, examining the companies around him and distilling the examples of good and bad practice that illustrate much of his writing.

Levitt's influence contributed to the rise of the marketing concept in the 1960s and its increasing incorporation into management thinking, initially in the United States but later also in Europe. His subsequent works may not have achieved the fame of "Marketing myopia," but they are nevertheless an important part of the evolving pattern of marketing writing that has gathered impetus through recent decades. By pointing out the myopic vision of many managers, Levitt set in motion a vigorous new way of thinking that was taken up by other management writers and practitioners and culminated in the rebirth of marketing in the 1980s. Other marketing gurus such as Philip Kotler acknowledge the influence of Levitt's work, and he is regularly quoted.

In retrospect, Levitt has been proven to have had remarkable foresight in his anticipation of the importance of marketing to organizations, his initial work predating the marketing boom by two decades. He also successfully predicted the value of relationship marketing, a topic which only became an identifiable discipline in the early 1990s, and the concept of the global village, which is now commonplace.

Levitt's assertion that there is no such thing as a growth industry is another tenet that proved influential and was taken up by writers such as Tom Peters and Richard Pascale in the 1990s.

For More Information
Books:
Drucker, Peter. *The Practice of Management*. New York: HarperBusiness, 1986.
Levitt, Theodore. *Innovation in Marketing: New Perspectives for Profit and Growth*. New York: McGraw-Hill, 1962.
Levitt, Theodore. *Marketing for Business Growth*. New York: McGraw-Hill, 1974. (first published in 1969 as *The Marketing Mode: Pathways to Corporate Growth*)
Levitt, Theodore. *The Marketing Imagination*. New York: Free Press, 1983.
Levitt, Theodore. *Thinking about Management*. New York: Free Press, 1991.

Journal Articles:
Levitt, Theodore. "Marketing Myopia." *Harvard Business Review*, Jul./Aug. 1960, pp. 45–56.
Levitt, Theodore. "The Industrialization of Service." *Harvard Business Review*, Sept./Oct. 1976, pp. 63–74.
Levitt, Theodore. "After the Sale Is Over." *Harvard Business Review*, Sept./Oct. 1983, pp. 87–93.
"The Globalization of Markets." *Harvard Business Review*, May/June 1983, pp. 92–102.

Niccolò Machiavelli

1469	Born.
1498	Secretary of Second Chancery, Florence.
1512	Falls from grace as Medici family returns to power.
1513	Publication of *The Prince*.
1527	Dies.

Summary

Throughout most of the five centuries since his death Niccolò Machiavelli has not been a popular figure. There have always been a few people who appreciated his genius, but most have too closely associated him with intrigue and dark deeds. Fortunately, in the last 100 years or so, a more reasoned view of his work has developed and the enormous value of Machiavelli's philosophy and its remarkable relevance to modern society has emerged progressively.

Life and Career

Niccolò Machiavelli was born in 1469, the son of a Florentine lawyer. He first came to public notice when in 1498, at the age of 29, he was appointed Secretary of the Second Chancery—part of the complex bureaucracy that ran Florence as a city state. His appointment came after the execution of Savonarola, the friar-politician who, after leading a revolt that expelled the Medicis and established a democratic republic, dominated Florentine life until he ran foul of the papacy and was burned for heresy.

Machiavelli held the post of Secretary for 14 years, during which time his influence was significant. He took part in 30 foreign missions, meeting most of Europe's key politicians and rulers. This opportunity to learn about government, politics, and economics must have been unique. Unfortunately, it was not to last. In 1512 the Medicis returned to power, and Machiavelli lost his post immediately. He was then suspected, quite wrongly, of plotting against the Medicis, for which he was arrested, imprisoned, and tortured. Although eventually found innocent, he was expelled from Florence and forced to spend the rest of his life in exile on an isolated farm. His many attempts to reenter political life failed and he died in 1527, still struggling to regain his lost influence. It was more than 300 years later that Italy became unified, as Machiavelli had wanted it to be.

While Machiavelli may not have enjoyed his time in exile, the world has gained immeasurably from it. The enforced idleness allowed him to write prodigiously about his experiences and ideas.

His written works include a history of Florence, several plays, and two books that established him as a great authority on power politics: *The Prince* and *The Discourses*. Professor Max Lerner, in his introduction to the 1950 Random House edition of *The Prince* describes the book as "a grammar of power." There can be no more fitting description of this seminal work.

Contribution

Machiavelli presents no instant management theories, no clever techniques for solving day-to-day problems. He deals mainly with broad strategies, and to get value from his writing one needs to interpret it and make comparisons. Perhaps the best approach is to first read Jay's introduction on the art of making such comparisons and then to read Machiavelli with a personal checklist of interests and questions.

Some pertinent insights

The following examples show how certain passages in Machiavelli's writing bridge the seemingly huge gap between sixteenth-century politics and twentieth-century business.

Leadership

Machiavelli provides several examples of good leaders and leaves his readers in no doubt about the importance of skillful leadership to the success of any enterprise. He dismisses luck and genius as the key to successful leadership and goes for "shrewdness." The dangers and risks a leader faces are dramatically illustrated (happily for us these are less terrifying today than in Renaissance Italy), and comparison is made between the relative ease of getting to a position of leadership and the difficult task of staying there.

Centralization versus decentralization

Anyone who thinks that the problem of choosing between centralized or decentralized control is a modern dilemma will be quickly persuaded otherwise by reading *The Prince*. Machiavelli's examples are drawn entirely from government and from military history, but the comparisons with today's business world are easy to make. Perhaps his best advice comes when he is talking about the government of colonies and outposts.

Poor communications in Renaissance times usually made decentralization the only option in such cases, and Machiavelli's recommendations center on what today we would call selection and training. A colonial governor must be carefully selected for his experience and loyalty, trained thoroughly in the state's way of doing things and made so familiar with "best practice" that however isolated from "head office" guidance he may be, the job will still get done in a highly predictable way. Shades of William Whyte's *Organization Man*?

Takeovers

The equivalent of a takeover in Machiavelli's world was the conquest of another country or the establishment of a colony. In such matters his advice is very clear. One either totally subjugates the original inhabitants, so that rebellion is unlikely and the cost of garrisoning the place reduced to a minimum, or, and Machiavelli makes clear this is his preference, the conqueror puts in a small team of "key managers."

This team will displace only a small number of the original inhabitants, who being scattered cannot rebel, and the remainder will quickly toe the new management line since they have everything to gain from cooperation and a clear indication of what happens to those who do not cooperate. Parallels with business takeovers are frighteningly stark.

Change

Machiavelli has little to offer in the way of ideas for coping with change, but shows very clearly that the problems of introducing change were just as awesome and hazardous in the sixteenth century as they are today. In *The Prince* he says: "It must be considered that there is nothing more difficult to perform, nor more doubtful of success, nor more dangerous to handle, than to initiate a new order of things."

Federations and Bureaucracies

Machiavelli compared the "management" of sixteenth-century France and Turkey. He saw France as a "federal organization"; a collection of independent baronies in which the retainers regarded their baron, and not the king, as the "key manager." Such organizations are difficult to control, impossible to change, and the ruler is easily overthrown. Turkey, on the other hand, was in Machiavelli's time a classic bureaucracy with a highly trained civil service. Civil servants were frequently moved around, hence they developed no local loyalties, and had a strict, hierarchical relationship with "top management." The ruler in such a state, being appointed by the "system," was secure, respected, and powerful. The points of comparison with today's large organizations need little emphasizing.

Context and Conclusions

The impact of Machiavelli's writing on politics has been accepted for some time, but the relevance of his ideas to business had to wait until the second half of the nineteenth century, when companies began to operate as large, complex organizations—the equivalent in Machiavelli's terms of a move from a tribal society to a corporate state. An English parson, writing in 1820, compares Machiavelli unfavorably with the devil, yet by the 1860s Victor Hugo was able to say, "Machiavelli is not an evil genius, nor a cowardly writer, he is nothing but the fact...not merely the Italian fact, he is the European fact."

Machiavelli's image is not helped by what many see as an amoral attitude toward power. It is easy to take offense when he unashamedly says, "A prudent ruler ought not to keep faith when by so doing it would be against his interest, and when the reasons which made him bind himself no longer exist."

Such statements are easier to accept if we remember they were made in times very different from our own. They were also the words of a man who was a true observer; he reported what he saw and measured results dispassionately in terms of practical success or failure. He had moral views, as can be seen in his other writing, but on political issues he is a cold realist. He had, as Professor Lerner so aptly observed, "the clear-eyed capacity to distinguish between man as he ought to be and man as he actually is—between the ideal form of institutions and the pragmatic conditions under which they operate."

He was centuries ahead of his time.

For More Information

Books:

Jay, Antony. *Management and Machiavelli*. London: Hodder and Stoughton, 1967.
Machiavelli, Niccolò. *The Prince and The Discourses* (introduced by Max Lerner). New York: Random House, 1950.

Ikujiro Nonaka

1935	Born.
1958	Graduates from Waseda University
1995	Publication of *The Knowledge-Creating Company*.
1995	Joins Japan Advanced Institute of Science and Technology (JAIST).
1997	Becomes dean of the school of knowledge science at JAIST.

Summary

The work of Ikujiro Nonaka is best known for its focus on the creation of knowledge within organizations. Nonaka believes that this is the most meaningful core capability for a company, particularly because it leads to innovation. He argues that the knowledge generated becomes the key source of competitive advantage for the firm.

Life and Career

Ikujiro Nonaka (born 1935) is the first Professor of Knowledge at the Haas School of Business, University of California, where he previously received his MBA and Ph.D. degrees. He is also dean of the graduate school of knowledge science at the Japan Advanced Institute of Science and Technology (JAIST) in Japan. He was formerly a professor and Director of the Institute of Innovation Research at Hitotsubashi University, Tokyo.

Professor Nonaka has described his work as comparative research on knowledge-creating processes in companies around the world, and research on the characteristics of innovative activities in Japanese companies. He seeks to answer questions about what knowledge is, how organizations create knowledge, and how we can promote knowledge creation.

Contribution

The Knowledge-Creating Company

In their book *The Knowledge-Creating Company: How Japanese Companies Create the Dynamics of Innovation*, Ikujiro Nonaka and Hirotaka Takeuchi argue that the success of Japanese companies is due to their skill and expertise in organizational knowledge creation, especially with respect to bringing about continuous business innovation. They use the metaphor of a journey, warning that there are new and foreign road signs to follow on the way. The book, which combines theoretical and philosophical analysis with practical case studies, attempts to convey the complex forces at work within creative organizational systems. It is not straightforward to read, but the authors justify this with the declaration that "...managers can no longer afford to be satisfied with simplistic ideas about knowledge and its creation."

Explicit and Implicit Knowledge

Nonaka and Takeuchi's starting point is a contrast between Western and Eastern philosophies. In the West knowledge is formal, unambiguous, systematic, falsifiable, and scientific, and a quest for knowledge normally involves the analysis and interpretation of data and information. New knowledge is documented and then transferred by means of formal training. The authors describe this form of knowledge as "explicit." It is primarily managed through databases and manuals. Human expertise, experience, and insights are, they claim, generally ignored as sources of knowledge.

In the East, however, knowledge is intuitive, interpretive, ambiguous, non-linear, and difficult to reduce to scientific equations. Instead of being created through data analysis and interpretation, it grows from the expertise and experience of many people, whose minds are probed for insights. New knowledge is distributed and retained through experience. The resulting Eastern form of knowledge is described as "implicit."

In the authors' view, implicit and explicit knowledge are not totally separate but mutually complementary entities. Successful Japanese companies are able to convert implicit knowledge to explicit knowledge, so that knowledge acquired by individuals becomes organizational knowledge shared among colleagues, and explicit knowledge is converted into implicit knowledge by individuals. Nonaka and Takeuchi refer to this interaction between implicit and explicit knowledge as knowledge conversion. They suggest four methods of knowledge conversion, otherwise known as the SECI process: socialization, externalization, combination, and internalization.

These are described as the mechanisms by which implicit knowledge is "amplified" throughout the organization, creating a spiral model of knowledge creation.

Middle-up-down Management style
Nonaka and Takeuchi argue that the two traditional Western management styles, "top-down" and "bottom-up," fail to foster the dynamic interaction necessary to create organizational knowledge.

Successful Japanese companies acknowledge the vital role played by middle managers in taking the top management vision of "what should be" and the frontline employees' realistic sense of "what is," and developing midrange concepts. Middle managers are, in effect, the real "knowledge engineers" of the knowledge-creating company, serving as facilitators between top and bottom as well as between theory and reality, and playing a key role in innovation.

A "hypertext" organization consisting of interconnected layers is put forward as the ideal structure for knowledge creation. It combines two traditional structures—the hierarchy and the task force. Surprisingly, the model for this organizational form is the U.S. military, which is bureaucratic in peacetime but highly task-oriented in war. Nonaka and Takeuchi provide two case studies of Japanese companies that have attempted to implement a hypertext structure—Kao and Sharp.

Transferring Knowledge
The Knowledge-Creating Company is rich in case studies, which are mostly based on large, well-established Japanese companies, including Matsushita, NEC, Canon, Honda, and Nissan. Many of the case studies describe a "transferring process," in which the organizational knowledge created during new product development in one division becomes transferred to other parts of the company. For example, the knowledge created within Canon while developing the mini-copier in the early 1980s was subsequently used in other areas. The product knowledge generated was applied to other equipment such as printers; the knowledge gained from the manufacturing process led to the automation of copier production;

and the organizational knowledge gleaned, especially with respect to the role of middle managers and cross-functional working, influenced the way the company was managed.

The transfer of knowledge can also take place at a global level across national boundaries, and one example given is of Nissan's experience of developing a car in the United Kingdom. The case of Shin Caterpillar Mitsubishi, a U.S.–Japanese alliance, shows how knowledge creation can cut across company as well as national boundaries. It refers to the experience of Mitsubishi of Japan and Caterpillar of the United States when they pooled their resources to develop and market hydraulic shovels. Nonaka and Takeuchi demonstrate that using the four stages of knowledge conversion within the alliance averted potentially damaging clashes of culture, overcame the weaknesses of both sides in knowledge creation, and led to effective knowledge creation and innovation.

Practical Implications

The authors finish with some recommendations as to what Western companies can do to become knowledge-creating companies. They should:

- create a knowledge vision (top management should define the boundaries of organizational knowledge and outline what kind of knowledge ought to be created);
- develop a knowledge crew (of employees with diverse talents);
- build a high-density field of interaction (an environment in which frequent and intensive interactions take place) at the front-line;
- piggyback on the new product development process;
- adopt middle-up-down management;
- switch to a hypertext organization;
- construct a knowledge network with the outside world (meaning external stakeholders such as customers).

The Concept of "Ba" or Shared Spaces

Since the publication of *The Knowledge-Creating Company*, Nonaka has developed the theory of "Ba," which provides a platform for creating knowledge. *Ba* means "place" or "shared spaces" and can be physical (for example, an office), virtual (for example, e-mail) or mental (for example, shared experiences, ideas, and, by extension, organization culture). Nonaka argues that knowledge cannot be separated from its context and is embedded in *ba*.

Nonaka describes four kinds of platform corresponding to the four stages of knowledge conversion mentioned above. Each space supports a particular conversion process and thereby speeds up overall knowledge creation.

- Originating (supports the socialization stage)—physical face-to-face experiences which provide the environment in which individuals share feelings and experiences. These are the key to the transfer of tacit knowledge.
- Interacting (supports the externalization stage)—a team-based environment, where individuals' mental models and skills are converted into common terms and concepts. This assists the process in which tacit knowledge is made explicit.
- Cyber (supports the combination stage)—interaction in the virtual world of cyberspace. This allows the exchanging and combining of different forms of explicit knowledge.

- Exercising (supports the internalization stage)—focused training with senior mentors and colleagues which assists the conversion of explicit knowledge into tacit knowledge.

"Knowledge Activists"

Knowledge activists support platforms and cultures by enabling knowledge creation. A knowledge activist can be an individual, group, or department that takes on a particular responsibility for energizing and coordinating knowledge creation throughout the organization. The activist has three roles: to act as a catalyst of knowledge creation, to coordinate knowledge creation initiatives, and to provide overall direction to these efforts.

Context and Conclusions

Peter Drucker first used the terms "knowledge worker" and "knowledge society" in the 1960s and more recently stated that knowledge has become the only meaningful resource. Nonaka acknowledges Drucker's contribution and takes it a stage further by looking at how knowledge is created and examining the processes and mechanisms involved.

The second half of the 1990s saw a huge surge of business interest in knowledge, led primarily by practitioners rather than academics. Nonaka, while not responsible for the attention given to knowledge management, provided ideas that gave purpose and direction to practitioner initiatives. No other writer in this field has made such a forceful business case for knowledge creation. Moreover, Nonaka reminds us that information technology is not enough and that human experience and implicit knowledge are important in creating new knowledge. Lastly, Nonaka emphasized the importance of middle management in organization information creation as early as 1988, and this was a significant departure from the Western view of middle management as a deadweight, potentially expendable part of the corporate structure.

For More Information

Books:

Nonaka, Ikujiro, with Hirotaka Takeuchi. *The Knowledge-Creating Company: How Japanese Companies Create the Dynamics of Innovation.* New York: Oxford University Press, 1995.
Nonaka, Ikujiro, Georg Von Krogh, and Kazuo Ichijo. *Enabling Knowledge Creation.* New York: Oxford University Press, 2000.

Journal Articles:

Nonaka, Ikujiro. "The Knowledge-creating Company."*Harvard Business Review*, vol. 69 no. 6, Nov./Dec. 1991, pp. 96–104.
Nonaka, Ikujiro, Georg Von Krogh, and Kazuo Ichijo. "Develop Knowledge Activists!"*European Management Journal*, vol. 15 no. 5, October 1997, pp. 475–483.
Nonaka, Ikujiro, and Noboru Konno. "The Concept of 'Ba': Building a Foundation for Knowledge Creation." *California Management Review*, vol. 40 no. 3, Spring 1998, pp. 40–54
Nonaka, Ikujiro, and Ryoko Toyama, and Noboru Konno. "SEC ba and Leadership: A Unified Model of Dynamic Knowledge Creation."*Long Range Planning*, vol. 33 no. 1, Feb, 2000, pp. 5–34.

Kenichi Ohmae

1943	Born.
1972	Joins McKinsey & Co.
1975	Publication of *The Mind of the Strategist*.
1987	Publication of *Beyond National Boundaries*.
1990	Publication of *The Borderless World*.
1995	Stands as candidate for governorship of Tokyo.
1995	Publication of *The End of the Nation State*.

Summary

Ohmae's fresh approach to business strategy challenged business leaders to think in innovative, simple, and unconventional terms. His work in the late 1970s and 1980s heralded the arrival of Japanese management techniques in the West. Ohmae was the messenger for the Japanese way of doing business, urging managers to think "out of the box," and challenge accepted norms with clear, simple ideas in order to gain, and sustain, competitive advantage.

Life and Career

Kenichi Ohmae was born in 1943 on the island of Kyushu, and graduated from Waseda University and the Tokyo Institute of Technology before obtaining a Ph.D. in nuclear engineering from the Massachusetts Institute of Technology. In 1972 he joined the consulting firm McKinsey & Co, becoming managing Director of their Tokyo office. As well as being a nuclear physicist, he is an accomplished clarinettist and a politician. In 1995, he ran for election as governor of Tokyo and also acted as an adviser to Japan's then prime minister, Nakasone.

Ohmae lives in Yokohama and advises some of Japan's most successful international companies in a wide spectrum of industries. His special interest and area of expertise is in formulating creative strategies and developing organizational concepts to implement them.

Ohmae's seminal book, *The Mind of the Strategist*, was published in Japan in 1975. It was, however, only when interest in Japanese management methods increased during the early 1980s that the book was published in the United States. This 1982 American edition was given the subtitle *The Art of Japanese Business*. In *The Mind of the Strategist* Ohmae argues that the success of Japanese companies can be attributed to the nature of Japanese strategic thinking. This, contrary to the Western stereotype of Japanese management, was largely creative, intuitive, and vision-driven. Ohmae went on to explain what this creativity involved and how it could be learned.

The view presented by Ohmae overturned traditional Western perceptions of Japanese managers and the idea that their success was founded on brilliantly rational, farsighted thinking. Ohmae heralded a revolution based on creativity and innovation, and showed how, in the hands of a single, talented strategist, creativity could transform a major corporation.

In 1990, Ohmae's book *The Borderless World* challenged Japanese companies and corporations around the world to take account of globalization in their strategic planning. He urged businesses to focus less on the competitive aspects of strategy (promoted so effectively by Porter and others), and instead to give greater focus to "country" and "currency," two key elements that in an interdependent world economy can make or break a business strategy. This approach reflected Ohmae's increasing focus on global business and the relationship between business and the nation state. The latter was also the subject of two other books, *Beyond National Boundaries* (1987) and *The End of the Nation State* (1995).

Just as *The Mind of the Strategist* had encouraged innovation in strategy in the 1980s, so *The Borderless World* highlighted the importance of the global interdependence that dominated trade in the 1990s.

Contribution
The Role of the Strategist

Ohmae has explored a number of features of successful business strategies (usually Japanese), and compared them with their typical counterparts in the West. He identified several key differences.

- *Vision and dynamic leadership.* Japanese businesses tend to have a single, driving force in the form of an effective strategist, a leader or visionary who possesses what Ohmae has described as an idiosyncratic mode of thinking. Through this, company, customers, and competition (described as the strategic triangle) merge into a dynamic interaction from which, eventually, a comprehensive set of objectives and plans for action emerges. This approach was in marked contrast to the large, strategic planning bureaucracies that were typical of many large Western corporations of the time (the early 1980s).
- *Customer focus.* The customer is at the heart of Japanese strategy and is virtually enshrined as central to corporate values. The focus of the business needs to be on delivering what the customer wants, or there will be no business.
- *Methodology.* Ohmae perceived that to develop effective strategies, managers must first gain a detailed understanding of the characteristics of each element in a situation, and then develop a holistic plan tying each part of the business, each separate resource, into a competitive and efficient operation. This is not a systems approach based on linear thinking, but instead relies on detailed analysis ("the starting point") and knowledge, combined with innovation, intuition, and creativity.

The Strategic Triangle

Ohmae claimed that, in constructing any business strategy, the three main players to be taken into account are the corporation itself, the customer, and the competition. Each of these three Cs is a living entity with its own interests and objectives, while collectively they form the strategic triangle. The three Cs influence strategy and planning in a number of important ways.

1. *Strategic business units (SBUs).* The need for strategic business units that understand all three elements and to which strategic decisions can be delegated is held to be essential, in order to take adequate account of the strategic triangle. This is particularly the case for a large company made up of a number of different businesses selling to different customer

groups (probably with different competitors). The definition of a business unit is always likely to be in dispute, so Ohmae suggests asking three key questions as a test:

- Are customer wants well defined and understood by the industry, and is the market segmented so that differences in those wants are treated differently?
- Is the business unit (an aspect of the corporation) equipped to respond easily to customer wants and needs?
- Do competitors have different sets of conditions that give them a relative advantage over the business unit?

If the business unit seems unable to compete effectively, then it should be redefined to better meet customer needs and competitive threats.

2. *Freedom of operation.* For Ohmae, the SBU must have full freedom of operation across the strategic triangle in order to develop and implement an effective strategy. In devising a strategy the SBU must be able to:

- address the total market for its customers;
- encompass all of the critical functions of the corporation, i.e., procurement, design, manufacturing, sales, marketing, distribution, and service, in order to respond with maximum freedom to the total needs of the customer;
- understand all key aspects of the competitor so that the corporation can seize an advantage when opportunities arise, and exploit any unexpected sources of strength.

3. *Matching the corporation with the market.* In the context of the strategic triangle, Ohmae sees the role of the strategist as matching the strengths of the corporation to the needs of a clearly defined market. Such matching, however, is relative to the capabilities of the competition. For this reason, Ohmae defines a successful strategy as one that ensures a better or stronger matching of corporate strengths to customer needs than that provided by competitors.

Four Routes to Strategic Advantage

In *The Mind of the Strategist*, Ohmae identifies four ways in which a corporation can gain advantage over its competitors.

- A business strategy based on Key Factors for Success (KFS). The business is required to identify what it does to give it an advantage over its competitors, or where the potential for advantage is greatest, and then concentrate resources there.
- Relative superiority. If a business is still unable to gain an advantage over its competitors and the KFS struggle is being waged equally, then any difference between the two competing businesses can be exploited. This might, for example, mean linking products together through the sales network to provide customers with better offers.
- Aggressive initiatives. When a competitor is established in a stagnant, low-growth industry, then Ohmae advocates an unconventional strategy aimed at upsetting the competitor's KFS. This can be achieved by challenging the accepted ways of doing business in the industry—upsetting the status quo.
- Strategic degrees of freedom. Success in the competitive struggle can be achieved by a business strategy based on the use of innovations. This may involve the vigorous opening up of new markets or the development of new products in areas untouched by the competition.

In each case, Ohmae believes that the main concern is to avoid taking the same approach in the same market as the competition.

Context and Conclusions

Gary Hamel, among others, has recognized Ohmae's immense influence and contribution, emphasizing the impact of his challenge to managers to think in new and unconventional ways. It is a testament to the strength and appeal of Ohmae's work that, although the growth of the Japanese economy faltered during the 1990s, his ideas are still regarded as fundamental contributions to strategic management.

It might be argued that Ohmae's emphasis on strategic creativity helped to lay the foundations for the radical, transforming management approaches of the 1980s and 1990s. Certainly, if one accepts the need for an intuitive, innovative strategist, then it seems likely that there will be widespread changes in the ways that organizations are managed. So it was with the arrival of lean production, business process reengineering, and strategies for innovation and empowerment. Ohmae's view of the strategist, in fact, is now the widely accepted norm, and the need for a questioning approach that is not constrained by tradition, fear, or habitual patterns of behavior has filtered down from the strategists themselves to all layers of organizations.

Later works by Ohmae have focused on the rise of the global business and the relationships between business and governments. In a sense, Ohmae has grown away from his starting point and now prefers to write about a time when the end of the nation state is imminent. For many this emphasis on the distant future—rather than on business approaches for the medium-term—is of more relevance to politicians and academics than companies competing today. Even so, his legacy of startlingly simple, unconventional, and effective approaches is still required reading for many executives.

For More Information

Books:

Ohmae, Kenichi. *The Mind of the Strategist*. New York: McGraw Hill, 1982.

Ohmae, Kenichi. *Japan Business: Obstacles and Opportunities*. New York: John Wiley, 1983.

Ohmae, Kenichi. *Triad Power: The Coming Shape of Global Competition*. New York: Free Press, 1985.

Ohmae, Kenichi. *The Borderless World: Power and Strategy in the Interlinked Economy*. New York: Harper Business, 1990.

Ohmae, Kenichi. *The End of the Nation State: The Rise of Regional Economics*. New York: Free Press, 1995.

Tom Peters

1942	Born.
1966–1970	Naval service, including a term of duty in Vietnam and being assigned to the Pentagon.
1973	Leaves Stanford with Ph.D. in organizational behavior; works for White House as senior drug abuse adviser.
1974–1981	Joins consulting firm, McKinsey, becoming a partner in 1977.
Late 1970s	Various collaborative research projects; development of the McKinsey 7-S Model.
1982	Publication of *In Search of Excellence*.
1982–present	Writing, lecturing, touring, and changing his mind; formulates ideas for a management agenda for the 1990s and beyond.

Summary

Tom Peters has probably done more than anyone else to shift the debate on management from the confines of boardrooms, academia, and consulting organizations to a broader, worldwide audience, where it has become the staple diet of the media and managers alike. Peter Drucker has written more and his ideas have withstood a longer test of time, but it is Peters—as consultant, writer, columnist, seminar lecturer, and stage performer—whose energy, style, influence, and ideas have shaped new management thinking.

Life and Career

Born in Baltimore in 1942, Peters repaid a navy scholarship to Cornell with a degree in civil engineering and four years' service in the navy, spending a term of duty in Vietnam in 1966 before being assigned to the Pentagon in 1968. He left Stanford in 1973 with a Ph.D. in organizational behavior and worked for the White House for a short while as senior drug abuse adviser. In 1974 he joined the top consulting firm, McKinsey.

Exposed to consulting assignments in America's blue-chip companies, Peters's curiosity and imagination led him in the late 1970s into various aspects of collaborative research, which brought about the development of the McKinsey 7-S Model. This model focuses on shared values, staff, systems, strategy, structure, skills, and style. It was in fact the first expression of the shift—characterizing all of Peters's work—away from the traditional numbers-centered, rational, analytical, and bureaucratic notion of management of McKinsey and many others toward a more innovative, intuitive, and people-centered approach.

In 1982, Peters copublished with Bob Waterman *In Search of Excellence*, which brought him worldwide fame, and set him off on a new career expounding his theories of excellence. Since then, his life has been a whirlwind of writing, lecturing, touring, and changing his mind.

Peters describes himself as gadfly, curmudgeon, champion of bold failures, prince of disorder, maestro of zest, corporate cheerleader, and irritator. *Fortune Magazine* calls him the Ur-guru (the original guru) and *The Economist* the Über-guru. He is the founder of the

Tom Peters Group and lives on his farm in Vermont, or on American Airlines, or on an island off the Massachusetts coast.

Contribution

In Search of Excellence resulted from the application of the 7-S model in an attempt to discover models of excellence in corporate America. Peters and Waterman identified eight lessons from their research.

- A bias for action—excellent companies got on with doing the job, unconstrained by the bureaucratic trappings.
- Be close to the customer—this has since become a key business "must."
- Autonomy and entrepreneurship—the entrepreneur has freedom to think, act and invest effort in the organization.
- Productivity through people—it was previously believed that large organizations held the key to productivity because only they could handle the economies of scale required for profitability.
- Be driven by hands-on values—the shared values of the 7-S model that matter to employees, as well as making the business tick with managers who are not afraid to get their hands dirty.
- Stick to the knitting—companies should stay with their core competencies, not diversifying for the sake of it.
- Simple form, lean staff—successful companies were not preoccupied with their size or procedures but with keeping things simple.
- Simultaneous loose-tight properties—examples of excellence derived from the faster-moving, more flexible features of smaller organizations, not the more cumbersome aspects of large ones.

When Peters declared in 1987, at the beginning of *Thriving on Chaos*, that there are no excellent companies, it was not only in recognition of the fact that many of the companies he had cited earlier had foundered. It was also because the rules had changed again; there was no single consistent route to excellence. Times change, so companies need to change their approach in order to continue to be successful. Peters has argued consistently that the eight lessons from *In Search of Excellence* remain valid—the companies he cited that later foundered merely failed to follow the lessons through.

A Passion for Excellence was published in 1985, intended as a sequel to *In Search of Excellence*, but this time with the focus on leadership. According to Peters (and his coauthor Nancy Austin) the successful leader becomes passionate about getting the most out of people, takes to heart the full people-centered implications of the 7 Ss, and lays the basis for the culture of empowerment. It is also in this book that Peters starts to return time and again to the centrality of the customer.

In *Thriving on Chaos*, Peters was one of the first to describe the emerging world of uncertainty and accelerating change. He was lucky with his timing: it was published in the same month (October 1987) that the stock market crashes in Wall Street, London, and Tokyo brought chaos to the world's money markets. The book was in fact a rejection of the secure world of the past, and a description of the uncertain world of the future. Some of the book's themes were already there in *In Search of Excellence*, customer responsiveness and flexibility through empowerment, for example. But already in 1987, the world was a fast-changing place where increased competition meant speed to market, and that meant fast-paced innovation. Most of all, Peters understood that organizations would need flexible systems to deal with a topsy-turvy world.

Thriving on Chaos encouraged managers to cast off their old thinking and be prepared for a world of change and uncertainty. But Peters had not yet drawn a map of how to get there. *Liberation Management* was his attempt to draw such a map. He advocated flexible, flowing structures that are antihierarchical and based on building up relationships with customers. As he had done in *Thriving on Chaos*, Peters quoted examples of companies that represent the lean, flatter, and responsive organization required now that the old rule-book had been torn up. Again, he focused on the need to innovate, on closeness to customers, and on empowerment. In *Liberation Management* he asserted that knowledge is becoming the key asset, the working capital of the organization.

Peters the Writer

Drucker may have written more, but Peters is beginning to catch him up. *Thriving on Chaos* is over 500 pages long; *Liberation Management* is over 800. His style of writing, as well as the content of his work, has changed over the years. One of the attractive features of *In Search of Excellence* was its accessible style. Peters's later works take this style to an extreme and reduce the language of management to monosyllabic expressions designed to shock the reader out of conventional thinking.

The Guru as Performer

This is an area that Tom Peters has made his own. Many gurus are academics or writers, but few would claim to have the impact of Peters on stage. He has been universally described as a brilliant performer, with great stage presence and unbeatable delivery technique. Sometimes delivering two seminars a day in different cities, Peters is acknowledged for his genuine interest, concern, even passion for getting people to reflect on the way they manage.

The Tom Peters Seminar: *The Circle of Innovation*

The message that comes over in *The Circle of Innovation* is one that has taken between 15 and 20 years to develop. The book attempts to push the management of organizations to anticipate the topsy-turvy markets that are emerging with global markets, the Internet, and the ever greater closeness of customer and producer.

- Beyond change—be prepared to try things out, but do not expect to get things right first time. Peters acknowledges the role of stability and regularity but attaches far greater importance to agility.
- Beyond downsizing—aim to be big and small at the same time, so that you get the benefits of a large organization (economies of scale, networking, and knowledge-sharing) along with those of the small (speed, independence, and responding to opportunities).
- Beyond empowerment—make every job entrepreneurial.
- Beyond loyalty—everybody learns to think about the future, the customer, and the bottom-line.

- Beyond reengineering—the conversion of units or departments into full professional service firms with responsibility and accountability.
- Beyond disorganization—as the organization spots and responds to opportunities, it becomes a network of partners, distributors, suppliers, and customers with boundaries that are transparent to outsiders.
- Beyond the learning organization—stimulating curiosity and creativity everywhere in the organization.
- Beyond TQM—toward sustainable product/service differentiation to escape the sameness of today's markets through design.
- Beyond management—from management to revolutionary leadership.

Context and Conclusions

Peters did not actually discover the concept of customers with *In Search of Excellence*, but he and Waterman bucked the dominance of strategy to remind management that customers come first. If he seems all for discontinuity and disorganization, it is principally to remind people not to get stuck in the rut of procedures and routine.

Peters has been criticized for not being thorough or academic enough in support of his assertions, for relying too much on his charisma as a performer, and for "dumbing down" management to a level of mundaneness and banality. However, his antennae have sensed where the world of business is heading before it arrives. It is also widely acknowledged that his approach, style, and energy have popularized management ideas to a wider audience than ever before.

Managers from all levels and from all types of organization say that Peters's influence has been positive rather than negative, and he is spoken of in the same league as Porter, Ohmae, Hamel, Handy, and even Drucker. If he has changed his mind, it is because the world of the 1990s and 2000s has altered radically from that of the 1970s. If he has been inconsistent, he has nonetheless stayed ahead of the management times and foreseen—or helped to set—the management agenda for the fast-changing world of the future.

For More Information

Books:

Crainer, Stuart. *Corporate Man to Corporate Skunk: The Tom Peters Phenomenon, a Biography*. San Francisco: Jossey-Bass, 1997.

Peters, Tom, and Bob Waterman. *In Search of Excellence: Lessons from America's Best-run Companies*. New York: Harper & Row, 1982.

Peters, Tom, and Nancy Austin. *A Passion for Excellence: The Leadership Difference*. New York: Harper Collins, 1985.

Peters, Tom. *Thriving on Chaos: Handbook for a Management Revolution*. New York: A. Knopf, 1987.

Peters, Tom. *Liberation Management*. New York: A. Knopf, 1992.

Peters, Tom. *The Tom Peters Seminar: Crazy Times for Crazy Organizations*. New York: Vintage Books, 1994.

Peters, Tom. *The Pursuit of Wow! Every Person's Guide to Topsy-Turvy Times*. New York: Vintage Books, 1994.

Michael Porter

1947	Born.
1969	Completes a degree in aeronautical engineering at Princeton University.
1971	Receives an MBA from Harvard Business School.
1973	Receives a Ph.D. from Harvard University. Joins the Harvard Business School faculty.
1980	Publishes *Competitive Strategy*, which sets him at leading edge of strategic thinking.
1994	Founds The Initiative for a Competitive Inner City, and becomes Chairman and C.E.O.

Summary

In an age when management gurus are both lauded by the faithful and hounded by the critics, Michael Porter seems to be one of the few who is both academically fireproof and largely without criticism from the business world. Porter has been at the leading edge of strategic thinking since his first major publication, *Competitive Strategy*, in 1980.

Life and Career

Born in 1947, Porter completed a degree in aeronautical engineering in 1969 and joined the Harvard Business School faculty at the age of 26. Like many academics, he has established a consulting company, Monitor, advising both leading-edge companies and governments on strategy.

His thinking on strategy has been supported by precision research into industries and companies. Over a period of almost 20 years, his thinking remains consistent as well as developmental—it has not stood still since *Competitive Strategy* became a corporate bible for many in the early 1980s.

Contribution

Before *Competitive Strategy*, most strategic thinking focused on either the organization of a company's internal resources and their adaptation to meet particular circumstances in the marketplace, or improving an organization's competitiveness by lowering prices to increase market share. These approaches, derived from the work of Igor Ansoff, were bundled into systems or processes that provided strategy with an integral place in the organization.

In *Competitive Strategy*, Porter managed to reconcile these approaches and provide management with a fresh way of looking at strategy—not just from the point of view of markets or of organizational capabilities, but from the point of view of industry itself.

Internal Capability for Competitiveness—the Value Chain

Porter describes two different types of business activity—primary and secondary. Primary activities are concerned with transforming inputs (raw materials) into outputs (products), and with delivery and after-sales support. These are usually the main "line management" activities and include:

- inbound logistics—materials handling, warehousing;
- operations—turning raw materials into finished products;
- outbound logistics—order processing and distribution;
- marketing and sales—communication and pricing;
- service—installation and after-sales service.

Secondary activities support the primary and include:
- procurement—purchasing and supply;
- technology development—know-how, procedures and skills;
- human resource management—recruitment, promotion, appraisal, reward and development;
- firm infrastructure—general and quality management, finance, planning.

To survive competition and supply what customers want to buy, the company has to ensure that all these value-chain activities link together, even if some of the activities take place outside the organization. A weakness in any one of the activities will impact on the chain as a whole and affect competitiveness.

The Five Forces

Porter argued that in order to examine its competitive capability in the marketplace, an organization must choose between three generic strategies:
- cost leadership—becoming the lowest-cost producer in the market;
- differentiation—offering something different, extra, or special;
- focus—achieving dominance in a niche market.

The skill is to choose the right one at the right time. These generic strategies are driven by five competitive forces that the organization has to take into account. These are the:
- power of customers to affect pricing and reduce margins;
- power of suppliers to influence the organization's pricing;
- threat of similar products to limit market freedom and reduce prices and thus profits;
- level of existing competition that impacts on investment in marketing and research and thus erodes profits;
- threat of new market entrants to intensify competition and further impact on pricing and profitability.

In recent years, Porter has revisited his earlier work. Such is the acceleration of market change that companies now have to compete not on a choice of strategic front, but on all fronts at once. Porter has also said that it is a misconception of his approach for a company to try to position itself in relation to the five competitive forces. Positioning is not enough. What companies have to do is ask how the five forces can help to rewrite industry rules in the organization's favor.

Diversification

Instead of going it alone, an organization can spread risk and attain growth by diversification and acquisition. While the blue-chip consulting companies such as Boston Consulting Group (market growth/market share matrix) and McKinsey (7-S framework) have developed analytical models for discovering which companies will rise and fall, Porter prefers three critical tests for success:
- the attractiveness test. Industries chosen for diversification must be structurally attractive. An attractive industry will yield a high return on investment, but entry barriers will be high; customers and suppliers will have only moderate bargaining power, and there will be only a few substitute products. An unattractive industry will be swamped by alternative products, high rivalry, and high fixed costs;

- the cost-of-entry test. If the cost of entry is so high that it prejudices the potential return on investment, profitability is eroded before the game has started;
- the better-off test. How will the acquisition provide advantage to either the acquirer or the acquired? One must offer significant advantage to the other.

Porter devised seven steps to tackle these questions:

- as competition takes place at the business unit level, identify the interrelationships among the existing business units;
- identify the core business that is to be the foundation of the strategy. Core businesses are those in attractive industries and in which competitive advantage can be sustained;
- create horizontal organizational mechanisms to facilitate interrelationships among core businesses;
- pursue diversification opportunities that allow shared activities and pass all three critical tests;
- pursue diversification through a transfer of skills, if opportunities for sharing activities are limited or exhausted;
- pursue a strategy of restructuring if this fits the skills of management, or if no good opportunities exist for forging corporate partnerships;
- pay dividends so that shareholders can become portfolio managers.

The National Diamond

Why do some companies achieve consistent improvement in innovation, seeking an ever more sophisticated source of competitive advantage? For Porter, the answer lies in four attributes that affect industries. These attributes are:

- factor conditions—the nation's skills and infrastructure capable of enabling a competitive position;
- demand conditions—the nature of home-market demand;
- related and supporting industries—presence or absence of supplier/feeder industries;
- firm strategy, structure and rivalry—the national conditions under which companies are created, grow, organize, and manage.

These are the chief determinants that create the environment in which businesses flourish and compete. The points on the diamond constitute a self-reinforcing system, in which the effect of one point often depends on the state of the others, and any weakness at one point will impact adversely on an industry's capability to compete.

The New Strategic Wave

Sometime between 1980 and 1990 a new wave of more subversive strategic thinking—with Gary Hamel and *Strategy as Revolution*, and Mintzberg with "The fall and rise of strategic planning" (*Harvard Business Review*)—emerged to replace the old rulebook. Porter's main contribution to date, *Competitive Strategy*, argues that strategic planning lost its way because managers failed to distinguish between strategic and operational effectiveness and confused the two.

The old strategic model was based on productivity, increasing market share, and lowering costs. Hence, total quality management, benchmarking, outsourcing, and reengineering were all at the forefront of change in the 1980s as the key drivers of operational improvements. But continuing incremental improvements to the way things are done tend to bring different players up to the same level, rather than differentiating them. To achieve differentiation therefore means that:

- strategy rests on unique activities, based on customers' needs, customers' accessibility, or the variety of a company's products or services;
- the company's activities must fit and link together. In terms of the value chain, one link is prone to imitation but with a chain, imitation is very difficult;
- it is important to make trade-offs. Excelling at some things means making a conscious choice not to do others—it's a question of being a "master of one trade" to stand out from the crowd, as opposed to being a "jack of all trades" and lost in the mass. Tradeoffs deliberately limit what a company offers. The essence of strategy lies in what not to do.

Context and Conclusions

It is a mark of Porter's achievement that much of his work on *Competitive Strategy*, researched in the 1970s, still has high value and relevance and still shapes mainstream thinking on competition and strategy.

While his work is academically rigorous, his ability to abstract his thinking into digestible chunks for the business world has given him wide appeal to both the academic and business communities. It is now standard practice for organizations to think and talk about "value chains," and the five forces have entered the curriculum of every management program.

For More Information

Books:
Crainer, Stuart. *Key Management Ideas: Thinking That Changed the Management World*. 3rd ed. Upper Saddle River, NJ: Prentice Hall, 1998.
Porter, Michael. *Competitive Strategy: Techniques for Analyzing Industries and Competitors*. New York: Free Press, 1980.
Porter, Michael. *Cases in Competitive Strategy*. New York: Free Press, 1983.
Porter, Michael. *Competitive Advantage: Creating and Sustaining Superior Performance*. Rev. ed. New York: Free Press, 1985.
Porter, Michael, ed. *Competition in Global Industries*. Boston: Harvard Business School Press, 1986.
Porter, Michael. *The Competitive Advantage of Nations*. Rev ed. New York: Free Press, 1998.

Journal Articles:
Jackson, Tony. "Dare to Be different." *Financial Times*, June 19, 1997, p 23.
Porter, Michael. "Corporate Strategy: The State of Strategic Thinking." *The Economist*, May 23,1998, pp. 21–22, 27–28.
Porter, Michael. "The Competitive Advantage of Nations." *Harvard Business Review*, Mar./Apr. 1990, pp. 73–93.
Porter, Michael. "From Competitive Advantage to Corporate Strategy." *Harvard Business Review*, May/June 1987, pp. 43–59.
Porter, Michael. "What Is Strategy?" *Harvard Business Review*, Nov./Dec. 1996, pp. 61–78.

Edgar Schein

1928	Born.
1949	Masters Degree in Psychology, Stanford.
1972–1982	Chairman of the Organization Studies Group of Sloan School of Management, Massachusetts Institute of Technology.
1978–1990	Sloan Fellows Professor of Management, Massachusetts Institute of Technology.
1985	Publication of *Organizational Culture and Leadership*.

Summary

Edgar Schein pioneered the concept of corporate culture with his landmark book *Organizational Culture and Leadership* (1985), which sparked off much research into the subject. He also coined the now much-used phrases "psychological contract" and "career anchor."

Life and Career

Currently the Sloan Fellows Professor of Management Emeritus and part-time senior lecturer at the MIT Sloan School of Management, Edgar Schein has had a long and distinguished academic career. He received his Ph.D. in social psychology from Harvard University, collaborated with Douglas McGregor at MIT, and worked for many years with the National Training Laboratory. In addition, he has made a strong contribution to the "helping" professions, mainly in the areas of organization development, career development, and organizational culture.

Schein has researched and written extensively about the factors that influence individual and organizational performance. The main themes underlying his work are the identification of culture(s) in the organization, the relationship between organizational culture and individual behavior, and the importance of organizational culture for organizational learning. Douglas McGregor invited him to MIT on the basis of his work on the repatriation of POWs following the end of the Korean War. This work strongly influenced Schein's whole career, and reemerged forcefully in 1999 in an article for the *Learning Organization* on brainwashing and organizational persuasion techniques ("Empowerment, Coercive Persuasion, and Organizational learning: Do They Connect?" vol. 6, no. 4, pp.163–172).

Contribution

Corporate Culture

Early in his career Schein found traditional approaches to understanding work behavior and motivation first too simplistic to explain the variety of experiences of individuals in organizations, and, second, too restrictive, since human and organizational needs vary widely from person to person, place to place, and time to time. In *Organizational Culture and Leadership*, he became the first management theorist to define corporate culture and suggest ways in which culture is the dominant force within an organization.

In his view, culture is a mix of many different factors, such as:

- observed behavioral regularities when people interact;
- norms that evolve in working groups;

- dominant values pushed by the organization;
- the philosophy guiding the attitudes of senior management to staff and customers;
- organizational rules, procedures, and processes;
- the feeling or climate that is conveyed without a word being spoken.

In *Organizational Culture and Leadership*, Schein defines culture as a pattern of basic assumptions, and discusses how these fall into five, often oppositional, categories:

- humanity's relationship to nature—some organizations seem to want to dominate the external environment, while others accept its domination;
- the nature of reality and truth—the ways and means by which organizations arrive at the "truth;"
- the nature of human nature—some people seem to avoid work if they possibly can, while others embrace it as a way of fulfilling their potential, to both their own and the organization's benefit;
- the nature of human activity—a focus on the completion of tasks on the one hand, and on self-fulfillment and personal development on the other;
- the nature of human relationships—some organizations seem to facilitate social interaction, others to regard it as an unnecessary distraction.

Organizational Socialization

Schein's thoughts on organizational socialization were triggered when, after arriving at MIT, he asked McGregor for guidance in the form of previous outlines and notes for a course he was preparing. McGregor suggested that Schein should make up his own mind. This lesson in acclimatizing to MIT led Schein to argue that companies should be conversant with their socialization practices and recognize the conflicts they can create for new recruits.

In "Organizational socialization and the profession of management" (*Sloan Management Review*, Fall 1988, pp. 53–65), Schein discusses how, when a new recruit enters the organization, a process of socialization—adaptation or "fit"—takes place. He argues that this process has more to do with recruits' past experience and values than their qualifications or formal training.

Usually, Schein suggested, organizations create a series of events that work to undo the new recruit's old values to some extent, so that he or she is more open to learning new values. This process of "undoing" or "unfreezing" can be unpleasant, and its success may therefore depend on either a recruit's strong motivation to endure it, or the organization's perseverance in making recruits endure it. There are three basic responses to this socialization process:

- rebellion—outright rejection of the organization's norms and values;
- creative individualism—selective adoption of key values and norms;
- conformity—acceptance of the organization's norms and values.

Noting similarities between brainwashing experienced by servicemen captured during the Korean War and the socialization of executives on programs at MIT, Schein argues that many forms of organizational development involve restructuring and change, and have serious implications for the way people work and their relationship with management.

Schein likens such processes to a form of coercive persuasion, or brainwashing, giving people little choice but to abandon, for example, older norms and values that fit badly with the new learning. If we are in tune with the goals and values of the change this will not be a problem, but if we dislike the values, we are likely to disapprove of the brainwashing. Schein concludes that, because the very concept of organization involves some restriction of individual freedom to achieve a joint purpose, the concept of a continually learning, innovative organization is something of a paradox, since creativity and learning are related to individual freedom and growth.

Organizational Learning

Organizational learning, Schein considers, needs to be fast in order to cope with growing market pressures, yet seems to be obstructed by a fear of, or anxiety about, facing change, particularly on the part of senior executives. This feeling is associated with reluctance to learn what is new, because it appears too difficult or disruptive. Schein argues that only a new anxiety greater than the existing one can overcome this, and his "anxiety 2" is the fear, shame, or guilt associated with not learning anything new.

Schein emphasizes the need for people to feel psychologically safe, if change is to happen. Achieving organizational learning and transformation therefore depends upon creating a feeling of safety and overcoming the negative effects of past incentives and past punishments—especially the latter. To learn, people need to feel motivated and free to try out new things.

Psychological Contract and Career Anchors

In *Organizational Psychology* Schein highlights a "psychological contract" (attributing the original concept to Chris Argyris) which he defines as an unwritten set of expectations operating between employees and employing managers and others in an organization. He stresses how essential it is that both parties' expectations of a contract should match, if a long-term relationship that will benefit both parties is to develop.

Closely linked to the notion of the psychological contract is the concept of the "career anchor," a guiding force that influences individuals' career choices and is based on their self-perceptions. Schein proposes that, from their varying aspirations and motivations, individuals—perhaps unconsciously—develop one underlying career anchor, which they are unwilling to surrender. On the basis of 44 cases, he distinguishes career anchor groups such as technical/functional competence, managerial competence, creativity, security or stability, and autonomy.

The Three Cultures of Management

Rather than a single culture, Schein identifies three cultures (or communities of interest) within an organization: the operator culture, which evolves locally within organizations and within operational units; the engineering culture of technicians in search of "people-free" solutions; and the executive culture, which is focused on financial survival.

The three often conflict rather than work in harmony. For example, while the executive culture requires systems and reporting relationships for evidence that operations are on track, the engineering culture attempts to design systems that cut across lines of control and the people manning these.

In his article "Three Cultures of Management: The Key to Organizational Learning"

(*Sloan Management Review*, Fall 1996, pp. 9–20), Schein suggests that, in many cases, either operators assume executives and engineers do not understand their work needs and covertly do things in their own way; or executives or engineers assume a need for tighter control over operators and force them to follow policies and procedure manuals. In either case, there is no commonly understood plan, and efficiency and effectiveness suffer.

Schein stresses the need to take the concept of culture more seriously and accept how deeply embedded are the assumptions of executives, engineers, and employees. He proposes that helping executives and engineers learn how to learn about, analyze, and evolve their cultures may be central to organizational learning.

Context and Conclusions

Schein's work now spans more than four decades and his great contribution has been in linking culture with individual development and growth, putting the accent on organizations as complex systems and on individuals as whole beings.

Schein was aware that the concept of corporate culture was no cure-all for ailing organizations. The fact, however, that culture is now generally recognized as a central factor in organizational change and development is largely attributable to his work.

For More Information
Books:
Schein, Edgar H. *Career Dynamics: Matching Individual and Organizational Needs*. Reading, MA: Addison-Wesley, 1978.

Schein, Edgar H. *Organizational Psychology*. 3rd ed. Englewood Cliffs, NJ: Prentice Hall, 1980.

Schein, Edgar H. *Organizational Culture and Leadership*. 2nd ed. San Francisco: Jossey-Bass, 1997.

Schein, Edgar H. *The Corporate Culture Survival Guide*. San Francisco: Jossey-Bass, 1999.

Journal Article:
Schein, Edgar H. "How Can Organizations Learn Faster? The Challenge of Entering the Green Room." *Sloan Management Review*, Winter 1993, pp. 85–92.

Adam Smith

1723	Born.
1748	Appointed lecturer in literature at Edinburgh University, Scotland.
1751	Appointed professor of literature at Glasgow University, Scotland.
1763	Publication of *The Theory of Moral Sentiments*.
1776	Publication of *The Wealth of Nations*.
1778	Accepts post of commissioner of customs in Scotland.
1787	Elected lord rector at Glasgow University.
1790	Dies.

Summary

Adam Smith (1723–1790) published his best-known book, fully entitled *An Inquiry into the Nature and Causes of the Wealth of Nations* but commonly known as *The Wealth of Nations*, in 1776. This is often described as one of the most important texts of our time, and its two main philosophical points stressed the supreme value of individual liberty, and the pursuit of self-interest as ultimately beneficial for society as a whole.

Life and Career

Smith was brought up in Kirkcaldy, Scotland by his widowed mother. He went, on a scholarship, to Glasgow University at 14, to study mathematics and moral philosophy; and then, at 17, to Balliol College, Oxford. In 1748, he was appointed to a lectureship in literature at Edinburgh, and in 1751, became Professor of Literature at Glasgow University. One year later, he was appointed Professor of Moral Philosophy and, despite a nervous disorder, faltering speech and a tendency to forgetfulness, became a teacher of high repute. His lectures focused on theology, ethics and jurisprudence.

In 1763, following the publication of his first book, *The Theory of Moral Sentiments*, Smith was asked to act as tutor and companion to the young Duke of Buccleuch during his "grand tour" of Europe. Through this he met several great philosophers and thinkers, including Voltaire and Rousseau, and his own ideas took firmer shape. On his return from Europe he retired to Kirkcaldy to concentrate on writing *The Wealth of Nations*.

In 1778, Smith accepted the post of commissioner of customs in Scotland, and was elected lord rector at Glasgow University in 1787. Although Smith had plans to add a third volume (on jurisprudence) to follow the other two, his writings remained limited to reissuing editions of *The Wealth of Nations*.

Smith never married and, despite his impressive mind, became known as somewhat eccentric, largely due to his tendency to forget everyday things, such as changing from his nightclothes into day wear. After the death of Smith's mother, he was looked after by a maiden aunt until his death in 1790.

Historical Background

To understand Smith's thinking fully, it is helpful to know a little about his background. He knew many of the most influential contemporary thinkers, and spent much time debating in the gentlemen's clubs of London. He was a friend of both John Locke and David Hume and was, for a time, a disciple of Quesnay, the leading French physiocrat. *The Wealth of Nations* undoubtedly drew ideas from many such sources.

In the later 17th and 18th centuries, there was increasing interest in the theory of "natural" law. The natural sciences had become established since the publication of Newton's *Philosophiae Naturalis Principia Mathematica* (1687) and there was a strong drive to uncover the natural laws that were thought to guide people's actions.

At the same time, burdensome government regulations were increasingly criticized, and the theory of natural order was being drawn into ideas about society and government. For example, John Locke's *Treatise on Civil Government* (1691) proposed that men are born free and equal, and are governed by "natural laws," arguing that, while executive power is necessary, this should be only by consent.

Such revolutionary ideas were taken up by many great thinkers, including Hume, Hutchison, the French physiocrats, and Smith himself. It was, however, impossible to prove the existence of a benevolent "natural order," ordained by God for men's happiness. While proponents of the concept considered it to be self-evident, it was always, in fact, an intangible hypothesis wide open to challenge.

The idea that human society should be based on a natural order encouraged ideas about individualism to develop further. The concept of an economic system founded on individual self-interest rather than government control is central to *The Wealth of Nations*, and to later social, political, and economic change.

The Wealth of Nations
Natural Law and "Laissez Faire"

The Wealth of Nations followed the French physiocrats in arguing that all human powers are subject to immutable, natural moral and physical laws. These laws, divine in origin, were thought to offer a basis for government that could leave things to work naturally, with results that would satisfy both individual and state interests.

Smith never actually used the term "laissez faire," but his book popularized associated arguments for government non-intervention in social, economic, and commercial matters. "Laissez faire" was first used by the French, and essentially meant that the government should let things alone, specifically in terms of trade, production of goods, and quantities or quality of products. This philosophy dominated much 18th and 19th century government, and assumed that:

- natural laws, if left to work freely, would create the best possible society;
- enlightened individual selfishness was ultimately in the public interest;
- men are born equal.

The Wealth of Nations took ten years to write, and the ideas within it challenged Smith's contemporary, mercantilist government and its protectionist laws. The author realized that his book would outrage those with vested interests in business or government, because of its arguments for government-enforced competition and against price-fixing.

Although often castigated as such, Smith was neither inhumane nor a proponent of "the law of the jungle" as an approach to social organization. He recognized the worst tendencies of some businessmen who "love to reap where they never sowed," and was extremely aware of how greed could lead to excesses of monopoly and corruption. Smith did, in fact, support some forms of intervention, especially in public areas such as defense. He did not, however, have our benefit of hindsight, or know how the Industrial Revolution would change society, creating some extremely wealthy businessmen, and a mass of extremely poor industrial workers, who would suffer greatly because of their lack of protection from regulatory laws.

The Law of Labor

Natural law was considered by Smith to encompass a "law of labor." According to this, the external environment could provide men with the products necessary for subsistence, in return for their labor, and all men should therefore have the right to perform activities to preserve their existence. Government's only role should be to promote the existence of natural law and to enable its free working.

The natural laws were assumed to work in the same exacting way as mathematical laws. Left to themselves, they should establish an order that would benefit both individuals and society. Individualism, for Smith and the other economists and philosophers of his time, meant relief from the constraints of mercantilism, the right to economic freedom, and the right of a people to legislate for themselves and be taxed by the government they chose.

The Division of Labor

Smith gives many examples of the advantages of the division of labor, with each worker focusing upon a single stage of manufacture rather than, as in traditional crafts, being involved in every stage. His ideas were based on life before 1760, and he did not foresee how the introduction of machinery would make the division of labor even more logical and sometimes a harsh necessity.

The Free Market

Smith's main thesis throughout *The Wealth of Nations* was the inefficiency of government interference, which he demonstrates with reference to the markets for both national and international trade. He envisions a free market as a customer-driven, democratic mechanism through which, by exercising their free choices about purchase or sale prices, people would act to regulate resources fairly. Although it was Dudley North who first related supply to demand and extolled the benefits of free trade, Smith recognized that buyers as well as sellers profit from trade, and saw international commerce as a source of wealth for both importers and exporters.

Smith had a very positive vision of how a free market would eventually realize a state of "universal opulence" for everyone. He argued that each nation should concentrate on those industrial areas where it enjoyed a "comparative advantage." These ideas were taken up by subsequent economists such as Ricardo and Malthus, and can be traced within the thinking of some contemporary strategists, particularly in Michael Porter's work on competitive advantage.

Morality

Smith is often criticized for a lack of moral focus in *The Wealth of Nations* but he did assume that its readers would already know of the moral base given in *The Theory of Moral Sentiments*. The earlier book sought to explore moral judgments within the context of Smith's assumption that people are essentially driven by self-interest, and proposed that we all have "social propensities" for sympathy, justice, and benevolence.

Context and Conclusions

The Wealth of Nations had a profound influence on English history, leading to the end of the mercantilist era and catalyzing a social and economic order based on individualism and the "natural laws" supposedly underlying competition and free market forces.

Smith's ideas have often been castigated for the support they gave to later businessmen who grew very rich while rejecting any regulations to protect industrial workers. He wrote his masterpiece, however, before the Industrial Revolution began to take effect, and it was intended as a polemic against restrictive government policies and monopolistic abuses, rather than as a panegyric for unregulated business. Also, just as Smith's first book, *The Theory of Moral Sentiments*, supplies a moral aspect to complement *The Wealth of Nations*, it is probable that his intended, but unwritten, third volume on jurisprudence could have contributed ideas for legal safeguards to protect the public from abuses resulting from greed and collusion, since he considered these typically to arise out of people's business activities and contacts.

For his time, Smith was actually a social radical, promoting liberty and equality and denouncing various pillars of the existing establishment. From our modern perspective, it is clear there was no factual base for his ideas about natural law and harmony, and that perfect competition could not erase social problems, particularly when factors from a future that Smith could not have imagined (including giant corporations, economic cycles and depressions, mass unemployment, and mechanical warfare) became more pertinent. Despite this, however, *The Wealth of Nations* remains a "milestone" book offering a composite analysis that shaped our social and economic world.

For More Information

Books:

Haakonssen, Knud, ed. *The Theory of Moral Sentiments*. New York: Cambridge University Press, 2002.

Smith, Adam. *Inquiry into the Nature and Causes of the Wealth of Nations* (abridged). Indianapolis, IN: Hackett Publishing Company, 1993.

Sun Tzu

c. 400 BC	Sun Tzu lived and wrote.
1780	First European translation of *The Art of War* published.
1910	English translation published.

Summary

Eastern business methods had already shaken Western management thinking long before Athos and Pascale published *The Art of Japanese Management* or Peters and Waterman popularized the McKinsey 7-S model in *In Search of Excellence*. The quality management techniques used by Japanese companies enabled them to put cheaper and better products into American and British stores than their domestic rivals. The search to discover how they achieved this led to an understanding that Japanese businesspeople have a different perspective on the marketplace from their Western counterparts.

Life and Career

Although the precise dates of his birth and death are not known, Sun Tzu is thought to have lived over 2,400 years ago, at roughly the same time as Confucius. Raised in a family of army officers, he became familiar with, and eventually expert in, military affairs. Historians are generally agreed that he was a general who led a number of successful military campaigns in the region currently known as the Anhui Province. It is recorded that the state of Wu, under whose sovereign he served, became a dominant power at that time. Since then, it has become standard practice for Chinese military chiefs to familiarize themselves with Sun Tzu's writings.

Contribution

The Art of War

Sun Tzu's *The Art of War* (the book's actual title is *Sun Tzu Ping Fa*, literally "The Military Method of Mr. Sun") is a compilation of his thinking on the strategies that underlie success in war. It has been translated into many languages, and there are several English versions. This account is based on the translation by Thomas Cleary, published by Shambhala Pocket Classics and available on the Internet. Two further editions, published by Tuttle and Wordsworth editions respectively, also were consulted.

Sun Tzu's anecdotes and thoughts, which fill no more than about 25 pages of text in all, are divided into 13 sections:

    1 strategic assessments
    2 doing battle
    3 offensive strategy
    4 formation
    5 force
    6 emptiness and fullness
    7 armed struggle
    8 adaptations

9 maneuvering armies

10 terrain

11 nine grounds

12 attack by fire

13 use of spies

Some of these have less current relevance than others, but they are all worth at least a glance. Hidden among advice such as not to dally in salt marshes when retreating or attacking (11), there is the odd gem that is striking in its modernity. For example: "when a leader enters deeply into enemy territory with the troops, he brings out their potential." (11) The advice given in section 10 on how to proceed in narrow or steep terrain (occupy the high and sunny side to await your opponent) can be quickly passed over, but a little further on in the same section Sun Tzu's castigation of poor leadership is much more pertinent: "When generals are weak and lack authority, instructions are not clear, officers and soldiers lack consistency, and they form battle lines every which way; this is riot."

On Strategy

Many commentaries focus on the first section, strategic assessments, at the expense of the others. It is certainly there that, helped by a little lateral thinking, Sun Tzu seems best to relate to the spirit of modern business. He refers initially to five key factors that determine the result of war:

- politics—that which causes people to be in harmony with their ruler;
- weather—the seasons;
- terrain—distances, difficulty or ease of travel, opportunities or safety;
- leadership—a matter of intelligence, trustworthiness, humaneness, courage, and strictness;
- discipline—organization, chain of command, logistics.

There are also seven issues to be appraised (the postscript following each question has been added to indicate the line most interpretations take).

- Whose moral influence is the stronger? (Whose followers are more willing to subscribe to common goals?)
- Which leader is the more able? (Who has the ability to combine benevolence and compassion with boldness and strict discipline?)
- Which army has greater advantage of nature and terrain? (Whom do politics, economic cycles, investment, and social and cultural factors favor? Who understands the bigger picture?)
- Whose laws and rules are more effective? (Do people understand what is expected as a result of clear instructions and procedures?)
- Whose troops are stronger? (How can things be arranged so that small can compete effectively with large?)
- Whose soldiers are better trained? (Who uses delegation and training for organizational effectiveness?)
- Whose system of rewards and punishments is clearer? (Who is therefore able to generate higher performance and a better competitive position?)

The theme of strategy is picked up again and again, apparently at random. One interpretation stretches section 6 to make it relate to market presence and strategies of deception employed to fool competitor intelligence. Sun Tzu argues that "there is no constant good or bad, right or wrong: therefore victory in war is not repetitious, but adapts its form endlessly . . .so a military force has no constant formation, water has no constant shape: the ability to gain victory by changing and adapting according to the opponent is called genius." (6)

On Information and Intelligence
". . .to fail to know the conditions of opponents because of reluctance to give rewards for intelligence is extremely inhuman, uncharacteristic of a true military leader. . .so what enables an intelligent government and a wise military leadership to overcome others and achieve extraordinary accomplishments is foreknowledge. . . [which] must be obtained from people who know the conditions of the enemy." (13)

On Tactics
"Making the armies able to take on opponents without being defeated is a matter of unorthodox and orthodox methods." (5)

"The difficulty of armed struggle is to make long distances near and make problems into advantages." (7)

On Competition and Competitor Intelligence
"So if you do not know the plans of your competitors, you cannot make informed alliances." (7)

"So the rule of military operations is not to count on opponents not coming, but to rely on having ways of dealing with them; not to count on opponents not attacking, but to rely on having what cannot be attacked." (8)

On Leadership and People Management
"If they rule armies without knowing the arts of complete adaptivity, even if they know what there is to gain, they cannot get people to work for them." (8)

"If soldiers are punished before a personal attachment to the leadership is formed, they will not submit, and if they do not submit, they are hard to employ." (9)

"Look upon your soldiers as you do infants, and they willingly go into deep valleys with you; look upon your soldiers as beloved children, and they willingly die with you." (10)

"If you are so nice to them that you cannot employ them, so kind to them that you cannot command them, so casual with them that you cannot establish order, they are like spoiled children, useless." (10)

On Communication
"When directives are consistently issued to edify the populace, the populace accepts . . . when directives are consistently issued, there is mutual satisfaction between the leadership and the group." (9)

Context and Conclusions
Historians tell us that the *Sun Tzu Ping Fa* is the oldest existing military treatise in the world, predating Clausewitz by 2,200 years. But so what? Does it have any relevance for people in

business today? How can the thoughts of a Chinese general who lived two and a half millennia ago possibly inform, enlighten, or inspire a modern manager, or have any bearing on his or her day-to-day concerns? And even if there are interesting links, do they do any more than show us that ancient Chinese strategists did not differ fundamentally from modern business people?

Sun Tzu's supporters, however, insist that his concepts are ageless. Although it is easy to stretch interpretation too far and find meaning anywhere if you look hard enough, such things as strategic intelligence, planning, attention to detail, cunning, deception, and theories of leadership in which the leader earns authority with the led, have universal value and are appropriate to any human arena and any period.

If part of Sun Tzu's modern appeal derives from the constant search for any nuggets of intelligence that may give an organization an edge over the competition, another part lies in the fact that the *Ping Fa* offers an opportunity to gain insights into the Oriental mind that do not come from someone with a modern ax to grind or reputation to make. In addition, the insights are couched in direct, no-nonsense, hard-hitting language that makes them seem more, not less, pregnant with meaning.

As globalization brings East closer to West, business relationships will hinge on understanding cultures and attitudes that may appear strange at first. And wherever managers set strategic goals, sell their goods abroad, or interrelate with their workforce, *The Art of War* may still have something to say to them. It is finding its way into many MBA programs.

For More Information

Books:

Kaufman, Stephen F. *The Art of War: The Definitive Interpretation of Sun Tzu's Classic Book of Strategy for the Martial Artist*. Rutland, VT: Charles E. Tuttle, 1996.

Sun Tzu. *The Art of War*. Trans. Yuan Shibing, interpretation Tao Hanzhang, foreword Norman Stone. Ware, Hertfordshire: Wordsworth Editions, 1993.

Sun Tzu. *The Art of War*. Trans. Thomas Cleary. Boston, MA: Shambhala Pocket Classics, 1991.

Journal Articles:

Crainer, Stuart. "Braingain." *Management Today*, April 1998, pp. 68–70.

Min Chen. "Sun Tzu's Strategic Thinking and Contemporary Business." *Business Horizons*, Mar./Apr., 1994, pp. 42–48.

Frederick Winslow Taylor

1856	Born.
1874	Becomes an apprentice pattern-maker and machinist at Enterprise Hydraulic Works.
1878	Takes unskilled job at the Midvale Steel Works.
1881	Gains master's degree in mechanical engineering.
1890	Becomes general manager of Manufacturing Investment Company (MIC).
1898	Becomes joint discoverer of the Taylor-White process, a method of tempering steel.
1911	Publication of *The Principles of Scientific Management*.
1915	Dies.

Summary

Peter Drucker is often called "the guru's guru." Drucker himself would suggest that the accolade should be given to Frederick Winslow Taylor (1856–1917). "On Taylor's 'scientific management' rests, above all, the tremendous surge of affluence in the last 75 years which has lifted the working masses in the developed countries well above any level recorded, even for the well-to-do," Drucker wrote in *Management: Tasks, Responsibilities, Practices*.

Life and Career

Although Taylor passed the entrance examination for Harvard College, failing eyesight meant that he could not become a student there. Instead he took the unusual step for someone of his background of becoming an apprentice pattern-maker and machinist at the Enterprise Hydraulic Works in Philadelphia.

Following his apprenticeship, Taylor took up an unskilled job at the Midvale Steel Works. After several different jobs and a master's degree in mechanical engineering, he was appointed chief engineer there. In 1890 he became general manager of Manufacturing Investment Company (MIC), eventually becoming an independent consulting engineer to management.

In 1881, Taylor won the doubles championships of the United States Lawn Tennis Association and a year later, the doubles in the Young American C. C. Lawn Tennis Tournament. Later in his career he developed a passion for golf and, in keeping with his love of experiment, attempted to make a putting green that was reliant on water below the surface rather than on natural rainfall. By the time of his death, Taylor's experiments had led to him filing at least 50 patents and had made him an extremely wealthy man.

Contribution

Scientific Management

Taylor's seminal work—*The Principles of Scientific Management*—was published four years before his death. In it, he put forward his ideas of "scientific management" (sometimes referred to today as "Taylorism"), which differed from traditional "initiative and incentive" methods of management. These ideas were an accumulation from his life's work, and included several examples from his places of employment. The four overriding principles of scientific management are as follows.

- Each part of a job is analyzed "scientifically," and the most efficient method for undertaking it is devised—the "one best way" of working. This consists of examining the implements needed to perform the work, and measuring the maximum amount a "first-class" worker can do in a day. Workers are then expected to do this much work every day.
- The most suitable person to undertake the job is chosen, again "scientifically." The individual is taught to do the job in the exact way devised. Everyone, according to Taylor, has the ability to be "first class" at some job. It is management's role to find out which job suits each employee and train them until they are first class.
- Managers must cooperate with workers to ensure the job is done in the scientific way.
- There is a clear "division" of work and responsibility between management and workers. Managers concern themselves with the planning and supervision of the work, and workers carry it out.

Taylor summed up the differences between his principles of management and the traditional method as follows: "Under the management of 'initiative and incentive,' practically the whole problem is 'up to the workman'; while under the scientific management, fully one-half of the problem is 'up to the management'...The principal object of management should be to secure the maximum prosperity for the employer, coupled with the maximum prosperity for each employee." Taylor could justify his methods because he felt that his long-term goal would lead to "diminution of poverty, and the alleviation of suffering."

His main reason for developing scientific management was that he wished to do away with "soldiering" or "natural laziness," as he believed that all workers spent little time putting in full effort. To do this, Taylor aimed to analyze every job in a scientific way so that no one could be in any doubt about how much work could and should be done in a day. He felt that "every single act of every workman can be reduced to a science." Much inconclusive argument has ensued as to whether he was the pioneer of time and motion study. Certainly, time study played as important a part in Taylor's scientific job and task analysis as the examination of a worker's movements and the implements he used.

Inherent in Taylor's management style was the setting up of planning departments, staffed by clerks who ensured that "every laborer's work was planned out well in advance, and the workmen were moved from place to place...very much as chessmen are moved on a chessboard, a telephone and messenger system having been installed for this purpose." He concluded that, in this way, "a large amount of the time lost through having too many men in one place and too few in another, and through waiting between jobs, was entirely eliminated." Such a policy did, however, require the setting up of a more "elaborate organization and system," which sowed the seeds for Max Weber's bureaucratic organization structure. Taylor's approach constituted one of the first formal divisions between those who do the work (workers) and those who supervise and plan it (managers).

Management and Workers

For workers on the shop floor, scientific management brought a dramatic loss in skill level and autonomy. As well as being subject to increased supervision, workers were no longer able to use their own tools, which they might have spent many years modifying to suit their own style. In many cases, however, Taylor's ideas were extremely effective. In the case of shovelers at the Bethlehem Steel Works, workers earned higher wages and the company saved between $75,000 and $80,000 per year through greater efficiency.

Although Taylor believed that disputes between managers and workers would be eliminated because what "constitutes a fair day's work will be a question for scientific investigation, instead of a subject to be bargained and haggled over," there were numerous occasions when his ideas came into conflict with labor organizations. His opinion of such unions was invariably derogatory, as he was convinced that their objective was to limit the output of their members. Because of this, Taylor focused on the individual, believing that where a group of workers was formed, peer pressure would be used to ensure each man did not work to his full capacity. In the Bethlehem Steel Works, he decreed that no more than four men could work together in a gang without a special permit.

Even the way he wrote about unskilled workers was condescending. "Now one of the very first requirements for a man who is fit to handle pig iron as a regular occupation is that he shall be so stupid and phlegmatic that he more nearly resembles in his mental make-up the ox than any other type" is a typical example.

Although Taylor's manner often appeared inhumane, he also wrote: "If the workman fails to do his task, some competent teacher should be sent to show him exactly how his work can best be done, to guide, help, and to encourage him and, at the same time, to study his possibilities as a workman. So that, under the plan which individualizes each workman, instead of brutally discharging the man or lowering his wages to make good at once, he is given the time and the help required to make him proficient at his present job, or he is shifted to another class of work for which he is either mentally or physically better suited."

Contemporary Reaction to Scientific Management

It is easy to see why Taylor's work was regarded as inhumane. However good his motives of bringing about the greater good for the worker on the shop floor, the alleviation of poverty, and the elimination of waste, his methods were extremely hard and sometimes had the opposite effect.

It took him three years to implement some of his methods in the Midvale Steel Works. The men resorted to breaking their machines in an attempt to prove to management that Taylor was overworking them. In response, he fined any man whose machine broke, until eventually "they got sick of being fined, their opposition broke down, and they promised to do a fair day's work."

Context and Conclusions

Many of Taylor's ideas are relevant to the modern day. Three in particular, taken from *The Principles of Scientific Management*, stand out:

- Rewards: "A reward, if it is to be most effective in stimulating men to do their best work, must come soon after the work has been done…The average workman must be able to measure what he has accomplished and clearly see his reward at the end of each day if he is to do his best." In Taylor's view, it was pointless to involve the shop floor workers in end-of-year profit sharing schemes.

- Quality standards: The use of written documentation for each part of a worker's job, inherent in scientific management, is strikingly prescient of the procedural documentation used in the ISO 9000 series of quality standards. "In the case of a machine-shop which is managed under the modern system, detailed written instructions as to the best way of doing each piece of work are prepared in advance, by men in the planning department. These instructions represent the combined work of several men in the planning room, each of whom has his own specialty , or function...The directions of all of these men, however, are written on a single instruction card, or sheet." The main difference is that today's best practice means involving staff in drawing up their own procedures.

- Suggestion schemes: Taylor proposed a form of incentive for employees to make suggestions if they felt an improvement could be made, either to the method or the implement used to undertake a task. If, after analysis, the suggestion was introduced into the workplace, the person suggesting it "should be given the full credit for the improvement, and should be paid a cash premium as a reward for his ingenuity. In this way the true initiative of the workmen is better attained under scientific management than under the old individual plan."

At the time of his death in 1917, Taylor's work was the subject of much debate, both for and against. His approach is now frowned on as "Victorian," but it should not be forgotten that he was a man of his times and sought solutions to the problems of his times. The main criticism of Taylor is that his approach was too mechanistic—treating people like machines or as unthinking creatures to be trained like dogs, rather than as human beings.

However, he was one of the first true pioneers of management through his scientific examination of the way work is done, and his thinking led directly to the achievements of other management gurus such as Max Weber and Henry Ford.

For More Information

Books:

Kakar, Sudhir. *Frederick Taylor: A Study in Personality and Innovation.* Cambridge, MA: MIT Press, 1970.

Nelson, Daniel. *Frederick W. Taylor and the Rise of Scientific Management.* Madison, WI: Wisconsin University Press, 1980.

Taylor, Frederick Winslow. *Shop Management* in *Scientific Management* (comprising *Shop Management, The Principles of Scientific Management, Testimony before the Special House Committee*). New York: Harper, 1947.

Taylor, Frederick Winslow. *The Principles of Scientific Management.* New York: W. W. Norton, 1967.

Max Weber

1864	Born.
1894	Professor of Political Economy, University of Freiburg, Germany.
1897	Professor of Political Economy, University of Heidelberg, Germany.
1904	First publication of *The Protestant Ethic and the Spirit of Capitalism*.
1919	Professor of Political Economy, University of Munich, Germany.
1920	Dies.

Summary

Since the early 1980s it has become fashionable to criticize bureaucracies for being out of touch with rapidly changing market conditions. As he was the first to develop the concept of bureaucratic organization any understanding of the way modern organizations work would be incomplete without at least a cursory study of Weber, who is commonly described as a founding father of sociology and whose work is also of historic importance from a managerial viewpoint. Weber's thoughts on the concepts of leadership, power, and authority are closely linked to his description of bureaucracy.

Life and Career

Max Weber was born on April 21, 1864, the first of seven children, and grew up in a cultured bourgeois household, ruled by a strong authoritarian father. At university in Heidelberg, Weber studied economics, medieval history, and philosophy as well as law. A period of military service brought him under the care of his uncle, Hermann Baumgarten, a historian, and his wife. Both uncle and aunt acted as mentors to Weber, the former as a liberal who treated him as an intellectual peer, the latter as a person who impressed him with her deep sense of social responsibility toward her charitable work. Both offered a stark contrast to Weber's father, who treated his son with patronizing authoritarianism.

It was probably during this formative period that Weber developed an aversion to the way people then most often gained positions of power and authority—through nepotism and accident of birth—factors he considered were lacking in legitimacy. He started to think of ways to free the individual as much as possible from personal judgments or from judgments clouded by emotion or self-interest.

After periods as a legal scholar at Heidelberg and then at the University of Berlin, Weber became professor of political economy, first at the University of Freiburg, and later at Heidelberg.

His principal contribution to the study of organizations stemmed from his interest in understanding why people obeyed commands. This interest led him to distinguish between power as the ability to force obedience irrespective of resistance, and authority as the ability to get orders obeyed as a matter of course, apparently voluntarily.

Contribution

Weber describes power as the probability of carrying out one's own will despite resistance or, at its extreme, as the ability to force people to obey. It is not necessarily the same as leadership or authority, but is invariably linked to them. Organizational power he links to structure and authority and considers inherent in any hierarchy or bureaucracy. Invariably the effects of power depend on who has it, how that person is perceived, and the particular situation in which power is invoked. Weber identified three types of legitimate authority.

Charismatic Authority

The leader is obeyed because of followers' faith in his or her special, "supernatural" qualities. Weber proposed in his *Theory of Social and Economic Organization* that the term "charisma" was associated with someone who possesses exceptional, supernatural qualities and who is thus set apart from ordinary people. These qualities constitute the basis on which that individual is considered to be, and is treated as, a leader.

Commentators at the beginning of the 21st century might conclude that very few business leaders could be said to have supernatural qualities. We must remember, however, that Weber was arguing from a philosophical standpoint, not a current, pragmatic management one; we may therefore understand "supernatural" as being "supernormal" and at the opposite end of a scale balanced by "rational." Although not considered supernatural, many business leaders have been deemed special in some way, and have had attributed to them qualities that set them apart from "ordinary people." Indeed, research in the 1970s and 1980s by Warren Bennis suggested that leaders do have qualities which set them apart, although he did not use the word "supernatural" and went on to suggest that leadership qualities can be developed.

Of his three models of legitimate authority, Weber thought charisma the least stable because its inspirational and motivational qualities disappear when the leader relinquishes the post. For Weber, charisma was not a sustainable option as the basis for authority. He advocated locating legitimacy in something more lasting and systematic.

Traditional Authority

Leaders have authority by virtue of the status they have inherited—the extent of their authority is determined by birth, custom, precedent, and usage. Although Weber derives his theory from a study of history, we can still sometimes witness today how many positions of authority are handed from one generation to another, as firms establish dynasties, and appointments have more to do with family ties than competence. Another characteristic of organizations based on traditional authority is that things tend to be done in a particular way just because "they have always been done like that."

In the competitive world of today, the dangers of this approach are only too apparent: larger organizations get caught up in their own systems and either fail to spot when competitors are catching them up or markets are slipping away, or else simply become trapped by their own inertia. Precedent, rather than rational analysis, becomes the reason in itself for doing things.

Weber's search for a sustainable form of organizational authority based on rational analysis led him to distinguish a third authority system.

Rational-legal Authority

Authority within a bureaucracy is both legal and rational when it is exercised through a system of rules and procedures attached to the "office"—the job role—which an individual occupies.

Weber described how bureaucracy-based, rational-legal authority works:

- the organization is structured around official functions that are bound by rules, each area having its own specified competence;
- functions are structured into offices organized into a hierarchy that follows technical rules and norms for which training is provided;
- the administration is separated from the ownership of the means of production;
- the rules, decisions, and actions of the administration are recorded in writing.

Weber stated that the bureaucracy was technically the most efficient form of organization because, within it, work is conducted with precision, knowledge of files, continuity, discretion, unity, strict subordination, and reduction of friction.

Bureaucracies

Within bureaucracies organized along rational lines, the abuse of power by leaders is minimized because:

- offices are ranked in hierarchical order;
- operations are conducted in accordance with impersonal rules;
- officials are allocated specific duties and areas of responsibility;
- appointments are made on the basis of qualifications and suitability for the position.

Weber was, however, also aware of the shortcomings of bureaucracy, inasmuch as:

- their characteristic information processing and filtering to the top makes them cumbersome and slow to react;
- their machinery makes it difficult to handle individual cases, because rules and procedures require all individuals to be treated as if they were the same;
- bureaucratization leads to depersonalization, because the roles of officials are circumscribed by written definitions of their authority, and there is a set of rules and procedures to cater for every contingency.

Weber recognized that the more efficient a bureaucracy becomes, the more it succeeds in excluding the personal, the irrational, and the incalculable in favor of emotional detachment and "professionalism." Perhaps this goes a long way toward explaining why Weber is held in low esteem in today's business climate of change and uncertainty.

Context and Conclusions

Weber recognized the dangers of bureaucratization and spoke of how measurement processes could turn people into cogs in a machine. In this respect his reflections are not too distant from Marx's theories of alienation. Although organizational bureaucratization increases efficiency and productive capability, its mechanical efficiency also threatens to dehumanize its participants. Weber also believed, however, that the only way people could make a significant contribution was to subjugate their personalities and desires to the impersonal goals and procedures of large scale organizations. Paradoxically, he believed that the only way to escape such a mechanical future was for a charismatic leader to transform the organization into something new.

Bureaucracy became the model for the 20th-century organization, and was encapsulated in Alfred Sloan's General Motors and Harold Geneen's ITT. Perhaps the mundaneness and regularity of bureaucratic, corporate life was best described in William Whyte's *The Organization Man* (1956), in which the individual is taken over by the bureaucratic machine, in the name of efficiency. A more recent and humorous interpretation of life in a bureaucracy has been depicted by Scott Adams in *The Dilbert Principle*.

Bureaucracy may have outlived its age of supremacy, but it is still hard to foresee a future without any need for the order, procedures, levels of authority, and controls that constitute a bureaucracy. The problem is how to develop systems that combine necessary bureaucratic features with a people-centered, flexible, and imaginative style.

As the foremost social scientist of his day—with little interest in management—Weber would have found it hard to believe that he was to exercise such a dominant influence on the way organizations have been managed. He would have also found it hard to credit the notion that he would be quoted as one of a trinity of management pioneers, along with Henri Fayol and F. W. Taylor, contemporaries whom he would not have known or read.

For More Information
Books:

Pugh, Derek S., and David J. Hickson. *Great Writers on Organizations*. 2nd ed. Burlington, VT: Ashgate Publishing, 1999.

Weber, Max. *The Protestant Ethic and the Spirit of Capitalism*. New York: Routledge, 2001.

Weber, Max. *Theory of Social and Economic Organization*. Trans. A.M. Henderson and T. Parsons. New York: Free Press, 1947.

Business Giants

Marc Andreessen

1971	Born.
1979	Aged eight, teaches himself BASIC computer language from a library book.
1993	Releases "Mosaic for X."
1993	Leaves National Center for Supercomputing Applications.
1994	Starts Netscape.
1995	Netscape I.P.O.
1998	Netscape revenues $534 million, but losing market share to Microsoft. AOL buys Netscape.
1999	Andreessen founds Loudcloud.
2001	Loudcloud I.P.O.

Summary

Marc Andreessen developed the first point and click graphical Web browser, Mosaic, which opened the Internet to the masses. Until its release in 1993, the Internet had been the domain of computer enthusiasts; the new software made the World Wide Web accessible to anyone with a computer and a telephone line. "Mosaic for X" was created while Andreessen was working at the National Center for Supercomputing Applications. Frustrated at his inability to develop his software commercially from within the NCSA, he left and in 1994 founded Netscape with the help of entrepreneur Jim Clark. Netscape achieved "first mover" status with the release of the Netscape Navigator browser. The browser was a hit, and in 1995 the company's I.P.O. (initial public offering) made Andreessen a multimillionaire. Soon, however, Microsoft muscled in on the browser market with Internet Explorer and, after a bruising corporate battle, Netscape was sold to AOL, the U.S. Internet service provider. Andreessen stayed on for a short period, but then left to start Loudcloud, where he is trying to build a one-stop-shop for hosting mission-critical IT systems.

Life and Career

Today the Internet is so pervasive that it is hard to believe that before 1993 it was relatively inaccessible to the majority of ordinary computer users, let alone the unwired masses. Two key events changed that: the creation of the World Wide Web by Tim Berners-Lee, and the development of the Mosaic point and click graphical browser, which was invented by a team of students led by Marc Andreessen.

Andreessen was born in Cedar Falls and was brought up in the small village of New Lisbon, Wisconsin, in the heart of the Midwest. At the age of eight he taught himself how to program in the computer language BASIC by reading a book borrowed from his local library. Andreessen was educated at New Lisbon High School, where he proved a formidable student. At the age of 12, his talent for computer programming blossomed when his parents bought him a computer to keep him busy while he was recuperating from an operation. Computer programming helped make rural life more exciting and allowed Andreessen to express himself creatively. After high school he went to the University of Illinois and, while there, got a computer programming job at the National Center for Supercomputing Applications (NCSA), a university-affiliated, federally funded research center.

Contribution

The NCSA had a budget of several million dollars a year. It also had a large number of staff who, in Andreessen's words, had "frankly not enough to do." Supercomputers by then had been superseded by the microcomputing revolution. Luckily, the NCSA had a relaxed attitude to the research interests of its students. Andreessen was allowed to lead a team on a project to develop a graphical browser client application for Tim Berners-Lee's World Wide Web.

Released in February 1993, "Mosaic for X" was a point and click graphical browser for the Web designed to run on a UNIX platform. Free versions for Macintosh and Windows operating systems followed in the fall of 1993. Mosaic changed the World Wide Web forever. With built-in support for Windows and Macintosh systems, the nontechnologically minded could access the Web. The browser also made use of the HTML < img > tag which made it possible to access images as well as text.

Then one day, out of the blue, he received an e-mail that was to change his life. "You may not know me," it began, "but I'm the founder of Silicon Graphics . . . "

Mosaic represented an important technological advance. But the NCSA wasn't set up to deal with commercial products. Instead, its policy was to license its inventions to other businesses. This arrangement did not suit Andreessen. He had no intention of allowing another company to exploit his new discovery, so he left. "It [the NCSA] wasn't a company, so it didn't have a clear, well-defined mission to be able to create and maintain great software," he later explained. "We basically reached the end of what we were able to do at NCSA. It [Mosaic] got popular and, after that, there's basically no way for an organization of that nature to maintain it."

Andreessen left NCSA in December 1993 and headed for Silicon Valley. He took a job with a software company, Terisa, put Mosaic to the back of his mind, and worked on security products for transacting commerce on the Web. Then one day, out of the blue, he received an e-mail that was to change his life. "You may not know me," it began, "but I'm the founder of Silicon Graphics . . . " Andreessen knew exactly who the founder of Silicon Graphics was: Jim Clark. Already a legend in Silicon Valley, Clark had sold his stock in Silicon Graphics and left the company in January 1994. He was impressed with the Mosaic browser. He contacted Andreessen and together they flew to Champaign-Urbana, the home of the NCSA, and signed up seven of the original Mosaic team on a salary plus stock options deal. The new company was called Mosaic Communications Corp., which subsequently became Netscape.

At Netscape Andreessen worked on a new browser called Navigator. It was rushed out before the rival Mosaic browser—by this time licensed to a company called Spyglass—could gain a dominant market share. To help boost Netscape's chances of succeeding, Andreessen and Clark adopted a radical business model. The plan was to give the browser away as a loss leader; the profits would come from selling server software to work with Navigator. The strategy worked. The Netscape Navigator was a huge success.

When the company was floated on Wall Street in August 1995, the stock price rocketed. Virtually overnight Andreessen was worth some $171 million. But Netscape's virtual monopoly in the browser market was to be short-lived. It soon dawned on others, including Bill Gates, the C.E.O. of Microsoft, that the browser could hold the key to the next generation of computing. Microsoft took the shortest route to market, sourcing its own browser from Spyglass, the company that had licensed the Mosaic browser. What followed was a period known as "the browser wars," in which Microsoft's Internet Explorer battled it out with Netscape's Navigator/Communicator browser. By mid-1998 Netscape's revenues had risen to $534 million, but its share of the browser market had slumped from 80% to some 60%.

> *When the company was floated on Wall Street in August 1995, the stock price rocketed. Virtually overnight Andreessen was worth some $171 million.*

After a bruising battle with Microsoft, Netscape finally threw in the towel, and in 1998 was swallowed up by America Online Inc. (AOL) for $4.2 billion. Andreessen lasted six months at AOL as chief technology officer before leaving to found another Internet start-up, Loudcloud, with fellow Netscapee Ben Horowitz. Loudcloud provides mission-critical hosting services to companies such as Ford and Nike. Despite his comparatively young age, Andreessen has amassed a wealth of experience in the IT industry. But Netscape is a hard act to follow. "This is a different business. Hopefully it will be a success, but it will be a different kind of success," he has noted. "One thing I've learned is nothing is duplicated, nothing is the same. I guess you could say it's just like having kids. Is your next kid going to be better than your first kid?"

With Loudcloud, Andreessen has produced something of an errant child. The company, based in Sunnyvale, California, had an uninspiring I.P.O. in March 2001, followed a few weeks later by the laying off of over 15% of its staff. As the United States threatens to tip into a full-blown recession, Andreessen will need all his entrepreneurial experience and skill to keep the company going.

Context and Conclusions

Just as Bill Gates and Steve Jobs became icons for one generation of entrepreneurs, so Marc Andreessen has become a role model for a new one. With his Internet browser, the tall whiz kid from Wisconsin democratized the Internet, which had previously been the province of fusty academics and geeks. The Mosaic browser and then Netscape Navigator opened a door into cyberspace. This process was accelerated by the radical business plan that Andreessen implemented at Netscape—giving the product away.

Since Netscape, Andreessen has moved on to new challenges. If he can make a success of Loudcloud, then his reputation as one of the great entrepreneurs of his generation will be secure. Even if he does not, he will be remembered as the man whose Web browser helped make the Internet the medium it is today.

CLOSE BUT NO CIGAR

LINUS TORVALDS

Swedish-born Torvalds is the man who developed Linux, an alternative computer operating system to Microsoft's Windows, which went on to threaten the Microsoft hegemony. Yet Torvalds's significance may ultimately rest not with the software he developed, but with the methods he used. Linux is one of the best examples of the open-source movement at work. Torvalds successfully managed a development process that was conducted by a hardened core of programmers spread across the globe. They could all work on the project because Torvalds had published his source code, the building blocks of his software, and permitted anyone to contribute to improving it. This puts Torvalds alongside the likes of Larry Wall and Eric Raymond in the pantheon of the open-source programmers.

For More Information

Books:

Clark, Jim, and Owen Edwards. *Netscape Time: The Making of the Billion-dollar Start-up That Took on Microsoft*. New York: St. Martin's Press, 1999.

Ehrenhafte, Daniel. *Marc Andreessen: Web Warrior*. Breckenridge, CO: Twenty-First Century Books, 2001.

Web site:

Loudcloud: **www.loudcloud.com**

Phileas Taylor Barnum

1810	Born.
1841	Opens American Museum in New York City.
1842	Introduces General Tom Thumb.
1850	Creates first American superstar, singer Jenny Lind.
1853	Starts New York's first illustrated newspaper.
1870	Starts The Greatest Show on Earth.
1875	Serves as mayor of Bridgeport, Connecticut.
1877	Elected to first of two terms in the state General Assembly.
1882	Purchases Jumbo the elephant from London Zoo.
1888	Proposed as a potential Presidential candidate.
1891	Dies.

Summary

A consummate showman and raconteur, P. T. Barnum was one of the most colorful figures to grace the business stage. He started out as a clerk and became a newspaper editor. His media career was cut short, however, when he was sued for libel and ended up in prison for 60 days. It was the nature of his release—40 horsemen, a carriage, and a band—that sold him on the power of spectacle.

Barnum went on to stage a series of extravaganzas, backed by astounding claims, each a little more exaggerated than the last. He paraded a woman called Joice Heth as the 161-year-old nurse of George Washington; exhibited "500,000 natural and artificial curiosities from every corner of the globe" in the American Museum on Broadway in New York City; showed an embalmed mermaid, to a mixed reception; and in 1842 hired the diminutive Charles Stratton as General Tom Thumb, who earned him an audience with Queen Victoria in England.

Toward the end of his career as a showman, he teamed up with James A. Bailey to take the Barnum and Bailey Greatest Show on Earth on tour across America. Fittingly for a man with such great powers of persuasion, he also tried his hand at politics. In 1875 he was elected mayor of Bridgeport, Connecticut, and went on to serve two terms on the state General Assembly. He was even touted as a potential Presidential candidate.

Life and Career

There is no proof that Phileas Taylor Barnum ever said, "There's a sucker born every minute." If he did, he was certainly not among their number. Born on July 5, 1810 in Bethel, Connecticut, Barnum was the eldest of five children. He was a bright child, who excelled at math. At the age of ten, he was woken one night by his teacher who had bet a neighbor that Barnum could calculate the height of a pile of wood in five minutes. He did it in less than two. He also demonstrated a flair for salesmanship, selling lottery tickets at the age of 12.

After his father died, Barnum traveled to Brooklyn, New York, where he found work at a general store. Captivated by the hustle and bustle of the city, he left the general store, but stayed on in New York, working at a weekly newspaper. His journalistic career was short-lived. Although promoted to the role of editor, he was successfully sued for libel and sentenced to serve 60 days in jail. In a sign of things to come, Barnum was greeted on his release by a band, a troop of 40 horses, and a horse and carriage.

Contribution

Barnum's career as showman and huckster extraordinaire started in earnest when he was 25. He paid the then considerable sum of $1,000 for the services of Joice Heth, who claimed to be both 161 years old and the nurse of the first U.S. President, George Washington. To a man with an innate sense of the dramatic, Heth was too good a business opportunity to pass up. "Unquestionably the most astonishing and interesting curiosity in the world!" was Barnum's handbill slogan. His investment in Heth paid off handsomely. Exhibiting in New York and New England, he pulled in $1,500 a week. When interest in Heth began to flag, he spread a rumor that she was not a living person but an automaton. It worked, drawing crowds who wished to see if it was true. Heth was exhibited until her death in February 1836. Even then, Barnum refused to allow her death to restrict his cashflow, arranging a public autopsy to verify her age. When the stunt backfired—the doctor said the woman was no older than 80—Barnum successfully spun the story in his own favor.

At the age of 60, Barnum started the business that he is probably most closely associated with—P. T. Barnum's Grand Traveling Museum, Menagerie, Caravan, and Circus, or The Greatest Show on Earth, as it became known.

Building on the success he enjoyed with Heth, Barnum bought Scudder's American Museum on Broadway in New York City, and populated it with "500,000 natural and artificial curiosities from every corner of the globe." In a wonderful example of his characteristic audacity, he put up a sign in the Museum bearing the words "This way to the egress." Unsuspecting visitors would follow the directions in pursuit of the mysterious "egress," only to learn that "egress" meant "exit" and they would then have to pay another quarter to get back in. Barnum's famous attractions included "The Feejee Mermaid," an embalmed mermaid (in reality half monkey, half dried fish), and in 1842 Charles Stratton, a.k.a. General Tom Thumb, the world's smallest man. Measuring just 25 inches in height, Tom Thumb was a worldwide hit, and earned Barnum an audience with Queen Victoria in England.

In 1850 Barnum conducted perhaps his most profitable business venture of all. He introduced America to the European opera star Jenny Lind, popularly known as "the Swedish Nightingale." When Lind disembarked at New York harbor in 1850, she was greeted by a crowd of 30,000, drawn by Barnum's publicity machine. He turned her into one of the first entertainment superstars. She performed over 90 concerts in all in the United States. When they parted company in 1852, Barnum had grossed over $700,000 from her performances.

Barnum ran the American Museum in New York City for 27 years. As well as dealing with the constant stream of visitors and sourcing new exhibits, he also had to deal with three major fires, which burned down the building. After the last of these in 1868, he retired from the museum business.

At the age of 60, Barnum started the business that he is probably most closely associated with—P. T. Barnum's Grand Traveling Museum, Menagerie, Caravan, and Circus, or The Greatest Show on Earth, as it became known."We ought to have a big show," said Barnum, "the public expects it, and will appreciate it." Barnum's show was the biggest circus in America, grossing $400,000 in its first year. On the road, Barnum teamed up with James A. Bailey and James L. Hutchinson, both Englishmen, and in 1881 toured as the Barnum and London Circus.

"The Towering Monarch of His Mighty Race, Whose Like the World Will Never See Again"—or Jumbo as he was better known—was another of Barnum's acquisitions. Purchased from London Zoo in 1882 for $10,000, the elephant became the subject of a transatlantic tug-of-war when, in an outbreak of Jumbo mania, the English public objected to his departure. As usual, Barnum got his way, shipping the creature to the United States. In a promotional tour de force, he arranged for Jumbo to walk across the brand new Brooklyn Bridge in 1883 to test its strength. Both survived. Sadly, however, Jumbo didn't survive a collision with a freight train in St. Thomas, Ontario. Undaunted, Barnum had him stuffed and continued to display both the elephant and its skeleton. In 1888 he teamed up once again with Bailey to tour as Barnum and Bailey's Greatest Show On Earth.

Throughout the years of his circus triumphs, the irrepressible Barnum also dabbled in politics. Not surprisingly for a man with such consummate PR skills, he had some success. In 1875 he was elected as mayor of Bridgeport, Connecticut, and in 1877 he was elected to the first of two terms in Connecticut's General Assembly. He was even put forward as a potential Presidential candidate in 1888, although this came to nothing.

In 1891 Barnum made a lighthearted remark to the effect that the press only said nice things about people when they were dead. Picking up on his comments, the *New York Sun* printed his obituary on the front page with the headline "Great and Only Barnum—He Wanted to Read His Obituary—Here It Is." Ironically, several weeks later Barnum was dead.

In a promotional tour de force, he arranged for Jumbo to walk across the brand new Brooklyn Bridge in 1883 to test its strength. Both survived. Sadly, however, Jumbo didn't survive a collision with a freight train in St. Thomas, Ontario.

He died quietly in his sleep on April 7, 1891. Professional to the last, his final words were reportedly about the show he was promoting at New York's Madison Square Garden: "Ask Bailey what the box office was at the Garden last night."

Context and Conclusions

Huckster, showman, impresario, and entrepreneur—P. T. Barnum was all these and more. The man who could justifiably be considered the father of advertising and public relations was the king of hyperbole. He invented the beauty contest, the baby contest, and the traveling show. He persuaded thousands to pay to see a "mermaid," which was in reality half monkey, half fish. In a manner that would make the most Svengali-like of pop managers blush, he discovered the diminutive Tom Thumb aged four and groomed him for stardom, teaching him to sing and dance live (no lip-synching in the 1800s). A man who knew the value of contacts, he hunted buffalo with General Custer and was friends with General Grant. He was said to be the United States's second millionaire and was so famous around the world that a letter sent from New Zealand addressed to "Mr. Barnum, America" still found its way to him. When he died the London *Times* printed the following editorial: "Barnum is gone. That fine flower of Western civilization, that *arbiter elegantiarum* to Demos, has lived. At the age of 80, after a life of restless energy and incessant publicity, the great showman has lain down to rest. He gave, in the eyes of the seekers after amusement, a lustre to America." A fitting epitaph.

CLOSE BUT NO CIGAR
DON KING

The shock-haired boxing promoter monopolized the money-spinning heavyweight division of the boxing world. Larger than life—although not quite as outsize as Barnum—King was especially noted for speaking at breakneck speed, quoting Shakespeare at press conferences, and having a Teflon-coated ability to deflect criticism and bad publicity.

For More Information
Books:

Barnum, P. T. *The Life of P. T. Barnum: Written by Himself.* Champaign, IL: University of Illinois Press, 2000 (originally published in 1854).

Barnum, P. T. *Struggles and Triumphs, or, Forty Years' Recollections of P. T. Barnum, Written by Himself.* New York: American News Company, 1871.

Werner, M. R. *Barnum.* New York: Harcourt, Brace & Co., 1923.

Fitzsimons, Raymond. *Barnum in London.* New York: St. Martin's Press, 1970.

Saxon, A. H., (ed). *Selected Letters of P. T. Barnum.* New York: Columbia University Press, 1983.

Lord Beaverbrook
(William Maxwell Aitken)

1879	Born.
1898	Moves to Halifax, Canada.
1905	Moves headquarters of Royal Securities to Montreal.
1906	Worth over $500,000.
1910	Moves to England and wins a seat in the House of Commons.
1911	Knighted.
1916	Acquires a controlling interest in the London *Daily Express*.
1917	Receives peerage—becomes the first Lord Beaverbrook.
1923	Buys the London *Evening Standard*.
1938	Active supporter of appeasement.
1940	Made minister of aircraft production.
1947	Appears before Royal Commission.
1964	Dies.

Summary

William Maxwell Aitken (1879–1964) was born the son of a poor Presbyterian minister and rose to become the first Lord Beaverbrook—politician and media magnate. A talent for striking a deal, coupled with an ability to make powerful friends, helped Beaverbrook move from selling bonds to building companies. By 1906, still in his twenties, Beaverbrook was worth over $500,000. When political opinion turned against his business interests he simply moved on to another challenge.

In 1910 Beaverbrook moved to England and effortlessly insinuated himself into British political life and polite society. He became a Member of Parliament in the year of his arrival and was knighted in 1911. In 1916 he began to build a newspaper empire, buying the London *Daily Express* and then, in 1923, the London *Evening Standard*. A confidant of Winston Churchill, Beaverbrook contributed to the war effort as minister of aircraft production. After the war he took more of a back seat, pulling the strings of his empire from his country house in Surrey until his death in 1964.

Life and Career

Born William Maxwell Aitken in Vaughan, northern Ontario, Canada, on May 25, 1879, the son of Presbyterian minister, he was brought up in the town of Newcastle in New Brunswick.

It was a religious upbringing in austere surroundings. His father may have been a minister, but Beaverbrook was no angel. He was the pupil best acquainted with the schoolmaster's strap. His teacher described him as "the wildest imp of mischief I ever knew," adding tellingly, "but a born leader of men from the day he left the cradle."

After failing to get into college, Beaverbrook became a clerk for a local lawyer. In 1897 he became involved in politics, helping future Canadian prime minister Richard Bedford Bennett win a seat in the Legislative Assembly of the Northwest Territories. Moving to Halifax in 1898, Beaverbrook made friends with a leading businessman, J. P. Stairs. Stairs and several other investors formed the Royal Securities Corporation and put Beaverbrook in charge. He soon organized a number of companies with wide-ranging interests in Canada and abroad, moved the company's head office to Montreal, and, by 1906, was worth a small fortune.

Beaverbrook's biggest deal in Canada was to consolidate the cement industry and create a cement trust. Although the deal made Beaverbrook even richer, it also made him some powerful enemies. Sensing that popular sentiment was turning against him, Beaverbrook made the decision that would set him on the path to his career as a media baron. In 1910 he moved to England.

Contribution

When Beaverbrook arrived in London his purpose was to raise money in the financial markets for another of his deals. But he found a new interest in British politics. Influential friends, such as Scottish-Canadian Bonar Law, encouraged him to run for Parliament. He ran as a Conservative candidate for the seat representing Ashton-under-Lyne in Lancashire. Before the election no one gave Beaverbrook a chance of winning; he was running against an experienced local politician. He won by just 196 votes. It was a remarkable rise for this young upstart from Canada. Incredibly, in 1911, having been in the country for less than two years, he was knighted.

Reluctant to return to Canada because of investigations into his business affairs and enjoying the influence his money and connections had secured, Beaverbrook settled in England. He continued to act as a catalyst for behind-the-scenes political maneuvering. In 1916, against the backdrop of World War I, he helped Lloyd George and Bonar Law depose Herbert Asquith as prime minister. As a reward he was given a peerage. Remembering the name of a place he had seen on a map of New Brunswick, Aitken became the first Lord Beaverbrook.

While Beaverbrook had been busy pulling political strings, he had also been steadily acquiring stock in one of the United Kingdom's major national newspapers, the London *Daily Express*. By 1916 he had obtained a controlling interest in the paper, which he subsequently used to wield political influence. In 1918 he served briefly as minister of information, but a major falling-out with Lloyd George, then prime minister, forced him to resign. Bloodied but unbowed, Beaverbrook retreated to the safety of his newspaper, and there he continued to wage war on Lloyd George.

For a time Beaverbrook concentrated on his newspaper interests. He introduced the London *Sunday Express* in 1918 and bought the London *Evening Standard* in 1923. The circulation of the flagship *Daily Express* increased from 400,000 in 1919 to 2,329,000 by 1938. He ruled his growing media empire from his country house, Cherkley Court, near Leatherhead in Surrey. There he sat like a general, surrounded by telephones, news tickertape, and soundscribing machines, dictating the day's orders to his editors. Beaverbrook may have been a good politician and a better newspaper proprietor, but he would have made a poor statesman. Too often he showed questionable judgment in international affairs. His newspapers toed the appeasement line as Hitler rose to power and threatened to rampage through Europe. Right up until September 1938 Beaverbrook and the *Daily Express* were proclaiming that there would be no war in Europe, "this year, or next year either."

However, Beaverbrook made up for his lack of judgment with a sterling performance as minister of aircraft production during World War II. He was appointed by Winston Churchill against the advice of King George VI. It was an inspired decision by Churchill and a particularly unselfish one, for he and Beaverbrook had not always seen eye to eye. Churchill said it was Beaverbrook's "vital and vibrant energy" that convinced him he was the right man for the job.

Even though Beaverbrook managed to galvanize the nation's fighter and bomber plane production, he still insisted on running his ministry as he had his newspaper. He compensated for less than absolute power with a degree of brinkmanship, repeatedly threatening to resign when he didn't get things his own way.

After the war Beaverbrook's interest in politics waned, as did his influence. He disliked Clement Atlee, who succeeded Churchill as prime minister, and the feeling was mutual. Opinion was also moving against Beaverbrook's pervasive influence in British society. In 1947 a Royal Commission was appointed to look into his activities. "I run the paper purely for propaganda purposes," was Beaverbrook's provocative response. Despite his comments, he somehow managed to avoid serious censure. Beaverbrook gradually withdrew from the day-to-day management of his business interests and took to traveling the world, writing, and spending time with his family. His last years were spent at Cherkley Court; from there he continued to make his presence felt by constantly checking up on his editors. The *Daily Express* continued to go from strength to strength. By 1960 its circulation was 4.3 million, making it the number one U.K. newspaper. Beaverbrook died at home in June 1964, shortly after his 85th birthday.

Context and Conclusions

Lord Beaverbrook's two great strengths were his flair for deal making and his natural networking skills. His astonishing ability to cut a deal owed much to his appreciation of the true value of things. "When I was a boy, I knew the value of every marble in my village," he once boasted. "I always had an intuitive value of the real and not the face value of any article."

He was also blessed with a knack for making the right friends at the right time—Stairs in Canada; Bonar Law, Lloyd George, and Winston Churchill in England. The small, dapper man from New Brunswick charmed and bludgeoned his way into U.K. society in equal measure. His influence was always evident in the editorials of his newspapers. He was undoubtedly one of the great newspaper proprietors of his time.

For More Information

Books:

Beaverbrook, Lord. *My Early Life*. Fredericton, New Brunswick: Brunswick Press, 1965.

Taylor, A. J. P. *Beaverbrook: A Biography*. New York: Simon & Schuster, 1972.

Jeffrey Bezos

1964	Born.
1986	Graduates from Princeton.
1990	Youngest Vice-President at Bankers Trust.
1992	Senior Vice-President at D. E. Shaw & Co.
1995	Amazon.com opens for business.
1998	Net sales of $252.9 million, an increase of 283% over the same period in 1997.
1999	Amazon.com, Inc. has a market capitalization of $6 billion. Voted *Time* magazine's person of the year.
2000	Adds toys and electronics to product range.
2001	Amazon.com, Inc. posts first quarterly profit and achieves highest ever score for service business in American Customer Satisfaction Index.
	Industry protest as Amazon.com seeks patents to protect systems for online payments and advertisement allocation.

Summary

Jeff Bezos, the founder and C.E.O. of Amazon.com, is the most famous son of the e-commerce revolution. The company he created became the best known online brand in the world.

After graduating from Princeton University in 1986, Bezos worked for a variety of investment firms, notably D. E. Shaw & Co., where he helped establish one of the most successful quantitative hedge funds on Wall Street. By 1992 he had made it to vice President, yet he gave up this glittering career to chase a dream. Amazon.com opened for business on the Internet in July 1995, and with relentless hype soon became the flagship for the New Economy. When the tide turned against dot-com stocks in 2000, Amazon.com looked as if it might be washed up. Yet Bezos rode the storm and is floating high once more, with growing additional business in toys and electronic products.

Amazon.com opened for business on the Internet in July 1995, and with relentless hype soon became the flagship for the New Economy.

Life and Career

Born on January 12, 1964 in Albuquerque, New Mexico, Jeffrey Preston Bezos was a clever child. At a very early age he took a screwdriver to his crib and dismantled it into its component parts. This set a pattern. A few years later, when his grandfather bought him a Radio Shack electronics kit, he concocted a "burglar alarm" to keep his siblings (one brother, one sister) out of his bedroom. Moving on to the garage, the venue of choice for so many budding entrepreneurs, the ingenious Bezos proceeded to build a microwave oven driven by solar power. There is no record of how well it cooked.

Mike Bezos was an engineer with Exxon, and the family moved several times because of his work. Jeff attended high school in Miami and spent most summers on his grandfather's ranch, living the life of a cattle farmer and driving the tractors.

Contribution

In 1986, after graduating in electrical engineering and computer science from Princeton, Bezos headed for Fitel, a high-tech start-up company in New York, where he built a computer network for financial trading. After Fitel Bezos joined Bankers Trust, becoming their youngest Vice-President in February 1990. From there he moved to D. E. Shaw & Co. The Wall Street firm interviewed him on the strength of a recommendation from one of its partners, who suggested, "he is going to make someone a lot of money someday." At Shaw, Bezos described his role as a "sort of an entrepreneurial odd-jobs kind of a person," effectively looking for business opportunities in the insurance, software, and Internet sectors. He excelled in the role, helping to establish one of the most successful quantitative hedge funds on Wall Street, and becoming Senior Vice-President in 1992.

Then came his epiphany. Sitting at his computer in the office one day surfing the Internet, Bezos came across an astounding fact. According to usage statistics, the Internet was growing at a rate of 2,300% a year. He sensed an opportunity. Online commerce, he realized, was a natural next step. Being a combination of Wall Street insider and computer nerd, he was perfectly positioned to cash in.

Bezos compiled a list of 20 products that were suitable for selling online. On the list were items such as CDs, magazines, PC software and hardware—and books. The shortlist was quickly whittled down to two contenders—books and music. In the end, he decided upon books. His logic was twofold. With more than 1.3 million books in print as against 300,000 music titles, there was simply more to sell. And, perhaps more important, the major book publishers appeared less intimidating than their record company counterparts. The six major record companies had a stranglehold on the popular music distribution business, but the biggest book chain, Barnes & Noble, had only 12% of the industry's total sales.

Quitting his job, Bezos headed out to Seattle. "I will change the economics of the book industry," he is reputed to have told one venture capitalist. Ironically, some of the fundraising took place in the coffee shop of a Barnes & Noble bookstore.

With no state tax, a wealth of high-tech talent, and a major book distributor on the doorstep—Ingram's warehouse, Oregon—Seattle seemed a perfect place to start his new business. In the garage of his rented home, Bezos and his first three employees booted up their computers and began writing software for the new business. He originally planned to call the company Cadabra—a reference to the magic incantation. Fortunately for him, his friends convinced him that, while the name might have spellbinding connotations, it also sounded very similar to "cadaver." Instead, Bezos opted for Amazon, after the world's largest river.

The company, according to its Web site, "opened its virtual doors in July 1995 with a mission to use the Internet to transform book buying into the fastest, easiest, and most enjoyable shopping experience possible." By the beginning of 1999, Amazon.com, Inc. had a market capitalization of an astonishing $6 billion—more than the combined value of Barnes & Noble and Borders, its two largest bookstore competitors. The fourth quarter of 1998 brought net sales of $252.9 million, an increase of 283% over the same period in 1997.

With Amazon awash with revenue, analysts and e-commerce commentators seemed unperturbed by the absence of profits.

Bezos, meanwhile, was a model of reassurance. Amazon would reach $1 billion in sales by 2000, he confidently asserted, and sure enough it did. Yet details about when Amazon would make a profit were hazier. Amazon was, said Bezos, in "an investment phase," as might be expected of a company that had only just celebrated its fourth birthday. For a while, investors were more than happy to go along for the ride.

Then, in June 2000, cracks began to appear in the almost unanimous support enjoyed by the star child of the Internet revolution. Holly Becker, e-commerce analyst at Lehman Brothers and a longtime Amazon believer, switched her recommendation on the company from a buy to a neutral. She was, she said, "throwing in the towel on Amazon." Many saw Becker's change of heart as a turning point in the company's fortunes.

> *Holly Becker, e-commerce analyst at Lehman Brothers and a longtime Amazon believer, switched her recommendation on the company from a buy to a neutral. She was, she said, "throwing in the towel on Amazon."*

Yet Bezos may well have the last laugh. With some 21 million satisfied customers in the year to June 2001, revenue over the same period up by 16%, and a strategic alliance with Internet service provider AOL in the bag, Warren Jenson, Amazon.com's chief financial officer, correctly predicted operating profitability in the fourth quarter of 2001. Customer satisfaction was officially recognized when Amazon achieved the highest ever scores for a service industry in 2001 and 2002. The Amazon range is growing too, with the introduction of toys and electronics in 2000. Bezos, however, came under fire for holding back the broader development of e-commerce when he applied for patents to protect Amazon's Honor online payment system and the company's system for allocating advertising space from multiple bidders. Whether, in the final analysis, Bezos will go down in the business history books as the creator of a viable and long-lived Internet business, or simply as an e-business pioneer, remains to be seen.

Context and Conclusions

Amazon is the totem stock of the Internet evangelists. What the critics will tell you is that through smoke and mirrors, PR, and puff, one man has succeeded in making a fortune through hyping his online business to previously unthought-of heights. What he has created, after all, is nothing more or less than a virtual bookshop, and one that in its first five years didn't turn a profit. But Amazon.com isn't a bellwether stock without reason. Bezos is the quintessential dot-com icon. He proved to the business world that the Internet was about more than the dissemination and exchange of knowledge. He proved that it was possible to overcome fears about purchasing online, that it was possible to drive down transaction costs, and that it was feasible to build an international e-commerce business over the Internet. Bezos is one of the great business pioneers. He had the courage to attempt something that people doubted could be done. Amazon has firmly entrenched itself as a dominant force in e-commerce and as a result of product additions and strategic alliances is now a virtual marketplace. The question is whether it can profitably exploit its position.

CLOSE BUT NO CIGAR
SCOTT BLUM

A colorful character, Blum survived a brush with the SEC while at his company Pinnacle Micro and went on to found buy.com. buy.com epitomized the gung ho, blindly optimistic philosophy of dot-com mania with its "make money by losing money" strategy. The idea was to sell goods on the Internet at a loss and make money through advertising. Critics sniggered. The "losing money" part went well; unfortunately the "make money" element was lacking. Critics laughed openly. Meanwhile Blum stepped down as C.E.O. in March 1999, and as Chairman in October of the same year. He put his less than 50% of shares into a blind trust, raised $100 million in finance, and moved on to Enfrastructure.com, providing "scalable, full-service technology and infrastructure for high-growth companies."

For More Information

Books:

Saunders, Rebecca. *Business the Amazon.com Way: Secrets of the World's Most Astonishing Web Business*. Oxford: Capstone, 1999.

Spector, Robert. *Amazon.com: Get Big Fast—Inside the Revolutionary Business Model that Changed the World*. New York: HarperBusiness, 2000.

Web site:

Amazon.com: **www.amazon.com**

William Boeing

1881	Born.
1908	Travels to Seattle.
1915	Takes first plane ride.
1916	Pacific Aero Products Company incorporated for $100,000.
1917	Pacific Aero Products changes name to the Boeing Airplane Company.
1919	Eddie Hubbard flies 60 letters from Vancouver to Seattle.
1922	Becomes Boeing Airplane Company Chairman.
1927	Signs contract to fly airmail from Chicago to San Francisco.
1928	Consolidates business as Boeing Airplane and Transport Company.
1929	Boeing Airplane and Transport Company becomes United Aircraft and Transport.
1930	Ellen Church, a registered nurse, is first female flight attendant.
1934	United Aircraft and Transport broken up. William E. Boeing resigns as board Chairman.
1956	Dies.

Summary

William Boeing soared to dizzying heights with his aircraft manufacturing company and airline, founded in 1916 as Pacific Aero Products. Son of a wealthy lumberman, Boeing looked set to carve out a business in lumber, until the day he first saw a manned airplane. From that point onward, until his retirement from the airplane industry in 1934, he strove to turn his obsession with flight into a profitable business. For the most part he succeeded. With the help of some brilliant engineers, he designed and built a biplane that no longer required the pilot to sit on the wing. Incorporating his first company, he turned out airplanes for the military, always improving the technology.

When the end of World War I temporarily dampened orders for military aircraft, Boeing switched to commercial planes. He secured contracts to supply airmail and, with the help of pilot and entrepreneur Eddie Hubbard, built a successful airmail operation. But, in 1934, his dreams crashed to the ground when the government of the day accused him of monopolistic practices and ordered the breakup of his company into three separate companies. Disillusioned, Boeing retired and spent the remainder of his years in property development and Thoroughbred horse breeding.

Life and Career

The birth of William Boeing in Detroit, Michigan on the first day of October 1881 goes down in history as one of the most significant days in the development of air travel. After an education in Detroit and Switzerland, Boeing studied at Yale Engineering College. His father was a wealthy lumberman, so in 1902 Boeing went to work for the family lumber interests in Aberdeen, Washington, working his way up to become President of Greenwood Logging Company.

In 1908, he traveled to Seattle. It was here that Boeing became interested in aeronautics. On the University of Washington campus during the Alaska-Yukon-Pacific Exposition in 1909, he saw a manned flying machine for the first time. To the modern eye, the contraption in which J. C. "Bud" Mars took to the skies seems laughable, as well as downright dangerous. To Boeing, the sight of the small gasoline-powered dirigible ascending above the university buildings was a marvel.

Contribution

Boeing's next view of the wonders of aeronautical engineering came at the American air show held in Los Angeles in 1910. At the show, "barnstormers"—stunt pilots who performed (hopefully) death-defying tricks—entertained an astonished crowd. Boeing left for the return journey to Seattle filled with a burning curiosity about aviation. In the next few years he discovered all he could about aeronautics. He joined the Seattle University Club, where he picked the brains of students like navy engineer Conrad Westervelt. As far as Boeing was concerned, Westervelt—who had taken a few aeronautics courses at the Massachusetts Institute of Technology—was as good as an expert on the subject.

Together, Boeing and Westervelt made a study of biplanes, sometimes from close quarters. The unflappable Boeing was a passenger in early biplanes made by firms such as the Curtiss Aeroplane and Motor Company, in which both the pilot and passenger were required to sit on the wing during flight—not an undertaking for the fainthearted. The more he found out, the more Boeing was convinced that it was possible to design a better biplane than any that existed at the time.

In 1915, with the help of Westervelt and another engineer, Herb Munter, Boeing established the Pacific Aero club in a boathouse at Lake Union. Together they began work on the B & W—a new twin-float seaplane.

Boeing was wildly enthusiastic about the prospects of his new enterprise. He anticipated that World War I would mean the U.S. government would need more planes. He produced two prototype seaplanes, "Bluebill" and "Mallard," taking the controls of "Bluebill" on its maiden flight. Encouraged by the trials, Boeing founded Pacific Aero Products Co. in July 1916. But things didn't go as planned. Lieutenant Westervelt was reassigned and consequently unable to continue working with Boeing. Worse still, the navy rejected Boeing's prototypes. Undaunted, he hired another engineer, Tsu Wong, and built a new improved "Model C" seaplane.

> *Together, Boeing and Westervelt made a study of biplanes, sometimes from close quarters.*

When America entered the war in April 1917, Boeing changed the name of Pacific Aero Products to Boeing Airplane Co., and obtained orders from the navy for 50 planes. A workforce of over 300 was assembled to construct the new planes in the "Red Barn" on the Duwamish River.

The end of World War I was celebrated throughout the allied nations. For Boeing, it was a bittersweet moment. Victory in Europe meant the end of an intense period of activity and without the war to fuel production, prospects looked bleak. Orders dried up. To keep the factory open, Boeing turned to speedboat and furniture manufacture. To all his ventures, Boeing applied exacting standards. The boats were so good that Canadian smugglers used them to evade the authorities. Small military contracts kept the company above water, but it was an entirely different type of business that was to save Boeing from bankruptcy.

Although Boeing didn't know it at the time, his future lay in the hands of a man called Eddie Hubbard. Hubbard was Boeing's chief test pilot, the second Seattle man to win a license from the Aero Club of America. Hubbard was convinced that the future of the airplane lay in transporting passengers and goods. In March 1919 he delivered the first international airmail to America, flying in from Vancouver, Canada. While Boeing struggled for survival, Hubbard organized an aerial taxi offshoot of the company. In 1920, Hubbard was awarded a contract to carry mail between Seattle and Canada. He left Boeing and started his own firm, buying a Boeing B1 seaplane to use as the delivery plane. It was Boeing's first commercial aircraft sale.

If this was good news for Boeing, the Kelly Act, passed in 1925, was even better. Until then, domestic airmail was carried under a virtual government monopoly. The Kelly Act allowed the Post Office to grant contracts to carry airmail on certain routes to private operators. In 1926, the Post Office invited tenders for its Chicago–San Francisco route. Hubbard personally persuaded Boeing to bid. Boeing won, founded a new subsidiary—the Boeing Air Transport Corporation—and welcomed Hubbard back into the fold to help organize the new company.

The end of World War I was celebrated throughout the allied nations. For Boeing, it was a bittersweet moment.

When it was clear that the transportation of passengers by airline, as Hubbard suggested, promised to be the savior of Boeing's airline manufacturing company, Boeing put all his energy into expanding that side of the business. He rushed out over 20 Model 40s in time to start the new airmail contracts on July 1, 1927. In 1928, he brought airline and aircraft manufacturing operations under the aegis of a new company—the Boeing Airplane and Transport Company—and then bought out one of his main rivals, Gorst's Pacific Air Transport. He introduced larger planes that were capable of carrying up to 18 passengers, attended by registered nurses—the first air stewardesses. In 1929, Boeing changed the name of his company to United Aircraft and Transport and proceeded to buy out most of the competition. When the balance of the Post Office mail contracts was handed out to private carriers, United picked up the northern routes.

Boeing's acquisitive activities had, however, brought him onto the radar of President Franklin D. Roosevelt and a new Democratic administration. The U.S. government, in a show of strength, was determined to rid the country of the monopolistic practices that had dominated industry throughout the late 19th and early 20th centuries. Boeing was directly in the government's firing line. All airmail franchises were canceled with effect from March 10, 1934. As a stopgap measure the routes were handed over to the army, which, ill-equipped to handle the airmail routes, lost ten pilots in two weeks. When the contracts were offered to private carriers again, aircraft manufacturers were prevented from bidding. This was a poorly disguised move to restrain Boeing's power. As a result of the government's actions, United Aircraft and Transport was divided into three separate companies: United Aircraft Co., Boeing Airplane Company, and United Air Lines.

The mail contracts arrived just in time to save Boeing. His company might have survived long enough to pick up lucrative military supply contracts, but the breakup of the government monopoly on airmail distribution made it a certainty and allowed Boeing to bring in much-needed cash and to rebuild the manufacturing business. When the airmail contracts were withdrawn, Boeing's company was in a strong enough position to survive without them.

Boeing, however, was disgusted with the government's actions. The loss of the mail contracts sapped his resolve. After the breakup of United Aircraft and Transport, the prospect of restructuring and steering his company through another difficult period depressed him. At the age of 50 he retired from the company he had founded and had little more to do with it, other than acting as a consultant during World War II.

After retirement he concentrated on property deals, buying tracts of land to the north of Seattle. These became the Blue Ridge housing development. Ironically the first houses erected were bought by Boeing Company managers. Boeing also became a successful breeder of Thoroughbred horses. He died in 1956.

Context and Conclusions

Boeing was one of the great business pioneers of the 20th century. Fascinated by aviation as a young man, he turned a passion for flying into a business. Although he was a competent pilot, his skill lay in spotting talented people and getting them to produce results. Navy Lieutenant Conrad Westervelt taught Boeing aviation and introduced him to other enthusiasts. Herb Munter, a brilliant engineer, helped Boeing build his first plane. Another engineer, Tsu Wong, helped improve it. Eddie Hubbard persuaded Boeing of the merits of the airmail industry and passenger airlines. By motivating these and other employees and colleagues and inspiring them with his leadership, Boeing built the first major commercial airplane manufacturer. After the government intervened to clip his company's wings, he left the industry a dispirited and bitter

As a stopgap measure the routes were handed over to the army, which, ill-equipped to handle the airmail routes, lost ten pilots in two weeks.

man. But, before he died, he witnessed the introduction of the jet airliner, by the company he founded over 50 years before.

For More Information

Books:

Cleveland, Carl M. *Boeing Trivia*. Seattle: CMC Books, 1989.
Serling, Robert J. *Legend & Legacy: The Story of Boeing and Its People*. New York: St. Martin's Press, 1992.

Richard Branson

1950	Born.
1964	Goes to Stowe school.
1966	Founds *Student* magazine.
1970	Starts Virgin mail-order operation.
1971	Opens first record store in London's Oxford Street.
1977	Signs Sex Pistols.
1984	Launches Virgin Atlantic Airways.
1986	Virgin Group goes public.
1988	Management buyout of Virgin Group.
1994	Unsuccessful bid for U.K. National Lottery franchise.
1995	Launches Virgin Direct Personal Financial Services.
1996	Starts Virgin Rail.
2000	Again fails in bid to pick up U.K. National Lottery franchise.
2001	*Forbes* estimates Virgin Group value at $1.8 billion.

Summary

Swashbuckling Richard Branson has brought a welcome sense of fun and adventure to some traditionally staid business sectors with his many-tentacled Virgin Group. As a boy, he thought he could do better at running his school than the principal, ran an abortive parakeet breeding business, and published a magazine entitled *Student*. A mail-order record business was followed by record stores, then a record label, and then an airline. It may seem like an improbable sequence, but Branson swiftly realized that a good brand could be stretched, with care, to encompass anything from condoms to clothes, personal finance to trains. By 2000 the value of Branson's unwieldy empire collected under the Virgin Group banner was estimated at some $1.8 billion by *Forbes* magazine.

Life and Career

Richard Charles Nicholas Branson was born on July 18, 1950. His was an affluent middle-class family; his father was an attorney and, although to begin with money was tight, the family rented a property in the village of Shamley Green, in the wealthy "stockbroker belt" in the county of Surrey. Branson had a privileged private education, first at Scaitcliffe preparatory school and then at Stowe, one of the United Kingdom's foremost private schools.

Branson took little interest in academic studies, and only slightly more in sports. But he had a sense of confidence and self-belief. This was evident from his assertion that, despite failing a basic math test three times, he could make a better job of running the school than the principal. He actually dispatched a memo to the principal outlining how, in his view, the school rules might be improved, including the suggestion: "Allow sixth-formers [final year students] to drink two pints of beer a day."

He was never to profit from his suggestion, since he dropped out of school at 16, keen to make his way in the world of business. His principal commented at the time that Branson would end up either a millionaire or behind bars. Fortunately, it was the former, although a skirmish with British Customs and Excise meant it was a close call.

Contribution

Branson's first serious business was a magazine called *Student* which he launched when he was only 16 years old. He already had two failed schoolboy businesses behind him: one breeding parakeets, another growing Christmas trees. The magazine business wasn't a resounding success either. But somehow, despite his scant knowledge of pop music, he came up with the idea of a mail-order record company. And when the checks began flooding into the mailbox, he knew he had his first hit on his hands. Casting around for a name for his company, Branson came up with the name "Virgin," which won out over alternatives such as "Slipped Disc Records." "I had some vague idea of the name being catchy and applying to lots of other products for young people," he said.

The next move for Branson was into record stores. This move was a fortuitous one, forced on him by a mail strike that decimated his mail-order business. It was also in the early days of his record business that he had a chastening encounter with the law. Attempting to exploit a tax loophole, he was arrested and threatened with prosecution. The threat was only withdrawn when a repentant Branson agreed to pay back the money he owed.

His charmed business life continued when he launched the Virgin record label and signed up Mike Oldfield as one of its first artists. Oldfield's first album, *Tubular Bells*, was to remain in the U.K. album charts for the next ten years. Cash flowed into the company from *Tubular Bells* and enabled Branson to expand. The Virgin record label continued to sign up hit artists. The label became synonymous with a radical new wave of musicians. It signed up the Sex Pistols, followed in 1982 by Boy George.

In 1984 Branson, for the first time but certainly not for the last, stretched the Virgin brand beyond its normal territory of music and media and launched Virgin Atlantic Airways. He cleverly positioned Virgin Atlantic as a David taking on the Goliath of British Airways. The theme of sticking up for the little guy was one carried through in future Virgin start-ups. In the case of Virgin Atlantic it was an apt metaphor, as Branson spent many of the ensuing years pursuing British Airways through the courts over allegations of "dirty tricks" and fighting the subsequent libel actions. In the end Branson beat his Goliath; British Airways settled, paying £610,000 plus all legal costs, in 1993.

A charismatic character, Branson used his own flair for publicity to help extend the Virgin brand to a host of other businesses. Mates condoms, Virgin Publishing, Virgin Cola, Virgin Direct personal financial services, Virgin Trains, Virgin Internet, and even Virgin Bride, were all businesses that became part of the Virgin empire between 1984 and 2000. During this time Branson has variously attempted to circumnavigate the globe in a hot air balloon; appeared at the inaugural press conference for the launch of his airline wearing a brown leather aviator's helmet, like Snoopy in pursuit of the Red Baron; driven a full battle tank down a busy New York City street to demolish a wall of cola cans during the launch of Virgin Cola in the United States; dressed up as an air stewardess, and as a bride in full regalia complete with wedding dress and high heels; and skied down a mountainside naked (not on camera). His PR genius has earned the company millions of dollars worth of publicity for next to nothing.

Not everything has gone Branson's way, however. In 1986 the Virgin Group was floated on the London Stock Exchange, but Branson's unorthodox style and the conventional traditions of the City made an uneasy alliance. In 1988, following the October stock market crash, Branson and a number of other Virgin Directors bought the company back, making it a private concern once more and making Branson answerable to himself and a small group of shareholders. Other notable scratches on the Virgin record include the barrage of criticism Virgin trains has encountered (not surprisingly, and partly forgivably, given the state of the rolling stock and railroad infrastructure it inherited), the failure to win the franchise to run the National Lottery in the United Kingdom (twice) and the ensuing rumbling disagreement about compensation, and the withdrawal of Virgin Cola.

Forbes magazine may have demoted Branson in its World Billionaire list for 2001—it put the value of the Virgin Group at $1.8 billion as opposed to the $3.3 billion of the previous year—but it is unlikely that we are facing the demise of the intrepid, sweater-wearing, grinning Branson. He is far too savvy to be affected by anything short of a total economic collapse. The critics speculate that his empire is too highly geared and that Branson is saddled with debt. Closer inspection reveals that Branson has sold a minority stake in many of the businesses that would be vulnerable to a recession: Singapore Airlines owns 49% of Virgin Atlantic, AMP jointly owns Virgin Direct and Virginmoney, and Virgin Rail is 49% owned by Stagecoach, to mention a few. A more likely scenario is that Branson will bounce back from his temporary setbacks with his customary panache and launch a myriad new business ventures.

Context and Conclusions

Richard Branson, the clown prince of U.K. entrepreneurs, has appeared in some faintly ridiculous garbs during his time in charge of the Virgin Group. At times the onlooker is tempted to demand, "Will the real Richard Branson please stand up?" But the Branson persona is the secret of his success. Whether by design or by good luck, Branson has become a national institution in the United Kingdom. He appears as an antiestablishment, slightly hip, relaxed businessman, willing to challenge the complacent established corporate orthodoxy. He is the consumer's champion, offering a value and Virgin quality choice where no choice previously existed. At pains to point out where the consumer is getting ripped off, he steps in and provides a Virgin alternative. Of course, Branson's creations make money just like traditional businesses. It's just that somehow the British seem happy to give their money to Branson; they actively want to fill the coffers of their avuncular friend. When the big corporations such as British Airways or Barclays Bank first saw Branson dressed as an old-fashioned aviator or decked out in bridalwear, no doubt they laughed—until they realized that he had mugged them of their market share. They're not laughing now.

For More Information

Books:

Branson, Richard. *How I've Had Fun and Made a Fortune Doing Business My Way*. New York: Times Business, 1998.

Jackson, Tim. *Richard Branson, Virgin King: Inside Richard Branson's Business Empire*. Rocklin, CA: Primo Publishers, 1996.

Web site:

Virgin: **www.virgin.com**

Warren Buffett

1930	Born.
1934	Publication of *Security Analysis* by Ben Graham and David Dodd.
1950	Attends Columbia Business School.
1951	Graduates from Columbia, starts to invest for a living.
1965	Acquires Berkshire Hathaway (invests $10,000; it is worth $51 million by 1999).
1967	Berkshire Hathaway buys National Indemnity Company and National Fire & Marine Insurance Company.
1969	Winds up investment partnership to concentrate on Berkshire.
1995	Buys major stake in McDonald's.
1996	Acquires GEICO, the sixth-largest U.S. automobile insurer.
1998	Buys Executive Jet Corporation.
2001	Becomes the United States's second richest man behind Bill Gates.
2001	Announces 21st century investment strategy focusing on bricks, paints, and housewares.
2002	Berkshire Hathaway announces first ever negative coupon security.
2003	Continues investment strategy by acquiring furnishing goods giant, Burlington Industries.

Summary

Warren Buffett (1930–) had an eye for a deal from an early age. He progressed from child-hood race tipster and paper-route king to property owner and stock picker extraordinaire. By the age of 14 the young Buffett had already accumulated enough money to buy 40 acres of farmland. Now in his seventies, he is a multibillionaire—though not one to flaunt his wealth. The Coca-Cola-swilling, ukulele-playing Buffett lives a modest life, occupying an average house and preferring to drive an older car rather than the latest model even though his personal fortune makes him one of the richest men in the world. He is justly one of the most influential people in the finance world.

Life and Career

In 1952, an aspiring 21-year-old money manager placed a small advertisement in an Omaha newspaper, inviting people to attend a class on investing. He figured it would be a good way to accustom himself to appearing before audiences. His preparation even involved investing $100 for a Dale Carnegie course on public speaking. Twenty others showed up that day. If that same young man were speaking today, the building would be besieged. He was Warren Buffett, one of the greatest investors of all time.

Born on August 30, 1930, in Omaha, Nebraska, Warren Buffett exhibited the talents that were to make him wealthy at an early age. At the age of six, he would buy six packs of Coca-Cola for a quarter, break them up, and sell the individual bottles for a nickel each. When the young Buffett was stricken

> *At the age of six, he would buy six packs of Coca-Cola for a quarter, break them up, and sell the individual bottles for a nickel each.*

with a mysterious illness, he lay in bed figuring out how to get rich. On his recovery, he became one of the youngest racing tipsters in the United States when he published *Stable Boy Selections*—his information on the hot horses of the moment.

When Warren was 12 his father, Howard Buffett, won a seat in Congress and the family moved to Washington, D.C. The move was initially unpopular with Buffett. However, he changed his mind when he realized the commercial potential of the city. He took on five paper routes at once, delivering a staggering 500 papers each morning and earning the equivalent of a man's full-time salary of $175. By age 14 he had earned $1,200—enough to enable him to buy 40 acres of farmland in Nebraska and rent it out for farming.

Contribution

After another business foray in high school, installing overhauled arcade games in barbershops, Buffett decided to enhance his natural flair for commerce with a formal business education. He was admitted to the Wharton School at the University of Pennsylvania.

But Buffett did not complete his studies at Wharton. He found the theoretical aspects of business dull and discovered nothing in the curriculum to slake his thirst for practical knowledge. He finished his studies in business and economics at the University of Nebraska, in the meantime organizing paper routes for the *Lincoln Journal* on the side. At 19 he applied to Harvard Business School, but was refused admission. He turned to Columbia Business School, where he studied finance under investment guru Ben Graham.

It was in reading the stock market that Buffett found his true vocation. His first foray into stocks had been as a boy of 11 (of course it helped that his father was a stockbroker). Young Buffett bought three shares in Cities Service preferred at $38 a share; the stock promptly fell to $27. When it had recovered to $40 he sold, making a small profit. The stock then rose to $200, leaving the boy kicking himself and teaching him the value of long-term investment.

Determined to make a living by investing, Buffett plowed his energy and all the savings amassed from his various enterprises into the stock market. From 1951 to 1956 he turned $9,800 into $140,000. News spread about the new whiz kid investor, and more and more people asked him to invest their money for them. What started with friends spread to the general public, and soon Buffett was forming limited partnerships and taking a 25% cut of any return above 4%.

Once Buffett started investing as a career, he developed his own personal investment strategy. He began by looking for stocks that offered outstanding value and then holding those shares for the long term. "Lethargy, bordering on sloth, should remain the cornerstone of an investment style," he has said. He was heavily influenced by the theories of Ben Graham, his former teacher at Columbia and the coauthor of the investment classic *Security Analysis* (1934). Buffett eventually took Graham's investing strategies a step further by seeking out companies whose shares were inexpensive compared to their growth prospects. This approach required assessing a company's intangible assets, such as brand value. In this Buffett was ahead of his time. The area of intangible assets is now the subject of growing interest from business academics, but in the 1950s it was largely neglected. Buffett, however, was not unduly interested in theoretical niceties.

Theory was all very well, as Buffett had noted at Wharton, but how would his strategy work in practice? The answer proved to be, phenomenally well. Between 1957 and 1966 the investment partnership that Buffett managed posted an amazing 1,156% return—against 122.9% over the same period for the Dow Jones Industrial Average. A partner's investment of $10,000 would, after deducting Buffett's share, have returned $80,420. Buffett continued to outperform the market, making a 36% return in 1967 and a 59% return in 1968 in a speculative market, which was not particularly suited to his particular investment strategy.

In 1969, to the surprise of his managers, Buffett, concerned about maintaining his performance in an uncongenial investment climate, decided to wind up the partnership.

Since 1969 his attentions have been focused entirely on his investment vehicle Berkshire Hathaway, the publicly listed company he acquired in 1965. The markets may go up or down, but over time Buffett has delivered consistently for his shareholders, earning him the epithet "the Sage of Omaha." On the strength of his company's performance, it's a tag he undoubtedly deserves. A $10,000 investment in Berkshire Hathaway in 1965 would have been worth over $50 million by the end of 2000. Investors who backed the S&P 500 Index would have accumulated some $500,000, a paltry amount by comparison. The only downside, so far, has been investments into insurance companies, which have hit problems since 2002. On the other hand, he has resisted the temptation to be drawn into media-fueled stock bubbles such as the Internet boom of the 1990s. "As a group, lemmings have a rotten image," notes Buffett, "but no individual lemming has ever received bad press."

He remains determined to avoid the technology sector, "We have embraced the 21st century by entering such cutting edge industries as bricks, carpets, insulation, and paint— try to control your excitement." From 2001, he has invested in companies like Fruit of the Loom, Pampered Chef and Burlington Industries, part of that "household" portfolio.

Buffett himself has remained relatively unaffected by the plaudits heaped upon him. A modest man, he has few indulgences other than a corporate jet. Even then he bought a small, used plane for Berkshire; when he traded up to a more expensive model, he named it "the Indefensible." Modesty apart, he moved into the position of the United States's second richest person in 2001 behind Bill Gates. He lives in an average home, famously drives an old car, and his main hobby, it seems, is reading company reports.

Context and Conclusions

Warren Buffett is one of the greatest investors of all time. What lifts him above his peers is a determination to stick to his investment principles. Companies have risen and fallen, one minute at the height of fashion, the next on the bankruptcy pile. Buffett has steadfastly refused to jump on any bandwagon. Unlike so many other investors who are nursing their burns, Buffett let the dot-com train roll on by. Instead Buffett has made a fortune for himself and his shareholders by investing in undervalued companies for the long term. It's Buffett's willingness to buck the trend that makes him worth his "Sage of Omaha" tag.

For More Information

Book:
Lowenstein, Roger. *Buffett: The Making of an American Capitalist*. New York: Doubleday, 1996.

Leo Burnett

1891	Born.
1930	Joins Erwin Wasey as creative Vice-President.
1935	Borrows $50,000 and starts his own agency.
1940	Leo Burnett agency lands first major new client, the American Meat Institute.
1950	Proctor and Gamble appoints Leo Burnett for an institutional campaign.
1955	Retained by Philip Morris to develop a campaign for Marlboro cigarettes.
1967	Retires—although he continues to work at his agency part time.
1971	Dies.

Summary

Leo Burnett (1891–1971) changed the face of advertising in the United States. After working his way through a number of agencies, including Homer McKee and Erwin Wasey, he resisted the lure of the Madison Avenue agencies in New York and in 1935 established his own business in Chicago. After a hesitant start, Burnett's distinctive style of advertising soon attracted major clients such as Procter & Gamble. The Leo Burnett advertising agency went on to produce some of the most striking advertising of its time, including the "Marlboro Man" campaign. Burnett's advertising philosophy gave rise to the Chicago School of advertising, and by his death in 1971 he was universally acknowledged as one of the most influential figures in his industry.

Life and Career

Leo Burnett was born George Noble Burnett in St. Johns, Michigan, on October 21, 1891. The name Leo was a result of hospital officials mistaking the abbreviated Geo. for Leo. The name stuck.

Burnett started out in advertising young. His father owned a dry goods store and Burnett would design and draw the display cards, little realizing that advertising would come to play such an important part in his life. He attended the local high school, moonlighting as a reporter for several weekly newspapers in the area. Immediately after graduation he briefly took up a position as a teacher in St. Johns's single-classroom village school before heading for the University of Michigan at Ann Arbor.

At the university, Burnett earned a degree in journalism. Once again he continued to work throughout his studies, this time both as a night editor at the *Michigan Daily* and producing display cards for a department store. Leaving the university he worked at the *Peoria [Illinois] Journal* as a reporter for $18 a week. He remained there for about a year, until the lure of the burgeoning automobile industry proved too great and he set off for Detroit.

In Detroit Burnett joined the Cadillac Motor Car Company as editor of an in-house magazine. He had been tipped off about the job by one of his old college professors and, as part of his application, wrote an essay on neatness that sufficiently impressed the people at Cadillac to win him the job. Soon Burnett had been handed responsibility for Cadillac's advertising. The pattern for his professional life was set.

Contribution

After a brief stint in the U.S. Navy during World War I—much of it spent building a break-water in Lake Michigan—Burnett, with several other Cadillac employees, broke away to form LaFayette Motors. He followed LaFayette to Indianapolis but when the company moved to Wisconsin he remained in Indianapolis as creative head at the Homer McKee advertising agency.

He settled at Homer McKee for ten years. In 1929 the stock market crash affected adver-tising agencies severely. Homer McKee was no exception, losing one of its major auto-mobile accounts. Now with a young family, Burnett needed a secure job and decided to move on. The family moved to Chicago in 1930, and Burnett signed up for Erwin Wasey as creative vice President. At the time Erwin Wasey was one of the leading advertising agen-cies in the world. Shortly after Burnett joined, the firm moved its headquarters to New York. The New York advertising agencies had developed a reputation for a hard sell approach. They were also perceived by their Western and Midwestern clients as favoring companies based on the East Coast.

Several of Burnett's clients approached him and suggested he open his own agency. Initially Burnett's loyalty prevailed. Then Art Kudner left Wasey to start his own agency, taking several automobile clients, including General Motors, with him. Burnett relented. It was 1935, Burnett was 44, and on August 5, his own agency opened for business.

Burnett borrowed $50,000 to start Leo Burnett Company, Inc. He was joined by a friend, Jack O'Kieffe, as well as three clients—Green Giant, Hoover, and Realsilk Hosiery—who brought in revenues of some $900,000. The agency's first year was a tough one. Despite attempts to win accounts from both Hershey and Wrigley Gum, Burnett ended the year with the same clients he started with.

The second year went the same way. Burnett had briefly recruited Dick Heath, who brought in some business. Unfortunately Burnett and Heath had a falling out within the year and Heath left. It wasn't until O'Kieffe persuaded Burnett to bring Heath back that things began to improve. In 1940 Leo Burnett landed its first major new client, the Ameri-can Meat Institute. Thereafter the agency gathered momentum, picking up prestigious accounts such as the Pillsbury Family Flour account, Kellogg's Cereals, and—the account that brought Burnett onto the radar of the Madison Avenue agencies—the Tea Council, a New York-based organization.

Burnett's agency made a name for itself through its distinctive style of advertising—what Burnett called "stressing the inherent drama in the product." The trickle of clients became a flood after Proctor and Gamble appointed Burnett's for an institutional campaign in 1950.

In 1955 Burnett's was retained by Philip Morris to

The Marlboro campaign with its imagery of the rugged Marlboro Man was one of the most memorable of the 20th century.

develop a campaign for Marlboro cigarettes. The Marlboro campaign with its imagery of the rugged Marlboro Man was one of the most memorable of the 20th century. There were many other notable campaigns in the years that followed. Clients included Schiltz Beer, Maytag, and United Airlines.

Burnett's influence on the advertising industry was so great that the term "the Chicago School of advertising" was coined to describe his and his followers' distinctive approach. It was a style that tried to capture the essence of the product in its advertising rather than just use clever words. It was also an inclusive approach that didn't try to play to either East or West Coast America in particular.

In the late 1960s, suffering increasingly from illness, Burnett took a back seat in the business he had created. In 1967 he "retired," although he continued to come into the office at least twice a week. On June 7, 1971 after a spell in the office, Burnett suffered a heart attack at his home and died that night. He was 79.

Context and Conclusions

Praised by competitors and clients alike, Leo Burnett made a unique contribution to the advertising industry. He created his own, highly influential school of advertising—the Chicago School. He was driven by a consuming passion for excellence and creativity that shone through in the work of his agency. He also adopted a socially responsible approach to business, demonstrated through the firm's pro bono work, conducted in part under the auspices of the Advertising Council.

Unlike some other agencies, the pressures of winning business never drove Burnett's company to employ unscrupulous or cut-throat practices. It was a testimony to its founder's even-handed approach that he was often praised by his closest rivals.

For More Information
Book:
Broadbent, Simon. *The Leo Burnett Book of Advertising*. London: Business Books, 1984.

Web site:
Leo Burnett: **www.leoburnett.com**

Andrew Carnegie

1835	Born.
1848	Family moves to Allegheny near Pittsburgh, Pennsylvania. Carnegie, aged 12, takes job in cotton mill.
1870	Builds first blast furnace. Experiments with the Bessemer process.
1874	Opens steel furnace at Braddock.
1880	Plant operating for 24 hours a day with profits of $2 million.
1881	Company reorganizes as Carnegie Bros & Co.
1882	Carnegie acquires coke-producing interests of Henry C. Frick.
1886	Writes *Triumphant Democracy*.
1889	Moves to New York to conduct R&D into the steel manufacturing process. "Gospel of wealth" article published. Steel production 332,111 tons.
1899	Steel production 2,663,412 tons. Carnegie buys out Frick.
1901	Frick and J. Pierpont Morgan purchase the Carnegie Company for $500 million.
1919	Dies.

Summary

Andrew Carnegie (1835–1919) was one of the finest of his generation. A significant proportion of his achievements fell within the 19th century, yet his impact on the commercial revolution that took place in the United States as the 19th century gave way to the 20th is huge. Carnegie was arguably the first of a generation of businessmen who pioneered industrial growth in the United States and throughout the world on the back of steel manufacturing and the building of railroads. At the end of his long career he had built the largest steel company in the United States and amassed a vast personal fortune.

Life and Career

Andrew Carnegie was born in Dunfermline on November 25, 1835. In 1848 economic depression persuaded Carnegie's father to emigrate with his family to the United States. The family settled in a colony of Scots gathered at Slabtown, Allegheny, near Pittsburgh, and the 12-year-old Andrew took work in a local cotton mill.

Leaving the cotton mill, he got a job at the Pittsburgh Telegraph Office as a messenger boy. Thomas A. Scott, superintendent of the western division of the Pennsylvania Railroad at the time, spotted Carnegie's potential and appointed him as his secretary at $50 a month, in those days a handsome salary for one so young. It was Scott who set Carnegie on the path to riches by showing him the likely gains of investing in startup companies. Acting on a tip from Scott, Carnegie bought stock in the Adams Express Company using money from his mother, who remortgaged her house. Shortly afterward he borrowed money to invest in a venture commercially exploiting the invention of the sleeping car for the railroad.

During the Civil War, Carnegie served with Scott in Washington. Then, with the Union victory secured, he took Scott's old position as superintendent of the western division of the Pennsylvania Railroad. But his entrepreneurial instincts were not satisfied, and he soon left the railroads to establish an iron bridge building firm, the Keystone Bridge Company. He was also involved in several other speculative ventures that proved successful.

Contribution

While Carnegie was busy hustling in the United States, Henry Bessemer, an inventor and businessman, was working on a manufacturing process in England that would change industry the world over. The Bessemer process allowed the industrialized production of steel from iron. Carnegie often visited the United Kingdom, and on one visit he came across the Bessemer converter. It was a revelation.

Hurrying back to the United States, Carnegie formed Carnegie, McCandless & Co., built his first blast furnace in 1870, and began experimenting with the Bessemer process. He opened a steel furnace at Braddock and, by 1880, the plant was operating 24 hours a day and producing annual profits of $2 million. In 1881 the company reorganized, becoming Carnegie Bros. & Co. Carnegie held the controlling interest. In 1882 he acquired the coke-producing interests of Henry C. Frick, who became his most trusted associate.

Carnegie was arguably the first of a generation of businessmen who pioneered industrial growth in the United States and throughout the world on the back of steel manufacturing and the building of railroads.

In 1889 Carnegie moved to New York to continue his research into the steel manufacturing process. He also spent six months of the year with his family in Scotland. In his absence Carnegie left Frick, as chair of Carnegie Bros., in charge of the day-to-day running of the company. When Frick took over, the company was a collection of disparate threads—the threads being individual mills and furnaces dotted about Pittsburgh. Frick wove these threads together into a fabric: an organization that would become the biggest steelmaking enterprise in the world. He centralized the management structure and integrated production. The firm was transformed into the Carnegie Steel Company, valued at $25 million.

Unfortunately for Carnegie, Frick also presided over one of the most notorious incidents in U.S. corporate history. In an attempt to drive down costs and boost profits, Frick reduced piecework rates. Incensed, the Amalgamated Iron and Steel Workers Union called its members at the Carnegie Homestead plant out on strike. Instead of settling through negotiation, Frick inflamed the situation by arranging to bring in 300 strikebreakers.

When the day came and the strikebreakers arrived on barges down the Monongahela River, complete with armed guard, all hell broke loose. At the end of a day of pitched battle, ten men lay dead and a further 60 were wounded. Homestead was placed under martial law.

Carnegie, in Scotland at the time, was irate. It was not just the disruption to the company that he rued; Frick had gone against his explicit instructions not to use strikebreakers. For Carnegie it was a matter of personal ethics. Nevertheless, being the controlling owner and, as such, ultimately responsible, he had to bear the dark stain of the workers' blood on his reputation for many years after the debacle.

Although Carnegie refrained from criticizing Frick in public, their relationship never recovered. The company continued to thrive, improving annual production of steel from

332,111 tons in 1889 to 2,663,412 in 1899, and profits from $2 million to $40 million. But, because of the deteriorating relationship between them, Carnegie took the opportunity to buy Frick out for a handsome $15 million in 1889. Even this act of severance failed to quell the personal animosity between the two men. In 1901 Frick returned with the backing of the notorious J. Pierpont Morgan and purchased the Carnegie Company for $500 million, establishing the U.S. Steel Corporation, which, valued at $1.4 billion, was the biggest steel company in the world.

Context and Conclusions

Carnegie played a leading role in the industrialization of the United States. As a poor Scottish boy who became one of the wealthiest men in the world, his rise from rags to riches was extraordinary. In his time he was criticized and praised in equal measure. Some saw him as a smug, tyrannical, autocratic, arrogant slave driver; others as a wise, benevolent, enlightened entrepreneur. Of the many qualities Carnegie possessed, one in particular stands out: he was an opportunist who acted on his instincts. He took any opportunity to promote his business interests. When he invited the Prince of Wales to ride a Pennsylvania Railroad engine, for example, he did it to secure business favors rather than to increase his social standing.

Some saw him as a smug, tyrannical, autocratic, arrogant slave driver; others as a wise, benevolent, enlightened entrepreneur.

Carnegie will be remembered as much for his philanthropy as for his business adventures. In later life, guided by his ethical beliefs, he gave away the greater part of his fortune. He established a trust fund "for the improvement of mankind." The Carnegie Institute of Pittsburgh, the Carnegie Institute of Technology, the Carnegie Institution of Washington, and three thousand public libraries were built with this trust money.

When the "King of Steel" died in August 1919, he had already given away $350 million of his fortune.

For More Information

Books:

Carnegie, Andrew. *The Empire of Business*. New York: Doubleday, Doran & Co., 1902.

Mackay, James. *Andrew Carnegie: His Life and Times*. New York: John Wiley, 1998.

Web site:

Carnegie Corporation of New York: **www.carnegie.org**

Willis Haviland Carrier

1876	Born.
1901	Graduates from Cornell University. Joins Buffalo Forge Company.
1906	Patents "apparatus for treating air."
1914	Buffalo Forge closes air-conditioning subsidiary.
1915	Forms Carrier Engineering Corporation.
1922	Invents the centrifugal refrigeration machine.
1924	Detroit's J. L. Hudson Co. becomes first air-conditioned department store.
1925	Installs air conditioning into Rivoli Theater in New York.
1928	San Antonio's Milam Building the first air-conditioned office tower.
1930	Air conditioning installed in over 300 theaters.
1940s	Turns over company facilities and expertise to war effort.
1950	Dies.

Summary

Willis Haviland Carrier invented his air-conditioning machine early in his career. He spent the rest of his life improving his product and building and leading the company that sold it. A brilliant student, he graduated from Cornell University in 1901 and carried his natural inquisitiveness into his first job. His initial research into heating and cooling devices resulted in one of the first commercial air-conditioning machines. When his company dropped the technology, Carrier started his own company. Then, with a mixture of charm, persuasion and inventiveness, he set about selling his idea to the whole country. He was so successful that by the time of his death in 1950, air conditioning was taken for granted by millions of Americans.

Life and Career

Willis Haviland Carrier was born and raised on a farm, on the eastern shores of Lake Erie in Angola, New York. Born on November 26, 1876, he was an only child. In later years it was said that Carrier had been something of a mathematical prodigy, but the reality was more mundane. As many children do, he struggled with math, especially fractions. His mother insisted on a novel way of teaching him. "My mother told me to bring up a pan of apples from the cellar," said Carrier. "She had me cut them into halves, quarters and eighths, and add and subtract the parts. Fractions took on a new meaning, and I felt as if no problems would be too hard for me—I'd simply break them down to something simple and they would be easy to solve."

Carrier put his problem-solving skills to good use studying for a mechanical engineering degree at Cornell University in Ithaca, New York. He was an exceptional student. "Carrier would start explaining an idea in class, and he was soon so far ahead of us in his thinking that not even the professor could keep up with him," said a fellow undergraduate.

Theoretical engineering came easy. Money didn't. Despite a four-year scholarship Carrier still struggled to survive, taking on a string of odd jobs so he could afford to eat and pay the rent. When he graduated in 1901, he went to work for the Buffalo Forge Company, designing heating systems.

Contribution

At Buffalo Forge, Carrier started at the bottom on the draftsman's board. He soon discovered a serious flaw in the design process. There was insufficient data available on the science of heating and cooling air to allow the design of well-engineered heating and drying systems. Carrier spent his evenings poring over books, compiling his own data tables. Finally he summoned the courage to ask his boss for funds to research the subject, requesting $3,000. His boss misheard the sum as $30,000. When he found out the true figure, he was so relieved that he agreed to Carrier's request on the spot.

Carrier established his own research team to investigate the basic engineering principles involved in heating buildings. The research, which enabled the company to calculate how much heating surface area is required to heat a building of a particular size, led to savings of $40,000. His research efforts paid off in other ways too. Carrier was promoted to head up the company's experimental engineering department.

In the sultry summer of 1901, the Brooklyn-based company of Sackett-Wilhelms Lithographing and Publishing had problems. The humidity affected its business badly. The ink ran and the moist paper swelled, costing the company money. Representatives came to see Carrier. Could he do something to regulate the humidity? He said he'd try.

Carrier didn't invent room-cooling machines. Primitive devices, aimed at making buildings more comfortable to live in during hot humid summers, had been around for some time, especially in the Deep South. Most were variations on a theme—air blown by a fan over a block of ice. Crude and impracticable, these devices did little to abate the oppressive heat, and even less to combat the humidity. In addition, the transport of ice—an industry in itself—was difficult and expensive.

It didn't take long for the inventive Carrier to improve upon the ice machines. Inspiration for his new work came to him out of a fog that enveloped him as he stood in a damp Pittsburgh train station. The paradoxical solution to the problem of how to control humidity in a room lay in creating an artificial fog, in which Carrier determined the amount of

In 1928, San Antonio's Milam Building opened the first air-conditioned office tower. An unexpected bonus was a staggering 51% increase in productivity among white-collar workers during the summer months.

air saturation. His first design was a contraption that pulled moist air through a filter, passed it over chilled coils, and then redirected it to where it was needed. It was the equivalent of melting 54 tons of ice a day. In 1906 he patented an improved version of the design to which he gave the name "apparatus for treating air." A competitor, Stuart Cramer, coined the term "air conditioner."

Carrier had hit the jackpot. Buffalo Forge, however, was blind to the opportunity. With the outbreak of World War I in 1914, the company canned its small but growing air-conditioning subsidiary. Undaunted Carrier took his invention and, in 1915, with several friends and

$32,600, formed Carrier Engineering Corporation. The company's slogan was "Every Day a Good Day."

In its first year the company was awarded 40 contracts for air conditioning systems. In 1922 Carrier produced another improvement to his system—the centrifugal refrigeration machine. This invention made it practical to introduce air conditioning into large spaces.

The government even removed the company's chillers from department stores such as Macy's to install them in war production plants.

Industry snapped up the company's new product. Carrier's air conditioning brought comfort to shoppers at Detroit's J. L. Hudson Co., when it became the first air-conditioned department store in 1924. Relief was in sight too for the millions of office workers slogging through summer days in their sweat-drenched shirts. In 1928, San Antonio's Milam Building opened the first air-conditioned office tower. An unexpected bonus was a staggering 51% increase in productivity among white-collar workers during the summer months.

Carrier's air conditioning also proved popular with theatergoers. Stifling heat in the summer left New York's theaters either empty or closed. In 1925, the owner of the famous Rivoli Theater in New York took a risk and asked Carrier to install air conditioning. Passers-by reading the advertising would have been forgiven for thinking that the air conditioning was a bigger attraction than the play. So it proved. The line snaked around the block for the first air-conditioned performance, which, after a sticky beginning when the 133-ton air conditioning machine was late starting up, was a great success. By 1930, Carrier had installed air conditioning into 300 theaters. With the benefit of air conditioning at work and at play, it wasn't long before the American public was demanding it in their homes.

In the 1920s, Carrier started to supply home air-conditioning units—the small "Weather-maker"—for residential use. But when the chill wind of the Great Depression blew, plans for air-conditioned homes were shelved. World War II further delayed the mass introduction of air conditioning into homes, when Carrier's production facilities were given over to the war effort. The government even removed the company's chillers from department stores such as Macy's to install them in war production plants.

Carrier never got to grips with the domestic market, failing to produce a small and reliable enough product to bring to the consumer mass market. It wasn't until the 1950s that companies like Westinghouse would introduce home air-conditioning on a large scale. Carrier never lived to see it—he died of a heart attack in September 1950.

Context and Conclusions

Known as "the Chief" by his workers, Carrier was both an inventor and a leader. Although he relied on the business skills of colleague Irvine Lyle to help build his company, Carrier was the driving force behind its success. Other people were investigating the means of controlling air temperature and humidity—Stuart Cramer, for example, was on the right track but failed to see the bigger picture. But Carrier realized the potential of his invention and, by installing it in theaters and offices, brought it to the public's attention, thus creating a growing tide of demand.

Air conditioning made new industrial processes possible and increased productivity and, more importantly, it made life comfortable for millions of people. It is difficult for anyone who lives in temperate climes to understand the significance of Carrier's achievement, but for those who step outdoors in the summer to the blast of hot air and the closeness of 80% humidity there is no need to explain.

CLOSE BUT NO CIGAR
STUART CRAMER

Carrier may be the man known for bringing air conditioning to the people of the United States, but he didn't invent the term. The man who did was Stuart Cramer of Charlotte, North Carolina. Trained as an engineer, Cramer built up substantial holdings in the textile industry of the southern states in the early 1900s. Driven by necessity, he designed a device to moisten the air in his textile factories and filed a patent for the "Cramer System of Air Conditioning." However he seemed to lack Carrier's vision, as the Parks-Cramer Company aimed its humidification primarily at the cotton industry rather than at a wider audience.

For More Information
Books:

Ingels, Margaret. *Willis Haviland Carrier: Father of Air Conditioning*. Reprint ed. Manchester, NH: Ayer Company Publishing, 1972.
Wampler, Dr Cloud. *Willis H. Carrier, Father of Air Conditioning*. New York: Newcomen Society, 1949.

Walter Percy Chrysler

1875	Born.
1905	Attends the Chicago Auto Show.
1908	William Crapo Durant founds General Motors.
1911	Employed as works manager at Buick, part of General Motors.
1916– 1919	To prevent him leaving, Durant ups his salary from $50,000 to $500,000.
1920	Leaves GM and retires.
1921– 1923	Rescues Willy's-Overland, then Maxwell-Chalmers, and builds the Chrysler Six.
1924	Chrysler Six car shown during New York Auto show. Chrysler Six goes into production.
1925	Maxwell Motors becomes the Chrysler Corporation. Chrysler is President and Chairman. Company turns in a profit of $17 million.
1928	Chrysler Corporation buys Dodge Brothers' dealership network. Renamed Chrysler Motors. The 1,048-ft. Chrysler building constructed in midtown Manhattan.
1940	Dies.

Summary

Walter P. Chrysler (1875–1940) was the founder of one of the largest U.S. automobile corporations of the 20th century, the eponymous Chrysler Motors. Even as a teenager Chrysler demonstrated a natural ability for engineering. His formidable engineering talents were later matched by his organizational and management skills. From Buick and General Motors in 1908 to the Chrysler Corporation in 1925, via Willys-Overland and Maxwell-Chalmers, Chrysler proved to be something of an automobile company doctor transforming ailing firms into healthy ones. By his death in 1940 he had put Chrysler firmly alongside Ford and General Motors as one of the big three U.S. automobile companies.

Life and Career

Shortly after Chrysler was born, his family moved from Wamego, Kansas, to Ellis, Kansas, where his father worked as an engineer for the Kansas Pacific Railroad. Chrysler attended the local school in Ellis, but also spent a great deal of time with his father in the engineering workshops of the Kansas Pacific Railroad, where he developed a fascination with engineering.

Leaving school he became an engineer with the Union Pacific Railroad (previously the Kansas Pacific Railroad) and by the age of 18 had already designed and built a miniature steam engine that ran on a homemade track.

When, at age 22, Chrysler finished his apprenticeship, he set out across the United States looking for work. He moved from job to job, working for the Rio Grande & Western Railroad, the Colorado & Southern Railroad, and the Chicago & Great Western Railroad, all the while enhancing his reputation as a skilled engineer.

It was in Oelwein, Iowa, while working as the Superintendent of Motive Power for the Chicago & Great Western Railroad, that Chrysler first saw the contraption that would change his life. Walking the streets of Oelwein one day, he came across several horseless carriages. Curiosity aroused, he made a point of attending the 1905 Chicago Auto Show.

Contribution

At the Auto Show Chrysler was entranced by a Locomobile Phaeton, with its red leather upholstery and white bodywork. Putting $700 down and financing the balance, Chrysler bought the car, had it shipped home, and then proceeded to take it to pieces—not once but several times. By the time Chrysler was done with dismantling and reassembling his new car he had a perfect understanding of how it was engineered.

His next career move took him to Pittsburgh, Pennsylvania, as works manager for the American Locomotive Company. It was an executive there who tipped him off about a job at the Buick automobile company. Chrysler met Buick's President, Charles W. Nash, and was taken on as works manager. It was 1911—Chrysler had entered the automobile industry.

The Buick plant in Flint, Michigan was the cornerstone of William Crapo Durant's General Motors, founded in 1908. Durant was ousted as President of GM in 1910, but staged a comeback, regaining the presidency in 1916 and firing Charles W. Nash. As Durant's fortunes rose so to did Chrysler's. Chrysler began by sorting out production at the Buick plant. Before long he was President and general manager of Buick. When Durant got wind of a rumor that Chrysler was planning to take over another auto company, Packard Motors, Durant made Chrysler an offer he couldn't refuse. He increased his salary from $50,000 a year to an astonishing $500,000.

Chrysler's meteoric ascent continued. As General Motors' Vice-President in charge of production and then executive Vice-President, Chrysler worked alongside Durant. But Chrysler wasn't impressed with Durant's handling of the company. Predicting disaster, he left GM in 1920. Shortly after, Durant was forced out by GM's financiers over the company's $80 million debt. Chrysler, however, had restored the good name of Buick and increased production from 40 to over 500 cars a day. In 1920, 45 and financially secure, he put away his desk diary and retired.

It was a brief retirement. He was approached by a group of bankers and asked to rescue the ailing Willy's-Overland company. He would have a two-year contract, the position of executive Vice-President, and a free hand. Chrysler asked for one extra thing—an annual salary of $1 million. The desperate bankers agreed; Chrysler set about saving the company.

His strategy was to build a brand new car—new design, new engineering—to revive W-O's fortunes. He assembled a team of automotive experts that included the independent engineering team of Carl Breer, Owen Skelton, and Fred Zeder. Work was well advanced on the new car when the bankers got cold feet and withdrew their support. Chrysler, however, motored on, forming the Chrysler Corporation as a separate entity within W-O and retaining the original design team at the production facility in Elizabeth, New Jersey. The new car was christened the Chrysler Six.

Before long Chrysler was on the move again when bankers called him in to save yet another automobile company in trouble—Maxwell-Chalmers. Chrysler negotiated with W-O to be allowed to work with Maxwell and took a $100,000 salary and stock options. When his two-year contract was up at W-O, Chrysler left for Maxwell-Chalmers.

When he arrived, Maxwell-Chalmers was in a mess. After some wheeling and dealing Chrysler merged Maxwell and Chalmers. Then, at the helm of the new Maxwell Motors, Chrysler refocused his attention on the Chrysler Six. He brought the Chrysler Six engineering team to Maxwell, and in 1923 the new car appeared in prototype. With its fast top speed, high-compression engine, and hydraulic brakes, the Chrysler Six was truly revolutionary.

Maxwell Motors was restructured in 1925, emerging as the Chrysler Corporation with Chrysler as president and chairman of the board. In 1925 the company turned in a profit of $17 million.

For once Chrysler struggled to raise the finance to put the car into production. Bankers were reluctant to bankroll an unproven and experimental product. Undaunted, Chrysler took the car to the 1924 New York Auto show. On discovering that, as a prototype, the car was ineligible for the show, he displayed it in the foyer of the Hotel Commodore—the show's headquarters—creating enough interest to persuade financiers Chase Securities to put up production money.

The Chrysler Six was in production in the same year. In that year alone 32,000 were sold. Maxwell Motors was restructured in 1925, emerging as the Chrysler Corporation with Chrysler as President and Chairman of the board. In 1925 the company turned in a profit of $17 million. New models rolled off the Chrysler production line. In 1928 Chrysler Corporation bought Dodge Brothers with its extensive dealership network and changed its name to Chrysler Motors. With Chrysler in command, the company flourished, survived the Great Depression, and outlasted many competitors by a combination of astute management and innovative products. Chrysler remained President until 1935 and Chairman until his death in 1940.

Context and Conclusions

The list of recipients of *Time* magazine's Man of the Year award is dominated by politicians and statesmen, with a few notable exceptions. One of those exceptions is the *Time* magazine Man of the Year in 1928—Walter P. Chrysler. Alongside Henry Ford and William Crapo Durant, Chrysler was one of the greatest automobile industrialists of the first half of the 20th century.

Of the three men, Chrysler arguably represented the most complete combination of technical, entrepreneurial, and managerial ability. Few men have taken on such demanding corporate challenges so frequently. It was no coincidence that, whenever an automobile company was ailing, the man the bankers called in to save it was Chrysler.

For More Information

Books:

Chrysler, Walter P., and Boyden Sparkes. *Life of an American Workman*. New York: Dodd, Mead & Co., 1950.

Breer, Carl, ed. Anthony J. Yanik. *The Birth of the Chrysler Corporation and its Engineering Legacy*. Warrendale, PA: Society of Automotive Engineers, 1995.

Curcio, Vincent. *Chrysler: The Life and Times of an Automotive Genius*. New York: Oxford University Press, 2000.

Web site:
Chrysler: **www.chrysler.com**

Jim Clark

1944	Born.
1961	Joins the Navy.
1971	Earns M.S. in physics from Louisiana State University.
1974	Earns Ph.D. in computing from University of Utah.
1978	Starts teaching at Stanford University.
1982	Founds Silicon Graphics.
1994	Leaves Silicon Graphics and founds Netscape.
1998	AOL acquires Netscape.
1999	Founds myCFO.com
2001	Healtheon Services becomes the third multi-billion dollar business founded by Clark.
2001	Starts project to remotely control luxury yacht Hyperion via Internet.
2002	Sells myCFO.com.

Summary

When it comes to technology startups, Jim Clark (1944–) is a man with the Midas touch. His companies have created billions of dollars of shareholder value. He epitomizes the restless, pioneering spirit of the new economy.

After a spell in the Navy, Clark embarked on a teaching career at Stanford University, expanding his interest in computer graphics research. When no one would invest in the technology he invented, he established his own company, Silicon Graphics. During his time at Silicon Graphics from 1982 to 1994, the company was at the forefront of computer graphics technology and its machines set the standard.

With one success behind him and already a wealthy man, Clark teamed up in 1994 with the cherubic-faced Marc Andreessen to found Netscape. It was another huge success: the Netscape browser dominated the market for several years. With a number of other startups to his credit, Clark marches on. His subsequent ventures, myCFO.com, a Web-based financial adviser for high-net-worth individuals, and Healtheon Services, an online healthcare business, have kept him busy since 1999.

Life and Career

James H. Clark was born in 1944 in Plainview, Texas. Initially he showed little interest in gaining an education and at the age of 16 dropped out of school. It was 1961. One story has it that Clark was suspended for telling a teacher to "go to hell" after being reprimanded for failing to read Samuel Taylor Coleridge's *Rime of the Ancient Mariner*. Had Clark read the poem, it might have appealed to his nautical impulse: after leaving school he promptly joined the U.S. Navy.

Clark's lack of interest in school wasn't due to a lack of aptitude; he simply wasn't ready to study at that point in his life. Military service changed that. While in the Navy Clark was required to take a standard math test. His score was so high that the administrators suspected him of cheating and insisted he retake the test. When he repeated the feat they moved him into an area that might tax his mind a little more: computers. The Navy was also the proving ground for Clark's shrewd business brain. He ran a surreptitious loan operation, lending money to other sailors to tide them over until payday. At 40% interest it was a lucrative enterprise.

Contribution

After the Navy Clark went to Louisiana State University and excelled, earning an M.S. in physics in 1971. In 1974 he earned a Ph.D. in computer science at the University of Utah. At Utah Clark met Ivan Sutherland, widely regarded as the man behind interactive computer graphics. It was a field in which Clark was to have a major impact.

The pattern of Clark's early working life was that of a bright individual seeking a challenge that would hold his attention. He embarked on a teaching career at the University of California, Santa Cruz, but he soon quit to take up consulting, which he liked even less.

Returning to academia in 1978, Clark joined the faculty of Stanford University. In addition to his teaching duties, he had obtained funding from the Defense Advanced Research Projects Agency (DARPA) to lead a team of students conducting research into computer graphics technology.

Clark worked with his team for three years. During that time they made several important technological breakthroughs. The team created a "geometry engine" that shifted 3-D graphics processing from software to hardware, with the instruction set embedded into a computer chip. Clark attempted to sell the technology to established computer companies, but when no one showed any interest, he determined to go it alone. "I concluded after talking to DEC and IBM and all these companies," he said, "that they didn't understand how to use what we had in the first place, so they would surely screw it up." Taking six of the Stanford team

In February 1994 Clark left the company that had made him rich. The split was the result of his growing frustration.

with him, he left in 1982 to found Silicon Graphics (now SGI). There Clark drove his team to create the ultimate 3-D engine, delivering interactive, real-time 3-D computer graphics to the humble PC. When he resigned from SGI in 1994, the company had had eight years of an astonishing 40% annual growth, with annual revenues reaching the $2 billion mark. The company employed more than 5,000 people; its name synonymous with the high end computer graphics market.

SGI machines enabled designers to visualize objects by rendering them onscreen using a computer. They could then rotate them, morph them, and manipulate them to give an accurate representation of how the object would appear and behave in the real world. When Hollywood caught on to the potential of the SGI technology, the studios used it to create out-of-this-world special effects in movies such as *Jurassic Park* and *Terminator II*, as well as the entirely computer-generated *Toy Story*.

In February 1994 Clark left the company that had made him rich. The split was the result of his growing frustration. SGI was no longer able to move at the speed Clark wanted. His vision was to bring expensive SGI technology within the reach of the average consumer. Others at the company were unconvinced. Clark left.

He was unemployed for approximately 24 hours. On the morning he resigned, he sent an e-mail to Marc Andreessen, a brilliant young computer programmer. Clark thought that an invention of Andreessen's, the NCSA Mosaic browser, would be perfect for interactive television. At the time the Internet was in its infancy, and many saw interactive television as "the next big thing." Andreessen persuaded Clark that the Internet was the best market for the browser, and in 1994 they established Mosaic Communications Corporation. It was the company that became Netscape.

Clark's genius was evident in the business plan. The strategy was a radical one: give the product—the Netscape browser—away. It was a masterstroke, and it worked. Soon the Netscape Navigator browser was familiar to virtually every Internet user. By 1996 Clark and Andreessen's company had captured over 80% of the market. If the browser was given away to noncorporate users, Clark made sure corporations paid for it and the compatible server software. At the company's I.P.O. in August 1995 it was valued at some $2 billion, making Clark the first Internet billionaire. Had it not been for Microsoft, Netscape would have become the dominant browser on the Internet. Although initially slow to recognize the potential of the Internet, Microsoft moved decisively into the browser market. Up against the might of the Redmond-based computer giant, Netscape eventually lost ground and was sold to America Online. Despite the fall, Clark, commenting on the move to split Microsoft, argued that Microsoft should be allowed to keep its own browser as part of the Windows operating system. Having played a significant role in making the Internet the pervasive means of communication it is, Clark became even wealthier after the AOL deal.

Since then Clark's enterprising spirit has seen him involved in several startups, including Healtheon, Shutterfly.com, and myCFO.com. Healtheon was Clark's vehicle to overhaul the ailing U.S. health service, and its success made it the third multi-billion dollar business he had founded. MyCFO.com, a web-based financial advisory service for high-net-worth individuals, proved successful before he sold it in 2002. When Clark is not working hard he's playing hard, flying his stunt plane or crewing his $30 million 155-foot sailboat *Hyperion*. Since 2001, he has been working on a project to control *Hyperion* remotely via the Internet.

Context and Conclusions

In the space of two decades Jim Clark built three incredibly successful companies. The first, Silicon Graphics, was part of the personal computer revolution; the second, Netscape, played a pivotal role in the development of the Internet; the third, Healtheon, is helping to reshape the U.S. health service. How? Clark attributes his fortune to "a combination of being persuasive, believing in what you're doing, having integrity...and knowing how to judge good people, because you can't afford to have anything but good people early on in a company."

Clark knows the value of a good team, surrounding himself with the right people. "I look for intelligence and a certain measure of humility," he observes. "People who are boastful or too proud may be really good, but they're not my kind of people. A business is about teams, and teams mean getting along with people. There's just not enough room for a lot of superegos in a company.".

For More Information

Web site:
myCFO.com: **www.myCFO.com**

Michael Dell

1965	Born.
1977	Aged 12, sells stamps by catalog.
1983	Enters the University of Texas at Austin.
1984	Drops out of college to found Dell Computer.
1988	Dell Computer's first year revenue is $257.8 million.
1994	www.dell.com launched.
1997	Dell's online sales, begun in 1996, exceed $3 million a day.
2000	Online sales reach $50 million.
2000	Problems with supply of Intel chips, Dell stock price falls.
2000	Accelerates investment strategy of acquiring companies in networking and storage.
2000	Introduces computers with open-source Linux operating system.
2002	Launches managed networking services.

Summary

Michael Dell (1965–) was always going to be a winner. After all, how many high school students earn more than their teachers? Dell progressed from selling newspaper subscriptions to selling computers.

Yet it wasn't the product that made him wealthy, it was the way he sold it. The Dell corporation pioneered direct selling of computers. It is also an excellent example of a company succeeding by sticking to its founding principles: build to order, keep low stocks, sell direct, understand your customer. And the Internet was a godsend for Dell. What better way of reaching the global consumer? Dell's success with the direct selling business model has made him the youngest C.E.O. ever of a *Fortune* 500 company.

Life and Career

Michael Dell started his business career as a boy. Born in Houston, Texas, on February 23, 1965, he came across his first commercial opportunity when he was just 12 years old. Like many children his age, Dell was an enthusiastic collector of stamps. Where he differed from his peers was in his approach. Dell didn't trade stamps with his friends at school, he contacted the auction houses and sent them his catalog. When anyone placed an order he went out to find the required stamps. His direct sales method and entrepreneurial acumen were an early sign of what was to come.

Dell brought new focus to his early commercial forays. As a summer job he sold newspaper subscriptions for the *Houston Post*. He quickly realized that calling people at random using the telephone list supplied by the company was not the best way to win new business. Instead he targeted two distinct groups, newlyweds and new homeowners. He obtained lists of applicants for wedding licenses and compiled a list of people who had recently applied for mortgages. He then wrote a personalized message and conducted his own mail campaign. Subscriptions poured in. When the new school term began Dell was asked as part of an economics assignment to complete a tax return. Dell estimated his income at $18,000. His teacher, assuming a mistake, corrected his return by moving the decimal point. She was dismayed to discover that the mistake was hers. Dell earned more than she did.

Contribution

Dell's career really started while he was studying at the University of Texas at Austin. By then the boy who had dismantled and reassembled the motherboard of his Apple II computer at 13 had grown into a fledgling entrepreneur, making money from his computing hobby. Dell would rebuild computers and sell them. Still at college, he started a company called PCs Limited, headquartered in his dorm room. Ignoring his parents' advice to concentrate on his studies, he decided the lure of business was too great and concentrated his efforts on his PC company.

In 1984 the Dell Computer Corporation was founded with just $1,000 in capital. With such a small investment Dell was forced to develop a business model that required little capital outlay. He decided to build to order. This eliminated the need to tie up working capital in inventory. The company carried only around 11 days' worth of inventory—and still does. Compare this to the 45 days' worth of inventory in an average, nondirect distribution channel and the cost savings are obvious. Building to order also allowed Dell to cut out the middleman, retaining more profit and reducing selling costs from a typical 12% of sales to a mere 4–6% of sales.

Low costs and high profit margins are a recipe for an exceptional business. In its first eight years Dell Computer grew at an astonishing annual rate of 80%.

Low costs and high profit margins are a recipe for an exceptional business. In its first eight years Dell Computer grew at an astonishing annual rate of 80%. Even when it slowed down, it was still growing at over 50% a year. By the middle of 2000 its yearly sales were up to $27 billion.

Such a successful business model has attracted its imitators. Companies such as Compaq and Gateway have adopted a similar model. None, however, seems to be able to capture the Dell magic. "There is a popular idea now that if you reduce your inventory and build to order, you'll be just like Dell. Well, that's one part of the puzzle, but there are other parts too," Dell has said. He explains the company's success as "a disciplined approach to understanding how we create value in the PC industry, selecting the right markets, staying focused on a clear business model, and just executing."

Dell has built more than a simple direct selling company. His company's success is closely linked to its relationship with the customer. He knows that the company must not only sell but deliver. Dell Computer has made good use of its direct communication with the consumer. The result? A strong brand, low customer acquisition costs, and high customer loyalty. Dell asks his customers to complain so he can keep the company at the cutting edge of consumer needs. The company once ran an ad that said, "to all our nit-picky, over-demanding, ask-awkward-questions customers. Thank you, and keep up the good work." Few computer companies—or any other company, come to that—would have the confidence to run an ad like this.

With his innate enthusiasm for technology Dell was quick to realize the potential of the Internet. Harnessing its power to reach a wide audience at little cost, the company swiftly moved its selling operations online. "The Internet for us is a dream come true," Dell has said. "It's like zero-variable-cost transaction. The only thing better would be mental telepathy." The figures support the point. Dell began e-commerce in 1996. By 1997 the company's online sales exceeded $3 million a day. The comparable figure for 2000 was $50 million. Half the company's sales are Web-enabled.

When it comes to strategy Dell is no slouch. As the year 2000 approached all the talk in the industry (apart from Y2K worries) was about the imminent demise of the PC. Analysts predicted that PC sales would slump as consumers sought mobile computing solutions. Donald Selkin, chief investment strategist at Joseph Gunnar, the New York securities and banking firm, said of Dell Computer, "I believe its glory days are over; I hate to say it, but it's old technology."

Others believe that Dell's success is founded on a business model rather than a particular product. As if to prove the point, Dell has expanded into areas such as servers and storage network devices. In the quarter ending April 30, 2000, for example, sales of these products accounted for 48% of the systems sales total. There was a 100% increase in sales of storage products, and Dell's machines accounted for 40% of the worldwide industry growth in the server market. Michael Dell says, "I believe we have the right business model for the Internet age. We have a significant lead in dealing direct with customers and suppliers."

In 2000, he indicated that he was accelerating investment into networking and storage companies. He also started to offer Linux open-source operating systems on PCs, broadening the appeal of the range. In 2003, he launched Dell-managed network services to strengthen the company's position in corporate computing. Despite those changes, the company was damaged by a shortage of Intel chips in 2000 and suffered its first stock price fall.

The Dell Computer Corporation had been consistently ranked number two in the world in terms of liquidity, profitability, and growth among all computer systems companies, and number one in the United States. With that sort of performance, many a C.E.O. would be pleased to take a bow. Michael Dell merely describes it as "a great start."

Context and Conclusions

The youngest C.E.O. ever to run a *Fortune* 500 company, Michael Dell has joined the ranks of the most revered entrepreneurs in America. He is credited as the man who took the direct sales model and elevated it to an art form. Dell Computer may not be the biggest company in the world—yet. Nor are its products the most innovative. Yet Dell has built a benchmark company, demonstrating how best to structure a business in order to reap the most reward from new technologies.

For More Information

Book:

Dell, Michael, and Catherine Fredman. *Direct from Dell: Strategies that Revolutionized an Industry*. New York: HarperInformation, 2000.

Web site:

Dell: **www.dell.com**

Walter Elias Disney

1901	Born.
1918	Tries to enlist for World War I, at age 16, but is rejected.
1920	Creates his first original animated characters.
1925	Marries employee Lillian Bounds.
1928	Creates Mickey Mouse.
1937	First feature-length musical animation, *Snow White and the Seven Dwarfs*, premiers.
1940	Disney and over 1,000 staff occupy the Burbank Studios.
1955	Disneyland opens.
1964	Conceives Experimental Prototype Community of Tomorrow (Epcot).
1966	Dies.
1971	Disney World opens in Orlando, Florida, with Epcot to follow in 1982.

Summary

Walt Disney (1901–1966) started with an idea for a cartoon and finished with a film studio. Over a 43-year career in Hollywood, he and his studio won 48 Academy Awards and 7 Emmys as well as a host of other awards. He pioneered the cartoon as an entertainment medium with full-length cartoon features like *Snow White and the Seven Dwarfs*, *Dumbo*, and *Fantasia*. Under his guidance the Disney entertainment machine also produced family film favorites such as *Mary Poppins* and wildlife features such as *The Vanishing Prairie* among its 100-plus films. Today the company that Disney created spans a huge entertainment industry that even his, the most fertile of imaginations, could never have conceived.

Life and Career

Born in Chicago, Illinois, on December 5, 1901, Walt Disney was raised by his parents on a farm near Marceline, Missouri. As a child he showed above average ability. At the tender age of seven he sold sketches to neighbors. His interest in the arts continued at McKinley High School in Chicago where he concentrated on drawing and photography. In the evenings he studied at the Chicago Academy of Fine Arts.

When World War I arrived, Disney tried to enlist in the U.S. Army. Unable to produce his birth certificate, he was rejected as being too young. Instead he traveled to France with the Red Cross and spent his time driving an ambulance decorated with his own cartoons.

Settling in Kansas City after the war, Disney embarked on a career as a cartoonist. In 1920, while working for Kansas City Film Ads, he created his first original animated characters. In May 1922 he started his own company, Laugh-O-Grams. The laughs were short-lived as the company quickly ran into financial difficulties, and Disney decided to skip town. Emboldened by the spirit of youth, he left for Hollywood armed only with his drawing equipment, an idea for a cartoon, and the suit he stood up in.

Contribution

Disney's new venture began where so many great U.S. corporate dreams have started—in a garage. Together with his brother Roy, Disney launched Disney Brothers Studio. He started out with $500 borrowed from his uncle, $200 from Roy, and $2,500 from his parents, who mortgaged their house to find the money. Before long Disney was out of the garage and into the back of a Hollywood real estate office. The first work that he sold was a series of featurettes based on Lewis Carroll's Alice character.

Mickey Mouse was born in 1928. There are several versions of how Disney came up with the idea of the little mouse. The most frequently recounted story is that a flash of inspiration came to him on the way home from a disastrous business meeting in which he was forced to relinquish control of his most successful character at the time—Oswald the Rabbit. Daydreaming on the train to Hollywood, he recalled the mice that had been frequent visitors to his old office. Disney wanted to call his new character Mortimer. His wife— displaying a more acute instinct for marketing—persuaded him to christen his creation Mickey Mouse. Mickey made his debut in the first ever sound cartoon *Steamboat Willie*. It was November 1928 and Disney was just 26.

Disney continued to innovate within the cartoon medium. *Silly Symphonies* introduced Technicolor to cartoons, and in 1937 he premiered the first feature-length musical animation, *Snow White and the Seven Dwarfs*. Disney took a huge risk with *Snow White*. The film was the first of its kind. The $2 million it cost to make was a huge amount in the 1930s, particularly in the middle of the Great Depression. Fortunately for Disney, the gamble paid off, and the studios followed *Snow White* with other full-length animated classics including *Pinocchio*, *Dumbo*, and *Bambi*.

By 1940 Disney and over 1,000 staff had occupied the Burbank Studios. Disney no longer drew any of the studio's output, nor had he done so since the early 1920s. In his own words he was "a little bee. I go from one area to another, and gather pollen and sort of stimulate everyone." The worker bees in Disney's hive weren't always impressed with him. Many resented his reluctance to acknowledge the contribution of the studio artists. Indeed, he wasn't an easy man to work for. Frequently neurotic and obsessive, he imposed strict rules at his studio.

During the 1940s the Disney studio became embroiled in a series of labor disputes. Disney was

The Disneyland theme park in Anaheim, California, was to be a living embodiment of the Disney movies; a magical land where children and adults could mingle with their favorite cartoon stars from the big screen.

also a member of the Motion Picture Alliance for the Preservation of American Ideals—an organization which sought out "communists, radicals, and crackpots" in the movie business. In 1947 he testified before the House Un-American Activities Committee, denouncing a number of employees at his studios as communist sympathizers. The fallout from these events took years to dissipate.

World War II had temporarily sidelined the Walt Disney studio's output. Most of the Disney facilities were given over to the making of propaganda and health films commissioned by the U.S. government. The small nongovernmental output consisted of comedy shorts to pep up morale. After the war Disney varied the studio's productions; cartoons were joined by films combining live action and animation, and "true-life adventures" portraying animals in their natural habitat.

In 1955 Disney took his brand in a new direction with the Disneyland theme park in Anaheim, California; a magical land where children and adults could mingle with their favorite cartoon stars. Disney's investment was $17 million. It was another big risk for him, but Disneyland was a great hit, with Mickey and his friends greeting a million people in its first seven weeks and many millions more since. At the same time, Disney continued to push his products on television. He supplied color television with the *Wonderful World of Color*.

From the mid-1960s onwards one project consumed Disney. The plan was to build a Disney World with a social dimension. Disney was interested in solving the problems afflicting urban living in America. His answer was the Experimental Prototype Community of Tomorrow (Epcot)—the equivalent of a gigantic Ideal Home Exhibition for urban life.

Disney World opened in October 1971. Located in Florida, it was built over 43 square miles and included a theme park, hotel complex, airport, and, 11 years later, the futuristic Epcot Center. Like its Californian relation, Disney World was a success. Disney, however, was not present to witness the fruition of his plans. He died on December 15, 1966.

Context and Conclusions

Walt Disney is an icon of the 20th century and an American folk hero. To many, his name conjures up an image of wholesome homespun entertainment laced with good old-fashioned American family values. While this may have been true of his studio's output, Disney himself was a tough, tenacious, and driven businessman with a sizeable ego.

His innovative work ranged from celebrated animated feature films to futuristic amusement parks. The magic of Disney is, however, nowhere more evident than in the fact that such a complicated and often difficult man could attract such talented individuals to his studios and somehow persuade them to produce their very best work. Critics may carp about his management style, but the vision and drive that spawned a billion dollar international entertainment company was down to one man—Walt Disney.

For More Information

Books:

Byrne, Eleanor, and Martin McQuillan. *Deconstructing Disney*. London: Pluto Press, 1999.

Giroux, Henry A. *The Mouse that Roared: Disney and the End of Innocence*. Lanham, MD: Rowman & Littlefield, 1999.

Nardo, Don. *Walt Disney*. San Diego, CA: Lucent Books, 2000.

Schickel, Richard. *The Disney Version: The Life, Times, Art, and Commerce of Walt Disney*. Chicago: Ivan R. Dee, 1997.

Sherman, Robert B., and Richard M. Sherman. *Walt's Time: From Before to Beyond*. Santa Clarita, CA: Camphor Tree Publishers, 1998.

Web site:

Disney.com: **www.disney.com**

James Buchanan Duke

1856	Born.
1881	Family business starts cigarette production.
1890	The big five tobacco companies merge to form the American Tobacco Company.
1905	Duke brothers start their own hydroelectric generating business, the Southern Power Company (becomes Duke Power in 1927).
1911	The American Tobacco Company is trustbusted and broken up into a new American Tobacco Company, Liggett and Myers, P. Lorillard, and R. J. Reynolds.
1924	Duke Endowment fund established.
1925	Dies.

Summary

James Buchanan Duke (1856–1925), or "Buck," as he was commonly known, was born into a tobacco business dynasty. His father, Washington Duke, had over many years and despite the interruption of the Civil War built up a thriving tobacco business in Orange County, North Carolina. Had it not been for Buck Duke the business might well have remained a successful but parochial tobacco company. Under his guidance, however, W. Duke, Sons and Company swiftly rose to cultivate a global tobacco empire culminating in victory in the "tobacco wars" and Duke's elevation to President of the American Tobacco Company. When the U.S. government dissolved the tobacco trust in 1911, a major setback for Duke, he merely switched his attentions to the energy business. The Southern Power Company, which he founded with his brothers in 1905, subsequently became Duke Power and remains so to this day.

Life and Career

Duke was born near Durham, North Carolina. His education—his academic education, that is—took place at New Garden School in Greensboro, North Carolina, and the Eastman Business College in Poughkeepsie, New York. A more direct form of education took place in the family business. The Duke family farmed and produced tobacco products, chiefly smoking tobacco. Under pressure from local competition, however, they eventually shifted to the production of cigarettes in 1881.

Initially this manufacturing process was performed by hand and was a slow and cumbersome one. Even an expert could roll only four cigarettes a minute. As cigarettes became more popular the tobacco companies sought to mechanize the process. The Allen and Ginter Company of Richmond, Virginia, offered $75,000 to any person who could invent a practical cigarette-making machine. The offer was taken up in 1880 by 18-year-old James Bonsack, who developed a machine of this type. However, Allen and Ginter discarded it after a trial period.

Sensing an opportunity, W. Duke, Sons and Company took up the machine (two, in fact). Once again the invention disappointed, but Buck Duke and a young engineer, William T. O'Brien, were able to alter it and make it reliable, cutting the cost of manufacturing cigarettes in half.

Contribution

At the age of 28 the young Buck Duke was called upon to open a branch of the family business in New York City. Within five years the New York City factory was rolling out half the entire country's total production of cigarettes. His talent for marketing helped. According to later commentators, Duke "was always an aggressive advertiser, devising new and startling methods which dismayed his competitors, and was always willing to spend in advertising a proportion of his profits which seemed appalling to more conservative manufacturers."

Duke wasn't allowed to celebrate his success for long as the "tobacco wars" loomed. Fought between the five principal cigarette manufacturers, the tobacco wars were a bitterly contested struggle for supremacy in the market. The four main combatants were the Allen and Ginter Company of Richmond, the F. S. Kinney Company and the Goodwin Company, both of New York, and William S. Kimball and Company of Rochester. Together with the Duke company these manufacturers produced 90% of North America's cigarettes in the 1880s. Each company thought that it could dominate the market, and an advertising war ensued. When no clear winner emerged, it became apparent that the most sensible approach would be to staunch the flow of spending and merge the five companies.

Although James B. Duke founded a power company that still survives to this day, as well as an endowment trust that has handed out billions of dollars to its beneficiaries, he is best remembered for the part he played in establishing the tobacco industry.

When the smoke cleared in 1890, the five companies had gone. In their place stood the result of the merger—the American Tobacco Company—with Duke at its helm as President. This tobacco giant became known as the "tobacco trust." During the following decade the victorious Duke steered the American Tobacco Company to global dominance.

In 1901 he visited Britain to thwart the transatlantic competition. In the space of a few days he bid for both Players and Ogdens, two large cigarette manufacturers. He succeeded in buying Ogdens, which prompted the formation of the Imperial Tobacco Company to fight off Duke's unwanted attentions. Duke in turn formed the British American Tobacco company.

Eventually, the American Tobacco Company fell victim to its own burning ambition. In 1911 the United States Supreme Court, in the trustbusting spirit of the times, ordered the dissolution of the tobacco trust as a "combination in restraint of trade." At the time of its break-up, American Tobacco had 80% of the market and revenues of some $325 million. From the ashes of the tobacco trust grew four major tobacco corporations: a new American Tobacco Company, Liggett and Myers, P. Lorillard, and R. J. Reynolds.

While Buck Duke was conquering the tobacco markets, his eldest brother, Benjamin Newton, was wrapping up the textile market. The Duke family had been involved in textiles as far back as 1892. As the textile empire grew, so too did the need for cheap power. This encouraged the Dukes, including Buck, to start up their own hydroelectric generating business, the Southern Power Company (subsequently renamed Duke Power), in 1905. As with everything else the Dukes touched, the energy business became very successful and before long was supplying electricity to over 300 cotton mills, plus factories, towns, and cities in the Piedmont region of North and South Carolina.

Duke was an ardent Methodist and conducted his professional life in a manner befitting his religious beliefs. He was the richest member of the Duke dynasty, and in later life he embarked on a philanthropic spree. In 1924 he established the Duke Endowment as a permanent trust fund. The prime beneficiary of the fund was Trinity College, a Methodist-related institution founded in part by Duke's father. A new university was built around Trinity College and renamed Duke University. The Duke Endowment, with offices in Charlotte, North Carolina, remains to this day one of the largest foundations in the United States. It has distributed more than one billion dollars.

James B. Duke died in New York City on October 10, 1925, and is interred on the campus of Duke University.

Context and Conclusions

Although James B. Duke founded a power company that still survives to this day, as well as an endowment trust that has handed out billions of dollars to its beneficiaries, he is best remembered for the part he played in establishing the tobacco industry. With the benefit of hindsight, it is clear that Buck Duke was successful in producing and marketing what turned out to be a pernicious product. Even so, he was a tenacious and formidable businessman with considerable marketing acumen.

Duke summed it up: "I have succeeded in business not because I have more natural ability than many people who have not succeeded, but because I have applied myself harder and stuck to it longer."

For More Information
Book:

Nall, James O. *The Tobacco Night Riders of Kentucky and Tennessee, 1905–1909*. Kuttawa, KY: McClanahan Publishing House, 1991.

Web sites:

The Duke Endowment Non-Profit Foundation: **www.dukeendowment.org**
Duke Energy®: **www.duke-energy.com**

George Eastman

1854	Born.
1874	Starts work at the Rochester Savings Bank on $15 per week.
1878	Takes up photography.
1880	Patents a dry plate and a machine for mass-producing it.
1881	Takes Henry A. Strong as partner.
1884	The Eastman Dry Plate and Film Company incorporated.
1885	Advertises his revolutionary new photographic film.
1888	The word Kodak registered as a trademark.
1899	"Wage dividend" strategy implemented.
1919	Hands one-third of his company holdings—$10 million—to his employees.
1932	Dies.

Summary

"You push the button, we do the rest." The well-known advertising phrase was coined by George Eastman (1854–1932), the U.S. industrialist who brought photography to the masses. Before Eastman's intervention, photography was the province of a small number of specialists who could both understand and physically maneuver the cumbersome technical machinery necessary to take a small picture. Eastman reduced photography to a simple process, making it accessible to all. In addition to his role as an innovator, he brought enlightened management practices to his company, the Eastman Kodak Company—practices that were far ahead of their time. During his tenure the Eastman photographic empire grew from one assistant to over 13,000 employees and from a small room to the 55-acre, 95-building Kodak Park Works in Rochester, New York.

Life and Career

The youngest of three children, Eastman was born in the village of Waterville, 20 miles southwest of Utica, in upstate New York. Aged five, Eastman moved with his family to Rochester. His father died unexpectedly, leaving the Eastman family in financial straits.

Finishing school at 14, Eastman was forced to get a job to contribute to the family finances. After a period with an insurance firm, he decided to study accounting at home in the evenings to increase his chances of earning more than $5 a week. In 1874, five years after starting in insurance, his studies paid off when he was offered a position as a junior clerk at the Rochester Savings Bank on a weekly salary of over $15.

Contribution

Eastman's life-changing moment came at age 24. He was planning a vacation in Santo Domingo when a colleague suggested making a photographic record of the trip. Eastman bought the equipment needed to take a photograph using state-of-the-art wet-plate technology. This comprised a camera the size of a 21-inch computer monitor and tripod, together with the glass plates on which the images were captured, and the chemicals, glass tanks, plate holder, and other paraphernalia required for developing them. There was also a tent in which the developing had to take place before the wet plates with the photographic emulsion on could dry out. To learn how to use all the equipment cost $5—a week's wages for Eastman only a few years earlier.

Eastman never made it to Santo Domingo. Instead he became obsessed with photography. Before long he was busy perfecting a dry-plate process in which a photographic plate was covered with a veneer of a special gelatin emulsion. This emulsion remained sensitive even when it was dry, enabling the plate to be exposed whenever the photographer wished, unlike the wet-plate process in which the print had to be developed immediately. It was an idea that Eastman had read about in a British magazine. He took the idea, perfected it, and in 1880, after three years of experimentation, patented a dry plate and a machine for mass-producing it. He gave up his job at the bank and at the beginning of 1881 took on a partner, Henry A. Strong.

Quick to recognize the commercial possibilities of his innovation, Eastman leased a building on State Street in Rochester and began to turn out dry plates for other photographers. Early on the company was faced with a crisis when the dry plates provided to dealers proved defective. Eastman recalled all the faulty plates and replaced them with good ones. "Making good on those plates took our last dollar," he later said. "But what we had left was more important—reputation." In 1884 the Eastman Dry Plate and Film Company was incorporated.

It dawned on Eastman that he could do more than make life easier for professional photographers. He could, in his own words, "make the camera as convenient as the pencil."

When Eastman perfected the transparent roll film and roll holder, the days of cumbersome plate photography were numbered. Photography was at last within reach of the amateur. Eastman took a hand in all aspects of promoting his new photographic film. He wrote the ads and came up with the famous slogan: "You push the button, we do the rest." He even dreamed up the word Kodak, registering the trademark in 1888, and devised the yellow color scheme associated with it. Its origins have been a subject of speculation ever since, but Eastman appears to have invented the name out of thin air. "I devised the name myself," he told his biographer. "The letter 'K' had been a favorite with me—it seems a strong incisive sort of letter. It became a question of trying out a great number of combinations of letters that made words starting and ending with K. The word Kodak is the result."

The KODAK camera was released in 1888 and before long KODAK advertising was inescapable. One of the first electric advertising signs in Piccadilly, London, bore the legend KODAK. In 1892 the company was renamed the Eastman Kodak Company of New York.

Eastman built his business using an enlightened humanitarian management style far removed from that of some of his contemporaries. In 1899 he distributed to his entire work force a substantial sum from his own pocket. It was the first act of Eastman's "wage dividend" strategy, a plan to reward employees in proportion to the dividend paid on the company stock. Continuing in the same vein, in 1919 he handed a third of his company holdings—worth some $10 million—to his employees. At the same time he instituted retirement annuities, life insurance, and disability benefits.

George Eastman's philanthropy extended beyond the confines of his corporation. The Massachusetts Institute of Technology (MIT) was particularly favored as two of its graduates, Frank Lovejoy and Darragh de Lancey, had become valued assistants to Eastman. He gave the institute $20 million under the name of "Mr. Smith"—and for years after there was intense speculation over the identity of the mysterious benefactor. Eastman was confident enough of his anonymity to join in a toast to Mr. Smith at an annual MIT alumni dinner.

In his final years Eastman was plagued by disability resulting from damage to the lower spinal cord. His inability to lead an active life frustrated him so much that he shot himself on March 14, 1932. He was 77.

Context and Conclusions

Eastman took a cumbersome scientific process and turned it into a commercial mass-market product. Through his pioneering and innovative work on photographic technology he brought the means of capturing the moment on film to the general public at a price it could afford. Eastman was also the father of a particular type of "trust what's in the box" branding. With its suggestion that consumers simply need to provide their imagination to complement its technology, Microsoft's "Where do you want to go today?", for instance, is a modern echo of that first Kodak promise, as is "Intel Inside." Both draw on Eastman's early inspiration that consumers could be persuaded to trust the brand to take care of the technological side, leaving them free to personalize the product to suit their own lives.

An enlightened manager, Eastman introduced business practices well ahead of his time.

Eastman's slogan captured a turning point in the history of consumerism unlike any other. Previously consumers had understood—even if only at a rudimentary level—how the products they bought worked. But in the late 19th and early 20th century, an explosion of new and technically complex inventions—which included the telephone, the electric light bulb, and film processing—changed the situation forever.

An enlightened manager, Eastman introduced business practices well ahead of his time. He recognized the importance of crisis management when faced with complaints from customers. He also understood that acknowledging the contributions of the work force with remuneration above and beyond their basic salary would in turn benefit the company. Few companies the size of Eastman Kodak were forward-thinking enough to implement employee stock ownership programs and the variety of employment benefits he instituted.

For More Information

Books:

Ackerman, Carl W., and Edwin R. Seligman. *George Eastman: Founder of Kodak and the Photography Business*. Boston: Houghton Mifflin Co., 1930.

Brayer, Elizabeth. *George Eastman: A Biography*. Baltimore, MD: Johns Hopkins University Press, 1996.

Collins, Douglas. *The Story of Kodak*. New York: H.N. Abrams, 1990.

Web site:

Kodak.com: **www.kodak.com**

Thomas Alva Edison

1847	Born.
1854	Family moves to Port Huron, Michigan.
1859–62	Sells newspapers on the Grand Trunk Railway.
1863	Works as a telegraph operator; travels across the United States.
1868	Patents his first invention, an electric vote recorder.
1869	Takes up inventing full time, moves to New York City, and starts his first business, making telegraph equipment.
1870	Opens a factory and laboratory in Newark, New Jersey.
1874	Develops a quadruplex system for the telegraph.
1876	Moves to Menlo Park, New Jersey.
1877	Invents the phonograph.
1879	Develops the first commercially viable electric light bulb.
1882	Opens Pearl Street Central Power Station in New York City.
1889	Forms Edison General Electric, and invents the kinetograph (an early motion picture camera).
1892	Edison General Electric merges with Thomson-Houston to create General Electric. Edison sells his interest.
1910	Invents a nickel–iron–alkaline storage battery.
1931	Dies.

Summary

"Genius is 1% inspiration and 99% perspiration," declared Thomas Alva Edison (1847–1931), the inventor and entrepreneur. It was a maxim he clearly lived by. Unlike many inventors, Edison was a great businessman. By the end of his extraordinary career he had accumulated 1,093 U.S. and 1,300 foreign patents. The inventor of the phonograph and the incandescent light bulb also found time to start up or control 13 major companies. Directly or indirectly, his endeavors led to the creation of well-known corporations like General Electric and RCA. Consolidated Edison is still listed on the New York Stock Exchange.

Life and Career

Thomas Edison was born in the town of Milan, Erie County, Ohio, of Dutch and Scottish extraction. The youngest of seven children, he was effectively an only child since his siblings were much older. His schoolteacher mother was loath to let the young Edison out of her sight and educated him mainly at home.

He was a voracious reader. Newton's *Principia Mathematica*, Parker's *Natural and Experimental Philosophy*, and Gibbon's *Decline and Fall of the Roman Empire* had all been devoured before he reached the age of 12. It was a pattern that continued as Edison embarked on a lifetime of discovery and self-education.

From an early age he displayed an entrepreneurial spirit. When, due to economic hardship, the family was forced to move to Port Huron, near Detroit, he sold vegetables from his home garden, operated a newspaper concession on the Grand Trunk Railroad, and eventually printed his own paper, the *Grand Trunk Herald*. In his spare time he conducted chemical experiments. In one particular episode, he set fire to a train's boxcar. This mishap aroused such anger in the guard, who had to put out the fire and burned his hands in the process, that he struck Edison on the ear, bursting his eardrum and leaving him partially deaf.

Contribution

Telegraphy turned out to be the catalyst for Edison's greatness. He was a natural with the Morse key, becoming one of the fastest transcribers of his day. As a night-duty telegrapher, he was required to key the number six every hour to confirm he was still manning the wire. Instead he invented a machine that automatically keyed the number and he spent the nights indulging himself at local bars. Fired from a succession of jobs, he crossed the United States working as a freelance telegrapher, finally coming to rest in New York. He had by this time filed his first patent—an automatic vote recorder for the Massachusetts Legislature.

It was in New York that Edison formed his first partnership, with Frank L. Pope, a noted telegraphic engineer, to exploit the potential of their inventions. The partnership was subsequently absorbed by Gold & Stock, a company controlled by Marshall Lefferts, former President of the American Telegraph Company, who paid $20,000 to the two partners for this privilege. Recognizing Edison's ingenuity, Lefferts conducted a side deal with him, securing Edison's independent patents for the then princely sum of $30,000.

In 1870, with the benefit of some financial security, Edison hired the talents of Charles Batchelor, an English mathematician, and John Kruesi, a Swiss machinist. He signed patent agreements with Gold & Stock and Western Union, took on a business partner, William Unger, moved into a four-story building at Ward Street, Newark, New Jersey, and started inventing on a grand scale. The fertile mix of minds at Ward Street quickly produced a stock printer, quadruplex telegraphy, and a machine to enable the rapid decoding of Morse.

Domestic life did little to change his work habits. Indeed he appeared to work even longer hours.

By 1876 the 29-year-old Edison had 45 inventions to his name and was worth some $400,000. Domestic life did little to change his work habits. Indeed he appeared to work even longer hours. Edison was notorious for his devotion to seeking a solution to the problem in hand. Not only would he work, sleep, and eat at the company premises, but he would lock the lab doors and tell his staff they were staying until they arrived at an answer.

The 1870s were the most creative phase of Edison's life. Needing to expand his premises he moved into buildings at Menlo Park, New Jersey. It was there that he and his team perfected the phonograph. The patents were filed in December 1877, but developing a commercially viable product proved difficult. Finally the phonograph came to market in a selection of models from large to miniature, motordriven or handcranked. The product was a huge success—so much so that Edison's creditors began creeping out of the woodwork.

Barely pausing to draw breath, Edison continued to invent. In early 1877 he began experimenting with incandescent filaments and glass bulbs. Some time before developing the light bulb, he managed to persuade a consortium that he could design a marketable lighting system based on such a product. As a result he signed a rights and remuneration agreement that laid the foundation for the Edison Electric Light Company.

In reality he was far from developing this product. Time passed with Edison making favorable noises about progress while actually making little headway in the lab. Feeling the pressure, at one point he retired to an understairs closet, took a dose of morphine, and slept for 36 hours.

It was on Wednesday, November 12, 1879 that Edison finally lit a bulb that lasted long enough to be considered of commercial value. It lasted for 40 hours 20 minutes and within two months Edison had extended its lifetime to 600 hours. Countless visitors trekked to Menlo Park to gaze in wonder at the lights that lit the roadway. Sadly, what followed for Edison was not the triumph of invention but a period of protracted patent litigation that lasted over ten years.

The invention of the light bulb and the formation of the Edison Electric Light Company mark the pinnacle of Edison's achievements. In the years that followed, a succession of innovations emerged: DC generators, the first electric lighting system, electrical metering systems, alkaline storage batteries, cement manufacturing equipment, synchronized sound and moving pictures, and submarine detection by sound. His labs attracted a great number of prodigious minds, most notably Nikola Tesla, famed for his work on the Tesla coil and AC induction motors. The wizard of Menlo Park, however, never quite recaptured the brilliance of his earlier years. Edison died, working to the last, on October 18, 1931.

Context and Conclusions

Part of Edison's genius lay in the realization that innovation alone was insufficient for commercial success. Edison focused on creating a commercially viable product. To do so, he assembled a team of brilliant minds at Menlo Park. In effect he created the first product research lab—a forerunner of facilities such as the celebrated Xerox PARC at Palo Alto, California. It was a practical and commercial approach to invention that proved immensely successful.

Edison's pragmatism also extended to patenting his ideas. He understood the value of intellectual property and the importance of being able to assert ownership of ideas.

A legend in his own lifetime, his achievements were acknowledged shortly before his death in a nationwide celebration attended by luminaries such as President Hoover, Henry Ford, John Rockefeller, and George Eastman. He remains an inspiration for inventors and entrepreneurs to this day.

For More Information

Books:

Baldwin, Neil. *Edison, Inventing the Century*. New York: Hyperion, 1995.

Israel, Paul. *Edison: A Life of Invention*. New York: John Wiley, 1998.

Jenkins, Reese V., et al., eds. *The Papers of Thomas A. Edison*. Baltimore, MD: Johns Hopkins University Press, 1989.

Josephson, Matthew. *Edison: A Biography*. New York: John Wiley, 1992.

Millard, Andre. *Edison and the Business of Innovation*. Baltimore, MD: Johns Hopkins University Press, 1990.

Web site:

Con Edison, Inc.: **www.conedison.com**

Michael Eisner

1942	Born.
1960	Starts at Denison University, Granville, Ohio.
1966	Works with Barry Diller at ABC.
1969	Joins Diller as Director of feature films and program development.
1971	Becomes head of daytime and children's programming at ABC.
1976	Becomes President of Paramount.
1984	Appointed C.E.O. of Disney Productions.
1987	*Three Men and a Baby* grosses over $100 million at the box office.
1992	Disneyland Paris opens.
1994	Katzenberg leaves. Shelves Disney America plans.
2000	Disney posts profit of $1.9 billion on revenues of $25 billion.
2002	Attacks IT industry for failing to adequately protect digital content.

Summary

Michael Eisner, Chairman and C.E.O. of Disney, is what the famous company lacked for many years: a true successor to Walt Disney himself. The big cheese that made the mouse roar, he breathed life into a moribund Disney when he joined it in 1984, with his own personal team of "mouseketeers," to work alongside President and C.O.O. Frank Wells. Eisner and Wells resurrected the magic kingdom. Eisner's insight was that Disney should be in the family entertainment business in all its manifestations, so the Disney brand was stretched to encompass a mountain of merchandising, stores, books, videos, games, movies, and theme parks. His other claim to fame is the size of his paycheck.

Born during World War II, Eisner got an early taste of the entertainment business when, still a student, he spent three months at NBC studios. With the help of his father's contacts, he obtained a job as a clerk at NBC. Next he worked at ABC (a company he later bought) with Barry Diller. In 1976, aged 34, he followed Diller to Paramount as President. Together with young, thrusting executives such as Jeffrey Katzenberg, Eisner helped make Paramount a hit factory. Katzenberg followed him when he moved to Disney to rejuvenate the ailing studio and make it an entertainment powerhouse once again. In the mid-1990s, however, the Disney magic lost its sparkle temporarily as Eisner contended with executive fallouts and the aborted Disney America project, and had heart bypass surgery. But by 2000 the company was back on track, and Eisner's status as one of the highest paid executives in the United States looked to be deserved.

Life and Career

Michael Eisner was born in Mt. Kisco, New York on March 7, 1942. An affluent family, the Eisners lived in a large apartment on Park Avenue on the Upper East Side of Manhattan, where Michael attended a local private school, Allen-Stevenson. More interested in sports than studies, he soon discovered he had a strong competitive drive and preferred to be a leader rather than a follower. He displayed a self-confident streak that belied his young age and that remained with him all his life. Attending a reunion of a summer camp many years later, he arrived at the hotel, joined the others, sat down for the feast, and even sang the camp song at the appropriate moment. It was only when the Director of his camp walked into the room, sidled over to him, and explained that he was attending the wrong reunion, that Eisner realized self-confidence could sometimes be misplaced.

After Allen-Stevenson came boarding school, and then, in 1960, Eisner started at Denison University in Granville, Ohio. The dissection class put paid to his idea of studying medicine so he switched to English as his major. During one summer vacation he managed to wangle a job at NBC—his father knew Robert Sarnoff, the son of RCA founder, David Sarnoff. Although he spent his three months at NBC as nothing more than a runner, working on the sets of shows such as *The Price Is Right*, he fell in love with the entertainment business.

Contribution

Despite his persistence and enthusiasm, however, and help of his father's contacts, Eisner struggled to find a job in entertainment. Eventually, he was offered the job of a clerk for $65 a week at NBC. He accepted immediately. Shortly afterward, he took a weekend job at WNBC radio as traffic researcher. His job was to "borrow" other radio stations' traffic reports and pass them on to the morning DJ. Eisner was in no position to argue about the ethics of the situation and did as he was told, although he occasionally embellished his traffic bulletins with imaginary streets named after past girlfriends.

By 1966 he had obtained a job working as Barry Diller's assistant at ABC (Diller was to become one of the most respected executives in the entertainment business). ABC proved an excellent training ground for the ambitious Eisner, who became involved in all aspects of the television business and quickly learned that hit TV shows were like gold dust. Eisner estimates the odds of achieving even an average success at only one in 4,000. In 1968 he turned down a job offer from the advertising agency Foote, Cone, & Belding, but recommended one of his superiors, who landed the job. Eisner promptly took up the position that had been vacated.

Diller, meanwhile, had been promoted to work on a partnership with Universal Studios to produce made-for-television movies. In 1969 Eisner joined him as Director of feature films and program development. In 1971 Eisner became head of daytime and children's programming at ABC. With ABC's daytime ratings languishing at the bottom of the table, it was a win–win situation for him. Sure enough, daytime television improved considerably under his control, so that, several Eisner-instigated shows later, he was back with prime-time development, this time as vice President.

In 1976 Eisner decided to move out to Los Angeles. After a string of successes, including *Happy Days* and *Starsky & Hutch*, he was headhunted by Barry Diller, now at Paramount, and offered the job of President of Paramount. He was only 34.

Between 1977 and 1982, profits at Paramount increased from $30 million to over $100 million, largely due to the new culture of aggressive creative risktaking introduced under Diller and Eisner. Hit TV shows such as *Taxi* and *Mork & Mindy*, together with movies such as *Saturday Night Fever*, *Elephant Man*, *Grease*, *Star Trek*, *Ordinary People*, *Airplane*, and *Raiders of the Lost Ark* brought the dollars flooding into the Paramount coffers. In 1984, after some political infighting at Paramount, Eisner, by now one of the top movie executives in the country, moved on to become C.E.O. of Disney.

When Eisner joined Disney in 1984 the company was in the doldrums. He set about transforming the declining movie and theme park company into an entertainment giant. Key to this transformation was an injection of new blood in the form of Jeffrey Katzenberg, still in his early thirties.

Under the labels Touchstone Pictures and Hollywood Pictures, Katzenberg greenlighted a string of hit feature films including *Down and Out in Beverly Hills* and *Three Men and a Baby*, a movie that grossed over $100 million at the box office, the first Disney movie ever to do so. Of their first 17 movies, 15 made money.

Eisner, with his tremendous experience in television, also rejuvenated Disney's TV output with top ten shows such as *Ellen* and *Home Improvement*. Eisner and Disney were attacking on all fronts. Eisner repackaged classic Disney animation for home video. Titles such as *Bambi, Cinderella,* and the more modern *Aladdin* and *The Lion King* elevated Disney to the number one Hollywood studio in home video sales.

By the early 1990s Disney, now trading as the more commercial sounding Walt Disney Company rather than Walt Disney Productions, was posting revenues of over $5 billion and profits close to $1 billion. The days of Disney being built on the fortunes of a small mouse were long gone. From 1985 right through to 1990 the company posted record profits for 20 quarters in a row.

It was only in the mid-1990s that the Disney magic began to lose a little of its sparkle. Although Eisner pulled off a major coup when he acquired the ABC broadcast network, this was counterbalanced by a spectacular and acrimonious falling-out with his longtime co-worker, both at Paramount and Disney, Katzenberg. This followed Katzenberg's departure to found DreamWorks with industry luminaries Steven Spielberg and David Geffen. Eisner got angry, reportedly, because of leaks of financial information to the media, which he attributed to Katzenberg. Katzenberg in turn claimed he was owed substantial bonuses, worth several hundreds of millions of dollars. In court, Eisner admitted he might have said of the diminutive Katzenberg, "I hate the little midget," and that he believed his one-time associate had a "dark side." The dispute rumbled on for several years before it was settled privately. It was an unfortunate end to what had been such a profitable partnership. A little later, Eisner had more executive problems when he hired Mike Ovitz, talent agent, as his number two, only to see him depart just over a year later.

On top of the problems following Katzenberg's departure, Eisner also had to handle the ongoing saga of Disney America. The plan was to build a park that provided a historical experience focusing on America's past. The problem was the proposed site for the venture outside the town of Haymarket, Virginia. What Eisner hadn't factored into his decision to locate Disney America in Virginia was the proximity of some of the richest families in the United States. Only hours after being publicly announced in November 1993, the project was facing a barrage of criticism. Up against some of most powerful and effective lobbyists in the country, Eisner eventually had to back down, despite the money and time spent on the planning. Then, to cap it all, he had to undergo heart bypass surgery.

Eisner's troubles were reflected in the balance sheet; profits dropped 28% from 1998 to 1999. But by 2000 Disney was back on track with a profit of $1.9 billion on revenues of $25 billion. And Eisner benefited personally from Disney's recovery; his base salary rose from $750,000 to $1 million, securing his position as one of the highest paid C.E.O.s in the United States.

Eisner watched the growth of digital media distribution with some trepidation, fearing that it could harm revenues and profitability. In 2002, he provoked anger by suggesting to a Senate Committee that IT and software companies had failed to provide adequate protection for digital media because "piracy helps sell computers."

Context and Conclusions

Michael Eisner has had three extraordinary careers. At ABC and Paramount he earned a reputation as a producer of hit shows. He carried that reputation to Disney and added to it by demonstrating an ability to revitalize a corporation. His instinct for what an audience wants was honed in the screening rooms of ABC where he nurtured hit shows such as *Happy Days*. And by surrounding himself with the best talent in the industry, he managed to stay in touch with viewer tastes. Hollywood can be incestuous, backbiting, and an extremely difficult environment to work in. It is testimony to Eisner's political skills and entertainment instincts that he has managed to stay at the top for so long and recover from potentially knockout blows such as the abortive Disney America scheme.

CLOSE BUT NO CIGAR
DAVID GEFFEN

Very close in this case, since David Geffen is undoubtedly one of the major powers in Hollywood. Like Mike Ovitz, Geffen started out in the mailroom at the William Morris talent agency. Working his way up, he made big money boosting the careers of rock acts such as The Eagles and Jackson Browne. At Warner Brothers, he discovered that life in a big studio didn't suit him, but he still managed to persuade them to help finance his own record label, Geffen Records, which had hits with artists such as Aerosmith, Guns 'n Roses, and Cher. At the same time, he enjoyed success with the Geffen Film Company and movies such as *After Hours* and *Beetlejuice*. He sold his record company to MCA. It in turn was sold to Matsushita, at which time his stock was worth some $700 million. In 1994 Geffen made his biggest claim yet for media moguldom when he linked up with Jeffrey Katzenberg and Steven Spielberg to found DreamWorks SKG, a new Hollywood studio.

For More Information

Books:

Eisner, Michael, and Tony Schwartz. *Work in Progress*. New York: Random House, 1988.

Grover, Ron. *The Disney Touch: How a Daring Management Team Revived an Entertainment Empire*. Homewood, IL: Business One Irwin, 1991.

Flower, Joe. *Prince of the Magic Kingdom: Michael Eisner and the Re-making of Disney*. New York: John Wiley, 1991.

Larry Ellison

1944	Born.
1964	Leaves University of Illinois, attends University of Chicago.
1969	Moves to Berkeley, California.
1977	Cofounds Oracle with Bob Miner and Ed Oates.
1986	Oracle I.P.O. Company revenue approximately $55 million.
1989	Oracle revenue approximately $571 million.
1990	Oracle hits financial difficulties.
Mid-1990s	Focuses Oracle on Internet-related products.
1998	Wins Sydney–Hobart boat race.
1999	Launches first electronic exchange for the automotive industry.
2000	Oracle praised for financial performance.
	Oracle admits spying on Microsoft.
2001	Proposes Oracle solution for controversial national identity card scheme.
	Loses position as the United States's second richest man.
2002	Oracle launches first fully-integrated relational database.

Summary

The man behind Oracle, Larry Ellison (1944–), was responsible for his company's transformation from a small software company in the 1970s to what is now a new economy, Net centric powerhouse. Raised on Chicago's tough South Side, Ellison was a self-taught computer programmer. Traveling out West, he struck the software equivalent of gold when he developed the Oracle database program.

At its I.P.O. in 1986, Oracle's revenues were some $55 million. Three years later that figure was $571 million. The company's early success owes a good deal to Ellison's leadership. At the time critics carped about his playboy lifestyle, flashy cars, and girlfriends, embellishing their stories with tales of his owning fighter aircraft. Ellison, in the meantime, worked like a driven man, making important decisions such as dropping his company's flagship product and betting the future of Oracle on the Internet. In 2001, his reputation was damaged when he admitted spying on Microsoft and he provoked further controversy when he proposed a national identity card scheme after the September 11th terrorist attack. Despite that, it's a brave person who bets against Ellison, the samurai warrior of Silicon Valley.

Life and Career

Born in 1944, Lawrence J. Ellison's childhood dream was to become an architect. Gifted at math and science, he attended the University of Chicago to study math; there he taught himself computer programming. Then, like another computer billionaire, Bill Gates, Ellison dropped out of college and headed in 1969 for California and the nascent computer industry. Armed with little more than his self-taught computing skills, Ellison took a job as a computer programmer.

Contribution

It was Ellison's good fortune to obtain a job with Amdahl. Founded by Gene Amdahl, the company was 45% owned by Fujitsu, so Ellison had the opportunity to travel to Japan on business. It was a trip that was to change his perspective on life and have a long-lasting influence on his approach to business.

Japanese culture, Ellison realized, was fundamentally different from that in the United States. He was intrigued by the apparent contradictions: the Japanese were aggressive yet incredibly polite; they were arrogant yet humble. He was also interested in the emphasis they placed on the group rather than the individual. This attitude, the antithesis of the individualistic, entrepreneurial ideals he had grown up with, pervaded Japanese corporations and society. Ellison's observations of Japan made a profound impression on him.

In 1976, IBM developed SQL (sequel), a computer language for accessing databases. Popular opinion at that time said that database programs were not commercially viable. Ellison didn't agree. He was quick to recognize the commercial possibilities. If he moved fast, he thought he could beat IBM to market with a database product.

Ellison was not a man to doubt his instincts, and he sought financing for a new company that would specialize in databases. Venture capitalists were less enthusiastic than he was about his business prospects. "They wouldn't even meet with you," said Ellison of prospective investors. "They would just leave you waiting in the waiting room for 45 minutes, until you finally got the idea they were not going to see you. And then the receptionist would search your briefcase to make sure you were not stealing copies of *Business Week* from the coffee table. We were persona non grata in the venture capital community."

Frustrated, Ellison and his partners Bob Miner and Ed Oates invested $2,000 of their own money in the startup. The company was named System Development Laboratories and was later renamed Oracle Corporation. The company's first product was two years in the making, with Ellison and colleagues supporting themselves by consulting.

Once news got out about Oracle's new software, the company never looked back. Profitable from day one, in the period up to 2000 the company lost money in only one quarter: 1990. Its rate of growth was incredible. When Oracle was publicly floated in March 1986, revenues were some $55 million. By 1989, when the company moved to its new campus-style location at Redwood Shores, California, revenues were approximately $571 million.

Oracle's success has been built on the strength of the product, coupled with an aggressive pursuit of market share. Ellison recalls that his attitude to competitors was informed by his experiences in Japan. On a business trip he got talking to a Japanese executive about competition. "We believe," said the executive, "that our competitors are stealing the rice out of the mouths of our children. In Japan we think anything less than 100% market share is not enough. In Japan we believe it is not sufficient that I succeed; everyone else must fail."

After recounting the tale to a newspaper reporter, Ellison was greeted with a story featuring his picture accompanied by the words "It's not sufficient that I succeed; everyone else must fail." Whether or not he needed any lessons in competitive drive is a moot point: his competitive instincts appear to be well developed. Oracle has for the most part shown itself unwilling to coexist peacefully with its rivals and has capitalized on its market position.

One element of corporate makeup Ellison did adopt from the Japanese is his fervor for building a team culture. He has said that he would "never hire anybody I wouldn't enjoy having lunch with three times a week." If everyone at Oracle gets along, Ellison figures there will then be less destructive internal conflict. This is one of his greatest strengths: an innate understanding of what motivates people and makes them tick.

In his private life Ellison has always liked to live life to the full. He has flown fast planes, driven fast cars, and sailed fast yachts. He is a world-class yachtsman and was first across the line in the Sydney–Hobart race in 1998—a race in which six lives were lost due to the appalling weather. Ellison's playboy lifestyle has proved a target for critics, who have accused him of neglecting his corporate responsibilities, but this is to underestimate Ellison's commitment to his business empire. His shrewd judgment is illustrated by his decision in the mid-1990s to refocus the company away from its flagship client-server software products to products that can run via a browser over the Internet. Ellison virtually bet the future of the company on this vision: "If the Internet turns out not to be the future of computing, we're toast. But if it is, we're golden."

To date, Oracle9i—the company's new Internet database software—has sold well, and the company has continued to launch a series of "firsts." In 1999, Oracle was involved in establishing the first industry electronic business exchange—Autoxchange. 2000 saw the first Internet file system, 2001 the first database with a built-in web server, and 2002 the first fully-integrated relational database. However, "off the field" incidents have also accompanied Ellison. In 2000, the company admitted to employing private investigators to spy on Microsoft and, in 2001 following the September 11th terrorist attacks, provoked controversy by proposing detailed recommendations for a national identity card scheme.

Although Oracle was hit along with other technical companies by the slowdown in 2000–2001, Ellison continues to remain one of the richest men in the world.

Context and Conclusions

Ellison is one of a select band of first-wave computer tycoons. In the same way that technological advances made the likes of Edison, Schwab, Gillette, and Ford rich at the beginning of the 20th century, so computers and the Internet have created a small group of billionaires in the final decades of the century. Ellison is in the mold of those earlier moguls. Critics have accused him of arrogance. They fail to appreciate the self-belief required to succeed. Ellison, like one of his heroes, Winston Churchill, is a man with the courage of his own convictions, the courage to stand alone and ignore conventional wisdom. It is not that he is beyond humility—he has, for example, learned much from Japanese culture and incorporated that knowledge into Oracle. But Larry Ellison is a man who sees his self-belief as integral to his success.

For More Information
Book:

Wilson, Mike. *The Difference between God & Larry Ellison? God Doesn't Think He's Larry Ellison: Inside Oracle Corporation*. New York: HarperTrade, 1998.

Web site:
Oracle Corporation: **www.oracle.com**

Enzo Ferrari

1898	Born.
1918	Nearly dies in flu epidemic.
1929	Starts Scuderia Ferrari.
1933	Clients Alfa Romeo withdraw from racing.
1937	Alfa Romeo sets up own racing team.
1939	Ferrari severs relationship with Alfa Romeo.
1947	Creates own racing car, the 12-cylinder 125S.
1969	Sells 50% interest in business to Fiat.
1988	Fiat increases stake to 90%.
1988	Dies.

Summary

The man who turned his eponymous sports car into a billion-dollar brand was forced to abandon his education by the outbreak of World War I and to take a job in a local workshop. But, having been fascinated by racing cars from the age of ten, Enzo Ferrari realized a dream when he joined a racing team, first as a test driver, then as the racing driver. In 1929 he started his own company, Scuderia Ferrari, to provide services to other racing teams. It gradually evolved, however, into a racing team in its own right.

After World War II, with the Scuderia factory relocated to Marinello, the 50-year-old Ferrari set about designing and manufacturing his own car. The first model, the 12-cylinder 125S, rolled off the production line in 1947. There followed a period of unrivaled success both in Grand Prix racing and in sports car manufacture. Ferrari would no doubt have liked to leave his business to his son, but, tragically, Dino Ferrari died young. In 1969 Ferrari sold a 50% interest in his business to Fiat, and in 1988 Fiat upped their stake to 90%. Ferrari died that same year.

Life and Career

Enzo Ferrari roared into the world on February 18, 1898 in Modena, northern Italy. His father was a metal fabricator who owned his own factory, so it was no surprise that Ferrari took a keen interest in engineering. As a young boy of ten, he was taken to his first motor race at the Via Emilia, Bologna. Entranced by the fast cars, he vowed that he would learn to drive, a feat that he accomplished by the age of 13. In 1914, as war broke out in Europe, Ferrari was forced to leave school and take a job in the workshop of the local fire station.

Ferrari enlisted during World War I. He survived the conflict only to be brought close to death by the flu epidemic that raged through Italy in 1918. When he had made a full recovery, he set out to find a job associated with racing cars and applied to Fiat but was rejected. Disappointed, but reluctant to give up his dream, he took work as a delivery driver for a local garage and raced cars in his spare time with moderate success. With the help of a friend, and on the strength of his growing reputation as a driver, he eventually landed a job at the Italian car company Alfa Romeo, which employed him initially as a test driver, and then as a racing driver for its works team.

Contribution

Ferrari's big opportunity came when he was selected to drive for Alfa Romeo at the French Grand Prix. It was one of the most prestigious races in the racing calendar, but Ferrari blew his big chance when he mysteriously pulled out of the race. His reasons for withdrawing from the Grand Prix can be only guessed at. There was speculation that he had lost his nerve and suffered a sudden crisis of confidence. If true, it was nothing to be ashamed of. Ferrari was the best person to judge his own ability, and he would have been foolish to risk his life. And if it was an attack of self-doubt, it didn't affect his success as a businessman.

Despite this setback Ferrari continued to work for Alfa Romeo and in 1929 started his own company, Scuderia Ferrari. It offered racing services to its clients, delivering their cars to the track and providing engineering backup and other support. As most of the cars were Alfa Romeos and Alfa Romeo was also a client of Scuderia, Ferrari maintained his close relationship with the car company. He even struck a deal whereby Alfa Romeo provided technical expertise in return for shares in his company. Shell and Pirelli also obtained stock in Scuderia.

The company ran into trouble in 1933, however, when Alfa Romeo decided to withdraw from racing. Suddenly Ferrari was without cars, an essential part of any racing team.

For a company emblem Ferrari selected the prancing horse, the squadron badge of the Italian World War I flying ace Francesco Baracca. The yellow background to the now familiar symbol was chosen because yellow is the traditional color of Modena. At first Ferrari and his team met with great success. Ferrari had signed up the best drivers. He could afford to do this because, to avoid a massive salary bill, he agreed to hand over a share of the prize money. With several victories coming in the first year it turned out to be a lucrative time for both the drivers and their boss.

The company ran into trouble in 1933, however, when Alfa Romeo decided to withdraw from racing. Suddenly Ferrari was without cars, an essential part of any racing team. For a while he managed to negotiate a halfway house deal whereby Alfa Romeo continued to supply cars and Ferrari's Scuderia became, to all intents and purposes, the Alfa Romeo racing team. But even this unsatisfactory arrangement came to an end in 1937, when Alfa Romeo decided to run its own racing team once more. Ferrari found himself answering directly to Alfa Romeo management, even though he ran his own company. It was an untenable situation. In 1939 Ferrari left, but only after Alfa insisted that he sign a contract agreeing not to use the Ferrari name in motor racing for two years. The contract was rendered meaningless, however, when World War II intervened.

During World War II, Ferrari moved the Scuderia premises from Modena to Marinello. The new factory was razed to the ground in the war and rebuilt from scratch. After the war, at the age of 50, Ferrari set about creating his own racing car. Production was revved up and the first car, the 12-cylinder 125S, emerged in 1947. Before long, Ferrari cars were winning Grand Prix races across Europe. Yet Ferrari was not satisfied. One problem was that constructing racing cars consumed a great deal of cash. His solution to this problem was to build sports cars, and so, by default, the Ferrari sports car marque was established.

Ironically, the success of the Ferrari sports car only caused more problems for its creator. Now he was struggling to meet demand for road cars at the same time as keeping the racing team going. In 1963 the Ford Motor Company made an offer for the business, but Ferrari turned it down because of the onerous terms. In 1969 he turned instead to a fellow Italian, Gianni Agnelli, who controlled the industrial giant Fiat. Agnelli agreed to acquire a 50% share in the Ferrari company.

After the war, at the age of 50, Ferrari set about creating his own racing car. Production was revved up and the first car, the 12-cylinder 125S, emerged in 1947.

Throughout the 1970s and 1980s Ferrari continued to build on the company's reputation as the most exclusive sports car manufacturer in the world. At the same time the Ferrari racing team sped to victory after victory. The last car created under Ferrari's control was the F40. In 1988 Fiat increased its holding in Ferrari to 90%. The Ferrari family retained the balance. Ferrari died, aged 90, that same year.

Context and Conclusions

Throughout his career in the automobile business, Ferrari displayed a tough streak that kept him at the top. Despite his love of cars, business came first, and if a model proved unsuccessful it was unceremoniously scrapped (one reason why very few early Ferraris are still around). For many years Ferrari remained unchallenged as the king of motor racing. Eventually, however, other manufacturers—such as Mercedes and the Japanese company Honda—stole some of the limelight. Away from the race track, Ferrari continued to cut a dash. He never set out to create a mass-market automobile. Instead, he showed how, through quality engineering and bold design, it was possible to make a car into a luxury brand. In Italy, a country that prides itself on its sense of fashion and style, the sleek and powerful Ferrari sports car transformed the son of the metal fabricator into a national icon.

CLOSE BUT NO CIGAR

FERDINAND PORSCHE

Born in 1875 in North Bohemia, later part of Czechoslovakia but then still within the Austrian empire, Porsche was a brilliant engineer whose only formal education came from sneaking into night classes at the Technical University in Vienna. After a career of varied success, including the design of the VW Beetle prototypes, Porsche became a motor design consultant. Hitler was one of his clients, and as a result Porsche was imprisoned for 20 months in the postwar period. During this time his son, working for the family firm, designed the first Porsche sports car, the Type 356.

FERRUCCIO LAMBORGHINI

Lamborghini came to sports car production via tractor manufacturing—he built the best tractors in Italy—and air conditioning. When the clutch on his Ferrari broke and the service he got from the manufacturer was less than impressive, Lamborghini decided to build his own sports car. The stylish flamboyant Lamborghinis were a roaring success—the Countach at 190 m.p.h. was the fastest road car of its time. Lamborghini died in 1993.

For More Information

Book:

Yates, Brock. *Enzo Ferrari: The Man, the Cars, the Races, the Machine.* New York: Doubleday, 1991.

Web site:

Ferrari: **www.ferrari.com**

Henry Ford

1863	Born.
1884	Attends business school for three months.
1896	Chief engineer at Edison electric factory in Detroit. Drives first vehicle out of garden shed.
1901	Ford drives to victory in Grosse Point car races.
1903	Founds Ford Motor Co.
1905	Model A produced.
1908	The first Model T rolls off the production line.
1914	Ford introduces wages for unskilled workers at a minimum of $5.
1918	The River Rouge plant built.
1919	Ford's son, Edsel, becomes President of the company.
1924	Ten millionth Model T produced.
1928	Brings out second Model A.
1945	Hands over power to his grandson Henry Ford II.
1947	Dies.

Summary

Henry Ford (1863–1947) was part engineer, part inventor, and part entrepreneur. A talent for engineering and curiosity drove Ford to develop a prototype automobile in his garden. His flair helped him found the Ford Motor Company to develop his prototype. By 1924 Ford had sold ten million Model T Fords—the car famously available in a choice of colors so long as it was black. On his way to ten million sales Ford broke the land speed record and the mold of manufacturing. During his lifetime his introduction of mass-production assembly line methods irrevocably changed the nature of manufacturing, something for which, for once, the use of the phrase "paradigm shift" is wholly justified.

Life and Career

Ford was born in 1863 on his father's farm at Greenfield, near Detroit, Michigan. As a boy he showed great interest in mechanics and engineering. He delighted in dismantling his friends' watches and then reassembling them, and while still a schoolboy he built an engine from junk. He was always looking for ways to improve things. "Even when I was very young I suspected that much might somehow be done in a better way," he later observed. "That is what took me into mechanics."

Leaving school at 16, Ford went to work as an engineer for James Flower & Co. in Detroit. To supplement his meager $2.50 a week, he worked at a jewelers in the evenings. Nine months of grueling hours later, Ford moved to the Dry Dock Engine Works to try his hand at a different type of engineering. By 1896, he was chief engineer at the Edison electrical factory in Detroit, but finding himself unable to confine his engineering to work, Ford continued to tinker with engineering projects at home.

> *His first prototype automobile was the Quadricycle, built in his garden shed.*

Ford's strategic planning skills appear to have been underdeveloped at this early stage in his career. His first prototype automobile was the Quadricycle, built in his garden shed. The Quadricycle was too big to drive out of the shed, which forced him to dismantle part of the shed to remove the innovative horseless carriage.

For eight years Ford continued to work 12-hour days and then come home to improve his invention. Yet despite the potential of his automobile, no one could be persuaded to invest in it. The turning point came when Ford built a car for the Grosse Point automobile races. Although inexperienced, Ford entered the races, drove the car himself, and won emphatically. He repeated the feat the following year, in 1902. The victory attracted financiers and, after a couple of corporate false starts, the Ford Motor Company was up and running. On the way Ford broke the world land speed record for a four-cylinder automobile, driving a mile over the frozen Lake Sinclair in 39.2 seconds, seven seconds faster than the existing record.

Contribution

Ford's idea was to produce a car for "everyday wear and tear," suitable for the masses. "Anything founded on the idea of the greatest good for the greatest number will win in the end," he said. Competitors like Cadillac were expensive, at many thousands of dollars, and so beyond the reach of the majority of ordinary people. Ford's first commercial automobile was the Model A Fordmobile, in 1905. Priced at $850, it undercut its rivals and, in its basic but solid design, it appealed to the mass market. It was followed in 1908 by the Model T.

The overwhelming demand for the Model T forced Ford to modify the production process and make it more efficient. Initially the cars moved along the production line on cradles. At each stop, men climbed over the cars attending to different tasks. Ford simplified the process and made it more predictable. First, he delineated tasks so that one man performed one task repeatedly, instead of several. Second, he roped the cars together so that they traveled at a steady speed through the plant. These simple but effective measures resulted in an increase in production from 100,000 to 200,000 with, at the same time, a reduction in the workforce of nearly 1,500 men.

So many prospective employees queued up at the factory gates that the fire brigade had to use its hoses to disperse the crowd.

Production line work was arduous and monotonous; staff turnover was high. In 1914 Ford reluctantly increased wages for unskilled workers to a minimum of $5, a move that brought in workers from far and wide. Tens of thousands joined the Ford automobile company. So many prospective employees queued up at the factory gates that the fire brigade had to use its hoses to disperse the crowd.

Ford's management style was not, however, benevolent. The company had its own sociological department to nanny the workers—making sure, among other things, that they were mindful of good personal hygiene. Ford's coercive managerial style grated among the workforce. To sweeten this he introduced profit sharing and an extensive welfare program.

He stopped short of allowing the workers to form a labor union, however. When

Roosevelt introduced the Wagner Act of 1935, allowing the unionization of the motor companies, Ford resisted the legislation bitterly, refusing to let labor unions operate at Ford auto plants. It was only after adverse publicity as a result of the infamous Battle of the Overpass in May 1937, when several United Auto Workers' officials were badly beaten, allegedly by Ford employees outside the River Rouge plant, that Ford was forced to back down and permit union organization at the company.

By 1924 Ford had manufactured 10 million Model Ts and built a new plant at River Rouge, with wages raised to $6 a day. Increasingly he spent less time managing—his son, Edsel, had become President in 1919—and more time pursuing his socially idealistic interests. He built an experimental rural idyll, a model U.S. village named Greenfield Village. He also launched the Peace Ship in an attempt to end World War I and hobnobbed with other magnates and entrepreneurs such as his good friend Henry Firestone. Although a pacifist, Ford was drawn into war manufacturing after Pearl Harbour when the Willow Plant was built to produce B-24 bombers. This gigantic production works, with its mile-long assembly line, produced one plane every hour, with a total of 86,865 aircraft between May 1942 and the end of the war. In 1943 Ford returned as C.E.O. after Edsel died.

More at home on the factory floor addressing engineering problems, Ford lacked the managerial skills and flexibility necessary to keep the company ahead of the competition. He was unable to keep pace with the beast he had created. Fixated on the Model T, he waited too long to develop the company's next model, the revamped Model A (launched in 1927), and so lost the initiative forever to General Motors. Like many entrepreneurs Ford was reluctant to give up his company. A poorly-managed succession further damaged the company, with Ford finally handing power to his grandson Henry II in 1945. Ford died at the age of 84 on April 7, 1947.

Context and Conclusions

Henry Ford is frequently cited as one of the most important and influential businessmen of the 20th century. Although he didn't invent that icon of modern society, the motor car, he was responsible for turning it into a mass-market commodity. Once the sole province of the wealthy, the car was, in its pre-Ford incarnations, a toy—unreliable, poorly engineered, impractical, and above all expensive. Ford changed all that. The champion of mass production, he started an entire industrial revolution of his own, founded on his Model T. It was a revolution that made Ford $1 billion richer and made travel a reality for millions.

For More Information

Books:

Doubleday, Ralph H. *The Triumph of an Idea: The Story of Henry Ford*. New York: Graves, Doran & Company, Inc., 1934.

Ford, Henry, and Samuel Crowther. *My Life and Work*. New York: Doubleday, Page & Co., 1923.

Web site:

Ford Motor Company: **www.ford.com**

Bill Gates

1955	Born.
1977	Drops out of Harvard to start up computer software company with Paul Allen.
1980	Agrees to license operating system to IBM.
1995	Windows 9X series introduced.
1997	Microsoft ordered to supply Windows 95 without a browser.
2000	Microsoft found guilty of anticompetitive behavior. Judge orders break-up of Microsoft.
2001	Break-up ruling set aside by appeal court. Launch of XP generation of OS and X-Box game console.
2002	Gates Foundation donates $300 million to world health research.
2003	Major focus on security of Windows operating system. Commitment to mobile computing.
2003	Microsoft passes $200 billion market capitalization.

Summary

Bill Gates's contribution to the development of computer technology is beyond dispute. At the age of 13 he was already plotting his business future, forming the Lakeside Programmers Group with some school friends. Its aim was to seek commercial opportunities for their computer skills. His early programming brilliance, his alliance with Microsoft cofounder Paul Allen, and his departure from Harvard to start Microsoft are well known.

Microsoft went on to become one of the most successful companies the world has ever seen. As the Internet market exploded, he beat off Netscape in the browser wars. But perhaps his biggest challenge to date has come from the Department of Justice and its antitrust lawyers. Despite protracted litigation Gates has so far managed to keep Microsoft intact, and enabled it to hold on to its dominant position.

Life and Career

William Henry Gates III was born in Seattle on October 28, 1955. He was a precociously brilliant boy. Before his tenth birthday he had read the family's encyclopedia from beginning to end.

At Lakeside, the exclusive private school he attended in Seattle, he developed an obsession with computers. Gates, then still only 13 years old, and some of his computer friends formed the Lakeside Programmers Group, dedicated to using their programming skills to make money.

He was a precociously brilliant boy. Before his tenth birthday he had read the family's encyclopedia from beginning to end.

At Lakeside he developed a friendship with another boy two years his senior. The boy, whose obsession with computers matched Gates's, was Paul Allen.

The intellectually driven Gates left Lakeside in 1973 to study law at Harvard. Law was a lot less appealing to him, however, than computing. He contacted Allen and the two teamed up to develop a version of an early computer language—BASIC.

Gates dropped out of Harvard in 1977 to start up a small computer software company with Allen. They called it Microsoft.

Contribution

A brilliant strategic decision in 1980 set Microsoft on the road to global dominance. At that time IBM dominated the IT industry through its mainframe business. By the late 1970s Microsoft was licensing its software to a number of customers. But the prevailing wisdom was that hardware was the business to be in and software merely an adjunct. Apple at the time was developing a proprietary in-house operating system (OS) that would provide a competitive advantage. Its strategy was to maintain control over what it regarded as its superior hardware by running it with its own software. Gates thought differently. As far as he was concerned the more people that used Microsoft software on their machines the better. So when IBM approached Microsoft to develop the operating system for its first PC, Gates recognized what an enormous opportunity this presented. IBM's dominance of the IT market meant that its PCs were destined to set the standard—both for hardware and for the OS. IBM failed to realize that, when the end user switched on the machine, the part of the computer he or she interacted with would be the OS, supplied by Microsoft. Gates capitalized on the situation, cannily retaining the right to license its OS to other PC manufacturers.

Yet in those early days the rest of the world still failed to understand the importance of Gates's coup. Even in 1984, Fortune magazine was criticizing Gates for failing to develop the management depth that would turn a temporary victory into long-term dominance.

The decision by IBM to use Microsoft's MS-DOS was a turning point for both companies. From that point onward, the fortunes of IBM, which singularly failed to grasp the significance of the OS, would inexorably decline, until Lou Gerstner came to its rescue as C.E.O. in 1993. For Microsoft the only way was up. Endorsed by IBM, MS-DOS displaced other competing OS offerings regardless of their technical merits, in much the same way that VHS had vanquished Betamax in the battle of the video standards.

Yet in those early days the rest of the world still failed to understand the importance of Gates's coup. Even in 1984, *Fortune* magazine was criticizing Gates for failing to develop the management depth that would turn a temporary victory into long-term dominance. Not for the last time the media underestimated Gates's drive, ambition, and strategic vision.

When ill health forced Allen to leave Microsoft, Gates's position as leader was confirmed. Microsoft's rapid growth soon made it the darling of Wall Street. From a share price of $2 in 1986, Microsoft stock had soared to $105 by the first half of 1996, making Gates a billionaire.

Microsoft has launched a succession of successful products. But Gates hasn't had things all his own way. When the Internet revolution took off in the early 1990s, Microsoft was momentarily caught off balance. A company called Netscape sprang up, giving away a nifty piece of software called a browser that transformed the Web from a techie's playground to a mass-market phenomenon. Microsoft desperately responded by licensing Mosaic browser technology from a company called Spyglass, tweaking it, and repackaging it as the Microsoft browser Internet Explorer. To cover all the bases, Microsoft also bought WebTV, eShops, Hotmail, and Vermeer, the original developers of the Front Page HTML editing software.

Critics regularly deride the company for buying technology rather than developing its own solutions. Microsoft has countered that it has developed a number of important technologies and is still doing so.

Criticism has also constantly been leveled at Microsoft, alleging that it abuses its dominant market position. Matters came to a head when the U.S. Justice Department investigated Microsoft to establish whether the company was in breach of antitrust law. In June 2000, after a lengthy trial and a mountain of depositions, U.S. District Judge Thomas Penfield Jackson ordered Microsoft to be split into two companies, holding that it had violated the nation's antitrust laws by using monopoly power to push aside potential competitors to the detriment of consumers. Microsoft took the case to the appeal court in February 2001, and in June of that year the court decided to overturn part of the original decision, withdrawing the requirement for Microsoft to be broken up. Despite that, the company continues to grow and, in 2003, it passed $200 billion market capitalization.

Ultimately it may not be the antitrust ruling that poses the biggest threat to Microsoft's bottom line. Microsoft risks being sidelined by the sheer pace of technological progress. Handhelds and mobile phones may be the PCs of the future, and those markets are not dominated by Microsoft. Even on its home ground of PC operating systems, open-source software such as Linux poses a threat. Gates hit back with the launch of Microsoft's next generation XP operating system toward the end of 2001. On this occasion it was the closer integration with the Internet and, in particular, the "smart tags" feature that worried some commentators. In the event, the feature was dropped, although that doesn't mean it won't resurface. Another big product for Gates in 2001 was the X-box. This new gaming system, due out in time for Christmas 2001, was Microsoft's shot at breaking into a lucrative market on the hardware side. It is too early to tell, however, whether the combined forces of XP and the X-box, plus the numerous partnership agreements Microsoft has forged with dot-com companies, will be enough to preserve its hegemony. But Gates, the architect of the world's greatest software company, won't go down without a fight.

Since 2000, Gates has moved from C.E.O. to Chief Software Architect to concentrate even more on the company's future direction. Software security is a major focus and Microsoft launched an initiative in 2003 called Trustworthy Software. The company is also targeting mobile computing as an important arena for future development.

Context and Conclusions

Bill Gates is lauded and reviled in almost equal measure. His charitable work, which tends to be overlooked, has grown rapidly and, in 2002, the Gates Foundation gave more than $300 million to tackle Aids and other global health challenges. The secrets that lie behind Microsoft's spiral of success have been dissected from every possible angle. Whatever you think of the dominance of Microsoft or Gates's methods, it cannot be doubted that when it comes to building and retaining a competitive advantage he has few peers. His technical skills, while not to be underrated, are not his greatest attribute. Far more important is his strategic thinking. It is this that has enabled him to outsmart his opponents at every turn. His other great attribute is the ability to hire the best talent and then motivate it to work at high tempo. He may appear awkward, geeky even, in public, but Gates is as sharp as a box of razors.

CLOSE BUT NO CIGAR

KEN OLSEN

Olsen was once hailed by *Fortune* magazine as the "most successful entrepreneur in the history of American business." Founding Digital Equipment Corporation (DEC) in 1959, he spent the next 35 years riding the IT roller coaster at the helm of his company. Olsen, the man who pioneered the minicomputer, was heavily influenced by the writings of Alfred Sloan and organized DEC along similar lines to GM (small business units) when under Sloan's control. He left in 1992 to found Advanced Modular Solutions Inc. After a disastrous spell in the early 1990s, DEC was finally bought by Compaq in 1998.

For More Information

Books:

Dearlove, Des. *Business the Bill Gates Way*. New York: AMACOM, 1999.

Gates, Bill. *Business @ the Speed of Thought: Using a Digital Nervous System*. New York: Warner Books, 1999.

Wallace, James, and Jim Erickson. *Hard Drive: Bill Gates and the Making of the Microsoft Empire*. New York: John Wiley, 1992.

Web site:

Microsoft: **www.microsoft.com**

Harold Geneen

1910	Born.
1934	Obtains a degree in accounting.
1934–1959	Works for number of firms including American Can, Bell and Howell, Jones and Laughlin Steel, and Raytheon.
1959	Joins ITT.
1966	ABC merger blocked.
1971	Acquires Hartford Insurance.
1977	Steps down as C.E.O.
1979	Steps down as Chairman.
1983	Resigns as Director.
1997	Dies.

Summary

Harold Geneen is the classic example of the C.E.O. as analyst. He joined the board of ITT in 1959 and set about turning the company into the world's greatest conglomerate. His basic organizational strategy was that diversification was a source of strength. Under Geneen, ITT's spending spree amounted to 350 companies. By 1970, ITT was composed of 400 separate companies operating in 70 countries.

By sheer force of personality, Geneen's approach worked. Between 1959 and 1977, ITT's sales went from $765 million to nearly $28 billion and earnings per share rose from $1 to $4.20. Geneen stepped down as Chairman in 1979. But a company built around the drive and energy of one man will not last longer than that man's career. His followers were unable to sustain Geneen's uniquely driven working style. In the month of Harold Geneen's death, ITT was taken over.

Life and Career

Son of a Russian Jewish father and an Italian Catholic mother, Harold Geneen was born in Bournemouth, England in 1910. His family moved to the United States before his first birthday, but his parents separated soon after they arrived. As a result, Geneen's childhood was spent at boarding schools and summer camps. When Geneen started work as a runner for the New York Stock Exchange, he continued to study at night at New York University. In 1934 his hard work was rewarded with a degree in accounting.

For the next 25 years his career took in a string of companies, starting with the forerunners of Coopers & Lybrand, followed by Montgomery (an accounting firm), then the American Can Co., Bell and Howell Co., Jones and Laughlin Steel Co., and Raytheon. After Raytheon, where Geneen was vice President, came the biggest challenge of his career and the job that made him famous: the International Telegraph and Telephone Company, more commonly known as ITT.

Contribution

When Geneen arrived at ITT in 1959, the corporation was a ragbag collection of businesses, loosely focused around telecommunications, with revenues of $800,000. During the 1960s the predominant organizational trend was one of diversification and conglomeration. C.E.O.s went into a purchasing frenzy, raiding the corporate aisles for any company, no matter what business it was in, so long as it turned a profit. Geneen was no exception.

Over the ensuing decade Geneen purchased over 300 companies, operating in over 60 different countries. There was no rationale to these purchases, no common thread, other than that of profit. Sheraton hotels, Avis car hire, Continental Baking were all tucked away in ITT's roomy locker. "I never met a business that I didn't find interesting," said Geneen, and the ITT balance sheet certainly bore him out.

It was a mammoth undertaking to manage so many disparate companies. Fortunately for ITT, Geneen was no slouch; on the contrary, he was a fiercely driven workaholic. His ITT office in New York was equipped with eight telephones and a clock that showed which parts of the world were in daylight and which were in darkness. Ten suitcase-sized leather attaché cases crammed full of documents were stacked along the window ledges. Six of the cases, stuffed with reports, communiqués, and memos from over 400 reporting corporations, followed Geneen around the country and the world. "If I had enough arms and legs and time, I would do it all myself," said Geneen. Well into his eighties, long after he left ITT, Geneen was still working a ten-hour day at his office in New York's Waldorf-Astoria hotel. A typical Geneen story is recounted by an old ITT executive. Dragging a group of executives in for an evening meeting,

> *Fortunately for ITT, Geneen was no slouch; on the contrary, he was a fiercely driven workaholic.*

Geneen worked them late into the night. At 11:45 p.m., the last of the executives made his way out of the office, pausing to wait for Geneen. Instead the C.E.O. peeled off his jacket, pulled on a sweater and kept on working—the last executive in the building.

Even so, it required all his energy to control the ITT conglomerate. To keep it together, Geneen employed rigorous financial accounting methods. Each month, 50 or more executives flew to Brussels to spend several days examining the figures. "I want no surprises," was one of Geneen's mantras. Full information was paramount, as was the ability to tell real facts from details masquerading as facts. "The highest art of professional management requires the literal ability to smell a real fact from all others," asserted Geneen.

And his approach seemed to work. From 1959 to 1977, ITT sales rocketed from some $765 million to approaching $28 billion, with earnings up from $29 million to $562 million. It was a success by most people's standards, not just Geneen's. Yet the more companies he acquired, the harder it was to keep all the plates spinning in the air. In 1974 and 1975 profits fell: Geneen may have been able to keep up a relentless pace, but his followers were either unable or unwilling to match it.

Geneen's efforts to support his company's share price sometimes strayed outside the boundaries of acceptable practice. In 1972, America's Securities and Exchange Commission discovered $8.7 million had been sunk into nefarious and illegal activities around the world. This allegedly included bribery, and colluding with the CIA in an attempt to undermine the Allende government in Chile.

Geneen stepped down as chief executive in 1977, as Chairman in 1979, and as a Director four years later—not that such a relentless man could ever retire to a life of quiet contemplation and gentle pastimes. He carried on working in a number of different companies of his own creation until his death from a heart attack in 1997.

ITT, however, was a different proposition. Without Geneen to support it, the house of cards collapsed. ITT limped on but eventually, after selling many of the companies acquired by Geneen, it was split up into three separate companies.

Context and Conclusions

Harold Geneen was one of the last of his breed. He came to power at ITT at the height of the mania for conglomerates. Size mattered, and if size mattered then Geneen was very, very important. It is doubtful if any other C.E.O. in corporate history acquired more companies—over 300—with less rationale. Of course acquisition is one way to grow earnings, but eventually the relentless growth has to stop and increased earnings must come from existing operations. Even a man with Geneen's drive and boundless energy will struggle to keep 300 plates in the air, and so it proved. In the decade following his departure from ITT, the cry from the boardroom was "stick to the knitting." Companies slimmed down, shed noncore business, and left ITT looking like a bloated dinosaur. Yet Geneen deserves his place in the pantheon of business greats. Why? Because he was the best of his type, the paragon of his age, the king of the conglomerates.

> *Harold Geneen was one of the last of his breed.*

CLOSE BUT NO CIGAR
CHARLES G. BLUDHORN

Who today remembers Charlie Bludhorn? Yet in the 1960s and 1970s, Bludhorn—then head of conglomerate Gulf and Western—was one of the most fashionable C.E.O.s of his time. Along with conglomerate kings such as James Ling, Henry Singleton, Charles "Tex" Thornton, and of course Harold Geneen, Bludhorn was fêted as a business visionary. Among the many corporate baubles he accumulated were Music Corporation of America, Madison Square Garden, and Paramount Studios. When conglomerates fell out of fashion, so did Bludhorn. Gulf and Western was whittled down to size until Paramount was pretty much all that remained.

For More Information
Books:

Sampson, Anthony. *The Sovereign State of ITT*. New York: Stein and Day, 1973.
Shoenberg, Robert J. *Geneen*. New York: Norton, 1985.

Louis Frederick Gerstner

1942	Born.
1964	Joins McKinsey & Company.
1978	Joins American Express.
1985–1989	President of American Express.
1991–1993	IBM's cumulative losses pass $15 billion, a new record for corporate misery.
1993	Joins IBM as new C.E.O. and Chairman of the Board.
1993–1995	Restructuring means over 80,000 jobs go.
1994	IBM posts $3 billion profit on sales of $60 billion.
1995	Buys Lotus Notes.
2000	Revenues $88.4 billion with net profits of $8.1 billion.
2001	Stock price breaks through $100 barrier. Company valued at $178 billion.
2002	Steps down as C.E.O.

Summary

Lou Gerstner's business career seems almost too good to be true. After a broad education, taking in engineering and business, Gerstner went to work for the management consultancy McKinsey. He made senior partner at 31—the youngest ever. There followed an equally impressive progression through blue chips American Express and RJR Nabisco. At Amex, Gerstner revitalized the fledgling credit card business. At RJR he made inroads into a mountain of debt, prepping the company for the mega merger of the century. The IBM job seemed like a no win scenario: the once-great company, holed below the waterline, looked to be sinking faster than the Titanic. Gerstner reportedly took the job only after headhunters Heidrick & Struggles persuaded him it was "for the good of the country." With Gerstner's ingredients in the mix, an apparently poisoned chalice turned out to be a refreshing brew. Eight years on and IBM was back, holding its own with the best of the IT heavyweights, both young and old. Much of the credit went to Gerstner.

Life and Career

Born in Mineola on March 1, 1942, Louis Frederick Gerstner was the second of four sons. His early education was courtesy of the local Catholic school. His higher education is a textbook progression for many of today's top executives. First he majored in a specialized discipline, in his case engineering science at Dartmouth, graduating in 1963. After Dartmouth he went on to obtain an MBA from Harvard Business School. Then he joined management consulting firm McKinsey & Company in 1964.

At McKinsey, Gerstner made rapid progress and was appointed Director at age 28. His early career post-McKinsey was no less impressive. At American Express during the 1980s, he revitalized the company's credit card division and saw net income grow by 66%. Then he went on to RJR Nabisco Holdings, where he cut a debt mountain of $26 billion to $14 billion, preparing the company for the largest leveraged buyout in corporate history.

When IBM cast around for an executive to replace C.E.O. John Akers and pull the company out of the mire, they chose Gerstner. The surprise was that Gerstner, with a glittering career ahead of him, entertained the offer to chase an apparently lost cause. But, to the relief of "Big Blue" and headhunters Heidrick & Struggles, in 1993 Gerstner joined IBM as its new C.E.O.

Contribution

When Gerstner arrived at IBM, it was in big trouble. For years "Big Blue" had been the dominant company in the information technology industry, reaping massive profits through sales of its mainframe computers. But by the late 1980s the company had become complacent, lazy, and slow. Full of its own self-importance, it ceased to innovate and lagged behind a rapidly changing IT market. Although it had introduced an IBM-badged PC, by outsourcing the two key components—the operating system and the processing chip—the company had handed the advantage to Microsoft and Intel. Bogged down in bureaucracy and bloated with top-heavy management, IBM ground to a halt. In 1990 gross profit margins were a healthy 55%, but by 1993 they had slumped to 38%. There was no sign of an end to the downward trend. Gerstner's response was immediate, dramatic, and effective. His recovery checklist was: cut costs; get customers back again; find strategic direction; and restore employee morale.

Cutting costs was comparatively easy, if painful. Gerstner budgeted for a restructuring cost of $8.9 billion, and set about laying off 35,000 employees before the end of 1995. The figure ended closer to 85,000. Elsewhere, measures such as centralized purchasing, better inventory management, and the eradication of duplication in areas like product development, all contributed to improving the balance sheet position. In a move to improve customer relations, Gerstner made a special effort to get out and see the customers firsthand. The feedback from thousands of customer contacts persuaded him to retrain his generalist workforce to become the product specialists that customers demanded.

As Gerstner got rid of staff, he also took the opportunity to get rid of some of the ingrained corporate culture. Out went the traditional IBM executive look of blue suits and white shirts. "This is a company that was very successful for several decades, but the curse of success is that people try to codify it," he said pointedly in an interview with the *Financial Times*. "My view is that you perpetuate success by continuing to run scared, not by looking back at what made you great, but looking forward at what is going to make you ungreat, so that you are constantly focusing on the challenges that keep you humble, hungry, and nimble."

When Gerstner landed at IBM, much was made of his lack of technological background. "He won't be able to spot technological opportunity," the critics said. And, when he gave a speech early on which included the line "the last thing IBM needs now is a vision," there was a chorus of disapproval from the media Cassandras. With hindsight, worries over a paucity of vision were unfounded. For a man with no vision, Gerstner has been remarkably consistent in his strategy for IBM.

Innovation is a central plank of Gerstner's strategy. In the year that he arrived, IBM filed for more patents than any other company in the United States. Thereafter, each year brought more innovative technologies from the supposedly directionless IT giant. Voice recognition technology, the world's fastest supercomputer, copper-wired semiconductors, promising new technology to replace silicon chips, nanotechnology...the list of IBM innovation under Gerstner runs on.

Much of IBM's creativity is aimed at e-business, an area Gerstner believes is vital to its future success. By the beginning of 2001, the fastest-growing segment of the roughly $90-billion company was its services business. Gerstner has repositioned the company as a major e-business company while hanging on to core business such as servers, storage, networking, and middleware. It's a neat trick. Cleverly, he has also abandoned the IBM closed, proprietary approach to technology and embraced the philosophy of the open source movement, opening up IBM's technologies to other companies in a flurry of partnering deals.

So what impact has Gerstner had on the bottom line? In 1994, nearly two years after his arrival, the company posted a $3 billion profit on sales of $60 billion. This came after three consecutive years of losses, totaling $15 billion. On the strength of the recovery in profits, the share price had improved to $89 by early 1994. Since then it's mostly been an upward trend, although IBM stock has been susceptible to the same sorts of fluctuation as other technology stocks. Performance has also looked solid. Revenues for 2000 were $88.4 billion, with net profits of $8.1 billion. By October 2001 the stock price had broken through the $100 barrier, and the company was valued at $178 billion. Whichever measure you use, Gerstner's performance was impressive. Some even believed it justified his $14 million salary.

The challenge facing Gerstner and IBM now is to sustain the transformation. For a company of IBM's size, perpetual motion is a necessary but elusive quality. Gerstner seems to have confounded the critics by creating an agile and innovative company from a stagnant behemoth without, as was predicted, splitting it into smaller units.

Context and Conclusions

By reputation, Lou Gerstner sits alongside management heavyweights of the post World War II period such as Jack Welch and Andy Grove. Is such exalted standing merited? The answer is unquestionably yes. Gerstner's timely arrival saved one of the largest and most famous IT companies in the world from extinction. He rediscovered the tradition of innovation and customer service, ingrained in the organization by its founder Thomas J. Watson, Sr. He was the right leader, in the right place, at the right time. In the late 1980s and early 1990s, IBM needed a manager who could make an unwieldy, bureaucratic, and tired company agile and hungry again. It took some painful restructuring, but Gerstner steered the company through its bad times and altered its course. The company emerged with a new focus that embraced e-business and IT services, while retaining its core manufacturing business and corporate values. The transformation was reflected in the bottom line as IBM regained favor among investors, analysts, and media alike. After a stellar career at companies such as McKinsey, American Express, and RJR Nabisco, Gerstner's triumph at IBM was a fitting capstone for one of the finest managers of his generation.

For More Information
Book:
Garr, Doug. *IBM Redux: Lou Gerstner and the Business Turnaround of the Decade.* New York: HarperBusiness, 2000.

Jean Paul Getty

1892	Born.
1914	Studies at Oxford University, England.
1916	Becomes a millionaire.
1923–39	Marries five times.
1930	Father dies, leaving Getty $500,000 of his $15 million fortune.
1949	Acquires oil concession in Neutral Zone, Middle East.
1953	Major oil find in Neutral Zone.
1953	Founds J. Paul Getty Museum in Malibu, California.
1960	Moves to Sutton Place, England.
1976	Dies.

Summary

Jean Paul Getty (1892–1976), son of an oil prospector, was born with a silver shovel in his mouth. Although his father was a multimillionaire, Getty inherited just $500,000 of the $15 million family fortune. Undaunted, he acquired control of his father's company and spent 20 years amassing a collection of oil interests, including Western Oil, Tidewater Oil, and Skelly Oil. He also dabbled in the property market, buying prestigious hotels in Mexico and the United States. When the Navy declined his offer to enlist during World War II, he helped the war effort instead by running an aircraft company.

In 1949 he struck the deal that gained him access to the oilfields of the Middle East. At the time there had been no major oil finds in the region, but, backing his instincts, Getty invested upwards of $10 million. Within three years of signing the contract Getty discovered a huge oilfield, securing his position as one of the world's wealthiest men. He lived out the latter years of his life at Sutton Place near Guildford in England, writing his memoirs and indulging in his passion for collecting art.

Life and Career

The son of oil executive and lawyer George Franklin Getty, Jean Paul Getty was born in Minneapolis, Minnesota, on December 15, 1892. His father took him on a tour of his oilfields when he was 11, teaching the boy about the oil industry. In 1906 Getty moved with his family to California.

A good scholar, Getty's studies took him through Harvard Military Academy and the Polytechnic High School, both in Los Angeles, and on to the University of Southern California and the University of California, Berkeley. In 1914 he completed his studies with two terms at Oxford University, England, where he took a diploma in politics and economics.

Getty returned to the United States after Oxford determined to enter the diplomatic corps. His father had other ideas. By this time the senior Getty had built a multimillion dollar oil business; he had only one son, and he was desperate for him to commit to the family business. Jean Paul agreed to try his hand. He struck a deal with his father: he would have a free hand to purchase leases on land he suspected might hold oil. His father would finance the operation and the younger Getty could keep 30% of any profits.

Contribution

J. Paul Getty started in business by buying oil leases and prospecting for oil. By June 1916 the 24-year-old had made a million dollars. He might just as easily have been a casualty of World War I—he volunteered to train as a pilot, but didn't receive a reply to his offer until 1919, after the end of the war.

With his newly acquired riches Getty gave free rein to the impulses of youth and headed for Los Angeles, where he spent the next few years living the life of a wealthy playboy. He dated a number of attractive women, built-—and crashed—his own sports car, and generally lived life to the full. But in 1919, tiring of his life of leisure, Getty returned to the oil business. He joined his father's company, starting at the bottom as a roustabout, working on the drilling operations and earning a meager $3 a day. It was tough manual labor, but Getty thrived on it. The experience taught him a valuable lesson: always supervise the drilling of wells in person.

While his business life was extremely successful, his personal life was less so. Between 1923 and 1932 Getty married no less than four times (with a fifth in 1939). He blamed the failure of most of his marriages on his commitment to work, and in truth any woman who married the workaholic Getty early in his career was destined to see little of her husband.

Although he had displayed a shrewd business mind while working with his father, it was his father's death in 1930 that set Getty on the path toward the oil empire he would eventually accumulate. His father, who was not impressed by Getty's frequent marriages and was aware that his son's personal wealth was considerable, left him only $500,000 of his $15 million fortune. The bulk of the estate was left to Getty's mother.

With less inheritance than he might have bargained for and with the control of the Getty oil empire vested with his mother, Getty was forced to start over. He set out to prove he had as much commercial acumen as his father. Through a series of shrewd deals Getty acquired Western Oil and, through a controlling interest in his father's company, Mission Corporation, Tidewater Oil, and Skelly Oil.

It took Getty 20 years to put in place the pieces that would eventually be controlled by the Getty Oil Company, of which he owned 80%. It was a long, protracted battle, and Getty admitted that had he known that it was Rockefeller's Standard Oil that owned Tidewater Oil, he would never have set out to buy it.

Oil wasn't the only industry Getty was interested in. In 1938 he expanded into the hotel business, buying the Pierre at Fifth Avenue and 60th Street in New York for $2,350,000. This was followed by other property deals such as the Pierre Marques Hotel near Acapulco, Mexico.

He offered his services to the U.S. Navy during World War II, declaring, "I am 49 but in good health, have owned three yachts, and am experienced in their care and maintenance." The Navy declined. Instead Getty was asked to assist with equipment production, and Spartan Aircraft, a subsidiary of Skelly Oil, turned out training planes and aircraft parts for the war effort under his personal guidance. After the war the company turned its energies to mobile home construction.

Getty's approach to business is well illustrated by one of his most celebrated deals. Backing a hunch in 1949, Getty negotiated the rights to a 60-year drilling concession in an area of desert lying between Saudi Arabia and Kuwait known as the Neutral Zone. No oil had ever been found there; no surveys had suggested oil would be found there. Getty nonetheless agreed to pay King Saud $9.5 million in cash plus $1 million a year regardless of whether he struck oil or not. The year 1950 came and went, as did 1951, and no oil in commercial quantities was discovered. When 1952 drew to a close and there was still no strike, observers began to doubt Getty's legendary knack for finding oil. In 1953 the doubters were silenced when Getty finally struck oil. It was an enormous find, and soon the field was producing more than 16 million barrels a year.

During the 1950s Getty moved to England, buying through his company one of the country's most celebrated Tudor mansions, Sutton Place, near Guildford, Surrey. From there he orchestrated his business interests in Europe and the Middle East. He founded the J. Paul Getty Museum in Malibu, California, in 1953 to display his art collection. His later life was spent dealing with personal tragedy—the premature death of two of his sons and the kidnapping of his grandson—writing his memoirs, and building his collection of art masterpieces, antiquities, and carpets. He died in 1976.

Context and Conclusions

J. Paul Getty had the confidence of a millionaire's son and the understanding of money that comes with it. "If you owe the bank $100, that's your problem. If you owe the bank $100 million, that's the bank's problem," he once observed.

His business instincts were invariably right, and he was resolute to the point of stubbornness in backing his hunches. He could have cut his losses in the Middle East when no oil was discovered. Instead he gritted his teeth and stuck it out, and in the end he was proved right. Getty's instincts made him exceedingly wealthy: in October 1957 *Fortune* named him the richest man in the world.

For More Information

Web site:

J. Paul Getty Museum: **www.getty.edu/museum**

King Camp Gillette

1855	Born.
1871	Gillette family hardware business burns down.
1890	Holds four patents.
1894	Writes *The Human Drift*.
1895	Works for the inventor of cork-lined bottle caps.
1901	Gillette and Nickerson form the American Safety Razor Company.
1903	Production begins on the new safety razor.
1904	The renamed Gillette company is awarded the patent for the new invention. Invents the double-edged blade—a concept still used to this day.
1906	Twelve million blades sold to date, generating revenues of $90,000.
1915	Sales of seven million blades a year.
1932	Dies.

Summary

King Camp Gillette, the safety-razor entrepreneur, made his fortune by taking a mundane everyday product and improving it. So confident was he of his invention that he formed the American Safety Razor Company in 1901 and persuaded investors to back him before he even had a commercial product. In the first year of production Gillette sold 51 razor sets and 168 blades. By 1905 the figure was 250,000 razor sets and 100,000 blade packages. Part of the secret of Gillette's success was his modern attitude towards branding. With his picture on the wrappers of his disposable blades, he was soon known the world over. By the time he had moved on to improving the world through his social theories, the Gillette safety razor was a permanent fixture in the grooming habits of a large proportion of the world's male population.

Life and Career

King Camp Gillette was born in Fond du Lac, Wisconsin, into a family of innovators. His father was a patent agent and small-time inventor. His mother wrote a cookbook based on a lifetime of culinary experimentation; the book was still in print a century later. When Gillette was four, his family moved to Chicago to start up a hardware business. Unfortunately, the business was ravaged by the Great Fire, and in 1871 the family moved once again, this time to New York City.

Gillette took a job as a traveling salesman. Not content with merely selling his products, he couldn't resist improving them. By 1890 he had accumulated four patents. In 1895 he was working for the man who had invented cork-lined bottle caps. He had some simple advice for Gillette: "Invent something people use and throw away." Gillette took his words to heart and turned his attention to the safety razor.

His father was a patent agent and small-time inventor. His mother wrote a cookbook based on a lifetime of culinary experimentation; the book was still in print a century later.

Traditionally, men of the time used the straight-handled razor blade to shave. The increasing use of the railroad, however, had prompted a rethinking of the design of this basic implement. The swaying of the carriages made it downright dangerous to use the traditional cut-throat. Safety razors had been invented—a heavy blade fitted at right angles to a short handle—but they still had major shortcomings. Gillette used a Star safety razor. This required continual sharpening on a leather strop just as the traditional razor did. Eventually the blade wore out.

Gillette had an idea. What if it were possible to take a small square of sheet steel and put a permanently sharp edge on it? Such a product would be sufficiently affordable to throw away when it became dull.

Contribution

To help him in his quest for a new improved safety razor, Gillette turned to metallurgists at the Massachusetts Institute of Technology. They assured Gillette that his idea was impossible. Undaunted, Gillette continued to search for someone who shared his belief and vision. That person was William Emery Nickerson, an inventor who, ironically, had been educated at MIT.

Gillette's search had taken six years. His doggedness was rewarded in 1901 when, together with Nickerson, he formed the American Safety Razor Company. Then in 1903 production began on the new safety razor. Razor blades were bundled up and sold as a package. The razor handle was sold as a one-time purchase. In 1904 the renamed Gillette Safety Razor Company was awarded the patent for the new invention. Initial sales were disappointing. After an intensive advertising campaign in men's magazines and newspapers in the United States and Europe, however, things improved. By 1906 12 million blades had been sold, generating revenues of $90,000.

The inevitable patent battles ensued. With a large proportion of the world's population as a potential market, sharp practices were rife. Competitors came to the market with modified versions of Gillette's product. Gillette responded with litigation or, in many cases, by buying the competition. And all the while he continued to tinker with his invention. In 1904 he came up with the double-edged blade, a concept used to this day. With his face plastered over the wrappers of his razor blades, Gillette became a celebrity.

Although the Gillette razor made King Camp Gillette a millionaire, he remained unfulfilled. He had strong philosophical and political beliefs. With his newly made millions he was now a powerful figure in North American commerce. He had an idealistic vision of a utopian society based on universal cooperation, and he now had the means to attempt to make it a reality.

Gillette wrote several books outlining his vision, beginning with *The Human Drift* (1894) that predated the invention of the Gillette razor. In a reaction against the mass pollution and sprawling urban development of the Industrial Revolution, he planned pollution-free cities contained in giant glass domes. In this new Utopia, one company would perform all production with the citizens as the shareholders. "Selfishness would be unknown, and war would be a barbarism of the past," he wrote.

One interesting byproduct of Gillette's obsession was his meeting with Henry Ford. In the years before World War I Gillette attempted to set the wheels of his World Corporation in motion. First he asked Teddy Roosevelt to be President. When Roosevelt unsurprisingly declined, Gillette approached the writer Sinclair Lewis, who in turn arranged a meeting between Gillette and Ford. The outcome of this meeting between two dogmatic, strong-willed millionaires should have been no surprise. At first the two merely talked over each other then, growing angrier, they began to shout at one another.

Context and Conclusions

Gillette's attempts at social engineering came to nothing. The stock market crash of 1929, coupled with boardroom machinations and constant patent litigation, wiped out his personal fortune. He spent a lot of time during his final years trying unsuccessfully to extract oil from shale. In the end he died, unfulfilled and frustrated, in 1932. The Gillette Safety Razor Company, however, thrived, carrying on its founder's tradition of innovation and remaining at the cutting edge of safety razor development. The company introduced foam shaving cream (Foamy), anti-perspirant (Right Guard), and continued to do what Gillette had always done—improve the safety razor with the twin-blade, pivoting-head, disposable, and triple-blade razors.

The stock market crash of 1929, coupled with boardroom machinations and constant patent litigation, wiped out his personal fortune.

King Camp Gillette will be remembered for creating a product used daily by people the world over. Not only did he pioneer the market for disposable products, but he also showed an early and prescient awareness of the power of both celebrity and the brand. His image on the packaging of his product made him famous and helped reassure the consumer about the product's quality. This in turn boosted sales and helped make the Gillette Safety Razor Company the leader in its market.

For More Information

Book:
Adams, Russell B., Jr. *King C. Gillette: The Man and His Wonderful Shaving Device*. Boston: Little, Brown & Co., 1978.

Web site:
The Gillette Company: **www.gillette.com**

Roberto Goizueta

1931	Born.
1953	Graduates from Yale University.
1954	Starts work for Coca-Cola in Cuba.
1959	Castro takes power in Cuba.
1960	Flees Cuba for Miami.
1964	Moves to Coca-Cola HQ in Atlanta.
1974	Made Senior Vice-President. Is told Coca-Cola's secret formula.
1979	Appointed Vice-Chairman of Coca-Cola.
1980	Becomes C.E.O. and Chairman of Coca-Cola.
1981– 1997	Coca-Cola's stockmarket value leaps 3,500%.
1982	Oversees launch of Diet Coke and purchase of Columbia Pictures.
1985	Launches and withdraws New Coke.
1996	Coca-Cola plays unofficial host to the 1996 Olympic games in Atlanta.
1997	Dies.

Summary

Roberto Goizueta (1931–1997) could have been the owner of his family's sugar refinery business. Instead he became head of Coca-Cola, one of the world's largest and most valuable companies. Fleeing from communist Cuba after Fidel Castro came to power in 1959, Goizueta arrived in Miami in 1960 and began working for Coca-Cola. He moved to the corporate headquarters in Atlanta in 1964. With the support of company legend Robert Woodruff, Goizueta worked his way steadily up through the management ranks until he was made C.E.O. in 1980.

During his tenure Goizueta improved Coca-Cola's stagnating share price and took the company into noncore but profitable areas such as entertainment. Despite his considerable successes, however, he is likely to be remembered as the man who authorized one of the biggest marketing gaffes of all time—the switch from the traditional Coca-Cola formula to New Coke in 1985. New Coke was a commercial and public relations disaster, but at least Goizueta was brave enough to admit his mistake. And there's no question that Goizueta was good for Coca-Cola. In the hospital, fighting the cancer that was eventually to kill him, he commented, "It's all right if people want to worry about me. But they shouldn't worry about the company, because it's in better shape than it's ever been."

Life and Career

Roberto Crispulo Goizueta was born in Havana, Cuba, on November 18, 1931. He was a bright child who had a privileged upbringing. He attended the Cheshire Academy in Connecticut, where he mastered the English language through an unusual combination of formal tuition and sitting through countless hours of American movies.

He earned a degree in chemical engineering at Yale University in 1953, graduating tenth in his class, and returned to Cuba to work in his family's sugar refining business. He wanted to carve out a career for himself, however, and on the off chance answered an ad in a

Havana newspaper for a bilingual chemical engineer. He got the job and started work on July 4, 1954, with the Coca-Cola Company.

In 1959, after leading a communist revolution, Fidel Castro seized power in Cuba. Eighteen months later Goizueta, his wife Olga, and their three children left for the United States, leaving everything behind except a suitcase, $200 in cash, and 100 Coca-Cola shares.

Contribution

Goizueta and his family settled in Miami, where he worked for Coca-Cola's Latin American division. In 1964 he was reassigned to the technical research and development department at the company's headquarters in Atlanta.

He was a hard worker known for his neatness and sharp dress sense. In Atlanta he found himself working closely with a company legend, Robert Woodruff. Woodruff had organized the syndicate that in 1923 bought out the Candler family's interests in Coca-Cola. He had overseen the company's global expansion and Coke's growth into one of the world's most valuable brands, and he was still a major player. Goizueta clearly made a good impression on Woodruff: in 1966 he was made company Vice-President. Aged just 35, he was the youngest executive ever to have held the post.

Goizueta's meteoric rise continued. He became Senior Vice-President in 1974 and a Vice-Chairman in 1979. Finally, in May 1980, he became C.E.O. and Chairman of Coca-Cola. At the time he was one of only two people who knew the formula for Coca-Cola, then, as now, one of the most closely held industrial secrets in the world. It was a long way from the family sugar refinery in Cuba.

When Goizueta took the helm, Coca-Cola was facing one of the toughest challenges in its history. Its chief rival, PepsiCo, was using a taste test dubbed the "Pepsi Challenge" to turn soda drinkers into Pepsi purchasers. In Pepsi's blind taste test it turned out that many consumers preferred Pepsi to Coke. Goizueta had promised that he was prepared to take risks in an effort to revitalize the company and in April 1985 he proved true to his word when he announced that Coca-Cola was replacing its traditional recipe cola. The switch to New Coke was, according to Goizueta, "the boldest single marketing move in the history of the consumer goods business." Unfortunately, it also proved one of the major marketing mistakes of the 20th century.

Detailed market research conducted by Coca-Cola had supported the move, indicating that most consumers preferred the new formula. But New Coke failed miserably on the shelves. After it was introduced, not only did Pepsi remain a threat, but the old-formula Coke was still selling in millions of units every day. The move weakened the Coca-Cola brand. Instead of shrugging off Pepsi's threat like the market leader it was, Coca-Cola

> *When Goizueta took the helm, Coca-Cola was facing one of the toughest challenges in its history. Its chief rival, PepsiCo, was using a taste test dubbed the "Pepsi Challenge" to turn soda drinkers into Pepsi purchasers.*

appeared worried. Furthermore, by producing a drink named "New Coke" the company dislocated its established brand values of tradition and authenticity from its new product. To call this the marketing own goal of the century would be to understate the effect. Goizueta was buried under an avalanche of criticism. Some Coke fans uncharitably said that the new formula tasted like "furniture polish"; others said "sewer water."

To his credit, Goizueta didn't let pride or stubbornness get in the way of good marketing. Realizing that the introduction of New Coke had been a disaster, he backtracked, and in July, after only 90 days, he reintroduced the original formula as Classic Coke. It has not been tinkered with since.

With the exception of the New Coke debacle, Goizueta's period at the helm of Coca-Cola was a huge success. In 1982 he oversaw the successful product launch of Diet Coke. That same year he led the company in a new direction, agreeing to purchase Columbia Pictures. Though the studio proved nearly impossible to manage, the acquisition turned out to be a smart financial deal: seven years later Coca-Cola sold Columbia to Sony, making a profit of nearly $1 billion.

Goizueta died in 1997, aged 65, leaving a personal fortune of $1.3 billion. When he died Coca-Cola was valued at $145 billion, compared with a value of $4 billion when he became chief executive.

Context and Conclusions

When Goizueta was appointed C.E.O. of Coca-Cola, the soft drinks manufacturer was beginning to show signs of vulnerability in a market it had dominated since it was first founded. Pepsi Cola was posing a threat to Coca-Cola through the Pepsi Taste Challenge. Pepsi's blind taste test results favoring Pepsi over Coke had the Coca-Cola executives rattled. Goizueta, a man willing to take risks, played Russian roulette with the Coke brand and lost: fortunately he only shot the company in the foot. Yet his response merely reinforced what a brilliant C.E.O. he was. Instead of trying to tough it out, he acceded to public demand. His prompt action prevented a marketing mishap from becoming a full-scale corporate disaster. It also reenergized the brand, reminding the public how much they loved "classic" Coke.

For More Information
Book:

Greising, David. *I'd Like the World to Buy a Coke: The Life and Leadership of Roberto Goizueta*. New York: John Wiley, 1999.

Web site:
Coca-Cola: **www.cocacola.com**

Andrew S. Grove

1936	Born.
1957	"Traitorous eight" start Fairchild Semiconductor. Grove escapes to United States.
1963	Gains Ph.D. from University of California, Berkeley.
1968	Gordon Moore and Bob Noyce start Intel.
1979	Becomes Intel's President and Chief Operating Officer.
1981	IBM decides to use Intel microprocessors.
1985	Shifts Intel's focus to microprocessors.
1987	Becomes C.E.O. of Intel.
1994	Flawed Pentium microprocessors recalled.
1998	Steps down as Intel's C.E.O.
1999	Intel launches Pentium 3 processors.
1999	Grove, a former journalist, warns media to adapt to threat of Web publications.
2001	Intel experiences product shortages and delays. 500 job cuts.
2001	Launch of Itanium high-end processor.
2001	European Commission launches antitrust case against Intel.

Summary

Andy Grove (1936–) managed to survive a childhood in Nazi-occupied Hungary only to find himself a victim of the Cold War. He escaped to the United States in 1957. After educating himself in New York and California, Grove joined Fairchild Semiconductor. In 1968 he followed colleagues Bob Noyce and Gordon Moore to form a new company, Intel. By 1979 he was chief operating officer.

In the 1980s Grove concentrated the company's efforts on manufacturing microprocessors. He was made C.E.O. in 1987. In 1994 he faced a crisis when a flaw was discovered in the company's flagship product, the Pentium processor. Under pressure, Grove made the decision to replace the chips rather than try to tough it out, reinforcing Intel's reputation.

Life and Career

Illness, discrimination, poverty: Andy Grove, born Andras Grof in prewar Hungary on September 2, 1936, suffered them all as a child. At the age of four he contracted scarlet fever, which left him with impaired hearing. Then another, more sinister, threat cast its shadow: as the Nazis swept to power in Europe, the Jewish Grof family feared for their lives. Grof and his mother assumed false identities and were sheltered by friends. The young Grof became Andras Malesevics.

Miraculously he and his family avoided the death camps and survived the war. Their celebrations were short-lived however, for in 1956 communist Russia invaded Hungary; Grof and the rest of his family found themselves on the wrong side of the Iron Curtain. Weighing up his options Grof, by now used to playing for high stakes, decided to escape.

He fled to Austria and from there to the United States, changing his name to Andrew S. Grove along the way. Arriving in the United States in 1957, he enrolled at City College of New York, graduating in 1960 with a degree in chemical engineering. After City College, he studied at the University of California, Berkeley, receiving his Ph.D. in 1963.

His first job after graduation was at Fairchild Semiconductor, a young company formed by several research scientists including Robert Noyce and Gordon Moore.

Contribution

Fairchild Semiconductor was the cradle of the computing revolution. It was formed by a disaffected group of researchers from William Shockley's research team at Shockley Semiconductor Laboratory in Palo Alto, California. Shockley had received the Nobel Prize for his work developing the transistor, and his academic reputation attracted some of the finest minds in electronics to his company, including Bob Noyce, Gordon Moore, Julius Blank, Victor Grinich, Eugene Kleiner, Jean Hoerni, Jay Last, and Sheldon Roberts.

Shockley's poor management style bred disaffection among his research team. The eventual exodus from his company of the so-called "traitorous eight" was one of the landmarks of computing history. The company they founded, Fairchild Semiconductor, revolutionized the world of computing with its work on the silicon transistor. The drain of talent from Shockley's lab went on after Fairchild to start up some of the best-known companies in Silicon Valley. Intel (Bob Noyce and Gordon Moore), Advanced Micro Devices (Jerry Sanders), and National Semiconductor (Charlie Sporck) were all spinoffs from Fairchild.

When Gordon Moore and Bob Noyce left Fairchild in 1968 to start Intel, they asked Grove to come with them. Noyce and Moore's original business plan involved manufacturing a new kind of computer memory using semiconductor technology, and in 1970 the first dynamic random-access memory (DRAM) for commercial use rolled off Intel's production lines. Intel had also been approached by a Japanese company, Nippon Calculating Machine Corporation (NCM), to produce logic chips. Intel had already been working on a smaller single chip and offered its own solution. A chip was eventually developed. Instead of the patent rights passing to NCM, Intel retained ownership and licensed manufacturing and selling rights. It was this key decision by Grove and the management team that paved the way for Intel to become the microprocessor giant it is today.

Intel's success was founded not only on its innovative skills but also on its skillful repositioning of what had previously been a commodity computer component into a household-name brand. TV commercials elevated the mundane microchip to an aspirational product. Encouraged by the "Intel Inside" ad campaign, consumers insisted on having an Intel chip inside their PCs. The Intel Pentium processor became as strongly associated with PCs as Microsoft's Windows operating system, another marketing success story.

Andy Grove's vision was instrumental in Intel's success. Grove steered the company from a fledgling producer of memory chips into a giant of the microprocessor industry. He got things done. In the early days he was the man who organized the office space and manufacturing capacity. He played a key role in the 1981 negotiations with IBM that saw Intel beat off competition from Motorola to supply the microprocessors for IBM's PCs.

In many ways Grove's childhood experiences had prepared him well for business life. He was a man who didn't avoid tough decisions. In the 1980s, when microprocessors looked as if they might be a better bet than memory, Grove made the bold and risky decision to refocus the company's efforts. It was a tough call that meant laying off thousands of employees. In 1987 Grove became the C.E.O. of Intel. The decisions didn't get any easier. Grove averted a potential crisis when a flaw was discovered in the company's flagship

Pentium microprocessor. With a technical problem probably discernible only by mathematicians threatening to balloon into a public relations disaster of epic proportions, Grove acted decisively. He could have used Intel's muscle to pass on the burden of replacement to the retailers and consumers. Instead Grove offered to replace the processors. The move may have cost a fortune—$475 million—but it safeguarded the Intel brand. Profits went up.

Grove was a godsend to the company's stockholders. During his tenure as C.E.O. Intel's stock value increased 24-fold. In May 1998 Grove resigned as C.E.O., remaining as Chairman of the board. Since stepping down he has focused on strategic thinking. Drawing on his experience as a journalist, he advised the media in 1999 to change its approach in light of the growing strength of Web publications.

Since Grove took a back seat at Intel the company has been wrestling with a number of difficult issues, not least a likely future decline in demand for microchips. Moore's Law (originated by Intel cofounder Gordon Moore) states that microprocessing power will double every 18 months. It has held true for over a decade, delivering revenue growth to Intel through consumer chip upgrades. Eventually, though, Moore believes that the rate of increase will slow, and he should know. Grove appears to be prepared for this. He is on record as saying that "all companies will be Internet companies." Backing this view, Intel has diversified its operations to embrace the Internet. Technical innovation continued after Grove's departure with the launch of the Pentium 3 processor in 1999, Pentium 4 in 2000, and the Itanium high-end 4-bit processor in 2001. However supply problems hit the company hard in 2000, leading to the loss of 500 jobs that year. In 2001, the company hit further problems when the European Commission launched an antitrust case against Intel for alleged abuse of a dominant position to stifle competition.

Context and Conclusions

Just as all companies need an entrepreneur to make things happen in the formative stages of a new venture, so too they need an organizer and steady hand to help guide a company from startup through the growth phase and beyond. Andy Grove is such a man. With resolve, vision, and an ability to take risks based on hard facts, Grove came from behind the Iron Curtain to become C.E.O. of one of America's technology bellwether stocks. As a child in war-torn Europe, Grove learned to assess a situation using all available information and then make a decision. It is a skill that has served him well throughout his life, both business and personal. Whatever his future achievements, his accomplishments at Intel alone merit a place alongside the great business leaders of the 20th century.

For More Information

Books:

Grove, Andrew S. *Only the Paranoid Survive: How to Achieve a Success that's Just a Disaster Away*. New York: Doubleday, 1999.

Grove, Andrew S. *Swimming Across: A Memoir*. New York: Warner Books, 2001.

Jackson, Tim. *Inside Intel: Andy Grove and the Rise of the World's Most Powerful Chip Company*. Collingdale, PA: DIANE, 2001.

Web site:

Intel: **www.intel.com**

William Randolph Hearst

1863	Born.
1887	Takes control of the *San Francisco Examiner*.
1889	The *San Francisco Examiner* makes a profit.
1895	Heads for New York to save the *New York Morning Journal*.
1896	Acquires New York's *Evening Journal*.
1902	Becomes a Democratic congressional representative for New York.
1920s	Builds a fabulous castle on San Simeon estate.
1930s	Forced to consolidate empire following the Great Depression.
1951	Dies.

Summary

Arguably the most famous media mogul of the 20th century, William Randolph Hearst (1863–1951) took the silver spoon of his inheritance and fashioned it into a gold one. Despite his patrician upbringing, he succeeded in keeping his finger on the pulse of his industry. Through a combination of media savvy and extraordinary stamina and persistence, he built an ailing newspaper, the *San Francisco Examiner*, into a billion dollar media empire. At his peak, Hearst owned over 40 major newspapers and magazines, not to mention a handful of radio stations and movie companies. In 1951 he died an immensely wealthy and powerful man, immortalized ten years previously, and much to his chagrin, in Orson Welles's movie, *Citizen Kane*.

Life and Career

Hearst was born in San Francisco on April 29, 1863. His father was a wealthy industrialist and speculator, and his mother a socialite and philanthropist. It was a potent cocktail of wealth, commerce, and culture that was to have a profound effect on him. An only child, he spent his early years shuttling between the family's huge estate at San Simeon, California, and their home in New York.

The classical academic route for the privileged awaited: a first-class prep school—St. Paul's Preparatory School in Concord, New Hampshire—followed by an Ivy League university—Harvard. At Harvard Hearst excelled in social activities. He was a member of the Hasty Pudding Theater and, more notably, business manager for the college magazine, the *Harvard Lampoon*. So much energy was put into his social life that he neglected his academic work. Hearst was eventually expelled and he never received his degree.

Shrugging off his academic failure, he took a job instead at the *New York World*. Joseph Pulitzer's newspaper was one of the leading newspapers in New York at the time. Hearst may not have paid attention in his Harvard classes, but at the *New York World* he received a first-class education in how to run a newspaper. However, he was soon summoned back to San Francisco by his father.

Contribution

In contrast to media moguls like Louis B. Mayer who worked their way up from the bottom of the pile, Hearst was handed his first newspaper as a gift. The *San Francisco Examiner* had been purchased by Hearst's father to provide him with a voice when he was running for the U.S. Senate. With the senate seat secured, the paper was surplus to requirements. Neglected, its circulation dwindled. The younger Hearst was desperate to take charge of it. His father was less enthusiastic and offered him as alternative inducements a one-million-acre ranch in Chihuahua, the 275,000-acre San Simeon ranch north of San Luis Obsipo, the Anaconda copper mines in Montana, and the Homestake gold mine in South Dakota. Hearst refused them all saying: "You are very kind but I would rather have the *Examiner*." Reluctantly, his father relented.

On March 4, 1887 Hearst took up residence at the *San Francisco Examiner*. He had discovered his métier. He was a brilliant newspaper owner. Thanks to a radical overhaul, by 1889 the *Examiner* was in profit. The staid format Hearst had inherited was replaced with hard-hitting investigative reporting, coupled with sensationalist, attention grabbing headlines. Increased sports coverage, serialized stories by well-known authors, banner headlines like "Huge Frantic Flames," biographical sketches, and exposés of the seedy underbelly of Californian life all contributed to the heady populist mix.

As circulation and profits rose, Hearst expanded the business. In 1895 he returned to his old hunting ground on the East Coast to save the *New York Morning Journal*. It was a decision that put him in direct competition with his onetime mentor, Joseph Pulitzer. Hearst pulled no punches in the ensuing circulation war. He added the *Evening Journal* to his collection in 1896 and poached some of Pulitzer's top writers. It was a period that gave rise to the term "yellow journalism," where newspapers assumed the role of opinion formers and determiners of morals. In scenes commonplace today, rival newspapers vied for scoops and used their front pages to boast of their achievements.

The most famous example of Hearst's proactive stance to newspaper reporting is the comment attributed to him when the illustrator Frederick Remington informed him that he wished to return from an uneventful Havana. Hearst supposedly responded: "Please remain. You furnish the pictures and I'll furnish the war."

His methods may have been controversial, but they worked. Hearst was unstoppable. He soon acquired newspapers in major cities throughout America. Following in his father's footsteps he became involved in politics. In 1902, Congress welcomed Hearst as a Democratic representative for New York. In all he served two terms in Congress and also became mayor of New York City.

With his newspaper empire firmly established, Hearst expanded into other areas of the media. As a publisher he produced titles that included *Cosmopolitan*, *Good Housekeeping*, and *Harper's Bazaar*. He also moved into the movie business, cutting his teeth with Hearst-Metronome News. Ultimately it was the movie industry, coupled with his infatuation for the actress Marion Davies, that was to prove his downfall.

His final years were spent trying to prevent the release of Orson Welles's film Citizen Kane, *a thinly disguised biopic of him. He failed.*

He formed W. R. Hearst's Cosmopolitan Productions as a vehicle for Davies, his Brooklyn-born mistress and a former Ziegfeld Follies girl. Abandoning his political career after failed attempts at the Senate and the presidency,

Hearst focused solely on films. Of the hundred films he sanctioned over the next 20 years, half featured his mistress. As well as sinking millions of dollars into making movies, Hearst spent more millions on a Beverly Hills mansion for Davies. Finally he embarked on the folly that was to prove his undoing, the construction of the Hearst Castle estate at San Simeon. The 25,000 acres of the estate and castle contained rare and priceless works of art, antiquities, a zoo, an airfield, and guest houses which were chateaux dismantled in Europe and flown to California to be reassembled stone by stone.

Hearst might have survived such profligate extravagance had it not been for the Great Depression. During the 1930s he was forced to consolidate his empire, selling newspapers and works of art to remain afloat. By the end of the decade he had halved his business interests and plundered the treasures at San Simeon. Marion Davies too, liquidated her personal assets and pumped $1 million into her lover's business. His final years were spent trying to prevent the release of Orson Welles's film *Citizen Kane*, a thinly disguised biopic of him. He failed. In the end, in ill health and bitter at the Welles episode, he retreated to San Simeon, handing over control of his empire to lawyers and managers. He died at the home of Marion Davies on August 14, 1951.

Context and Conclusions

Although Hearst's final years were marred by what must have been for him a humiliating fall from grace, he will still be remembered as one of the greatest media barons of all time. While he was born with all the advantages wealth brings, Hearst turned around the *San Francisco Examiner*, invented a new style of popular journalism, and fashioned a media empire through hard-nosed determination, incredible stamina, and a common touch that belied his background. Hearst was truly a paradox. A man with wealth beyond the dreams and understanding of most, he was blessed nevertheless with the innate ability to appreciate the hopes and fears of ordinary people.

To the last he saw himself as the people's champion. He believed that the criticism and misfortunes that had befallen him were the result of his willingness to take a stand on behalf of the masses. "Any man who has the brains to think and the nerve to act for the benefit of the people of the country," he said, "is considered a radical by those who are content with stagnation and willing to endure disaster."

For More Information

Books:

Davies, Marion. *The Times We Had: Life with William Randolph Hearst*. New York: Ballantine Books, 1975.

Nasaw, David. *The Chief: The Life of William Randolph Hearst*. Boston: Houghton Mifflin Co., 2000.

Proctor, Ben. *William Randolph Hearst: The Early Years 1866–1910*. New York: Oxford University Press, 1998.

Web site:

The William Randolph Hearst Foundations: **www.hearstfdn.org**

Milton Snavely Hershey

1857	Born.
1871	Drops out of school at age 13.
1872	Apprenticed at Joe Royer's Ice Cream Parlor and Garden.
1876	Opens a store making and selling candy in Philadelphia.
1882	Closes business in Philadelphia; opens and fails in Chicago.
1883	Opens candy store in New York City, which closes in 1886.
1886	Starts the Lancaster Caramel Company.
1893	Visits Chicago World's Fair and orders chocolate making equipment.
1895	Starts selling chocolate.
1900	Hershey's chocolate bar introduced. Lancaster Caramel Company sold for $1 million.
1906	Derry Church becomes Hershey Town.
1916	Builds sugar mill in Cuba.
1920	Loses $2.5 million on sugar futures. Forced to borrow from banks.
1942	U.S. Army asks Hershey to develop chocolate bar for field rations.
1945	Dies.

Summary

Milton Snavely Hershey (1857–1945) is the entrepreneur who brought the world the Hershey chocolate bar. He was a late starter in business, his first attempts in the confectionery industry ending in failure. Real success finally came in his late thirties with the Lancaster Caramel Company, a business he eventually sold to a rival for a large sum. The break that put Hershey in the history books came in 1893, when he stumbled across chocolate manufacturing equipment at the World's Fair in Chicago. Hershey concentrated on chocolate, perfected a recipe for milk chocolate, introduced mass production, and built a thriving chocolate business as well as a town called Hershey.

Life and Career

Born on September 13, 1857, Milton Snavely Hershey was brought up in Hockersville, Pennsylvania. It was a small rural town and he was educated in a one-room schoolhouse. His parents were farmers and, from a very early age, Hershey was expected to help out on the farm tending the livestock and doing other chores.

After attending a string of schools—including a private high school, the Village Academy of Green Tree, where he did not do well—Hershey gave up on education and took a position as an apprentice with a German-language newspaper based in Gap, Lancaster County. It was soon clear that his talents did not lie with either journalism or publishing. He left the paper and joined Joseph H. Royer of Lancaster as an apprentice confectioner.

He was an ambitious young man. Aged 19 he founded his own company, M. S. Hershey, Wholesale and Retail Confectioner. The business failed and was sold in 1882. Over the following few years Hershey traveled the country trying to set himself up in the candy business. In Denver, Colorado, he learned how to make caramels. In New York City he sold his candy on the street. None of these ventures prospered, so he headed back to Lancaster.

It was in Lancaster, the scene of his first business failure, that Hershey finally met with some success.

Contribution

Hershey put his caramel making skills to work. From the outset his business was based on quality of product. "Give them the quality, that's the best kind of advertising in the world" was his motto. The business took off when Hershey's caramels came to the attention of a candy importer who bought some to sell in England.

Hershey put his caramel making skills to work. From the outset his business was based on quality of product.

In 1893, however, while visiting Chicago, Hershey met the manufacturer of a German-made chocolate-making machine. He ordered one of the machines and had it shipped to Lancaster. The eventual result was a change of direction and the development of his most famous product, Hershey chocolate.

With the caramel business, Hershey had excelled in creating a variety of candies. Now he concentrated on perfecting a single product—chocolate. In 1900 he sold his caramel business for $1 million to the American Caramel Company of Philadelphia. With the proceeds, he invested in a new chocolate factory near his family home—he was married by now—in Derry Church.

When it came to making chocolate, Hershey had no recipe book or magic formula to rely on. Together with a few trusted colleagues he locked himself away and labored over the perfect milk chocolate recipe. "Nobody told Mr. Hershey how to make milk chocolate. He just found out the hard way," recalled one of his employees. Hard work though it was, Hershey struck chocolate gold. The result of his research—the Hershey chocolate bar—soon became a byword for quality in the United States.

Hershey continued to consolidate his chocolate business. He produced variations on the standard bar including: Mr. Goodbar, a milk chocolate and peanut candy bar, in 1925; Krackel, a chocolate bar filled with crisped rice, in 1938; and Hershey miniatures—small versions of all Hershey's chocolate bars—in 1939. To secure his sugar supply and guarantee its quality he built a sugar mill and small town in Cuba along the lines of Hershey, Pennsylvania.

In 1920 Hershey suffered a setback when he lost $2.5 million on the sugar futures market. He was forced to borrow from the bank, and, as a condition of the loan, the bank put a representative in Hershey's factory. It took him two years to pay the loan off and eject the overseer.

As Hershey's business grew, so too did the town surrounding the factory. Hershey wanted to build a town in keeping with his social philosophy in the same way that other chocolate philanthropists, like Joseph Rowntree and George Cadbury, had done in England. He drew up plans for an idyllic community that would not only house its inhabitants but provide for their every need, including employment at the Hershey chocolate factory. When the town was completed it contained parks, churches, a school, a hotel, a golf course, and even a zoo. Townsfolk would walk along streets such as Areba, Caracus, and Para, all named after cocoa bean producing regions. Hershey held a competition to name the new town. The winning entry, Hersheyoko, was vetoed by the U.S. Post Office, so he settled for plain old Hershey Town. He also constructed a mansion, High Point, overlooking the chocolate factory, to house his family.

Shortly before his death, one last act assured the name of Hershey a place in business history. When the United States entered World War II, the U.S. military instructed him to develop a chocolate bar for the troops—one that wouldn't melt. He once again set about chocolate innovation. The resulting Field Ration D Chocolate Bar formed an essential part of the army's personal kit. Not only was it a great favorite of the U.S. personnel, but with the stationing of American troops in England and the subsequent D-Day invasion of Europe, it became part of World War II folklore. Hershey died on October 13, 1945 at age 88.

Hershey wanted to build a town in keeping with his social philosophy in the same way that other chocolate philanthropists, like Joseph Rowntree and George Cadbury, had done in England.

Context and Conclusions

First and foremost Hershey pioneered the mass production of food and, in particular, chocolate. It may only have been milk chocolate, but Hershey manufactured it on an unprecedented scale. Besides his single-minded approach, Hershey possessed a number of other qualities that contributed to his success. He was innovative, creating the Hershey Kiss and inventing his own recipe for milk chocolate. He was a bold risk-taker, making decisions like the one to build a sugar plant in Cuba. Perhaps his defining characteristic, however, was his enlightened attitude toward corporate social responsibility. It makes sense to keep the work force happy, but few can claim to have gone to such lengths as Hershey to do so. The business history books tell how successful the Hershey chocolate bar was and still is. Hershey Town with its schools, parks, churches, and chocolate factory is a more permanent record.

For More Information

Books:

Brenner, Joël Glenn. *The Emperors of Chocolate: Inside the Secret World of Hershey and Mars*. New York: Random House, 1999.

McMahon, James D. *Built on Chocolate: The Story of the Hershey Chocolate Company*. Santa Monica, CA: General Publishing Group, 1999.

Web site:

Hershey Foods Corporation: **www.hersheys.com**

Conrad Nicholson Hilton

1887	Born.
1907	Helps with family hotel.
1912	Serves a term in the first New Mexico state legislature.
1919	Buys first hotel, Mobley Hotel in Cisco, Texas.
1925	Constructs his first hotel, the Dallas Hilton.
1925–1930	Opens new hotel every year.
1929	The Wall Street crash and great depression hits Hilton's business.
1933	Forced to sell his hotel in El Paso. Joins forces with William L. Moody. Forms the National Hotel Company.
1934	Leaves National Hotel Company.
1946	Hilton Hotels incorporated. Hilton becomes Chairman.
1948	Hilton Hotels International formed.
1949	First international hotel opens—Caribe Hilton in Puerto Rico.
1954	Pays $111 million for the Statler hotel chain.
1960	Hilton owns 188 hotels in 38 cities in the United States, as well as 54 abroad.
1960s–1970s	Expands international business and devotes his time to Conrad N. Hilton Foundation.
1979	Dies.

Summary

Conrad Nicholson Hilton pioneered the development of the hotel chain in the United States and across the world. He started as a boy, helping with his parents' small hotel in San Antonio, New Mexico. After a spell in the army during World War I serving as a lieutenant, Hilton set out to buy a small bank in Texas. Instead he bought a hotel. One hotel led to another, and despite tough times during the great depression, by the 1950s Hilton had acquired more than 150 hotels in the United States and abroad. His board of Directors advised Hilton against expanding his business abroad after World War II. He ignored them, founding Hilton Hotel International. The international hotels proved extremely popular, especially with Americans who knew they could rely on a Hilton hotel to provide them with a small oasis of United States culture and quality in a foreign country. When Hilton died in 1979, he left behind one of the foremost hotel companies in the world, as well as a philanthropic body—the Conrad Hilton Foundation—devoted to promoting, among other things, Hilton's firm belief in world peace through economics.

Life and Career

The son of a Norwegian immigrant father and a German-American mother, Conrad Nicholson Hilton was born in San Antonio, New Mexico on Christmas Day, 1887. He was educated at the Goss Military Institute in Albuquerque, the New Mexico Military Institute at Roswell, and St. Michael's College in Santa Fe. His first taste of the hotel business came in 1907. During the "panic" of 1907, money was scarce for the Hilton family. At Hilton's suggestion, part of the family's general store was converted into a small hotel. To drum up trade Hilton went to the local train station, where he offered travelers a room for $1.

Hilton's early flirtation with the hotel industry ended when he was left the family business to attend the New Mexico Institute of Mining at Socorro. After finishing his courses at the Institute, he made quick progress in business—and politics. In 1912, he was elected to serve a term in the first New Mexico state legislature. Still in his early twenties he founded the New Mexico state bank, but was considered too young to serve as C.E.O. When World War I came, he enlisted and served as a lieutenant in the Quartermaster Corps of the American Expeditionary Force.

Contribution

When Hilton was discharged from the army in 1919, he made a more serious start in the hotel business. In June of that year, he visited the town of Cisco in Texas. The small town was close to the Ranger oil fields and Hilton intended to buy a bank in the town. Instead he bought the Mobley Hotel, hoping to capitalize on his brief experience of the hotel business. It was a good decision. In the great depression of the late 1920s and 1930s, 11 of the region's 13 banks failed. Hilton's fledgling hotel business survived by a smart tactical move, when he rented his rooms out on eight-hour shifts to match the working patterns of the oil men. It was the beginning of Hilton's hotel empire.

Hilton bought a hotel in Fort Worth in 1919, then two smaller hotels in 1920. In 1925 he constructed his first hotel, the Dallas Hilton. In the five years from 1925 to 1930, Hilton was opening a new hotel every year. In 1929, the Wall Street crash and the great depression that followed hit Hilton's business badly. By this time he had eight hotels. Advertising in national magazines helped, but by 1931 travel had dipped throughout the United States, bringing him close to bankruptcy. In 1933 he was forced to sell his hotel in El Paso. Help arrived in the guise of William L. Moody, Jr. of Galveston. Moody was the son of a Texan millionaire, who had made a fortune primarily through the cotton business. To survive, Hilton joined forces with

> *By 1939, Hilton had paid off his debts and started to expand his business.*

Moody to form the National Hotel Company, with Hilton as general manager. But Moody and Hilton disagreed on how to run the business. In 1934 Hilton left the National Hotel Company and started on his own again, this time with five hotels.

By 1939, Hilton had paid off his debts and started to expand his business. He took advantage of the weakness of the economy to buy a string of hotels. These included prestigious names such as the Plaza and the Waldorf-Astoria Hotel in New York, the Palmer House in Chicago, and the Sir Francis Drake in San Francisco.

Hilton's operation of the Palmer House hotel in Chicago serves as an illustration of why he was so successful. During World War II there was a rush for accommodation. Hotels were booked up and travelers became frustrated in their efforts to find a room. In the Palmer House a sign said "Sorry! No rooms today without reservations." Day after day Hilton saw the sign and, growing sick of it, realized the demoralizing effect it must have on customers arriving at the hotel looking for accommodation. He had the sign removed and, in its place, made available desks to help visitors find accommodation elsewhere in the city if none were available there. Another problem was the inconvenience to guests who had to wait until the 3:00 p.m. checking-out time. To ease their plight, Hilton arranged for facilities where guests could wash and take a shower. Tailoring service to customers' needs in this way marked Hilton's hotels out from the competition.

As well as excellent customer service, Hilton used other techniques to make his business more efficient than those of his rivals. He introduced innovative financial controls, requiring department heads to calculate departmental costs and evaluate the actual cost of operations each month. This meant that, for the first time, hotel managers could estimate costs needed to deal with required service levels, and still get the best possible maximum gross operating profits.

Hilton was a master of squeezing profits out of his hotels. Take the landmark Hilton hotels, for example. The Plaza House was bought in 1943; Hilton instigated decorative improvements and boosted revenues by 8%. This in turn allowed him to spend $500,000 on improving facilities. Hilton called this tactic "mining for gold." He used it in all his flagship hotels. In its first year, the Waldorf-Astoria increased revenues by over $1.5 million, with 95 fewer employees. In the Mayflower Hotel, profits on food increased from 7% to 19%. Between 1948 and 1950, Hilton increased profits from 18% to 26%. In the same period the payroll came down by 4.5%, with other expenses down by 3%. Hilton's "magic formula" meant that hotels were profitable even in times of low occupancy.

Hilton Hotels was incorporated on May 29,1946, with Hilton becoming Chairman. After the war he traveled to Europe to assess the commercial opportunities, wanting to operate hotels outside of the United States. His board of Directors was not convinced and advised him against it. Nevertheless, he went ahead and incorporated Hilton Hotels International in 1948.

Hilton opened his first hotel outside America in December 1949. The 300-room Caribe Hilton hotel was built in Puerto Rico at a cost of $5.5 million. In its first year, it made a profit of $100,000 and went on to be very lucrative venture. And, just as importantly, it paved the way for Hilton's international ambitions. He expanded extensively, with hotels in cities across the globe including Berlin, Cairo and Istanbul. By the late 1950s, he owned 188 hotels in 38 American cities, as well as 54 abroad. On October 27, 1954, Conrad Hilton paid $111 million for the Statler hotel chain. At the time it was the largest commercial real estate deal in history.

Customer service is vital for any business today, and Hilton was ahead of his time.

Between 1960 and his death in 1979, Hilton increasingly devoted his time to the Conrad N. Hilton Foundation, which he had founded in 1944. The foundation was instrumental in building the famous Mayo Clinic, as well as setting up the Conrad N. Hilton College of Hotel and Restaurant Management at the University of Houston.

Hilton Hotels' corporate motto was "World Peace through International Trade and Travel." It was also Hilton's personal belief. He reasoned that through his business, he could contribute to global economic stability. When he died in 1979, the administrators of his estate (once they had sorted through his 35 separate wills) discovered that the bulk of it had been left to his foundation.

Context and Conclusions

Conrad Hilton was not the only man who built a hotel chain during the early and mid-20th century. He was not even the first. What made him so successful was his approach to business. Customer service is vital for any business today, and Hilton was ahead of his time. He insisted that service was tailored to the needs of his customers, even if that sometimes went beyond serving his own commercial interests in an effort to keep the customer happy. This in turn secured the reputation of the Hilton brand as a customer-oriented company. He also introduced stringent financial controls to keep on top of operating costs, and reinvested profits to upgrade service continually. Through his "magic formula" he brought customers into the hotels and used the increased revenues to improve facilities. Finally, he anticipated the approach of franchises such as McDonald's by applying brand consistency across the globe. Travelers could always rely on of the quality of a Hilton hotel, regardless of what country they were staying in. It was this forward-thinking approach to the building of his hotel empire that set Hilton apart from his peers.

CLOSE BUT NO CIGAR
ELLSWORTH STATLER
Statler built his first hotel as a temporary and speculative venture to provide accommodation for the 1901 Pan American Exposition. With the profits, he built more hotels. His 2,002-room Pennsylvania Hotel in New York City was the largest hotel of its day. Innovations included novelties such as private bathrooms, closets, telephones, and electric light switches by the doors. He was also the first to sell railway tickets in the hotel. Statler died prematurely in 1928. His business was successfully carried on by his widow, and eventually sold to the Hilton Hotel Corporation in the largest real estate deal since the Louisiana Land Purchase.

For More Information
Books:
Hilton, Conrad. *Be My Guest*. New York: Prentice Hall, 1957.
Jarman, Rufus. *A Bed for the Night: The Story of the Wheeling Bellboy E. M. Statler and His Remarkable Hotels*. New York: Harper and Bros., 1952.

Soichiro Honda

1906	Born.
1937	Founds Tokai Seiki Heavy Industry (TSHI).
1948	Cofounds Honda with Takeo Fujisawa.
1949	D Type motorcycle—the Dream—manufactured.
1952	Production of Cub begins.
1954	Honda motorcycle team is founded.
1959	Opens dealership in United States. Super Cub goes into production.
1963	Honda becomes top-selling motorcycle brand in United States.
1973	Officially retires.
1984	Ten million Honda 50s sold in United States.
1992	Dies.

Summary

Soichiro Honda started in business as a car mechanic and then, bypassing the time-honored Japanese networking system or *gakubatsa*, he made his own way in business with no help from cronies. The Honda Company was founded in 1948 and its first motorcycle—the Dream—was produced a year later. Success followed success. In 1959 Honda became the leading motorcycle manufacturer in Japan, and the Honda sports motorcycle team won the team prize at the Isle of Man TT races. In the same year the first Honda motorcycles were sold in the United States; soon they were outselling every other brand. The company went into the automobile business in the 1960s. Until Soichiro Honda's death in 1992, the company continued to be the most popular motorcycle manufacturer in the world and remained high in the international rankings of leading automobile manufacturers.

Life and Career

Born in the small Japanese town of Komyo in 1906, Soichiro Honda spent his early childhood helping his father with his bicycle repair business. At 15, without the benefit of a formal education, Honda traveled to Tokyo to look for work. He secured an apprenticeship at a garage, but ended up babysitting for the garage owner. Frustrated and dispirited, he returned home, only to be called back within six months. This time he stayed for six years, working as car mechanic before returning home once more to start his own car mechanic business. He was 22.

Honda's love of cars extended to racing them, and he set a new average speed record in 1936. Unfortunately he suffered a bad crash, breaking several bones, including both wrists. His wife, fearing for his safety, persuaded him to give up his hobby. Without the distraction of racing, Honda concentrated his energies on his business, and in 1937 he expanded into piston ring manufacture, founding Tokai Seiki Heavy Industry (TSHI). He was still conscious of his lack of education, however, and enrolled at the Hamamatsu School of Technology. As it turned out, he needn't have bothered.

Honda made a poor student. The demands of his business made it difficult to keep up with his classwork. He was reluctant to pay attention to engineering lectures that didn't involve piston rings, and he refused to take notes or attend written examinations. When the school's principal warned Honda that if he did not submit to examination he would not receive his diploma, Honda was unrepentant. "I am not impressed by diplomas. They don't do the work," he later said. "My marks were not as good as those of others, and I didn't take the final examination. The principal called me in and said I should leave. I told him that I didn't want a diploma—it had less value than a cinema ticket. A ticket at least guaranteed you would get in. A diploma guaranteed nothing."

Giving up on the diploma and therefore shunning the *gakubatsa*, the Japanese old-boy networking system, the maverick Honda set out to make his fortune on his own terms.

Born in the small Japanese town of Komyo in 1906, Soichiro Honda spent his early childhood helping his father with his bicycle repair business.

Contribution

By 1948 Honda had sold TSHI to Toyota for 450,000 yen (worth about $1 million today). He had established the Honda Technical Research Institute in 1946 and had tried to retire but found he couldn't resist the lure of engineering.

In 1948 Honda met a kindred spirit in financier Takeo Fujisawa. The two men had similar opinions on Japan's postwar industrial strategy. Both believed in long term investment, and in partnership with Honda, Fujisawa agreed to invest in a new company to manufacture engines. Honda retained responsibility for engineering, while Fujisawa dealt with marketing and sales.

By the 1950s Honda had signed a contract to sell the company's entire output of motorcycle engines to a company called Kitagawa. This wasn't as good a deal as it first appeared: Honda was geared up to produce 100 engines a month, while Kitagawa only produced 80 motorcycles at the most during the same period. Honda addressed the resulting cash flow problem by tearing up his contract with Kitagawa and replacing it with deals to supply complete motorcycles to distributors.

The company's first big hit was the Cub, which offered customers the choice either of buying an engine to fit to their bicycles or buying a complete motorcycle. In less than a year the Cub was selling 6,500 units a month and had captured over 70% of the Japanese domestic motorcycle market.

While Honda's reluctance to play by the rules caused problems in some areas, particularly with the Japanese Ministry of International Trade and Industry, it served the company well in others. Honda adopted a refreshingly open recruitment policy. Although the company had problems recruiting graduate students because of Honda's unwillingness to play the *gakubatsa* game, it attracted many high caliber employees who had been rejected by other Japanese corporations.

Honda was a perfectionist when it came to product design. He traveled the world conducting market research in person. He attended motorcycle races, taking notes on the competition. By using the best of the competition as a benchmark, Honda managed to turn the Honda motorcycle from an average product into the best racing motorcycle in the world. Success in motorcycle racing (Honda launched its own motorcycle racing team in 1954) raised the public profile of the company, added to the brand value, and enabled racing technology to filter down to the standard production model.

In 1959, the company went into large scale production of a new model that would sweep all before it, the Super Cub. To manufacture it Honda constructed the world's largest motorcycle plant in Suzuka City, which turned out 30,000 machines a month. In the same year the Honda team won first prize in the Isle of Man motorcycle races. Success on the track translated into sales.

> *Honda was a perfectionist when it came to product design. He traveled the world conducting market research in person.*

Also in 1959 Honda Motorcycles opened its first dealership in the United States. Instead of selling through the existing U.S. motorcycle distributors, Honda sold the small Honda motorcycles wherever he thought he might attract customers. At the time, total motorcycle sales in the United States were less than 5,000 a month. But by 1963 the company was selling 7,800 units; by 1984 Honda had sold some ten million Honda 50s. This remarkable success was due to the quality of the product and a brilliant advertising campaign. Instead of targeting its product at conventional motorcycle enthusiasts, Honda authorized a campaign with the slogan "You meet the nicest people on a Honda." The campaign targeted the family market and was a huge success.

The company Honda built went on to dominate the motorcycle market and make a big impact in the car market. At the end of the 20th century the company was still the world's number one motorcycle manufacturer. Honda retired in October 1973, keeping himself busy with work connected with the Honda Foundation. He died in 1992.

Context and Conclusions

Along with Konosuke Matsushita, Akio Morita, and Eiji Toyoda, Soichiro Honda was one of Japan's greatest industrialists. Notable for his independent streak, Honda spurned the traditional methods of building a business, deciding instead to go it alone. Turning a hobby into a business, he built a billion dollar company that produced the best selling motorcycle in the world. So good were their design and build quality that Honda motorcycles were soon outselling Triumph and Harley-Davidson in the U.K. and U.S. markets. To achieve this Honda used a combination of excellent engineering and clever marketing. By making a sports motorcycle that was faster than its competitors, the Honda company gained cachet for its consumer models and stayed at the cutting edge of technological development.

Above all, Soichiro Honda was determined to make his dreams a reality. "Many people dream of success," he said. "To me success can only be achieved through repeated failure and introspection. In fact, success represents 1% of your work which results from the 99% that is called failure."

For More Information

Web site:

Honda: **www.honda.com**

Howard Robard Hughes, Jr.

1905	Born.
1909	Father forms Sharp-Hughes Tool Company.
1925	Hughes moves to Hollywood, California. Starts making movies.
1927	*Two Arabian Knights* wins the Academy Award for comedy.
1934	Sets up Hughes Aircraft Company.
1935	Breaks airspeed record.
1936	Aged 30, breaks U.S. transcontinental speed record in a self-built plane.
1938	Smashes record for New York–Paris flight with time of 16 hours and 35 minutes.
1939	Obtains majority share in Transcontinental & West Airline.
1948	Saves airline (now renamed Trans World Airlines) from bankruptcy.
1954	Sells large part of RKO and concentrates on TWA.
1955	Establishes the Howard Hughes Medical Institute in Miami, Florida.
1966	Sells TWA shares for $750 million.
1975	Dies.

Summary

Howard Robard Hughes, Jr. (1905–1975) was born into wealth. His father founded a company that exploited a new design of oil drill. The Sharp-Hughes Tool Company was to provide a safety net of wealth throughout Hughes's life that made it possible for him to indulge his every whim. Indulge he did. Before the age of 25 he had moved to Hollywood and made several successful movies, founded a new drill bit company, bought over a hundred movie theaters, and learned to fly. By the time of his death in 1975, he had a built a successful airline (TWA), run a movie business, bought a piece of the gaming action on the Strip in Las Vegas, broken several airspeed records, survived three plane crashes, and become a legendary recluse. Few people have packed as much into one lifetime as Howard Hughes.

Life and Career

There is much disagreement about the facts surrounding the life of Howard Hughes. The disagreement even extends to his birthplace. Was it the city of Houston or the oil town of Humble? But there is no argument that Hughes was born on December 24, 1905 in Texas. His father was a wealthy man with a business degree from Harvard and a law degree from Iowa State University. In 1909 Howard Sr. formed the Sharp-Hughes Tool Company, manufacturing drilling bits for the oil industry. It was his invention of a new bit that propelled the Hughes family to the kind of wealth that even his son's noted profligacy could not dent.

As a boy, Howard Jr. was especially interested in engineering. He showed an impressive knack for building machines, constructing his own radio set as well as his own motorcycle. Away from engineering, Hughes's Uncle Rupert, a novelist and playwright, would take the boy to visit the Goldwyn studio where he developed a fascination with the movies.

Both Hughes's parents died before he was 20. On the death of his father, he somehow persuaded his relatives to sell him the Hughes Tool Company. Then, in 1925, he married a wealthy woman, Ella Rice, and moved to Hollywood, California.

In Hollywood Hughes began to exhibit the almost maniacal energy and drive that sustained him throughout his varied career.

Contribution

By 1925 Hughes had created the Caddo Rock Drill Bit Company, bought a controlling interest in Multi-Color, Inc., moved into a house on Muirfield Road in Los Angeles, and hired Noah Dietrich, ostensibly as an assistant. Dietrich was to become the "fixer" for the Hughes empire in the coming years. Hughes also purchased over a hundred movie theaters to assist him in his latest venture—moviemaking.

Hughes's first movie, *Swell Hogan*, was a flop. His third, *Two Arabian Knights*, made money and won the 1927 Academy Award for comedy. Hughes had another hit with *Scarface* and followed it with *The Front Page*. The difficulties involved in making *Scarface*, which stemmed partly from antagonism toward his anti-Semitic beliefs, took their toll on him and he temporarily abandoned moviemaking. For a time he restricted his interest in the movies to dating some of the most beautiful women of the time, including Ida Lupino, Katharine Hepburn, Ginger Rogers, Ava Gardner, and Lana Turner. Instead of making movies he turned his attention to the aviation business.

Hughes decided to form an aircraft company, so he hired a brilliant aeronautical engineer, Glen Odekirk, and set up business in a hangar in California. In the interval between shooting *The Front Page*, and setting up the Hughes Aircraft Company in 1934, he disappeared from sight. At about the same time, however, there appeared on the scene a gangly employee of American Airways, 6 feet 3 inches tall, called Charles Howard, who, irritatingly, asked endless questions about the airline's operations. Charles Howard, it transpired, was none other than Howard Hughes himself. Hughes also spent some of this "missing" period traveling as a hobo, and as a society photographer, a business he started from scratch in Huntsville, Texas, under the name R. Wayne Rector.

In 1939 Hughes helped finance Transcontinental & West Airline, obtaining a majority share in the process. The airline was later renamed Trans World Airlines (TWA). By 1940 the dynamic Hughes was running several businesses simultaneously, in different fields. He still owned the tool manufacturing company he had bought from his father's estate, which made him $2 million a month. In addition he was back in the movie business, running an airline, and gearing up for wartime manufacturing.

In the first half of the 1940s Hughes ordered commercial aircraft from Lockheed, made and released the film *The Outlaw*, created a new starlet in Jane Russell, opened a manufacturing plant to assist the U.S. war effort, and crashed yet another aircraft. He had already crashed two planes, killing two passengers.

In 1946, after another period of absence, Hughes reappeared to test his experimental reconnaissance aircraft, the XF-11. At 400 mph the plane became unstable. To the consternation of the members, he tried to land on the Los Angeles Country Club golf course. Luckily for the club, but unluckily for him, he didn't make it, plowing into a house on the way down. He was admitted to the Cedars of Lebanon Hospital, and the doctors predicted he would not last through the night. His injuries were extensive: a crushed chest, 12 broken ribs, a collapsed left lung, fractured shoulder, crushed vertebrae, and third-degree burns.

Remarkably, the apparently indestructible Hughes made a good recovery. He was left with burn scars and a deformed left hand, but very much alive.

Discharged from the hospital, he set about turning TWA around. He saved the ailing airline by obtaining a subsidy from the Civil Aeronautics Board in 1948, and a $10 million loan from the Reconstruction Finance Corporation. He also bolstered his movie business, buying the struggling RKO studio (Radio-Keith Orpheum) for $9 million. In 1954 Hughes sold most of RKO to concentrate on TWA. In 1955 he established the Howard Hughes Medical Institute in Miami, Florida, in an attempt to reduce his tax liabilities. On May 3, 1966 he sold 78% of his TWA stock for $750 million. It made him, temporarily, the richest man in the world.

The remainder of Hughes's career, until his death in 1975, was characterized by obsessive-neurotic behavior and flight from the IRS. Yet, despite his continual dislocation—moving from one hotel to another, one country to another—his increasingly bizarre behavior, and his dependence on pain-killing drugs, Hughes somehow managed to control his businesses from the end of a phone. He even expanded into hotels and casinos, buying the Desert Inn, Sands, Castaways, New Frontier, and Silver Slipper on the Strip in Las Vegas, as well as thousands of acres of land and over 500 mining concessions in an incredible spending spree.

The fact that Hughes's disparate collection of companies fell apart within 12 years of his death is evidence, if any were needed, that his bizarre personality was the glue that bound his business empire together.

Context and Conclusions

Of all the business leaders and entrepreneurs of the 20th century, Howard Hughes is one of the most colorful, controversial, and bizarre. An examination of his life reveals a man driven by the most basic of instincts: power, greed, lust, enmity. He ended his days a compulsive-obsessive, drug dependent hypochondriac, but consistently conducted business deals with a shrewdness beyond most of his peers. His achievements encompass movie making, aviation, and the hotel and gaming industry. In the movies Hughes notoriously pushed back the boundaries of decency and showed that it was possible to make successful movies outside the studio system. In Nevada he succeeded in loosening the Mob's grip on Las Vegas. In aviation he was among those who pioneered commercial airflight.

For More Information

Books:

Brown, Peter Harry, and Pat H. Broeske. *Howard Hughes: the Untold Story*. Brentwood, CA: Dutton, 1996.

Keats, John. *Howard Hughes*. New York: Random House, 1972.

Rummel, Robert W. *Howard Hughes and TWA*. Washington, D.C.: Smithsonian Institution Press, 1991.

Thomas, Tony. *Howard Hughes in Hollywood*. Sacramento, CA: Citadel Press, 1985.

Lee Iacocca

1924	Born.
1946	Joins Ford as a trainee engineer.
1949	Becomes sales manager.
1956	Introduces a new finance plan called the "56 for '56."
1970	Becomes President of Ford.
1978	Fired by Henry Ford II.
1979	Iacocca becomes Chairman and C.E.O. of Chrysler.
1983	Writes out check for $813,487,500 to clear Chrysler's federal debt.
1992	Retires from Chrysler.
1999	Starts E.V. Global Motors.

Summary

The lionization of chief executive officers began in earnest with Lee Iacocca. In the 1980s his remarkable turnaround of car giant Chrysler made him a corporate hero. The myth he helped to create culminated in the extraordinary worship of GE's Jack Welch in recent years. Arriving at the Ford Motor Corporation as a trainee engineer in 1946, Iacocca received the best education available in the industry. He worked his way up through Ford, not in engineering but in sales. Iacocca always claimed he wasn't a natural salesman, but he made a big impact at Ford with his revolutionary financing plan. He introduced the Ford Mustang, and was promoted to President of the company. After an internal power struggle, instigated by Henry Ford II, Iacocca was fired in 1978. He switched sides, joining Chrysler and becoming C.E.O. in 1979. Since retirement in 1992, he has concentrated on the healthy lifestyle, launching electric-powered vehicles and supporting healthy foods.

Iacocca received the best education available in the industry. He worked his way up through Ford, not in engineering but in sales.

Life and Career

Lee Iacocca was born on October 15, 1924 in Allentown, Pennsylvania. Iacocca's father ran a small hot dog business. For the Iacoccas, as for many other families during the late 1920s and 1930s, times were hard. Iacocca Sr. lost all his money and nearly lost the family home. Even though Lee Iacocca was only seven at the time, the harshness of the Depression ingrained frugality so deeply that, while he may not have been risk-averse in his business dealings, he always invested money conservatively and to this day dislikes waste.

Contribution

As a trainee at Ford's famous River Rouge plant, Iacocca got to see every stage of automobile production, from the extraction of coal and limestone, through the production of steel, to the manufacturing of the cars on the assembly line. It represented the best training the auto industry had to offer. Graduating from his trainee course, Iacocca decided against engineering and instead went to work in the Ford sales office in Chester, Pennsylvania. He was not a born salesman, yet through practice and experience he improved quickly, moving from a bashful, stammering sales clerk to become sales manager in 1949.

The 1950s were good years for Iacocca. In 1956, to combat poor sales of Ford motor cars, he introduced a new finance scheme called the "56 for '56." Credit financing was just beginning to take hold as a way of purchasing cars. The scheme allowed the cash-strapped purchaser to make a modest down payment of 20% and then follow up with three further payments of $56. The scheme was a success, and was adopted company-wide, making Iacocca an overnight star within the Ford ranks. One promotion quickly followed another. By 1960 he was head of the Ford division. Aged 36, Iacocca was general manager of the largest division in the world's second biggest automobile company.

He soon stamped his authority on the company, playing an influential role in the decision to abandon a proposed new model, the Cardinal, which was dropped despite the company incurring a $35 million loss. In its place, the first Ford Mustang rolled off the assembly line. The new car had been designed from scratch and was priced at an affordable level. Its launch created a wave of publicity, simultaneously featuring on the covers of *Time* and *Newsweek* magazines. The Mustang was the car the market had been waiting for. In its first year it sold a record 418,812, making a profit of $1.1 billion.

For Iacocca, who had championed the Mustang, the car's popularity had certain unwelcome side effects. There was no such thing as a private life anymore for the man who had brought Ford's most popular car to market. When Iacocca was returning from a trip to Europe on the Ford company plane, the pilot was contacted by two other pilots and a radio operator from a ship below, all of them wanting to speak to his celebrated passenger. "Is nothing sacred? It's Sunday morning. I am in the middle of nowhere, and I can't get away from this Mustang mania!" was Iacocca's reply. But Iacocca had much to thank the Mustang for. In January 1965 he was promoted to Vice-President of the corporate car/truck group, and on December 10, 1970 he became President of the Ford empire.

President he may have been, but Iacocca was not the most powerful person at Ford. That honor was reserved for the founder's grandson, Henry Ford II. Ford operated an unorthodox management style; he ruled through fear. Executives could find themselves clearing their desks for the most unlikely reasons. For several years Iacocca managed to walk the tightrope, on the one hand not seeming to threaten Ford's authority yet, on the other, doing a good enough job to avoid being fired. It is to his credit that Iacocca managed to stay in the job as long as he did.

In ill health, with his marriage strained, Ford became increasingly paranoid and his decisions increasingly bizarre. There was even an internal investigation within the company at Ford's request into Iacocca's activities which allegedly cost over $1,500,000 and came up with nothing damaging. Then, in 1977, Ford turned to the management consulting firm McKinsey & Company, calling them in to reorganize the company's management structure. McKinsey recommended a new structure with a Chairman/C.E.O., Vice-Chairman, and President at the top. Iacocca now became number three in the ruling triumvirate, and to humiliate him further, Ford insisted on parading this apparent demotion in public.

Then in 1978 Ford fired Iacocca. The reason—in Ford's own words—was: "Sometimes you just don't like somebody."

Iacocca was 54. He could have retired. Yet a few months later he joined the Chrysler Motor Corporation, becoming Chairman and C.E.O. in September 1979. During his time at Chrysler Iacocca executed one of the most impressive turnarounds in automobile history. When he arrived, the Detroit press was full of gloomy headlines such as "Chrysler losses are worst ever." The company was struggling, but, when he joined, Iacocca had not realized how serious its problems were. He soon found out—Chrysler was running out of money, and fast. Iacocca took swift remedial action: he eradicated excess inventory, renegotiated contracts with car rental companies Hertz and Avis, recruited a slew of top talent, and made substantial layoffs. Most important of all, he went cap in hand to the government and applied for a loan guarantee for $1.2 billion. It required new legislation. To secure government support Iacocca had to give testimony in Washington before the House of Representatives and Senate hearings. But the request was granted.

That it was attests to Iacocca's powers as a salesman. As he cut costs at Chrysler (he cut his own salary to $1), and the automobile market picked up, Chrysler's flagging fortunes revived. In 1983 Chrysler made a profit of $925 million and, not long after a new stock offering, Iacocca wrote out an historic check for $813,487,500 to clear the balance of the debt outstanding on the government loan.

Iacocca went on to steer Chrysler to greater success. He engineered the company's $1.5 billion acquisition of American Motors, and incorporated the Jeep into Chrysler's product offering. Iacocca retired from Chrysler in 1992, but his enthusiasm for business remained undiminished. Leaving the motor giants behind him, he founded a small start-up company, E.V. Global Motors, selling electric powered bicycles. In 2001, he took "clean transport" a stage further by launching the LIDO, an electric-powered vehicle designed for local driving, that resembled a cross between a golf buggy and Chrysler's retro PT Cruiser. Critics claimed that he had spent his career putting polluting vehicles on driveways and now it was payback time. Iacocca also invested in diabetes research through his support for Olivio Premium Products, a company marketing products based on olive oil. Iacocca pledged the equivalent of 25 percent of Olivio sales to research.

Context and Conclusions

Brilliant businessmen such as Henry Ford, Walter Chrysler, and Billy Durant long ago earned their place in the auto Hall of Fame. But among the postwar generation, only a few deserve to sit alongside the founding fathers. Lee Iacocca is one of them, successfully running not one but two of the big three U.S. motor manufacturers.

A rare combination of talented salesman and empathetic man-manager, Iacocca had an instinctive feeling for which models would sell and which would not. He introduced the Ford Mustang and revitalized Ford's prospects when the company was drifting directionless, following the death of the first Henry Ford. At Chrysler Iacocca performed one of the most breathtaking turnarounds in corporate history; in the process he became a corporate icon.

CLOSE BUT NO CIGAR
BOB LUTZ
Ex-Marine fighter pilot Lutz paid his dues in the motor business, working his way through General Motors, BMW, and, finally, Ford, where he was Vice-President. After Ford he became Iacocca's right-hand man at Chrysler and played a big part in the company's revival. Many think he should have gotten the C.E.O. job when Iacocca left. In 2001 he left Chrysler to join General Motors as Vice-President.

For More Information
Books:

Iacocca, Lee, and William Novak. *IACOCCA—An Autobiography*. New York: Bantam Books, 1984.
Iacocca, Lee, with Sonny Kleinfield. *Talking Straight*. New York: Bantam, 1989.
Wyden, Peter. *The Unknown Iacocca*. New York: William Morrow & Co., 1987.

Web site:
Chrysler: **www.chrysler.com**

Steve Jobs

1955	Born.
1976	First product, the Apple I, marketed.
1977	Apple II. Apple incorporated; Mike Markkula buys shares in the company and becomes Chairman.
1980	Apple goes public.
1982	$1 billion sales; John Sculley becomes C.E.O.
1984	Launch of Apple Macintosh.
1985	Jobs leaves Apple.
1986	Founds NeXT. Cofounds Pixar.
1993	Sculley leaves Apple.
1996	Jobs returns as consultant.
1997	Becomes "interim C.E.O."
1998	iMac launched.
2000	Drops "interim" from job title.
2001	Apple launches iPhoto to move into digital photography.
2003	New iMac launched.
2003	Launch of world's first 17-inch portable computer.
2003	Oracle announces it may buy into Apple.

Summary

Steve Jobs, cofounder of Apple Computer, is one of the folkhero C.E.O.s. The company was started in a garage by Jobs and his cofounder Steve Wozniak—and its Apple PCs changed the face of computing. Unfortunately, Apple got its strategy wrong, tying the Mac operating system software to Apple hardware. Microsoft went in the opposite direction, licensing the MS-DOS operating system to any and every PC manufacturer. The rest is history.

In 1985, former Pepsi Chairman John Sculley, brought in to add beef to Apple, removed Jobs from the company he had founded. Sculley himself was removed in 1993, and Jobs was eventually asked to return.

Since his comeback, Jobs has breathed new life into the company. To his many fans, Apple's revival confirms Jobs's status as one of the greatest technology entrepreneurs ever.

Life and Career

In February 1955 Paul and Clara Jobs adopted an orphan, Stephen. Jobs was brought up in Los Altos, California.

Out of school, he attended lectures at the Hewlett-Packard electronics company, and while working at Hewlett-Packard one summer he met Stephen Wozniak, a University of California dropout. Wozniak was an engineering whiz kid who was continually inventing gadgets. Jobs hooked up with Wozniak, attending meetings of the "Homebrew Computer Club." Most of the members were geeks. Jobs was different; he had an eye for style, utility, and marketability. He persuaded Wozniak to work with him to build a personal computer. The Apple I computer was designed in Jobs's bedroom and the prototype constructed in his garage.

After moderate success selling their first computer, a local electronics retailer ordered 25. Some helpful advice from a retired C.E.O. of Intel inspired Jobs and Wozniak to start their own company. To do so they sold their most treasured possessions, and with the $1,300 they raised, the two started a new company, which they named Apple.

Contribution

The company's first product, the Apple I, was marketed in 1976, priced at $666. Sales of the Apple I brought in $774,000 and soon the two entrepreneurs were working on the Apple II, a resounding success. This was not just down to its engineering, it was also due in large part to Jobs's marketing savvy. He brought in Regis McKenna, the best public relations man in Silicon Valley, who went on to popularize relationship marketing.

In 1980 Apple went public. Originally priced at $22 per share, the stock rose on the first day to $29, capitalizing the company at $1.2 billion. Between 1978 and 1983, in the absence of any real competition, Apple forged ahead in the personal computer market; its compound growth rate was over 150% per annum. Then, in 1981, IBM introduced its first PC, using an operating system called MS-DOS, licensed from a small software company called Microsoft. Within two years, IBM had exceeded Apple's dollar sales of PCs. Furthermore, Microsoft was causing a stir in the PC market, even though it didn't manufacture PC hardware. Microsoft licensed its operating software to PC producers. Jobs realized that if IBM and Microsoft were allowed to dominate the market then Apple could become marginalized.

To restore Apple's fortunes, Jobs turned to John Sculley, C.E.O. at Pepsi. The result of this unlikely alliance was the personal computer that cemented Apple Computer's status as the computer enthusiast's favorite computer company—the Apple Macintosh.

Instead of writing commands in computerese, Macintosh owners used a mouse to click on easily recognizable icons—a trash can and file folders, for example. Suddenly, you didn't need a degree in computer science to operate a personal computer. Other companies followed where Apple led, most significantly Microsoft. Apple became the darling of the creative world with an iconic status that Bill Gates and his crew never achieved. But what Microsoft did do was to dominate the PC software industry, commanding 80% market share as against Apple's 20%. In the end that proved critical.

The Apple fairy tale came to a sticky end in 1985 when white knight Sculley did the unthinkable and removed Jobs from the company he had founded. A fired-up Jobs proceeded to plow $250 million of investors' money into another startup, NeXT Computer. It disappointed, selling only 50,000 units. Pixar Animation Studios was a different story, however. This investment eventually paid out with the computer-animated blockbusters *Toy Story* and *A Bug's Life*. Back at Apple, Sculley himself was booted out in 1993 after a disastrous period that saw Apple's market share plummet from 20% to just 8%. He was replaced by Michael Spindler who lasted until 1996, by which time Apple's market share had fallen to just over 5%. Apple was staring oblivion in the face and Spindler was shown the door; Gil Amelio took over in the hot seat. After 500 days in the job, and with Apple's market share unmoved, Amelio invited Jobs back to help in a consulting role. It wasn't long before Amelio was on his way out too, and Jobs, now Apple's self-styled interim C.E.O., was back where he started.

Jobs dumped the NeXT operating system that he had sold to Apple, ditched loss-making licensing contracts, and most significantly launched the new iMac. The iMac was the embodiment of everything Jobs believed in: eye-catching design and simple operation. It was also the product of a different vision of the computer itself. It had no disk drive because Jobs believed they had been superseded by external storage devices such as zip drives and the Internet. The stylish Internet-ready machine, which Jobs hoped would restore the company's fading fortunes, was launched with the slogan "Chic Not Geek" blazed across advertising posters. The iMac sold 278,000 units in the first six weeks, an achievement that had *Fortune* magazine describing it as "one of the hottest computer launches ever." Wall Street, too, recovered its confidence in Apple: the company's share price doubled in less than a year. Fiscal 2000 revenues were some $7.98 billion, with net earnings of $786 million, and Apple has started to open a series of retail stores across the United States. Since then Apple's share price has been caught up in the same vortex as other technology companies. Product development has continued to follow the Steve Jobs theme of cool computing. 2001 saw the launch of iPhoto, Apple's strategy to win a strong position in digital photography. This was followed in 2003 by an even more powerful version of the iMac plus the world's first 17-inch portable. However, despite the continuing innovation, Apple's financial performance remained poor and, in 2003, Oracle announced that it might buy into the ailing company. What the future holds is unclear, but with Jobs back on the Apple throne, at least the company looks more like its old successful trailblazing self.

Context and Conclusions

Described by one newspaper as a "corporate Huckleberry Finn," Steve Jobs is one of a select group of IT whiz kids, but where Jobs differs from his peers is in his sense of style. IBM brought computers to the business world, Microsoft gave the PC its MS-DOS operating system, but Jobs made computing easy. By taking the graphical user interface that he had first seen in a Xerox PARC laboratory and incorporating it into the Apple Mac, Jobs enabled the technologically nonliterate to use a computer by simply pointing and clicking.

Jobs developed one of the first computer animation film studios, Pixar, and then returned to Apple just in time to save it from rotting. With the introduction of the iMac, Jobs once again demonstrated the imagination and design flair that made him a multimillionaire and made Apple the computer of choice for millions of devoted followers.

For More Information

Books:

Deutschman, Alan. *The Second Coming of Steve Jobs*. New York: Broadway Books, 2000.

Young, Jeffrey S. *Steve Jobs: The Journey Is the Reward*. New York: Lynx Books, 1988.

Web site:

Apple: **www.apple.com**

Phil Knight

1938	Born.
1959	Gains BS in Business Administration at University of Oregon.
1962	Travels to Japan in search of a track shoe manufacturer.
1964	Forms Blue Ribbon Sports with his old track coach, Bowerman.
1971	Company brand renamed Nike (after the Greek goddess of victory).
1972	Carolyn Davidson paid $35 for designing the "swoosh" logo adopted by Nike. The Cortez, the first shoe to appear under the Nike brand, arrives.
1975	Steve Prefontaine dies in a car crash. Introduction of the waffle sole.
1978	Blue Ribbon Sports renamed Nike Inc. Revenues of $71 million.
1980	Nike goes public.
1983	Revenues of $149 million.
1985	Launch of the Air Jordan.
1986	Revenues hit $1 billion.
1993–1994	Company rethinks strategy.
1998	Commits company to responsible employment practices.
1999	Nike cofounder Bill Bowerman dies.
2000	Nike designs uniforms for Sydney Olympics.
2000	Withdraws donation of $30 million to University of Oregon.
2001	Nike admits to worker exploitation.
2001	Congress briefing on Nike employment practices.

Summary

Phil Knight (1938–) followed his early promise on the running track at the University of Oregon with an equal talent for running a successful business. The product was, fittingly, the track shoe, which Knight, along with his partner and ex-track coach Bill Bowerman, revolutionized, transforming a basic accessory into a high-tech piece of athletics equipment. With a stroke of marketing genius, Knight chose the name Nike, Greek goddess of victory, for his brand in 1971, and the "swoosh" as his logo in 1972. Nike really hit the big time in the 1980s when its track shoes, starting with the Air Jordan in 1985, ran off the track and into mainstream fashion. The issue of child labor and Nike's manufacturing processes threatened to tarnish Knight's and the brand's reputation in the late 1990s, but strong management and a willingness to face ethical issues has seen Nike emerge in a better shape than some other multinationals.

Life and Career

Philip H. Knight was born in Portland, Oregon. At high school he played a lot of sports as well as becoming a roving reporter for the school paper. After high school he attended Oregon University, where he earned a BS in Business Administration. An avid runner throughout his childhood, Knight also joined the university track team. His track coach at university was Bill Bowerman, a man who, in coaching terms, was way ahead of his time. As well as training his athletes, he would experiment with their equipment to try and reduce their times. As part of that experimentation he constructed prototype track shoes with lightweight leather, and later nylon, uppers. The shoes may have only made a difference measurable in fractions of seconds, but in athletics a fraction of a second makes the difference between a gold medal and a silver.

After graduating from Oregon, Knight went to Stanford Graduate Business School to study for an MBA. As part of his master's degree he wrote a marketing paper. The thrust of his argument in the paper was that cheaper labor coupled with efficient manufacturing processes could threaten the dominance of German companies, such as Adidas and Puma, in the track shoe market. When Knight graduated, he decided to back his hunch and in 1962 traveled to Japan in search of a track shoe manufacturer. He found the Onitsuki Tiger Company and convinced them to supply him with shoes to import to the United States.

Back in America in 1964, Knight teamed up again with Bowerman to form Blue Ribbon Sports. They each invested $500 in the new company. Knight's first retail outlet was the back of his car, from which he would sell track shoes at high school track meets.

Contribution

Knight was unable to earn enough income from his shoe enterprise to support himself. Instead he was forced to take a job teaching accounting at Portland State University. In 1971 Knight and Bowerman decided to change the company's name to Nike. Bowerman's experimentation with shoe design paid off when he made an outsole by pouring rubber into a waffle iron. Sports shoe technology would never be the same again.

Later that year Knight was looking for a designer to prepare some charts for a business meeting when he came across graphic design student Carolyn Davidson, who was working on an assignment in the hallway at the university. Knight asked her if she could design a logo for the company. The brief was simply that the logo should suggest movement. From a selection of designs, Knight chose the "swoosh" sign, adopting it as the brand logo in 1972. Davidson was paid $35 for her endeavors. Today the "swoosh" logo is synonymous with Nike and recognized throughout the world. The Nike brand was #30 in the Interbrand Most Valuable Brands 2000 survey, valued at $3.015 billion.

Knight's marketing savvy helped the Nike brand gain public recognition. Before sneakers became mainstream fashionwear, Knight had the idea of associating the Nike product with top sports stars. The first star selected was middle-distance runner Steve Prefontaine, who was paid by Nike to wear its sports shoes. Prefontaine won a series of races wearing Nike shoes and narrowly failed to capture a medal in the 1972 Olympics. Tragically, he died in a car crash in 1975. By this time, however, Nike products were firmly associated with outstanding sporting achievement in the mind of the consumer.

By 1978 Blue Ribbon Sports had been officially renamed Nike Inc. In the same year Nike's revenues were $71 million. The company went public in 1980. In 1983 revenues were $149 million and by 1986 a massive $1 billion.

Chicago Bulls superstar Michael Jordan succeeded Steve Prefontaine as the Nike sports personality. This association helped propel Nike to even greater heights as Jordan became a U.S. sports icon, and Nike sports shoes became everyday wear for devotees of hip and happening youth culture. Knight continued to push technical innovation in Nike products with the launch of the Air Jordan in 1985. Whether the revolutionary product's air cushioning was a gimmick or actually increased performance didn't appear to matter, as the trendy sneaker outstripped the competition, becoming Nike's best-selling shoe.

In the early 1990s the company's phenomenal growth slowed. Nike had profited up to then thanks to the big trend in jogging as a means to keep fit and the popularity of basketball in the United States. But by 1993 these markets were flagging, and Knight decided to broaden the company's appeal and by extending it across a greater variety of sports, the company managed to stay ahead of the pack. The strategy involved more stars, such as golfer Tiger Woods and tennis star André Agassi; more sports, such as soccer and tennis; and more innovations, including the Predator soccer boot.

The main threat to Nike' success in the late 1990s was the issue of worker exploitation and child labor. Knight looked to head off the protests. In a statement to the National Press Club in May 1998 he said that "the Nike product had become synonymous with slave wages, forced overtime, and arbitrary abuse," and pledged to change things. He implemented a series of high-profile initiatives at the company that attempted to address the issue of exploitation. These measures sit uneasily, however, with Knight's cancellation of a financial contribution to his old university because of its decision to join the Workers' Rights Consortium. The most visible initiative was to commit the company to responsible employment policies in 1998. However, the criticism continued. In 2001, the company admitted to exploiting workers, but tried to regain some ground by committing to continued production in Indonesia. It was also the subject of a Congress briefing on its "sweatshop" practices.

In product terms, the range continued to grow. The death of co-founder Bill Bowerman in 1999 was a blow, but Nike responded by launching the successful "Bowerman" range of track shoes. Nike golf equipment sales soared in 2000 when Tiger Woods won a succession of titles. The 2000 Sydney Olympics proved a valuable platform for a new generation of high-tech sports equipment.

Context and Conclusions

Phil Knight's is one of the great marketing stories of the 20th century. Turning the humble track shoe into a must-have street fashion item was a masterstroke of marketing genius. It was a leap that he had to make in order to take Nike from a niche manufacturer of sporting footwear to a clothing and footwear giant and internationally recognized brand. Knight has also proved an astute strategist, guiding Nike in a different direction where necessary and facing up to the exploitation issues that threatened to elbow Nike off the track.

For More Information

Books:

Strasser, J. B., and Laurie Becklund. *Swoosh: The Unauthorized Story of Nike, and the Men Who Played There.* Orlando, FL: Harcourt Brace Jovanovich, 1991.

Katz, Donald. *Just Do It: The Nike Spirit in the Corporate World.* New York: Random House, 1994.

Goldman, Robert, and Stephen Papson. *Nike culture: The Sign of the Swoosh.* Thousand Oaks, CA: Sage Publications, 1998.

Web site:

Nike: **www.nike.com**

Ray Kroc

1902	Born.
1922	Begins work as sales representative for Lily Tulip Cup Company.
1954	Visits McDonald's burger restaurant in San Bernardino, California.
1955	Opens his first McDonald's in Des Plaines, Illinois.
1961	Buys out the McDonald brothers for $2.7 million.
1963	Number of hamburgers sold reaches one billion.
1965	Ronald McDonald introduced.
1967	First overseas branch opened.
1974	Buys the San Diego Padres.
1984	Dies.

Summary

Ray Kroc (1902–1984) was looking forward to retiring after a comfortable career selling milkshake mixers. All that changed one day in 1954 when he walked into a small restaurant in San Bernardino, California. It was called McDonald's Famous Hamburgers, and Kroc's visit was the catalyst for a global food revolution. He cut himself a deal with the McDonald brothers and set about creating a franchise network. In 1961 he bought out the brothers for a bargain $2.7 million.

The company went public in 1965. By the 1970s Kroc had turned a $2.7 million investment into a $500 million fortune. The public bought McDonald's burgers by the million. By the time of Kroc's death in 1984, the McDonald's golden arches were recognized the world over as a symbol for convenient and cheap fast food. Despite being a target in the 2000s for antiglobalization demonstrators, the company continues to go from strength to strength.

Life and Career

Raymond A. Kroc was born in Oak Park, Illinois, on October 5, 1902. His life and career can be divided up into two periods—before McDonald's and after it. Before McDonald's Kroc tried a variety of jobs before carving out a role as a milkshake-mixer sales rep.

At 15 he lied about his age so he could take part in World War I as a Red Cross ambulance driver. Disappointingly for him, the nearest he got to Europe was Connecticut. He was still finishing his training the day the war ended.

Having missed out on the war, Kroc looked for a job. He spent some time playing the piano for a living, and in 1922 landed a job selling paper cups for Lily Tulip Cup Company. Kroc was good at sales and had an eye for business. When one of his customers, Earl Prince, patron of Prince Multimixers, showed Kroc the five-spindle mixer he had invented, Kroc switched companies. He got a contract to sell the mixers nationally, and for the next 17 years that was exactly what he did. At 52 Kroc had spent most of his working life selling mixers. He was comfortably off and was thinking about his retirement, until, that is, the fateful day in 1954 when he walked into the small burger restaurant in San Bernardino run by the McDonald brothers.

Contribution

What impressed Kroc about the burger restaurant run by brothers Dick and Mac McDonald, apart from the large number of mixers they ordered and the lines of customers down the street, was the way the business was run. It was as if Henry Ford had applied his mass-production formula to the food business. The brothers ran a burger assembly line. There were eight five-milkshake mixers churning out 40 milkshakes at a time. To speed up the cleaning, the brothers dispensed plastic utensils and paper napkins. So efficient was the McDonalds' operation that customers received their meal within 60 seconds. Furthermore, the brothers offered a very limited menu at extremely competitive prices. For Kroc it was commercial love at first sight. "I felt like some latter-day Newton who'd just had an Idaho potato caromed off his skull," he later wrote.

Kroc was convinced that fast food, McDonald's style, could be the next restaurant revolution. Using all the skills he had acquired in 25-plus years of selling, he sold himself to the McDonald brothers, persuading them to license their name to him. In return they would receive a percentage of the sales for each franchise he created. To the McDonald's model Kroc brought dynamism and a homespun business philosophy. "Luck is a dividend of sweat," he once observed. "The more you sweat, the luckier you get."

The four pillars on which Kroc built the McDonald's empire were quality, service, cleanliness, and value. He introduced some innovations of his own such as standardizing the size of the burger and the amount of onions served with each one. He even built a laboratory in Chicago to research the ultimate french fry. Kroc's obsession with perfecting the McDonald's business formula cost him his marriage.

Kroc was convinced that fast food, McDonald's style, could be the next restaurant revolution.

Kroc's first restaurant opened in Des Plaines, Illinois, in 1955. Several others quickly followed. Kroc insisted that franchisees run their restaurants according to his strict guidelines. Although he had little trouble convincing franchisees to open McDonald's restaurants, Kroc still encountered severe financial problems that nearly bankrupted him in the early years. In 1960 sales of $75 million translated into a profit of $139,000. His solution was to buy the land where the restaurants were to be located and then lease them to the franchisees. In this way Kroc retained closer control over the business and made more money.

Soon Kroc's financial problems were a thing of the past and he was eyeing a bigger prize. In 1961 he bought out the McDonald brothers for just $2.7 million. It was one of the best deals in business history—for Kroc at least. He then embarked on a massive advertising campaign. The McDonald's landmarks kept coming: a billion hamburgers by 1963; the five hundredth restaurant; the brilliant concept of the burger clown, Ronald McDonald, universally appealing to children. In fact, so popular was Ronald McDonald that not long after his first national ad appearance in 1965, more children knew his name than that of the U.S. President.

When the company went public in 1965, Kroc was $3 million richer. It was a fortune that grew to $500 million by the mid-1970s as McDonald's franchises sprang up everywhere.

With the company firmly established in the United States, Kroc expanded overseas. In 1967 he took the golden arches to Canada, followed by Europe, Asia, and the rest of the world.

Kroc's great wealth affected him very little, since he spent much of his time ensuring that the McDonald's franchises maintained his high standards. One small indulgence was his acquisition of the San Diego Padres in 1974. He died at the age of 81 in San Diego, California.

Context and Conclusions

Few people can claim to have changed the way the world eats. Ray Kroc is one such individual. It took vision and courage to turn his back on a comfortable retirement for a new business opportunity at the age of 52. Kroc's idea was

Few people can claim to have changed the way the world eats. Ray Kroc is one such individual.

perfect for his time. The United States was suburbanizing, prospering, and depending more and more on the automobile; Kroc provided an increasingly mobile nation with fast, cheap, convenient food. His genius was not only to spot the opportunity but to package the experience carefully. Through franchises, strictly-regulated service and food production values, and innovative marketing, Kroc single-handedly invented the modern concept of fast food. He also pioneered the global brand, cooking up a McDonald's-style food revolution across the world.

For More Information

Books:

Kroc, Ray, with Robert Anderson. *Grinding it Out: The Making of McDonald's*. New York: St. Martin's Press, 1992.

Love, John F. *McDonald's: Behind the Arches*. Rev. ed. New York: Bantam, 1995.

Web site:

McDonald's: **www.mcdonalds.com**

Edwin Land

1909	Born.
1926	Leaves Harvard University after his freshman year.
1928	Invents the first synthetic sheet polarizer.
1929	Files for a patent.
1933	Forms Land-Wheelwright Laboratories.
1937	Forms Polaroid Corporation, Boston. Polaroid day glasses are introduced.
1939	Polaroid moves its offices from Boston to Cambridge, Massachusetts.
1948	First instant camera and film go on sale.
1957	Polaroid lists on the New York Stock Exchange.
1963	Color instant camera goes on sale.
1977	Invention of Polaroid Instant Movie Camera.
1982	Retires as President of Polaroid.
1991	Dies.

Summary

Edwin Land (1909–1991) pioneered instant photography for the masses with his invention of the Polaroid camera. The original idea was inspired by a question from his daughter on a sunny day in 1944 and a leisurely walk around the dusty streets of Santa Fe. Other important enterprises such as Land's groundbreaking work into light polarization at his Harvard University laboratories during the 1930s are less well known. And few people realize that it was a friend's fishing trip that led to the invention of Polaroid sunglasses, or that Land released a revolutionary new instant movie camera at the same time Sony was introducing videotape in 1977.

Land's life was a synthesis of invention and business. "An essential aspect of creativity is not being afraid to fail," he observed. Even after he retired from Polaroid in 1982, he devoted his time to his hobby—inventing. He built a research laboratory complex and filled it with like-minded people.

Life and Career

Born in Bridgeport, Connecticut, on May 7, 1909, Edwin Herbert Land was the only son of Harry and Martha Land. Theirs was a comfortable household; Harry Land owned property and ran a scrap-metal yard. As a boy Land was an enthusiastic scholar, albeit a tired one—he is said to have slept with a copy of R. W. Wood's *Physical Optics* under his pillow. According to his high school yearbook, the young Land was a "star in his studies." He was a student first at Norwich Free Academy, from which he graduated with honors, and later at Harvard University.

Land's academic interests weren't sufficient to keep him at Harvard. As a freshman he was already developing a cheap, effective polarizer of light that he called "Polaroid." In 1926, after that first year, he abandoned his formal physics studies, continuing his education instead at the New York Public Library. Although he didn't graduate, Harvard University awarded him an honorary doctorate in 1957, one of many honorary degrees.

Contribution

Land is best known for the invention of the Polaroid camera. Although the idea came to him in a moment of inspiration, he had already laid the foundations for instant photography with his advances in the field of light polarization.

When Land began to apply his mind to the subject, the main tool in use was the Nicol prism. Developed in 1828, it was a bulky and expensive piece of equipment. Land was convinced that he could improve on William Nicol's invention. His idea, following observations based on his studies in the New York Public Library, was to place a large number of aligned crystals in transparent plastic. The plastic would then be set, fixing the position of the crystals. Land gave a lecture on his idea at Harvard after a few preliminary experiments.

He patented his invention in 1929 and then created companies to develop and exploit it. The first, in 1933, was Land-Wheelwright Laboratories, established with Land's Harvard physics instructor George Wheelwright III. Next came Polaroid Corporation, founded in Boston in 1937. The next task was to find commercial applications for the invention.

The Polaroid camera was a phenomenal success. Land could easily have retired to a life of luxury. Instead he continued to conduct his research into the nature of light.

Land's original idea had been to use the technology to reduce glare in car headlights. Because this application involved an increase in wattage with a commensurate increase in fuel consumption, however, Land was unable to persuade automobile manufacturers of its benefits. This rejection led him to develop a string of products that used the new technology. Many of them were inspired by chance discoveries.

The world has a trout fisherman to thank for the invention of Polaroid sunglasses. One of Land's colleagues went on a fishing trip and took a piece of Polaroid film with him. When he returned he told Land that looking through the Polaroid reduced the surface glare from the water and enabled him to spot the fish. This discovery led to the manufacture of Polaroid glasses. At first these were sold in specialist hunting and fishing stores, but eventually they became the ubiquitous Polaroid sunglasses. The sunglasses led to the development of other products such as camera filters and antiglare screens.

Land attracted the finest minds he could find to his Boston laboratories and led his research team in developing a variety of products. He invented a new method of 3-D photography that was used extensively for reconnaissance during World War II. Then there were inventions such as nighttime goggles and the polarizing ring sight. Land also contributed to the technology used during the Cold War, including the surveillance equipment employed in the high-altitude U2 spy planes and spy satellites.

Land is probably best known for his invention of instant photography and the Polaroid camera. The idea came from a conversation with his three-year-old daughter Jennifer in 1944. It was a sunny day in Santa Fe, New Mexico, and Land took a snapshot of her. Why, she asked, couldn't she see the picture he had taken of her right away? This set Land thinking, and after pacing around the town for an hour he arrived at a solution.

The first demonstration of Land's revolutionary new instant camera took place in February 1947, at a meeting of the Optical Society of America. The commercial model was on sale within a year at a retail price of $89.50. Land was well aware that correct pricing was a key to the camera's success, and he priced it for the mass market.

The Polaroid camera was a phenomenal success. Land could easily have retired to a life of luxury. Instead he continued to conduct his research into the nature of light. He also invented a number of other products, including the Polavision instant movie camera, which hit the stores in 1977. Unfortunately it was an advanced product in a soon-to-be-defunct technology: the invention of magnetic videotape spelled the beginning of the end for 8mm film.

Land retired as President of Polaroid in 1982, but he continued his research. He built himself a research institute, the Rowland Institute for Science in Cambridge, Massachusetts, where he continued to experiment along with a group of fellow researchers until his death in 1991.

Context and Conclusions

Edwin Land was an inventor–business executive in the tradition of Thomas Edison. He possessed the rare combination of an inventive mind and the discipline to address the often mundane but challenging demands of running a big corporation. In a world in which commercial research is often jealously guarded, Land profited from his openness. He was happy to show friends and colleagues his research, and to challenge them to find commercial applications for his work. This led to the development of a number of new products, most famously Polaroid sunglasses. Had it not been for the advent of Betamax and VHS videotape, Land's invention of the instant movie camera might have been his crowning achievement.

Sadly, with Land gone, the company he founded struggled. In 2001, faced with debts of $950 million, the company laid off some 25% of its work force and was fighting to avoid bankruptcy.

For More Information

Book:
Olshaker, Mark. *The Polaroid Story: Edwin Land and the Polaroid Experience*. Lanham, MD: Madison, 1983

Estée Lauder

1908	Born.
1924	Uncle founds New Way Laboratories.
1944	Lauder sets up her own office.
1947	Estée Lauder Inc. founded.
1948	First retail account at Saks Fifth Avenue, New York City.
1960	First international account at Harrods, London.
1968	Revenues of $40 million.
1972	Son Leonard made President. Lauder becomes Chair.
1980s	Lauder steps back from running the company.
1995	Company I.P.O.

Summary

Much of the U.S. cosmetic queen Estée Lauder's (1908–) early life is shrouded in mystery. What is known is that she started in the cosmetics business selling her uncle's Six-in-One Cold Cream in 1924. By 1944 she had acquired a husband, an office in New York City, and a cosmetics concession in Saks Fifth Avenue. Lauder formally incorporated Estée Lauder Inc. in 1947. Resisting calls to go public, she kept her company in family hands and used her formidable sales and marketing talents to drive the business forward. In 1968 revenues were an estimated $40 million with profits of $4 million. Lauder ceded control to her son, Leonard, in 1972. By 1999, Estée Lauder, Inc. was earning over $3 billion in revenue from over a hundred products.

Life and Career

Estée Lauder was born Josephine Esther Mentzer in Queens, New York City, in 1908, the youngest of nine children. Her father ran a hardware store, and Lauder went to school nearby.

The young Lauder was introduced to the cosmetics business through her uncle Dr. Schotz, a chemist. His business, New Way Laboratories, was founded in 1924. Among the various potions and lotions he made—which included a poultry-lice killer, paint stripper, varnish, and embalming fluid—were several beauty treatments. Lauder helped her uncle out by selling products with names like Six-in-One Cold Cream and Dr. Schotz Viennese Cream.

In 1930 she married Joe Lauder, but by 1939 the couple had separated. A subsequent reconciliation led to their remarriage in 1942, at which time Lauder vowed to direct all her energies to selling cosmetics products. She continued to sell her uncle's products, setting up her own office at 39 East 60th St. in February 1944.

Soon afterward Lauder won a sales concession in the Bonwit Teller department store. She then set her sights higher. The prize concession was in Saks Fifth Avenue. When she told Bob Fiske, cosmetics buyer at Saks, that the department store should give her a concession, Fiske demurred, explaining that there was no demand for her products from his customers. Undeterred, Lauder created a demand by giving her products away at a talk at the Waldorf-Astoria Hotel. When she returned to Fiske, he relented.

In the late 1940s, with $60,000 or so at her disposal, Lauder was unable to persuade the BBD&O advertising agency to create a campaign for Estée Lauder. Instead she chose a more direct route to her customers. Using Saks's mailing list, Lauder sent out samplers and gifts as an enticement for customers to visit her store concessions.

Contribution

Lauder's breakthrough came with the invention of her first fragrance, the bath oil Youth Dew. Her principal competition, firms like Arden and Rubenstein, had all started with skincare products and gravitated to fragrances.

Accounts of how Lauder created her first fragrance differ. It seems that an old friend, A. L. van Amerigan, President of van Amerigan-Haebler (which subsequently became International Flavors and Fragrances), was involved. Similarly Ernest Shiftan, an employee of IFF and one of America's top perfumers, may well have been responsible for the development of the fragrance. Whether Amerigan gave the fragrance to Lauder is unclear. What is certain is that Youth Dew, introduced at Bonwit's as a bath oil, was an instant success. For $8.50 customers got a perfume that lasted a whole day.

Shrewdly, Lauder used the demand for the new perfume to sell her other cosmetics. The Youth Dew line was eventually extended across a variety of cosmetics including a pure fragrance. With Lauder shamelessly promoting it at every opportunity, it wasn't long before Estée Lauder was the third-largest cosmetics business in the United States behind Arden and Rubenstein.

Lauder's marketing acumen was again evident when a new breed of skincare products making dubious scientific claims began to spread from Europe to the United States. In France an emphasis on "feeding" the skin had given rise to products that made various health claims about their effects. The Food and Drug Administration, however, imposed tough regulations on products making any such claims. There were, for example, a host of placental-based products that ran afoul of the FDA and were withdrawn. Lauder, instead of making scientific claims for her new skin product, simply named it Re-Nutriv. The product's health enhancing attributes were implied in the name. She was also careful not to cross the line in her advertising. It focused instead on the high price of the product, and how a price of $115 a pound was justified by the inclusion of the "costliest" ingredients.

The "little business" that Leonard Lauder once said his mother was growing now controls over 40% of the cosmetics market in U.S. department stores.

At the time Estée Lauder's headquarters were at 666 Fifth Avenue, on the second floor— Lauder had a fear of heights. Competitors were close at hand. Charles Revson, founder of Revlon, was on the top floor of the same building and Helena Rubenstein was across the street. As Lauder made progress commercially she was also climbing socially. Her house in Palm Beach, Florida, afforded her the opportunity to meet rich people from the upper echelons of U.S. society. Lauder's efforts at networking were not entirely without mishap. One story has it that, arriving for dinner at the home of Dorothy Munn, wife of financier

Charles Munn, she gave a box of cosmetics (presumably her own) to her hostess. This was viewed as a gauche gesture as Dorothy Munn was wealthy enough to have her cosmetics made privately—a kind of haute-perfume.

By the 1970s Estée Lauder had bested its corporate competition and added the Clinique brand to its beautifying armory. Lauder herself had outlasted her personal rivals as both Elizabeth Arden and Helena Rubenstein had died within a year of each other in the 1960s. Lauder had since moved her headquarters to the new General Motors Building (with the ever-present Revlon camped on the top floors); she had also, by virtue of her friendship with the Duchess of Windsor, firmly placed herself at the pinnacle of the social scene. Her son Leonard became President of the company in 1972, with Lauder becoming chair.

The "little business" that Leonard Lauder once said his mother was growing now controls over 40% of the cosmetics market in U.S. department stores. Available in 118 countries, Estée Lauder products bring in over $3 billion in revenue.

Context and Conclusions

Estée Lauder Inc. is an astonishing example of how an international business can be built up from humble beginnings through one woman's relentless drive, networking, belief in her own products, and brilliant marketing. In particular, Lauder was responsible for a number of innovative marketing techniques for the cosmetics business, most notably the free gift with purchase.

Her strength of leadership was emphasized through her determination to keep the company in the control of her family. Estée Lauder remained an entirely private company until its I.P.O. in 1995. The Lauder family still holds a significant proportion of the shares. Although Lauder has progressively taken a back seat since the 1980s, her sons Leonard and Ronald, daughter-in-law Evelyn, grandson William, and great-granddaughter Aerin remain actively involved in the company.

For More Information

Books:

Israel, Lee. *Estée Lauder: Beyond the Magic: An Unauthorized Biography*. New York: Macmillan, 1985.

Lauder, Estée. *Estée: A Success Story*. New York: Random House, 1985.

Web site:

Estée Lauder, **www.esteelauder.com**

Ralph Lauren

1939	Born.
1962– 1964	Serves in the U.S. Army.
1968	Forms Polo.
1971	First store opens.
1986	Flagship store opens on Madison Avenue, New York City.
1993	The Polo Sport store opens.
1997	Awarded 1996 Menswear Designer of the Year by the Council of Fashion Designers of America.
1997	Polo Ralph Lauren I.P.O.
2000	Revenues of $1.6 billion.

Summary

Today designer stores are commonplace, and designer brands sell everything from sunglasses to perfume. But it wasn't always like that. In the days before DKNY, CK, and Armani, there was Polo by the American designer Ralph Lauren (1939–).

Lauren's early life suggested little of the success that lay ahead, other than a predilection for expensive suits. But, in the late 1960s, after persuading the New York store Bloomingdale's to sell his unfashionably wide ties, Lauren never looked back. From a single store in 1971, the Lauren fashion empire now numbers over 130 stores with revenues of over $1 billion. As Lauren designs on into a new millennium, the Polo brand continues to reflect his ability to capture the essence of a certain American way of life.

Life and Career

Born in New York City in 1939, Ralph Lauren always had an eye for fashion. The youngest of four children, his fashion flair and sense of color may have been inherited from his father, who was a mural painter. His education was highly conventional. After high school it wasn't fashion college that awaited him but City College, Manhattan, and a business degree. As a teenager Lauren was a snappy dresser. He didn't stint on quality, preferring to pay $100 for a suit (at that time a lot of money), rather than buy a cheaper, less well-made one. This was not always a popular policy with his parents.

Two years into his business degree program, Lauren took a job as a salesman at a glove company. This was followed by a similar job at a tie manufacturer's. It was while still at the tie firm, A. Rivetz & Co., that Lauren took the first tentative steps towards building his fashion empire. He began to create his own tie designs. With $50,000 and his designs, Lauren left Rivetz to form his own company, Polo, with his older brother. It was 1968.

Contribution

Lauren chose the name Polo because of its preppy connotations. Polo began life as a tie store. His ties were distinctively wide—wider than was fashionable at the time. While the customers appreciated the new designs, the stores weren't convinced. Lauren tried to get the famous New York City store Bloomingdale's to stock his products. Bloomingdale's was interested but asked if he would modify his designs by narrowing the ties to make them more in keeping with the fashion of the day. They also insisted he remove his brand label. The plucky Lauren called the store's bluff and refused. It wasn't long before Bloomingdale's was back, agreeing to stock Polo designer ties on Lauren's terms.

Lauren could never have succeeded without an innate sense of style and an innovative eye for fashion. Equally important was his understanding of how to build a brand. Lauren made Polo and its associated brands a lifestyle, as well as a design choice. Throughout the 1980s the Polo brand was backed by distinctive advertising that conjured up a variety of associations, from safaris to the English aristocracy.

Ralph Lauren's first store opened in 1971. In the seventies the concept of the designer store was still in its infancy. Lauren was one of the first men's fashion designers to open a store in his own name. With the help of his brother Jerry, he continued to establish the brand with season after season of clothes that aimed to be stylish, classic, and timeless. As more stores opened, Lauren extended his range to women's wear, and then to his "home collection" line, comprising linen, towels, furniture, and other similar products. The flagship store, Rhinelander Mansion on Madison Avenue, was opened in 1986, and in 1993 the Polo Sport store opened across the street.

Lauren could never have succeeded without an innate sense of style and an innovative eye for fashion. Equally important was his understanding of how to build a brand.

While the 1980s saw an extension of the Polo brand into new areas, it also brought new competition. Suddenly businessmen were wearing a new brand of suit—the Giorgio Armani power suit. Lauren modified his designs to produce crisp-looking sophisticated suits. What he would not do was abandon the ethos of the Polo brand for short-term gain. "I'm a long-term person," he has said. "I'm long-term about my work. I'm a builder. Everything I do is an extension of my life." Lauren's long-term perspective proved astute. What was considered the height of fashion in the 1980s seemed unduly ostentatious in the altogether more reserved 1990s.

In June 1997 the company went public. The I.P.O raised $767 million for Polo Ralph Lauren and made Lauren a very wealthy man. As befits the man behind one of the hottest fashion properties of the 20th century, Lauren lives a stylish life. He has properties in Jamaica, Long Island, and Fifth Avenue, as well as an estate in Bedford, New York, and a ranch in Colorado. An avid driver, Lauren has amassed a collection of prestigious cars that includes a 1937 Alfa Romeo and a 1938 Bugatti.

Context and Conclusions

Ralph Lauren led where many have since followed. His concept of the men's designer store was adopted by many other famous names, including Giorgio Armani and Calvin Klein. Lauren built Polo into a global brand with its quintessential, clean-cut, preppy look. His success was in selling not only clothes, but a way of life—a glimpse of which was revealed through stylized advertising. As Lauren says: "I don't design clothes, I design dreams." Today the company's brand names include Polo, Polo by Ralph Lauren, Polo Sport, Ralph Lauren, Lauren, RALPH, Ralph Lauren Purple Label Polo Jeans Co., and many others. There are now over 130 Polo/Ralph Lauren stores around the world selling a variety of products from fragrances to footwear, fabric to furniture, as well as the classic menswear Lauren made his name designing. For $150,000 you can even buy a Ralph Lauren trailer—a gleaming silver Airstream with a choice of four differently themed interiors.

For More Information

Book:

Trachtenberg, Jeffrey A. *Ralph Lauren: The Man behind the Mystique*. New York: Little, Brown, 1981.

Web site:

Polo.com: **www.polo.com**

Henry Robinson Luce

1898	Born.
1920	Graduates from Yale. Voted "most brilliant student."
1922	Leaves Baltimore for New York. Time, Inc. incorporated on November 28.
1923	The first issue of *Time* hits the stands.
1927	First profit posted—$3,860.
1928	Profits of $126,000.
1929	*Fortune* magazine launched.
1936	*Life* magazine launched.
1954	*Sports Illustrated* magazine launched.
1958	Suffers heart attack.
1967	Dies.

Summary

Henry Robinson Luce's strict Presbyterian upbringing at a missionary station in China seemed to do him no harm. His early academic record was outstanding, and his performance at Yale University no less impressive. When he graduated in 1920—voted "most brilliant" student of the year by his peers—he had already shown a talent for editing by radically overhauling the Yale newspaper, the *Daily News*. Following a whistle-stop tour of Europe, he worked on the *Chicago Daily News* and then the *Baltimore News*, where he linked up with fellow Yale alumnus Briton Hadden. Together they were unstoppable, launching a new publication *Time: The Weekly News Magazine* in March 1923 and nursing it from a paltry circulation to one of 118,000 in its third year. In 1929 they followed this success with the launch of the business magazine *Fortune* to chronicle the ups and downs of the Wall Street crash and the ensuing Great Depression. Taking sole control after the untimely death of Hadden in 1929, Luce went on to publish one successful magazine after another. *Life* magazine, founded in 1936, broke the company's circulation records, and they were broken again by *Sports Illustrated*, launched in 1954. After threatening to retire for many years, Luce died of a heart attack in 1967, still at the helm of his empire.

Life and Career

Henry Robinson Luce was born on April 3, 1898 in Tengchow, China, where his Presbyterian missionary parents were teaching at a Christian mission. The first of four children, Luce's upbringing was an austere one. His daily schedule began at six in the morning with a cold bath, followed by half an hour of Bible study. With six hours of Chinese lessons a day, the young Luce was fluent in the local tongue before he was able to speak English.

Barring a brief visit to America in 1906, Luce was to remain in China until he was 14. A precocious scholar, he attended the British-run boarding school in Chefoo. It was a tough environment with strict discipline. Fortunately for Luce, a strong work ethic, combined with a keen mind, kept him at the top of the class and away from the master's cane. The school's pupils were predominantly English, and Luce frequently found himself sticking up for the United States. "My Anglo-Americanism is deeper than any words," he once said. "Indeed, it is written in the blood of that shameful, and futile, endless two hours one

Saturday afternoon, when I rolled around the unspeakably dirty floor of the main school-room with a British boy who had insulted my country."

After Chefoo in China came the Hotchkiss School in Connecticut with a brief three-week tour of Europe in between. There Luce continued his excellent scholastic record: outstanding marks in his Greek exams, the honor roll, and leader of the class in most subjects. Outside his classes he discovered a new talent as editor-in-chief of the *Hotchkiss Literary Monthly* and assistant managing editor of the weekly school newspaper, the *Record*. Luce had found his vocation.

Contribution

It was at Yale that Luce started his career in publishing in earnest. Together with fellow student and ex-Hotchkiss pupil Briton Hadden, Luce revolutionized the Yale newspaper, the *Daily News*. On graduation in 1920 Luce was voted "most brilliant" and Hadden "most likely to succeed." The combination proved irresistible. After Yale, Luce continued his tour of the world's most prestigious educational establishments, heading for Oxford, England, where he studied history. Then, after a whistle-stop tour of Europe, he returned to the United States, obtaining work first on the *Chicago Daily News* and then on the *Baltimore News*. It was in Baltimore that Luce rejoined his old friend Hadden and together they developed a plan to launch a new weekly news magazine called *Facts*. When the magazine was finally launched it was called *Time: The Weekly News Magazine*.

The pair left Baltimore for New York in February 1922. There they rented a small one-room office, acquired a third partner in Culbrith Sudler, who was reportedly an expert at selling advertising, and spent the next few months seeking advice and capital. Advice was forthcoming—mostly along the lines of "don't do it"—but capital was less plentiful. Eventually, however, they managed to raise sufficient funds (partly through a share issue) and incorporated the business on November 28, 1922, having moved to a small loft in the printing trades building on Eighth Avenue. To decide who should edit the magazine and who should manage the business side of things, Hadden and Luce tossed a coin. It was to Luce's everlasting chagrin that he lost and, in the intervening three-year period before he was able to take up the post of editor, Hadden had the opportunity to stamp his mark on *Time* magazine. The first issue of *Time* hit the newsstands in March 1923, with a cover price of 15 cents.

The distribution of the first issues was farcical. A string of debutante acquaintances was entrusted with the task of addressing the first three issues and dispatching them to subscribers, who could read all three before making a financial commitment. In the ensuing mix-up some subscribers received three copies of the same issue, only one issue, or no issue at all. Of the 25,000 who agreed to take a look, only 9,000 ever received a copy. And of the 5,000 sent to the newsstands, 3,000 were returned unsold.

After this inauspicious start, however, circulation grew steadily. By the third year it had reached 110,000, with advertising revenue of $283,000, yet a profit remained elusive. Indeed, it wasn't until 1927 that the new magazine made a profit, and then it was just $3,860. In 1928 a more respectable figure of $126,000 was posted, and from that point onward figures improved rapidly. By then, Luce was editor. He ensnared his readers with an array of literary devices: compound words such as "sexational" and the more successful "socialite" made their debut on the pages of *Time*. Foreign words such as "tycoon"—from the Japanese *taikun*, meaning prince and "pundit" from the Hindu *pandit*, meaning sage—were popularized by Luce; and he also made common the use of euphemisms such as "great and good friend"—meaning mistress—to skirt around potentially libelous issues.

By 1927 *Time* had moved again, not once but twice, coming to rest eventually in Manhattan, just off Fifth Avenue. Luce's lifelong friend Hadden had always said his aim was to make one million dollars by the age of 30. As it turned out he made more than that, but in February 1929, nine days after his 31st birthday, he died from a streptococcus infection. Luce was left in full charge of the magazine.

> *Over the next 30 years, Luce built a publishing business with a worldwide circulation of over 13 million. To* Time *and* Fortune *he added the even more successful* Life *magazine, founded in 1936.*

Fortune magazine was the second major venture under the Time, Inc. banner. Founded in 1929, it was Luce's idea, based on his instinct that "business is obviously the greatest single common denominator of interest among the active leading citizens of the United States—our best men are in business." *Fortune* was two years in the planning. The magazine owes its name to Luce's wife Lila, who preferred *Fortune* to *Power*. To head up the editorial staff, Luce chose Parker Lloyd Smith, a brilliant Oxford graduate who did an excellent job in the magazine's early days, until in 1931 he threw himself to his death from a hotel window, for no apparent reason.

With catastrophic timing, the first issue of *Fortune*, 30,000 copies in all, rolled off the presses just three months after the spectacular stock market crash of October 1929. In spite of, or perhaps because of, its timing, the first issue was well received, and the magazine managed to survive the economic depression that followed. By 1937 revenues were up to $500,000 and circulation in excess of 460,000. Through the ensuing decades *Fortune* magazine cataloged the ups and downs of U.S. business life.

Over the next 30 years, Luce built a publishing business with a worldwide circulation of over 13 million. To *Time* and *Fortune* he added the even more successful *Life* magazine, founded in 1936. In 1954 when *Sports Illustrated* was introduced, it broke the circulation records set by *Life*. Luce successfully steered the company through World War II, adroitly negotiated the communist witch hunts that swept postwar America, and fended off hundreds of threats to sue the company for invasion of privacy or libel each year.

In 1967 the circulation of Luce's flagship magazine was some 7,500,000. Advertising, which was twice as much as for any other magazine, brought in $170 million to Time, Inc. *Time* magazine itself sold some 3,500,000 copies, yielding $86 million in advertising revenue. The company that Luce founded on a budget of $86,000 had total revenues in excess of $500 million, with profits of $37 million. For much of his later career Luce regularly threatened to retire. "At 40 I will retire and let the young take over," he used to say. But it was always the same story; even after his heart attack in 1958, he could not drag himself away. In February 1967 he was still in command of his empire when he finally succumbed to another heart attack.

Context and Conclusions

Flamboyant media moguls such as William Randolph Hearst, Lord Beaverbrook, and Lord Thomson are better remembered today than Henry Robinson Luce, especially outside the United States. Luce, the man with a Presbyterian upbringing, was content to remain in the shadows. He neither sought political power, as Beaverbrook did, nor did he go in for ostentatious shows of wealth like Hearst's mansion in San Simeon. Yet Luce's contribution to publishing was just as important, if not more so, as that of his peers. He created a number of magazines that have survived him and gone on to become national institutions.

For More Information

Books:

Cort, David. *The Sin of Henry R. Luce: An Anatomy of Journalism*. Secaucus, NJ: Carol Publishing Group, 1974.

Swanberg, W. A. *Luce and His Empire*. New York: Scribner, 1972.

Web sites:

Time.com: **www.time.com**

Fortune.com: **www.fortune.com**

Konosuke Matsushita

1894	Born.
1918	Starts Matsushita Electric Appliance Factory.
1929	Formulates the "basic management objective."
1933	Introduces the "five guiding principles."
1935	Matsushita Electric Appliance renamed Matsushita Electric Industrial Company (MEI).
1937	Adds two more guiding principles.
1946	Founds the Peace and Happiness through Prosperity (PHP) Institute.
1950	Returns to the company.
1961	Becomes Chairman of MEI.
1965	Introduces five-day workweek.
1973	Steps down as Chairman.
1989	Dies.

Summary

For a man who never left his native country before the age of 56, Konosuke Matsushita (1894–1989) made a big impact on the world. Matsushita started work at the age of nine. After spells as a coal worker and at an engineering company, Matsushita started his own company, Matsushita Electric Appliance (later Matsushita Electric Industrial Company, or MEI) in 1918. Through a combination of product innovation, clever marketing, and forward-thinking management, Matsushita developed the company into one of the largest of its kind in prewar Japan.

After a difficult postwar period, Matsushita rejoined his company in 1950. Reasserting his business values, he transformed MEI into an industrial giant that today consists of over 300 subsidiaries.

Life and Career

The youngest of eight children, Konosuke Matsushita was born in 1894 in the farming village of Wasa in Wakayama Prefecture, Japan. His father was a landlord who received income from the local tenant farmers, enabling the family to live in reasonable comfort. That changed in 1898 when Matsushita's father decided to speculate on the rice market. The investment was spectacularly unsuccessful and left the family in financial ruin. The changed circumstances spelled the end of Matsushita's rudimentary schooling. At the tender age of nine, he was asked by his father to go to Osaka to work in a charcoal brazier shop. This was followed by an apprenticeship in a bicycle shop.

In 1910 the young Matsushita was taken on as a wiring assistant at the Osaka Electric Light Company (OELC). He was a quick learner and despite his age, just 16, his skill at wiring earned him rapid promotion. But in 1917 he decided to leave OELC, partly due to health problems. Matsushita suffered from a debilitating lung condition and frequently took days off from work to rest. He decided that if he could start his own business he would be able to accommodate his poor health. He also wanted to market a new light socket he had invented, and his employers at OELC had done little to encourage his inventiveness.

Contribution

In 1918, at the age of 23, he founded Matsushita Electric Appliance Factory (the company became Matsushita Electric Industrial Company—MEI—in 1935). He had three employees, the equivalent of $50, and a prototype for a new type of electrical socket. Business was tough at first. Matsushita's first socket design turned out to be a dud. But the next product, an electrical attachment plug, sold well, especially since Matsushita undercut the competition by up to a third. The product that kept the company going, though, was a battery powered bicycle lamp shaped like a bullet. The lamp was unique in being able to run for up to 40 hours. Some Japanese even used it to light their houses.

Matsushita was a good engineer, but he was even better at marketing. He used the demand for his bicycle lamp to build a sales network throughout Japan. Once he had established countrywide distribution, he put the trademark "National" on Matsushita products and lowered prices to make his lamp a mass-market product. He also pioneered the use of national newspaper advertising, a relatively rare sight in Japan in the 1920s.

In 1929, with the company firmly established, Matsushita put into practice the management practices and philosophy for which he was to become famous. He was an extremely enlightened manager for his time. This much is evident from the slogan he adopted for the company: "harmony between corporate profit and social justice." Matsushita followed this in 1933 with his "five guiding principles" (two more were added in 1937), which shaped the conduct of the company. The principles, still adhered to today, are service to the public, fairness and honesty, teamwork for the common cause, untiring effort for improvement, courtesy and humility, accord with natural laws, and gratitude for blessings.

During the 1930s Matsushita made a number of decisions illustrating the leadership style that was to earn him the nickname "the god of management." During the recession of 1930 Matsushita refused to make wholesale layoffs. Instead he recruited underemployed factory workers to go out and sell stockpiled inventory. Later in 1931 he bought the rights to a radio patent, which he then made freely available to the market. This was an expensive ploy, but it had the effect of stimulating the market and so ultimately profited the company. It presaged a similar move by David Sarnoff, the head of RCA, with the patent for building color television sets, and anticipated the stance taken much later by the open source movement in computing. In 1932 Matsushita declared that entrepreneurs and manufacturers should aim "to make all products as inexhaustible and as cheap as tap water."

Somehow Matsushita managed to hold the company together during World War II. In postwar Japan, MEI came under the severe restrictions imposed on certain Japanese companies by the Allies. Matsushita was almost removed as President, but was saved in part by a petition from 15,000 employees. For a time he devoted his energies to the Peace and

Matsushita's first socket design turned out to be a dud. But the next product, an electrical attachment plug, sold well, especially since Matsushita undercut the competition by up to a third.

Happiness through Prosperity Institute, which he founded in 1946, returning to his company duties only in 1950. He reinvigorated the company, reorganizing it along divisional lines. At the same time he reassessed processes to make them more efficient and refocused the company on the core values he had expressed in the 1930s.

From 1950 until his retirement as Chairman in 1973, Matsushita oversaw a huge expansion of the company as its "three treasures"—washing machines, refrigerators, and televisions—as well as other electrical goods were exported around the world. The company grew to become one of the world's largest manufacturers of electrical goods, controlling a stable of global brand names including Panasonic, Technics, and JVC.

A measure of the man's attention to his business is revealed by an incident at the Matsushita Pavilion during the Osaka World's Fair in 1970. The exposition had been open for a few days when the pavilion's staff were surprised to see Matsushita waiting in line outside. When they rushed out to usher the founder of their company indoors, he told them that he had stood in line to find out how long visitors had to wait before they were admitted. Later that day he ordered that the system be redesigned to speed up admission and that shade from the sun be provided for the people waiting outside.

From the 1970s onward Matsushita concentrated much of his time on developing and explaining his social and commercial philosophies, mainly in his 44 published books. His most popular title, *Developing a Road to Peace and Happiness Through Prosperity*, sold over four million copies. He continued to teach his unique concept of management until his chronic lung problems claimed his life. He died of pneumonia on April 27, 1989. He was 94.

Context and Conclusions

Konosuke Matsushita founded one of Japan's greatest corporations, Matsushita Electric Industrial. Yet he is remembered for much more than the creation of an electrical goods empire. At MEI Matsushita implemented management practices that were far ahead of their time. He abandoned the conventional centralized management structure. He drew up a corporate creed and identified corporate values. He pioneered advertising in the press and competed both on price and quality.

Matsushita's philosophy can best be summed up by the "basic management objective" he formulated in 1929: "Recognizing our responsibilities as industrialists, we will devote ourselves to the progress and development of society and the well-being of people through our business activities, thereby enhancing the quality of life throughout the world." It was something Matsushita did to great effect.

For More Information

Books:

Gould, Rowland. *The Matsushita Phenomenon*. Tokyo: Diamond Sha, 1970.

Kotter, John P. *Matsushita: Leadership Lessons from the Life of the 20th Century's Most Remarkable Entrepreneur*. New York: Free Press, 1997.

Matsushita, Konosuke. *Quest for Prosperity—The Life of a Japanese Industrialist*. Tokyo: PHP Institute, 1988.

Web site:

Panasonic USA: **www.panasonic.com**

Louis B. Mayer

1885	Born.
1907	Buys rundown movie theater in Haverhill, Massachusetts.
1915	Shows D. W. Griffith's *Birth of a Nation* at his theaters.
1918	Starts movie production firm in Los Angeles—Louis B. Mayer Pictures.
1924	Louis B. Mayer Productions, the Samuel Goldwyn Company, and Metro merge to form Metro Goldwyn Mayer, or MGM.
1926	*Ben Hur.*
1927	Formation of the Academy of Motion Pictures Arts and Sciences.
1932	*Grand Hotel.*
1936	Rival Irving Thalberg dies.
1951	Ousted from MGM after a power struggle with Dore Schary.
1957	Dies.

Summary

The real-life story of movie tycoon Louis B. Mayer (1885–1957) reads like a script from one of his movies. Mayer hauled himself up from his humble beginnings as the son of an immigrant scrap-metal dealer to become a Hollywood legend. Starting in 1907 with a small chain of movie theaters, by 1924 he was Vice-President of Metro Goldwyn Mayer, arguably the greatest studio in Hollywood history.

Over the following decades the studio with the famous lion emblem was a roaring success as Mayer exerted his despotic influence over every aspect of the moviemaking process. Like many dictators, benign or otherwise, Mayer was ousted from MGM in 1951 after a bitter power struggle.

Life and Career

Louis B. Mayer was born Eliezar Mayer on July 4, 1885 in Minsk, Russia (now in Belarus). In 1888 Mayer emigrated with his family to New Brunswick, Canada. In Canada Mayer's father built a small junk-dealing business into a profitable scrap-metal organization. After elementary school Mayer joined his father's business, preferring the world of commerce to that of academia. Soon he had his own scrap business in Boston.

In 1907 Mayer took his first small step on the road to Hollywood. Relinquishing his position in the family business, he bought a small dilapidated movie theater in Haverhill, Massachusetts, at a knockdown price. He completely overhauled the theater and made a decision to show only quality movies. His gamble paid off. Soon he was the owner of the largest theater chain in New England. Film exhibitors fought to show new movies at Mayer's theaters. In 1915 he showed D. W. Griffith's *Birth of a Nation*, one of the most popular movies of its time. The huge profit Mayer made from showing the movie helped finance his ensuing adventures in Hollywood.

Contribution

By 1918 Mayer was camped out in Los Angeles, operating as a movie promoter through his company, Louis B. Mayer Pictures. It was the start of his personal main event. At first productions were funded from the proceeds of the theater chain business. He made a star of the actress Anita Stewart and, fired up by the acclaim received for his first production, *Virtuous Wives*, continued to use her as his main attraction for the following five years.

Hollywood was still in its infancy. For aspiring moguls there remained a once-in-a-lifetime opportunity to stake a claim in the city of celluloid. Mayer may have been wealthy because of his movie theater business, but his fortune was small change in an industry dominated by fabulously rich powerbrokers. And the mogul of all moguls was Marcus Loew. He commanded his fiefdom from the East Coast; 3,000 miles away in his New York City office Loew pulled the strings that made Hollywood dance.

Mayer ruled MGM "as one big family, rewarding obedience, punishing insubordination, and regarding opposition as personal betrayal."

In 1924 Mayer hit the jackpot. Loew decided that he wanted his own studio, Metro, to merge with Louis B. Mayer Pictures and the Samuel Goldwyn Company. What Loew wanted, he generally got, to the point that when Samuel Goldwyn backed out of the deal, Loew retained the Goldwyn name, calling the newly-formed company Metro Goldwyn Mayer (MGM). Mayer was appointed Vice-President. With his inherited stable of stars he was finally in a position to dominate Hollywood.

At MGM Mayer ostensibly shared his power with Irving Thalberg, hired in from Universal by Loew. In reality, Mayer ruled the roost, conducting a bitter battle behind the scenes with Thalberg that ended only with Thalberg's death in 1936.

By all accounts Mayer was an autocratic, manipulative despot who ruled MGM using extreme cunning. He was described by Ephraim Katz, the late respected film scholar and author of the classic resource, *The Film Encyclopedia*, as "a ruthless, quick-tempered, paternalistically tyrannical executive." Mayer ruled MGM "as one big family, rewarding obedience, punishing insubordination, and regarding opposition as personal betrayal." His political acumen must truly have been brilliant to control the egos of movie stars such as Lon Chaney and Greta Garbo, as well as Directors like King Vidor and Erich von Stroheim.

Unashamedly populist, Mayer was said to abhor intellectualism. Like many other media moguls he had an innate sense of what the masses wanted. He was also a hands-on operator. To the frequent annoyance of the studio employees, who considered themselves the true auteurs, Mayer not only constantly intervened in moviemaking but also managed to take many of the plaudits.

Inexorably MGM's power grew, and with it, Mayer's. The studio churned out a movie a week and created its own town, Culver City, where thousands of studio employees participated in the American dream. Off screen, Mayer was as ruthless as ever. He was equally adept at cutting film or cutting staff. He used the rise of the talkies as an excuse for a purge of the studio stars. Names that Mayer had helped make he now discarded: Buster Keaton, Erich von Stroheim, even Greta Garbo, were swept off the lot as Mayer and MGM marched on through the 1930s and 1940s.

Mayer cleverly managed to thwart objections to MGM's increasing dominance of the movie industry by forming an alliance of sorts under the banner of the Academy of Motion Pictures Arts and Sciences. Mayer, along with Douglas Fairbanks, Sr., was a prime mover behind the Academy's creation in 1927.

Like most dictatorial leaders, however, his ruthlessness eventually caught up with him. In the 1950s, lacking the energy of the emerging generation of would-be studio executives, he was finally ground down by the behind-the-scenes scheming. Outmaneuvered, he was ejected from MGM in 1951 to be replaced by Dore Schary. Grittily determined to the last, Mayer spent his final years failing to persuade the shareholders of MGM's parent company, Loew, to reinstate him and dump Schary. He died as a result of leukemia in 1957.

Context and Conclusions

In many ways Mayer's life was a drama in which he himself played the roles of both hero and villain. On his journey to moguldom he made countless enemies. It was said at the time of his death that the reason that half of Hollywood attended his funeral was to check that the great man was indeed dead. Mayer also earned the grudging respect of his competitors, who harbored a sneaking admiration for his commercial acumen.

At MGM Mayer presided over a golden age of moviemaking. He was responsible for a host of hits like *Ben Hur* (1926) and *Dinner at Eight* (1933). At his zenith he commanded the highest salary in the world—over a million dollars a year. Bob Hope said of Mayer that he "came out west with 28 dollars, a box camera, and an old lion. He built a monument to himself—the Bank of America."

Perhaps Mayer's most fitting epitaph is one of his own observations. Commenting on survival in the movie business, the combative son of a scrap dealer who became the most powerful man in Hollywood eloquently put it thus: "Look out for yourself or they'll pee on your grave."

For More Information

Books:

Altman, Diana. *Hollywood East: Louis B. Mayer and the Origins of the Studio System*. Secaucus, NJ: Carol Publishing Group, 1992.

Gabler, Neal. *An Empire of Their Own: How the Jews Invented Hollywood*. New York: Doubleday, 1988.

Schulberg, Budd. *Moving Pictures*. New York: Stein and Day, 1982.

Zierold, Norman. *The Moguls*. Los Angeles: Avon Books, 1972.

Web site:

MGM: **www.mgm.com**

Cyrus Hall McCormick

1809	Born.
1830	Given ownership of his father's prototype reaper invention.
1831	Produces viable working machine.
1834	Receives 14-year patent for the threshing machine.
1843	Head-to-head showdown with rival Obed Hussey.
1847	Moves business to Chicago.
1851	Awarded prize at Crystal Palace Grand Exhibition.
1859	Production at 4,119 machines a year.
1861	Beginning of American Civil War.
1870	Production of 10,000 machines a year.
1871	Great fire of Chicago destroys McCormick's manufacturing plant.
1873	New production plant opens.
1884	Dies.

Summary

Cyrus Hall McCormick had invention in his blood. He grew up with a father who was constantly inventing strange contraptions. On the family farm in Virginia, McCormick perfected the design of one of his father's crazy ideas—the mechanized reaping machine. Aged only 22, he started a small-scale home-manufacturing operation in Virginia Valley, producing two machines in 1840. It ended up as a massive manufacturing concern, based in Chicago. In 1884, the McCormick Harvesting Machine Company sold 54,841 harvesting machines to farmers from the United States to Australia.

A millionaire by the age of 50, McCormick paved the way for an agrarian revolution through the invention of his reaping machine and a host of innovative marketing techniques, from the installment plan to the money-back guarantee.

Life and Career

The son of a farmer and inventor, Cyrus Hall McCormick was the oldest of eight children. Born on February 15, 1809 in Rockbridge County, Virginia, McCormick grew up on the 532 rolling acres of farmland belonging to the family. His father Robert, in addition to running the farm, spent a lot of time tinkering with inventions aimed at easing the burden of farming. The most significant of his inventions was a horse-drawn reaping device, abandoned when he failed to perfect it. McCormick's father lacked the business sense, the will, and the drive necessary to turn any of his various inventions into a commercial venture.

The young McCormick had already demonstrated an ability for invention when, at the age of 15, he built a light-weight cradle for harvesting grain. When he was still 21, his father gave him a head start in life, handing over the ownership of his reaper invention. In 1831, McCormick worked six weeks nonstop to perfect the invention, to produce a viable working machine.

Contribution

In the summer of 1831, the 22-year-old McCormick used his horse-drawn reaper to mow down the field of wheat at John Steele's farm in Rockbridge County, Virginia. The assembled audience—farmers, laborers, and slaves—had witnessed the beginning of the mechanization of agriculture. Quality control would come later.

McCormick wasn't the first to invent the reaper. Others, such as Obed Hussey, were also thinking along the same lines. In 1834, McCormick applied for and received a 14-year patent for his threshing machine. Hussey had obtained a patent for his reaping device a year earlier. In the end it was McCormick's marketing genius that would make his product the standard for mechanical threshing.

Despite the obvious advantages of the reaper, developing the business proved difficult. McCormick swiftly set about remedying the situation. He started by eliminating the competition in the minds of the consumer. He arranged a head-to-head showdown with his rival in 1843, in which the McCormick reaper cut down 17 acres in the time it took Obed Hussey to clear just two. Word soon traveled through the farming community about the disparity in performance between the two machines.

Next, McCormick developed a licensing system. Manufacturers close to market were granted a license to produce the McCormick reaping machine. In some cases the agreement operated like a franchise, demarcating area in return for a franchise fee; in others it was simply a question of paying McCormick $20 for each reaper produced and sold.

To obviate the need to walk alongside his machine, McCormick designed a seat so the operator could sit above the reaper. This design, known as the "old reliable," became the standard model.

In 1840, from his Walnut Grove base, McCormick sold two machines—they both broke down. The following year, he sold seven. In 1844, still in the Virginia Valley, production had risen to 75 machines, 25 manufactured under license.

In 1847, McCormick moved to Chicago. The decision was motivated by the knowledge that, although he had manufactured 75 reapers in 1846, this was still a long way short of the demand. Devotion to his father, Robert, had kept McCormick in his hometown. When his father died in 1846, there were few reasons for him to remain in the backwoods of Walnut Grove. In Chicago, McCormick built a plant on the banks of the Chicago River. Over 7,500 square feet of factory space and river frontage meant completed machines could be loaded onto river transport. This allowed McCormick to expand production rapidly. In 1849, before completion of the factory, McCormick's company produced 1,500 reapers. By 1859, in a new factory premises, production had rocketed to 4,119 machines a year.

By 1860, some 70% of the country's wheat harvest was gathered using McCormick's reaper. Before the reaper, it took a man 40 hours to harvest an acre of

He arranged a head-to-head showdown with his rival in 1843, in which the McCormick reaper cut down 17 acres in the time it took Obed Hussey to clear just two.

wheat. With the McCormick reaper, two people could harvest an acre of wheat in a day. In the decade leading up to 1859, U.S. production of wheat boomed from 100 million bushels to 173 million. The agricultural revolution made McCormick a millionaire. It also made him a worldwide celebrity. The machine, first described by the *London Times* as a "contraption seemingly a cross between a wheelbarrow, a chariot, and a flying machine," won the main prize at the Grand Exhibition at Crystal Palace in 1851. This award was followed by prizes at the Hamburg Exposition, the Vienna Exposition and the Paris Exposition.

McCormick continued to manage his business well into his seventies. It was quite a feat, considering some of the severe setbacks the business suffered. Production was slack for the duration of the American Civil War, starting in 1861, during which time McCormick took the opportunity to promote his machine in Europe. By 1870 his factory was producing a staggering 10,000 machines a year. Then in 1871 a devastating blow was dealt to his business when the great fire of Chicago destroyed $188 million worth of property at his manufacturing plant. The resilient McCormick built an even bigger factory and production complex that sprawled over a 160-acre site. It opened in 1873.

McCormick died in 1884, with the business safely in the hands of his enterprising son, Cyrus McCormick, Jr. In the final years of his life McCormick successfully promoted his business abroad, taking the reaper to the both the Pacific and South America.

Context and Conclusions

In 1831, the year that McCormick invented his mechanized reaping machine, 80% of all workers in the United States worked in farming. By the 1930s this figure was down to just 2%. That dramatic reduction, which freed up the workforce to better mankind in other ways than through the drudgery of manual agricultural work, is largely due to Cyrus Hall McCormick and his "Virginia Reaper." The effects of his achievements cannot be overstated. The commercial success of his machine accelerated the colonization of America's West Coast, and allowed for the wholesale exploitation of the bread basket of the Midwest, which in turn allowed for a rapid expansion in the United States population. This growth, coupled with the release of workers from work on the land, was a significant factor in the growth of the United States as the biggest economy in the world.

McCormick continued to manage his business well into his seventies. It was quite a feat, considering some of the severe setbacks the business suffered.

Would this have happened without McCormick? Possibly, but McCormick was blessed with talents that many of his competitors lacked. His inventiveness extended beyond the creation of machines. He pioneered marketing innovations such as installment plans, commission sales, and money-back guarantees, that ensured every farmer who wanted a McCormick reaper could have one.

CLOSE BUT NO CIGAR

JOHN DEERE

Inventor and entrepreneur John Deere was a contemporary of Cyrus Hall McCormick. A blacksmith by trade, Deere invented the first self-polishing steel plow in the 1830s, just as McCormick was testing his reaping machine. In the end, McCormick's invention proved the more significant of the two. By 1855 Deere was selling 13,000 plows a year. He went on to found Deere & Company in 1868, today a million-dollar company. He survived McCormick by two years, dying in 1886.

OBED HUSSEY

The "almost-ran" of agricultural invention, Obed Hussey could justifiably lay claim to the invention of the reaping machine. A former whaler, Hussey patented his device in 1833, a year before McCormick. However his big mistake was to stay in Baltimore, Maryland, miles from his market. McCormick bit the bullet and moved from Virginia to Chicago in the Midwest. Hussey also lacked McCormick's flair for marketing and was unwilling to accommodate improvements to his design suggested by others.

For More Information

Books:

Casson, Herbert N. *Cyrus Hall McCormick: His Life and Work*. Chicago: A. C. McClure & Co., 1909.

Dobler, Lavinia. *Cyrus McCormick: Farm Boy*. Indianapolis, IN: The Bobbs-Merrill Co., 1961.

McCormick, Cyrus. *The Century of the Reaper—Cyrus Hall McCormick and Business*. Boston: Houghton Mifflin Co., 1931.

Scott McNealy

1954	Born.
1972	Attends Harvard University.
1978	Admitted to Stanford Business School's M.B.A. program.
1982	Joins startup company called Sun Microsystems.
1984	Three-year, $40-million deal to supply Sun-2 workstations. Made interim C.E.O. in place of Vinod Khosla.
1985	Becomes permanent C.E.O.
1986	Company has its I.P.O.
1988	Revenues reach $1 billion.
1991	Network, the greater Swiss mountain dog, born.
1992	Revenues reach $3 billion.
1994	John Gosling and others develop Java.
2001	Revenues reach $17 billion.

Summary

An amateur ice-hockey player and a 3-handicap golfer, Scott McNealy combines the charm and easygoing affability of a best buddy with the competitive drive required to be a successful athlete or business executive. Breezing through Harvard University and Stanford Business School, McNealy managed to combine his interests in beer and sport with the academic study necessary to obtain an economics degree and an M.B.A.

A laid-back start in the manufacturing industry gave way to the job of C.E.O. at Sun Microsystems in 1984, when his friend and cofounder Vinod Khosla was persuaded to step down. Since then life has been one long crusade against arch foe Bill Gates and the Microsoft vision of a PC-dominated world. Enlisting the help of some unlikely allies along the way, including a 135-lb. greater Swiss mountain dog and an animated character called Duke, McNealy continues to give his competitors a run for their money. With revenues of $17 billion and rising in 2001, the future looks bright both for him and for Sun.

Life and Career

Scott McNealy was born on November 13, 1954, in Columbus, Indiana. His father was an executive with American Motors, and much of McNealy's early childhood was spent in towns scattered across the Midwest. The McNealy family finally rolled to a standstill in Bloomfield Hills, Michigan, where McNealy attended Cranbrook, a private prep school. Academic achievement and social popularity came easily to him. He devoted a great deal of his time to sports, yet still managed to get a perfect 800 on his math SATs, earning him a place at Harvard University.

At the time McNealy's ambition was to become a doctor, but he ended up majoring in economics. When he wasn't studying, he was immersing himself in the Harvard social scene. An excellent golfer (*Golf Digest* ranked him number one among *Fortune* 500 C.E.O.s in 1999), McNealy captained the university golf team. By an interesting quirk of fate, he was at Harvard at the same time as his longtime business adversary Bill Gates. McNealy, however, has no memory of their paths crossing.

When he left Harvard, McNealy embarked on a career in manufacturing, working at a tractor body panel factory in Illinois. Life in the agricultural machinery business didn't appeal to him; he applied to Stanford University's Business School and, accepted on his third attempt, packed his bags and headed for California.

Contribution

McNealy graduated with the Stanford M.B.A. Class of 1980 and went to work for FMC Corporation, building military vehicles. In 1982 another Stanford alumnus, Vinod Khosla, contacted McNealy about a possible job. Khosla and graduate student Andy Bechtolsheim had combined forces to develop a workstation for computer networks. Bechtolsheim had been working on the Stanford University Network project, and so the two took the initials S.U.N. for the name of their startup.

Khosla wanted someone with manufacturing expertise, and he tapped McNealy, by then working for hardware company Onyx, for operations. McNealy accepted the job of vice President for manufacturing and operations at a celebratory meal in a McDonald's restaurant. The company enjoyed early success, winning a three-year, $40 million deal in 1984 to supply Sun-2 workstations to a company called Computervision.

This commercial success masked internal conflict over how the company should be run. Khosla, who had been the catalyst for starting Sun Microsystems, found the skills that had proved essential for getting the startup off the ground were not necessarily those needed to lead the company through the next phase. The uneasiness over Khosla's stewardship of Sun placed McNealy in an awkward position. He had joined the company at the request of Khosla, a personal friend. Nevertheless the two other founders, Bechtolsheim and Bill Joy, wanted a change at the top. Together with McNealy they persuaded Khosla that he should step down. McNealy was installed as C.E.O. in Khosla's place. It was an inspired appointment. His operational know-how and improbable combination of easygoing bonhomie and relentless drive kept the workforce engaged while pushing the company through a phase of rapid expansion. "We wanted to make a Ferrari out of spare parts," McNealy told the *New York Times*. "We were either going to be incredibly successful or we were going to empty the pool out with a belly flop." The company had its I.P.O in 1986. Sales continued to accelerate, from $1 billion in 1988 to over $3 billion in 1992.

McNealy realized early that one of the main obstacles to Sun's success would be the so-called "Wintel alliance" (Windows operating system and Intel chips). He decided to meet this threat to the Sun UNIX platform head on. Shrewdly, he embarked on a campaign of antagonism directed at Microsoft's Bill Gates that attracted the attention of the media and created a buzz around Sun. McNealy took the position of network evangelist (a view diametrically opposed to Gates's), preaching that "the network is the computer." He even named his dog Network and gave it its own page on the Sun corporate Web site.

In 1994 McNealy was handed a secret weapon in his battle against the Microsoft hegemony when John Gosling's team of Sun programmers developed a new computer language. Provisionally named "Oak," it was a cross-platform, write once, run anywhere language. Here, thought McNealy, was the big stick he could beat Microsoft with. He put the full might of the company behind the new language, which, when "Oak" failed to clear the lawyers, was renamed Java.

The story of how McNealy learned about Gosling's project is indicative of his management methods. Sun may ostensibly have a hierarchical management structure, but McNealy was quick to grasp one indicator of the de facto organizational structure—the e-mail trail. Find out who is receiving the critical e-mails, he reasoned, and you know where the power is concentrated within the company. When McNealy kept coming across e-mails on "Java group meeting," he reckoned Java was something he ought to find out about.

He was right. With its strong branding and open standards, Java has become a universal language. NASA's 1997 Mars mission gave a real boost to the product by allowing interactive participation in the mission via the Internet. Java is seen as key to future domination of computing. The company's "Sun One" vision sees an integrated set of Java-based hardware and software running on any platform, in contrast to proprietary systems like Microsoft Windows. By 2001, more than 2.5 million programmers were developing for Java and Sun had established the Liberty Alliance of 34 leading companies who would allow secure Internet transactions based on Java. The company's success is also attributable in part to McNealy's excellence as a communicator. *Forbes ASAP* described him as one of the top ten speakers in the technology industry. *60 Minutes* called him "one of the most influential businessmen in America"—and he was quick to proselytize users to the benefits of Java. McNealy's enthusiasm for selling Sun systems extends to some high profile networking. He famously challenged Jack Welch, General Electric's celebrated C.E.O., to a round of golf. McNealy lost, but so impressed Welch that he received a place on the GE board.

With McNealy in charge Sun has blazed a trail of innovation through the technology industry. In 2000 the company's annual revenues were over $12 billion. Still driven by McNealy's war cry of "the network is the computer," the company continues to provide "industrial-strength hardware, software, and services that power the Internet and allow companies worldwide to dot-com their businesses."

Context and Conclusions

Scott McNealy showed few signs of making a successful leader during his early career in manufacturing. Content to go along for the ride, he was thrust by chance into the driving seat of Sun Microsystems, the company he helped found. Like his business contemporaries Bill Gates and Larry Ellison, McNealy has created a multibillion dollar company that is strongly associated with its founder and C.E.O. Think Sun Microsystems and you automatically think of Scott McNealy. McNealy has taken the competitive drive that makes him a good golfer and an even better executive and instilled it throughout the company. He has also proved himself a media savvy leader. This is an essential quality in an age when the right words can propel a C.E.O. to cult status, and the wrong ones can sink a company.

For More Information

Book:

Southwick, Karen. *High Noon: The Inside Story of Scott McNealy and the Rise of Sun Microsystems*. New York: John Wiley, 1999.

Web site:

Sun© Microsystems: **www.sun.com**

Charles Merrill

1885	Born.
1907	Moves to New York to work for Patchogue-Plymouth Mills.
1911	Article "Mr. Average Investor" published in *Leslie's Weekly*.
1914	Founds Merrill, Lynch & Co. with Edmund Lynch.
1928	Writes to clients advising them that "now is a time to get out of debt."
1940	Pierce & Co. merges with Merrill Lynch.
1944	Suffers multiple heart attacks.
1947	Merrill Lynch largest retailer of stocks in United States.
1956	Dies.

Summary

Cofounder of the first chain of stockbrokers, Charles Merrill brought stock ownership to the masses. In doing so he helped to shift capitalism from a relatively small base of rich investors to a much broader cross section of U.S. society, a process that has continued in recent years with the advent of online trading. Merrill came to stockbroking by chance. A broken romance led him to the hubbub of Wall Street when he left the textile company Patchogue-Plymouth Mills and joined the bond department of George H. Burr & Co.

As early as 1911 Merrill was contemplating the merits of wider share ownership. He articulated his radical ideas in the article "Mr. Average Investor." He also became an expert on the financing of the relatively new concept of chain stores. It was a chain store approach that he brought to stockbroking. With drinking buddy Edmund Lynch, he founded Merrill, Lynch & Co. in 1914. He then successfully steered the firm through the maelstrom of the 1929 Wall Street Crash. After World War II, with the expanded firm of Merrill Lynch, EA Pierce, and Cassatt, Merrill fulfilled his vision of bringing share ownership to the masses. By 1947 Merrill Lynch was the largest retailer of stocks in the United States, with $6,200,000 worth of sales and an advertising bill of some $400,000. Plagued by ill health, Merrill was forced to take a back seat, and died in 1956.

His academic career was cut short when financial difficulties forced him to drop out of Amherst College without completing his degree. He later dropped out of law school.

Life and Career

The son of a shopkeeper and doctor, Charles Merrill was born in 1885 in the small village of Green Cove Springs, Jacksonville, Florida. His academic career was cut short when financial difficulties forced him to drop out of Amherst College without completing his degree. He later dropped out of law school. A stint as a semiprofessional baseball player in Mississippi was followed by a reporting job on a West Palm Beach newspaper.

Through a girlfriend's father, Merrill obtained a job at the textile company Patchogue-Plymouth Mills and moved to New York. It was 1907, the year in which J. P. Morgan bailed out the U.S. financial system. The financial crisis presented the young Merrill with an unexpected opportunity. He was dispatched to the National Copper Bank to obtain a loan that would save the company he worked for. It was a tall order, but the persuasive Merrill somehow managed to obtain a $300,000 loan from the bank President. Merrill thrived in the bustling environment of New York City. When his budding romance with the boss's daughter ended, he extricated himself from an awkward situation by taking a job at the newly created bond department of George H. Burr & Co. on Wall Street.

Contribution

While Merrill was at Burr, two events occurred that were to shape his future professional life. The first was the realization that it was possible to sell bonds and stock to the public, rather than just to powerful institutional investors. Merrill propounded his thoughts on this topic in his 1911 article "Mr. Average Investor," published in *Leslie's Weekly*. The second important event was Merrill's involvement in a financing deal for a chain of retail stores. At the time, chain stores were a new phenomenon. The economics involved made a significant impression on him.

Remarkably, amid the rampant speculation of the 1920s, Merrill was one of the few who advocated caution. To his partner Lynch, he wrote, "The financial skies are not clear. I do not like the outlook and I do not like the amount of money we owe."

In 1914 Merrill and his drinking buddy and colleague, Edmund Lynch, left Burr to form Merrill, Lynch & Co. In the first year of business Merrill won a contract to underwrite a $6 million chain-store financing deal. After a brief interlude due to the closing of the stock exchange at the outbreak of World War I, the chain store was successfully brought to market in May 1915, earning him $300,000.

Recognizing that chain stores would become an essential feature of U.S. postwar retailing, Merrill specialized in financing chain-store developments throughout the country. He retained a significant amount of stock in each deal. This not only made him a wealthy man but also gave the firm a decision-making role in the management of the companies it helped finance. Merrill used that power to great effect. At one point he even took control of a chain of grocery stores.

Remarkably, amid the rampant speculation of the 1920s, Merrill was one of the few who advocated caution. To his partner Lynch, he wrote, "The financial skies are not clear. I do not like the outlook and I do not like the amount of money we owe." When the financial storm came in 1929, Merrill Lynch was one of the few financial institutions to remain afloat. Clients who had taken Merrill's advice when he had written to them in 1928 advising them that "now is a time to get out of debt", had much to thank him for. Anticipating a lengthy downturn,

Merrill transferred his clients' accounts to another brokerage firm and devoted his time to managing a retail chain and looking after his own personal investments.

Merrill returned to Wall Street through the broking firm EA Pierce & Co., which merged with Merrill Lynch in January 1940. Through the newly created company of Merrill Lynch, EA Pierce, and Cassatt, Merrill brought stockbroking to the masses. It was the start of a financial revolution that introduced the chain-store approach to the elite world of stockbroking. Merrill ruthlessly drove down costs. With business conducted predominantly by phone, it was pointless having a large expensive building as the firm's headquarters, so he moved it to a cheaper, less prestigious location–70 Pine Street. He also needed to whip up enthusiasm among his employees. To do this he recruited brokers from a wider base. The newcomers were unencumbered with traditional Wall Street ways. Merrill trained them in a specially established school for trainee brokers.

Having marshaled his forces, Merrill took his operation to the U.S. public, building a chain of branch offices throughout the United States. The new brokers were paid salaries rather than working only for commission. This alleviated concerns on the public's part that the brokers would sell any stock, regardless of merit, merely to line their own pockets with commission. He backed up his campaign to broaden the appeal of stock buying by investing large amounts of money on advertising the firm's services. By 1947 Merrill Lynch was the largest retailer of stocks in the United States, with $6,200,000 worth of sales and an advertising spend of some $400,000. Its business was helped by the benign economic situation following World War II, as the United States began to reinforce its economic superpower status. During the Cold War much was made of the power of the free market economy in the United States, and individuals were actively encouraged to buy stock in American companies through initiatives such as a monthly investment plan scheme, introduced in 1954, which allowed the purchase of stock by installments.

After suffering multiple heart attacks during 1944, Merrill was forced to enjoy the company's success from the sidelines at the behest of his doctors. He did, however, continue to run and organize the business by phone from a variety of destinations including Palm Beach and Barbados. Merrill died in 1956, by which time he had succeeded in broadening the base of stock ownership to include over two million ordinary Americans.

Context and Conclusions

Charles Merrill took stockbroking out of the closeted world of Wall Street and onto the street. Influenced by his work financing deals for early chain-store development, he adopted the same model for selling shares. He strongly believed that the public would buy shares if they were readily available, an opinion he expressed in his 1911 article "Mr. Average Investor." He predicted the Wall Street Crash in the 1920s and saved his clients' fortunes. Through the firm of Merrill Lynch, EA Pierce, and Cassatt, he then took share ownership to the masses. A chain of branches throughout the country, low transaction costs, an expensive advertising campaign, and the help of a government push to finance share purchasing among the U.S. public, all helped make Merrill one of the leading stockbrokers in the United States.

CLOSE BUT NO CIGAR
WILLIAM ALBERT PAINE
Born in 1855 in Amesbury, Massachusetts, Paine worked as a bank clerk before founding his own stockbrokers, Paine, Webber, and Company in 1879 with partner Wallace G. Webber. The firm went on to acquire a host of other brokerages as it grew, and it is still in business today. It merged with UBS in 2000 and is now one of the biggest financial services firms in the world.

For More Information
Book:
Perkins, Edwin J. *Wall Street to Main Street: Charles Merrill and Middle-Class Investors.* New York: Cambridge University Press, 1999.

Web site:
Merrill Lynch: **www.ml.com**

J. P. Morgan

1837	Born.
1857	Joins Duncan, Sherman, and Co.
1862	Founds Dabrey, Morgan, and Co.
1871	Teams up with the firm of Drexel to form Drexel, Morgan, and Co.
1879	Puts together stock offering of $18 million for the New York Central Railroad.
1887	U.S. government passes the Interstate Commerce Act.
1895	Helps avert U.S. financial crisis.
1907	Bails out U.S. government again.
1912	Appears before Pujo Committee.
1913	Dies.

Summary

J. P. Morgan was one of the greatest financiers of his age. As a child he kept a close account of the receipt and expenditure of his allowance. As an adult he parlayed his attention to cash flow into a large fortune. He saw the Civil War as an opportunity to make money, and in 1862 he founded his own company, Dabrey, Morgan, and Co. By 1871 he had teamed up with the firm of Drexel to form Drexel, Morgan, and Co. He swiftly established himself as one of the leading financiers in New York. Industrialists and governments regularly turned to him for advice, and he helped avert a U.S. financial crisis in 1895. Morgan attempted to unify the railroad bosses in opposition to the U.S. government. A powerful influence in the formation of so-called industry "trusts," his business empire was eventually cut down to size by President Theodore Roosevelt.

Life and Career

J. P. Morgan was born in Hartford, Connecticut, on April 17, 1837. In the year of his birth America was plunged into financial gloom. Morgan, however, was unaffected; his father was a rich commodity broker who managed to make the most of the financial downturn. While he was still a boy, his father moved the family to Boston, where he became involved in the cotton trade.

Morgan took an early interest in business. Spurning childhood games, he spent much of his time poring over his accounts (a habit he carried with him throughout his life), detailing the receipt and expenditure of his allowance. He had a bookish nature—partly a result of his interest in business and money, and partly a result of a sickly constitution. Morgan was never a popular child at school. His aloof manner failed to impress his classmates, just as it would later alienate the U.S. public. His habits, such as writing to Paris in fluent French to order a pair of $900 boots, only served to reinforce the impression of arrogance.

Morgan's education was in keeping with his privileged status. When his family moved to London, he was dispatched to a private school in Switzerland. He then studied at the University of Göttingen in Germany and so impressed his tutors that he was asked to stay on as an assistant to one of the professors. The ambitious Morgan declined, insisting that he had to start out in business.

Contribution

Returning to America, in 1857 Morgan joined Duncan, Sherman, and Co., a firm with which his father had an association.

When the Civil War broke out in 1861, Morgan treated it not as a calamity but as an opportunity. He avoided enlistment through the accepted practice among the wealthy of paying a substitute to take his place. (The going rate was $300.) In 1862 he left Duncan Sherman and founded his own company, Dabrey, Morgan, and Co. While the war raged, Morgan piled up the profits. By 1864 he had amassed over $50,000. The war ended, but Morgan continued to go from strength to strength. By 1871 he had teamed up with the firm of Drexel, based in Philadelphia, to form Drexel, Morgan, and Co., based on the corner of Wall Street and Broad Street in New York.

Morgan was never a popular child at school. His aloof manner failed to impress his classmates, just as it would later alienate the U.S. public.

Morgan swiftly established a reputation as one of the leading financiers in America. His salary was more than $500,000—an astronomical amount at the time. It was during the 1870s that his association with the railroads began. The financing of the railroads required significant private capital, something that Morgan was only too happy to arrange.

His importance in the railroad business grew to the extent that leading players would turn to him to resolve disputes and offer his opinion. In an industry where companies fought increasingly hostile battles to gain supremacy, Morgan found himself playing the role of mediator.

When the U.S. government passed the Interstate Commerce Act in 1887, banning price-fixing collusion among railroads, the railroad companies naturally turned to Morgan again to organize a response. Obtaining a lasting consensus among the distrustful company bosses proved a task beyond even his talents. The misguided effort suggests a man whose ego was beginning to run out of control. Not only did he fail to unite the railroads against the government, he succeeded in setting himself up as the head of a conspiracy and thus an obvious target for the U.S. government, which was aiming to cut powerful business interests down to size.

By the 1890s Morgan had turned into a figure of hate among the U.S. public. Yet, despite this perception, Morgan's greatest public service lay ahead of him. In 1893 the withdrawal of funds from the United States by British investors sparked a financial crisis. As banks failed and the stock market collapsed, the U.S. government resorted to shoring up the financial system with its gold reserves. Statute prohibited the value of the reserves from falling below a prescribed level. The magic figure was $100 million in gold. In January 1895 gold reserves collapsed to $58 million and the treasury secretary John Carlisle turned to Morgan to save the day. Morgan proposed a syndicate of investors who would sell gold coin to the U.S. Treasury, paid for with newly issued bonds. It was a brilliant solution, as it provided not only an economic way out but also a politically expedient one. Morgan went further and guaranteed the scheme to the then President, Grover Cleveland. The Morgan syndicate intervention succeeded in stopping the financial slide and made Morgan a considerable profit, estimated at anywhere between $250,000 and $16 million.

This episode merely reinforced Morgan's already legendary financial prowess. He followed his rescue of the U.S. financial system with a series of breathtaking deals such as the financing of United States Steel, the largest steel corporation in the world. From the 1900s onward he devoted his attention to consolidating the railroad companies through his concern The Northern Securities Corporation, and to building a shipping trust. Unfortunately for him, however, the incumbent President, Theodore Roosevelt, had decided that political advantage could be gained by cracking down on the so-called trusts. As the well-known figure of Morgan stood behind The Northern Securities Corporation, Roosevelt decided that it should be made an example of. This time Morgan had met his match. Apart from a brief respite in 1907, when a U.S. President again turned to him for salvation during a financial crisis, Morgan's power waned.

By then in his 70s, Morgan devoted more time to his hobby of collecting art and to his private life. He died in Rome at the age of 76.

Obtaining a lasting consensus among the distrustful company bosses proved a task beyond even his talents. The misguided effort suggests a man whose ego was beginning to run out of control.

Context and Conclusions

J. P. Morgan was a remarkable businessman. His success owed much to his self-belief and opportunism, and a little to his wealthy and well-connected father. He suffered ill health throughout his life, particularly the periodic embarrassment of a large red bulbous nose, a result of eczema, the appearance of which would inevitably send him into deep melancholia. Yet despite frequent periods of illness-induced rest and recuperation, Morgan managed to build a string of business interests in the fashionable industries of the day—railroads, shipping, and electricity. He also, on more than one occasion, financed the U.S. government out of a mess.

Although not as wealthy as the likes of Carnegie or the Vanderbilts, Morgan amassed a fortune worthy of Croesus. He also accumulated a fabulous hoard of art treasures—a who's who of the old masters, including works by Vermeer, Gainsborough, Rembrandt, and da Vinci—as well as one of the finest libraries in the world. His reputation as a proud, vain, arrogant, and greedy man is justified. But he could be generous when it interested him. To a woman who offered him one of a missing pair of porcelain figures, he gave a handsome sum of money and a cottage in Wales.

CLOSE BUT NO CIGAR
JAY GOULD

A U.S. financier born in 1836, Gould was the most despised and underhanded of the "robber barons." He started out as a mapmaker and publisher of local history, then inveigled his way into a tannery business. He gained full control when his partner committed suicide. In the 1860s he took to speculating on the railroads. There followed a period of unscrupulous dealings, bribery of officials, and dubious financial practices that would rival if not surpass the worst examples of modern times. Gould emerged from the 1860s/1870s with a fortune of some $25 million (many others lost the shirts from their backs). A neurotic man who suffered terribly from dyspepsia and took his personal chef with him wherever he traveled, Gould was the driving force behind the expansion of the railroads across vast tracts of the United States. He died from tuberculosis, aged 57.

For More Information
Books:

Wheeler, George. *Pierpont Morgan and Friends: The Anatomy of a Myth*. Englewood Cliffs, NJ: Prentice Hall, 1973.

Winkler, John. *Morgan the Magnificent: Life of J.P. Morgan*. New York: The Vanguard Press, 1932.

Web site:

JPMorgan: **www.jpmorgan.com**

Akio Morita

1921	Born.
1946	Cofounds Tokyo Tshushin Kyogu.
1953	Travels to United States to license transistor technology.
1958	Company changes name to Sony.
1960	World's first all-transistor television.
1961	First Japanese company to list on New York Stock Exchange.
1963	Moves with his family to United States to establish Sony America.
1980	Sony produces Sony Walkman.
1982	Sony produces first CD players.
1993	Suffers stroke while playing tennis.
1999	Dies.

Summary

Akio Morita passed up the opportunity to lead an easy and secure life at the helm of the family sake business. Instead he chose to pursue his love of electrical engineering and start his own business, with all the risks that entailed. Starting with a prototype for a humble rice cooker, Morita's small company TTK grew into the electronic products giant Sony. In a lifetime devoted to his company, Morita gave the world a stream of innovative technologies and gadgets, from the portable transistor radio to the Sony Playstation. He was also the man responsible for making music portable, introducing the word "Walkman" into the global lexicon. In later life Morita refused to take a comfortable retirement, choosing to remain at the helm of Sony until he was forced to step down because of ill health.

Life and Career

Akio Morita was born on January 26, 1921 in Nagoya, an industrial city in Japan. By Japanese standards, his family was affluent middle class. Morita was heir to the family rice-wine brewing business, although he showed little interest in his father's company. Instead he preferred to tinker with electronics equipment. He soon became an avid amateur electronics enthusiast, neglecting his studies to build electronic gadgets, including a radio and a record player.

Morita continued to pursue his interest in electronics in college by studying physics. He joined the Japanese army during World War II and rose to the rank of lieutenant.

After the war Morita passed up the easy career route of working in the family sake business. Instead, in 1946 he traveled to Tokyo, where he joined his future partner Masaru Ibuka. With a $530 loan, the two started a new company, Tokyo Tshushin Kyogu (TTK). It was housed in a bombed-out department store.

Contribution

Morita eventually built one of the world's largest electronics companies, famed for its sophisticated miniaturized products. His first product prototype was a little less glamor-ous—a specialized rice cooker. But radio components and radio upgrades followed, and in the 1950s Morita produced his first major product, the tape recorder. It was the first in Japan.

Morita's biggest breakthrough was the transistor radio, despite the fact that the transistor was a U.S., not a Japanese, invention. Nor was the miniature radio that Morita produced using transistor technology the first of its kind. Morita had traveled to the United States in 1953 to license the technology from Bell Laboratories, but it was a joint venture between Texas Instruments and Regency Electronics that produced the world's first commercial transistor radio, the Regency TR-1, in October 1954.

TTK's first model was the TR-55, a set for which serious transistor radio collectors today would happily trade their grandmothers. Made in August 1955 in limited numbers, its production was restricted to Japan. TTK's first radio for export was the TR-63, produced in 1957.

Morita's small TR-63 was extremely successful for two main reasons. First, it was a truly innovative design, sold in a presentation box complete with a soft leather case, antistatic cloth, and earphone.

The second factor was Morita's dogged persistence. Taking the product direct to the distributors, he trekked around New York convincing electronic store owners to stock the TTK radio. He even turned down one large order because the potential purchaser didn't want the TTK company name on the product. He returned to Japan with a full order book.

In 1958 Morita pushed through a change of name for the company. A keen proponent of globalization, he was quick to realize that a name like Tokyo Tshushin Kyogu would prove an obstacle to capturing foreign markets. "We wanted a new name that could be recognized anywhere in the world, one that could be pronounced the same in any language," Morita said. He settled for Sony. This was a combination of the Latin word for sound—*sonus*—and the colloquial U.S. term "sonny." Morita's strategy clearly worked. When U.S. radio dealers were asked in a survey, "Have you ever handled Japanese radios?" they answered no. Asked whether they had ever dealt with Sony radios, they returned an unequivocal yes.

> *Morita's biggest breakthrough was the transistor radio, despite the fact that the transistor was a U.S., not a Japanese, invention.*

Over the years TTK/Sony produced a steady stream of innovative electronic products: the pocket radio in 1957, the world's first all-transistor television in 1960, and in 1968 the first home videotape recorder.

In 1963 Morita moved to the United States with his family and establish the Sony Corporation of America. It was a bold move for a man from a country whose businessmen were traditionally isolationist and protectionist in outlook. Morita pushed Sony's products in the United States, positioning the brand as premium quality. Soon the company's products were available nationwide.

When Morita noticed that young people liked listening to music wherever they went, he proposed that the company develop a portable tape cassette player. Morita's colleagues were unconvinced there was a market for a tape player of any size that lacked a recording facility. Morita stuck to his guns and persuaded his colleagues, and the Walkman was born in 1980. In a characteristically idiosyncratic move, there was no market research to back Morita's hunch. "The public does not know what is possible. We do," he said.

Interestingly, "Walkman" was not the product's universal name in the early days. Sony America thought the name poor English and changed it to "Soundabout" for the U.S. market. In Sweden it was known as "Freestyle" and in the United Kingdom, "Stowaway." Morita wasn't enthusiastic about this approach. As soon as he received a bad set of sales figures he used it as an excuse to change the name to Walkman throughout the world. The word has since become part of the global lexicon.

Another Sony innovation was video technology. Sony's Betamax technology lost out to VHS in the video standards war, but the company was instrumental in making home video recording a mainstream technology.

As the company's profits grew, Morita relentlessly pursued his vision of globalization. He used the expression "think globally, act locally" to describe his philosophy of corporate values that transcended national boundaries. Management thinkers such as Theodore Levitt and later Kenichi Ohmae popularized the phrase.

Having built Sony into a multibillion dollar company, Morita, by now a billionaire himself, refused to let up. Still brimming with energy, he spent time indulging in pastimes such as scuba diving, skiing, and tennis, all of which he started when he was past 50. He pursued a relentless schedule until he suffered a stroke while playing tennis. Ill health forced him to resign as President of Sony in 1993, and he died in October 1999.

Context and Conclusions

Akio Morita ranks as one of Japan's greatest business executives. Blessed with extraordinary drive, Morita was a risk-taker who would doggedly pursue his instincts. Time and again he followed his intuition, beginning with his original rejection of the safe option of working in the family business in favor of starting an electronics company with virtually no experience. The scale of his ambition was apparent in his decision to take his business to the United States at a time when Japan was not yet celebrated for its manufacturing techniques or the quality of its products.

It was Morita who helped put Japanese innovation on the world map by pushing through his globalization agenda, and, by backing his vision, he established Sony as a truly global company. He is responsible for making Japanese electronics a byword for innovative design and function.

For More Information

Books:

Morita, Akio, Edwin M. Reingold, and Mitsuko Shimomura. *Made in Japan: Akio Morita and Sony*. New York: Dutton, 1989.

Nathan, John. *Sony: The Private Life*. Boston: Houghton Mifflin, 2001.

Web site:

Sony: **www.sony.com**

Rupert Murdoch

1931	Born.
1950	Attends Oxford University, England.
1952	Works in Fleet Street on the London *Daily Express*. Returns to Australia.
1960	Buys the *Sydney Daily Mirror*.
1964	Founds the *Australian*.
1969	Buys the *News of the World* and the *Sun* in the United Kingdom.
1976	Buys the *New York Post*.
1981	Buys *The Times* of London.
1986	The "battle of Wapping."
1990	Saves business empire by restructuring debt.
1993	Buys into Star TV in Asia.
1997	Fox releases *Titanic*, biggest grossing film ever.
2002	Attempts to merge Sky TV with GM's Direct TV founder.
2002	Collapse of ITV Digital leaves Murdoch in control of 30% of U.K. media.
2002	Worldwide assets $42 billion, revenue $16 billion.

Summary

Rupert Murdoch (1931–) is one of the best known media barons of the modern age. After finishing his education at Oxford and a stint at the *Daily Express* newspaper, Murdoch returned to his native Australia to take over from his father at the helm of the *Adelaide News*.

He moved on to expand his media empire through a spate of acquisitions across the globe. In the 1980s he branched into movies and television, acquiring 20th Century Fox and Fox TV. In the United Kingdom he bought *The Times* and *The Sunday Times*, and emerged victorious from a bitter battle with the print unions. By the end of the 1980s the empire was mortgaged to the hilt, but after a major debt rescheduling exercise, Murdoch marched on into the 1990s, acquiring Star TV in Asia.

Life and Career

Now a U.S. citizen, Keith Rupert Murdoch was born in Melbourne, Australia, on March 11, 1931. His early education took place at Geelong Grammar school in Geelong, Victoria. He was not an impressive student—he admits he was "bone lazy" at school—other than in English, where his grades were above average. He also lacked sporting prowess. A restless child, he was more likely to be found cartwheeling across the outfield during play than participating in the school cricket match. His lack of interest on the athletic field led to him being disciplined on more than one occasion.

In 1950 he was sent to England to study economics at Worcester College, Oxford. While there, he stood unsuccessfully for President of the Labour Club—an interesting choice for a man whose political sympathies lay with the brand of right-wing ideology later embodied by Margaret Thatcher. His real education, however, took place on the *Daily Express* newspaper in Fleet Street, where he worked before returning home to Australia in 1952.

Back in Australia Murdoch, like the media baron William Randolph Hearst before him, was handed the opportunity to run a newspaper. On the death of his father, the Melbourne publisher Sir Keith Murdoch, he inherited the *Adelaide News*. It was the start of Murdoch's mercurial career as a news proprietor and media mogul.

Contribution

To begin with the board was reluctant to hand over complete control of the newspaper to the young tyro. But Murdoch wasn't a man to take no for an answer, even at this early stage in his career. He steered the newspaper in an avowedly populist direction. Headlines like the sensationalist "Queen eats a rat" boosted its circulation and gave it a new lease on life.

Murdoch's success with the *Adelaide News* spurred him on. He bought the *Daily Mirror* in Sydney and dabbled in television. His newspaper acquisitions were driven by opportunity rather than rationale at this point. "We tended to take the sick newspapers, the ones that weren't worth much, that people thought were about to fold up," he later observed. In 1964 he made his boldest move yet, founding the *Australian*—a national newspaper. The *Australian* gave Murdoch political clout and influence and made him a national figure, though commercially it was less successful.

A restless child, he was more likely to be found cartwheeling across the outfield during play than participating in the school cricket match.

Murdoch moved on from these early triumphs to expand his media empire through a spate of acquisitions across the globe. In the United Kingdom in 1969, he galloped in as an improbable white knight to save the *News of the World*, a downmarket and populist paper, from falling into enemy hands. The enemy in this case was Robert Maxwell, the Czech-born entrepreneur and budding media mogul. The owners of the paper, the Carrs, were reluctant sellers and strongly opposed a sale to a "foreigner." However when no home-grown business executive would come to their aid, they turned to the Australian Rupert Murdoch. It was the deal that gave Murdoch a toehold in the United Kingdom. Later that year he bought the newspaper the *Sun* for £500,000. In 1976 he added the *New York Post* to his growing empire. He subsequently lost, then regained, control of the newspaper. All the newspapers he acquired received the Murdoch treatment, adopting a right-wing, populist tone.

In 1981 Murdoch made an acquisition that was to have a long-lasting impact on newspapers in the United Kingdom. Fighting off fierce competition, he bought *The Times* of London. A serious newspaper, it seemed an unlikely target. Yet it was a clever purchase as it allowed him to reach a far broader cross-section of the British public. What followed was even more unexpected. Murdoch set himself on a collision course with the powerful U.K. print unions, challenging their inefficient working practices. He built a new printing plant at Wapping, away from Fleet Street, the traditional home of the London press, introduced computerization, and cut out the unions. The unions decided to make Wapping their Waterloo, and for most of 1986 the plant was under virtual siege, becoming the site for a pitched battle between the progressive Murdoch troops and the traditionalist unions. The outcome was a victory for Murdoch and his no-nonsense approach to business.

Wapping was a defining moment not only in union history in the United Kingdom but in the world's perception of Murdoch. He emerged from the episode as a tough, ruthless proprietor who would go to almost any lengths to achieve his aims. The truth was a little more prosaic. If Murdoch hadn't challenged the unions, someone else would have: Margaret Thatcher's Conservative government and the introduction of tough new antistrike legislation had provided a political context that was bound to result in such a battle. And there could be no resisting the march of technological progress—even in the printing industry.

The rest of the 1980s saw Murdoch branch into movies and television, acquiring Fox Studios in the United States in 1985, and seven Metromedia TV stations in 1986. By the end of the 1980s, however, Murdoch had overstretched himself, and a massive debt rescheduling exercise was required in 1990. This successfully shored up his empire. Murdoch then marched on through the 1990s, one deal coming hard on the heels of another. Today his business empire is a truly global one: in all, he has over 750 businesses in over 50 countries. At the end of 2002 his holding company, News Corporation, was worth some $42 billion, with revenues of $16 billion. Companies in the News Corporation empire include Harper-Collins Publishers, BSkyB, News International, the Los Angeles Dodgers, Fox TV, and Star TV.

Murdoch made his first move into Internet business in 1999 by taking a stake in WebMD, the company set up by Jim Clark as Healtheon. By 2002, News Corporation held 30% of U.K. media. BSkyB was given a boost by the demise of ITV Digital, a situation frustrating to the British Office of Fair Trading who had criticized the station just a year before for its dominant position. Murdoch attempted to build similar domination in the United States with an attempt to merge GM-owned Direct TV with his own Sky TV, but the merger was blocked by the Federal Communications Commission.

Murdoch continues to work long days at a fast pace and shows little sign of slowing down. There is endless speculation in the media about who will eventually succeed him, his children—Lachlan, James, and Elisabeth Murdoch—being the main candidates. His third wife, Wendy Deng, is another possible. For now, though, as demonstrated by his recent attempts to merge GM-owned Direct TV with his own Sky TV, megabillionaire Murdoch retains an iron grip on his empire.

Context and Conclusions

Murdoch has more than his share of critics, many strident. He is accused of a variety of sins from wielding too much power to "dumbing down" his media vehicles. Perhaps the criticism is overdone. Murdoch has an innate sense of what the public wants, and he makes sure he provides it. He is an astute pragmatist and brilliant entrepreneur who has built the world's first global media empire through instinct, talent, and hard work.

For More Information

Books:

Crainer, Stuart. *Business the Rupert Murdoch Way*. New York: AMACOM, 1999.

Regan, Simon. *Rupert Murdoch: A Business Biography*. London: Angus & Robertson, 1976.

David Ogilvy

1911	Born.
1938	Travels to the United States.
1948	Starts new advertising agency, Hewitt, Ogilvy, Benson, & Mather.
1960	Challenges the advertising industry practice of charging 15% commission.
1963	Publishes book *Confessions of an Advertising Man*.
1965	Merges firm with Mather & Crowther to form Ogilvy & Mather.
1975	Steps down from position as creative head.
1999	Dies.

Summary

It was fortunate for the world of advertising that David Ogilvy eventually found his way to its door. But he took a circuitous route. After working in Paris, he returned to England and pursued a career as an Aga cooker salesman. Next he dallied with advertising at the agency Mather & Crowther, enjoying the bright lights of London before packing his bags and heading for America. A job as a pollster for Dr. George Gallup was followed by a stint as a tobacco farmer with the Amish community in Pennsylvania. Finally in 1948, in his late thirties, Ogilvy started his own advertising agency. With a flair for copywriting, he was soon acknowledged by competitors and clients alike as one of the most brilliant advertising executives of his generation. He retired in 1975 after building Ogilvy & Mather into a business with annual billings of $800 million.

Life and Career

The son of a stockbroker, David Ogilvy was born on June 23, 1911. He was dispatched to Fettes School, a prestigious private school near Edinburgh, Scotland. What Ogilvy lacked in natural academic ability he made up for in scholarly application, securing a scholarship to study history at Christ Church at Oxford University.

When he left Oxford, the young Ogilvy sought adventure abroad. In France he worked in the kitchens of the Hotel Majestic. When Ogilvy had tired of *la vie parisienne*, he returned to England to sell a new type of stove, the Aga. As a salesman Ogilvy proved a great success, so much so that he was asked to write a manual for the Aga salesforce on how to sell the stove. (Thirty years later, the editors of *Fortune* magazine announced that it was probably the best sales manual of all time.) Ogilvy sent his manuscript, "The Theory and Practice of Selling the Aga Cooker," to his brother, who was working at the London-based advertising agency Mather & Crowther. His winning way with words earned him a place as a trainee at the agency.

Contribution

Ogilvy enjoyed the London lifestyle, partying till dawn at every available opportunity. He combined his social life with hard work, showing a natural aptitude for his new vocation. Very early on he began to develop his own theories about advertising. "Concrete figures must be substituted for atmospheric claims; clichés must give way to facts, and empty exhortations to alluring offers," an enthusiastic Ogilvy wrote in a presentation to his colleagues in the early 1930s.

In 1938 he left his job and embarked on another adventure. This time it was the United States that attracted his interest. He enjoyed himself so much that he decided to stay, moving to Princeton, New Jersey, where he worked with Dr. George Gallup, the man behind the Gallup polls. The experience he gained working for Gallup was invaluable, if poorly paid, as it provided him with insights into U.S. consumer preferences and the way they were formed.

During World War II Ogilvy worked for British intelligence in Washington. When the war ended, he decided to try his hand at tobacco farming, acquiring several acres of land in the heart of the Amish community in Lancaster County, Pennsylvania. Exactly what possessed Ogilvy to pursue an agricultural career is unclear. What is certain is that he was most unsuited to it, and before long he was back in New York.

It is fair to say that, without the help of his brother Francis, Ogilvy might never have become one of the great advertising figures of the 20th century. Casting around for a job, the 37-year-old enlisted the help of his brother to establish his own advertising agency in America. His brother not only rounded up $45,000 to help finance the new venture but also persuaded another British advertising agency, S. H. Benson, to invest a further $45,000 in return for a partnership. The newly created agency, Hewitt, Ogilvy, Benson, & Mather, opened for business in 1948. As an Englishman, Ogilvy struggled to win over U.S. clients, although the addition of ex-J. Walter Thompson employee Anderson Hewitt helped. It was Hewitt who saved the day when the business threatened to run out of capital after only a few months. Fortunately, Hewitt's uncle was the Chairman of JP Morgan and he lent the agency $100,000 with no security. And it was Hewitt who brought in the first major account, Sun Oil, worth some $3 million.

Despite the agency's diminutive size, it was clear from the beginning that Ogilvy's advertising intuition set the company apart from its competitors. His style was evident in an early campaign for shirtmakers, Hathaway. Ads featured a man with an eye patch, known as the man from Hathaway, who supported the small shirtmakers from Maine in their efforts to take on the giant shirtmaker Arrow. Ogilvy used photographs, then still a rarity in advertising, featuring a male model complete with eye patch performing a variety of unusual tasks. The Hathaway campaign made Ogilvy's reputation and was an early example of his approach to brand building and supporting brands through brand image. He followed the success of the Hathaway campaign with a campaign for

During World War II Ogilvy worked for British intelligence in Washington. When the war ended, he decided to try his hand at tobacco farming, acquiring several acres of land in the heart of the Amish community in Lancaster County, Pennsylvania.

Schweppes, the soft drink manufacturer. Putting to good use the knowledge he gained with Gallup, Ogilvy assuaged U.S. consumer sensibilities about class with Commander Edward Whitehead, the distinguished-looking gentleman who was boss of Schweppes at the time. Schweppes sales in the United States bubbled up by 500% over the following nine years.

Ogilvy's role at the agency was to be jack of all trades, master of most. The exception was administration, for which he had little time. To his credit he realized that this weakness was hampering the firm and employed Esty Stowell, a Benson & Bowles executive, as Vice-President in 1957. Stowell took responsibility for managing the entire agency, with Ogilvy retaining control of the creative department only.

Ogilvy's role at the agency was to be jack of all trades, master of most. The exception was administration, for which he had little time.

"At 60 miles an hour the loudest noise in this new Rolls-Royce comes from the electric clock." This was Ogilvy's slogan for his Rolls-Royce campaign. It exemplified his approach of putting the product center stage. "Make your product the hero of the commercial," he famously entreated. In 1960 he challenged one of the industry's prized but anachronistic practices—the 15% commission. As usual Ogilvy's stance was not merely ethical, but one guaranteed to attract publicity. It succeeded, bringing in new clients such as Shell who were only too happy to be rid of the 15% commission in exchange for a flat fee.

The 1960s was a big decade for Ogilvy. In 1963 he published his book *Confessions of an Advertising Man*, which sold well over half a million copies and cemented his position as an advertising guru. In 1965, the year after his brother's death, his firm merged with Mather & Crowther to form Ogilvy & Mather.

By 1975 Ogilvy & Mather was one of the top five advertising agencies in the world with around a thousand clients, offices in 29 countries, and billings of some $800 million. In the same year Ogilvy stepped down from his position as creative head to spend more time at his home in the south of France. In 1989, following a wave of mergers in the industry, Ogilvy's remaining share in the business was acquired by the WPP group.

Context and Conclusions

David Ogilvy said the secret of success was simple: "First, make a reputation for being a creative genius. Second, surround yourself with partners who are better than you are. Third, leave them to get on with it." But the most important things that Ogilvy acquired in his time on Madison Avenue were the ability and creative flair needed to lead by example. "The most important ingredient in any agency is the ability of the top man to lead his troops," he said. He was a late starter in advertising at 39. Yet he still made it to the top of his profession—and made an indelible mark there too. Ogilvy died on July 21, 1999.

CLOSE BUT NO CIGAR

LORD SAATCHI

Charles Saatchi built not one but two successful advertising agencies. First there was Saatchi & Saatchi, the U.K. agency that helped win a general election with its "Labour isn't working" posters for the Conservative party. Then, when Charles and brother Maurice got a little overambitious and were kicked out of their own company after an ill-conceived bid for a well known bank, they started up another agency. The new agency was M&C Saatchi. They took a few prestigious clients with them. Soon Maurice received a peerage, and M&C Saatchi overtook Saatchi & Saatchi in the billings rankings.

JAMES WALTER THOMPSON

J. Walter Thompson bought out William James Carlton, owner of advertising "broker" Carlton & Smith, for $500 in 1877. The furniture cost $800. In 1887 the JWT Company became the first agency to write advertisements for their clients rather than just sell them advertising space. By 1909 JWT had opened in London. It went on to become one of the world's most successful agencies.

For More Information

Books:

Ogilvy, David. *Confessions of an Advertising Man*. New York: Atheneum, 1963.

Ogilvy, David. *Blood, Brains and Beer*. New York: Atheneum, 1978.

Ogilvy, David. *Ogilvy on Advertising*. New York: Crown, 1983.

Web site:

Ogilvy: **www.ogilvy.com**

Jorma Jaakko Ollila

1950	Born.
1976	Studies at the University of Helsinki.
1978	Studies at the London School of Economics.
1981	Studies at the Helsinki University of Technology.
1985	Joins Nokia as Vice-President of international operations.
1986	Becomes C.F.O.
1988	C.E.O. Kairamo commits suicide.
1990	Assumes control of cellular phone business.
1992	Becomes C.E.O. of Nokia.
1994	Nokia listed on the New York Stock Exchange.
1999	Profits hit $4 billion.
1999	Nokia introduces world's first mobile phone with Internet access.
2000	Shares drop by 26%, wiping out $60 billion worth of market value in a single day.
2000	Nokia launches professional mobile radio with Internet access.
2001	Nokia launches first mobile phone with multimedia messaging.
2002	Nokia achieves first commercial 3G data calls.

Summary

In Europe, high-tech corporate superstars are conspicuous by their absence. Names like Philips and Siemens just don't set the pulse racing. The exception to the rule is the Finnish company Nokia. It has created a buzz around its products unmatched by other European companies in recent years. Much of the credit goes to Jorma Ollila, who became C.E.O. in 1992.

Ollila took a 147-year-old company, comprised of an assortment of businesses from timber to rubber boots, and transformed it into a cellular phone colossus. In 1998, it passed the United States company Motorola as the world's number one cellular phone manufacturer. In less than eight years, Ollila had made Nokia the most valuable company in Europe.

The product of an eclectic education including Atlantic College, the London School of Economics, and Helsinki University, Ollila came to power at Nokia at a difficult time. The suicide of the company's C.E.O., Kari Kairamo, followed by the collapse of the U.S.S.R. and difficult trading conditions, had left Nokia in need of a makeover. After turning the cellular phone division around, Ollila became C.E.O. in 1992. He shed all noncore, nontelecoms business and refocused on cellular phone manufacturing. Profits soared from zero in 1991 to $4 billion in 1999. By 2000 the company was being feted by analysts, investors, and the media. The year 2001 brought more trying times, but Ollila continues to apply his unique style of management as Nokia tries to navigate a downturn in the telecoms market.

Life and Career

Jorma Jaakko Ollila was born on August 15, 1950 in Seinäjoki, Finland. His education was a little more unorthodox than most. Aged 17, he was recommended for a scholarship at Atlantic College by his school headmaster. Atlantic College, in Wales, is a unique educational establishment founded in 1962 by Kurt Hahn, a German national who evolved a distinctive educational philosophy. The rationale behind the college is to bring together individuals with leadership qualities who then go on to become political or commercial leaders throughout the world. Ollila was part of the school's first intake.

Ollila followed Atlantic College by earning a postgraduate degree in Political Science in 1976 at University of Helsinki, an MSc in 1978 at the London School of Economics, and an MSc in 1981 from the Helsinki University of Technology. With his academic career behind him, he joined Citibank where he worked on the Nokia account. In 1985, he joined the Finnish company as Vice-President of international operations. A year later, aged 35, he became chief financial officer.

Contribution

The Nokia of today started life as three separate companies: the Finnish Cable Works, the Finnish Rubber Works, and the Nokia Forest Products Company. When the three merged in 1967, the new company took its name from the timber mill, which in turn took its name from the Nokia River in southern Finland.

The Scandinavian countries gained a head start in wireless telephony when they joined forces to develop technology first researched in Bell Laboratories in the United States. Despite the head start, Nokia almost managed to give the market away to Motorola in the 1970s. It was the beginning of a bleak period in the company's history. Nokia's C.E.O., Kari Kairamo, hedged his bets. The company took revenues from its more traditional businesses to fund its high-tech operations. Nokia bought a computer business from Ericsson, for example, and a German TV company, as well as making cellular phones. But Kairamo underestimated how big the cellular telephone business was going to be. Struggling to cope with the demand for cellular phones as well as to manage the other businesses it owned, Nokia lost market share to Motorola, which was well equipped for mass production.

Ollila had successfully dragged Nokia back from the precipice. One reason for the transformation was his focus on brand image.

One problem after another beset Nokia. In 1988 Kairamo committed suicide, and in 1991 the U.S.S.R. disintegrated, taking one of Nokia's principal markets with it. The company's largest shareholder even tried to sell its stake in Nokia to its rival Ericsson. Fortunately for Nokia, Ericsson wasn't interested. Into this difficult situation stepped Ollila in 1990, when he was put in charge of the cellular phone business. His first decision was a bold one: to keep the cellular phone unit rather than opt for the easy option of selling it. He set about raising morale and reorganizing the unit.

By 1992, Ollila was C.E.O. He turned his attention to the rest of the company's divisions. He rationalized the company, ditching noncore activities like the paper, rubber, cable, computer, and TV businesses. Putting his telecoms strategy into action required cash, so Ollila turned to the United States for investment. Nokia was already listed on the European stock exchanges, but a United States listing was a prerequisite for raising the kind of money Ollila needed. In 1994 Nokia was listed on the New York Stock Exchange. In the period before tech stocks fell out of favor, Nokia's stock performance was nothing short of miraculous. Between 1994 and 1999, the share price rose over 2,000%.

Ollila had successfully dragged Nokia back from the precipice. One reason for the transformation was his focus on brand image. He abandoned the existing array of cellular phone brands produced by Nokia, concentrating on a product line emblazoned with the Nokia name. His strategy was "telecom-oriented, global focus, value-added"—a slogan that came out of a brainstorming meeting. Competitors were obsessed with continually shrinking the size of the cellular phone. Ollila went further, hiring designers to make Nokia's cellular phone a fashion statement. He also brought in technicians to create revolutionary scrolling text displays and other refinements that made the phone as user-friendly as possible. At the same time Nokia hedged its bets, backing a variety of technical standards from the European GSM to the Japanese PDS. The first digital offering by the company in 1993 was predicted to sell at least 400,000 units—it sold over 20 million. Profits soared from zero in 1991 to $4 billion in 1999.

Ollila cut out noncore business, and he also cut out internal bureaucracy. Out went hierarchical management structures; in came a flat organizational structure. Today things get done in the company through networks of individuals. It's an entrepreneurial, innovative environment within a large corporation. Then there is "the Nokia Way"—a means of tapping into root feeling in the company. Brainstorming at a series of meetings throughout the company is synthesized into a vision statement by the top managers, and this is disseminated back through the organization via a series of presentations. The Nokia Way keeps the employees plugged into the company.

As the new millennium approached, the future looked bright for Nokia. The company was the most valuable in Europe. It was tipped in *Red Herring* magazine's must buy stocks for 2000. But Ollila hadn't reckoned on a change in market sentiment that left telecoms stocks out in the cold. Investors, used to year after year of astonishing growth, ran for cover when Ollila warned of disappointing third-quarter results in 2000. Shares dropped by 26%, wiping out $60 billion worth of market value in a single day. Once the darlings of the stock market, suddenly telecoms companies were out of vogue. Worse, there was the threat of mobile Internet and other forms of mobile data transfer. "It's a big paradigm shift," said Ollila. "We have the challenge of sailing in much more uncertain waters."

The future of Nokia is clouded with uncertainty. As a handset manufacturer, Nokia faces a number of threats, not least that of commoditization. Some 40 multinationals and more than a dozen companies in China have the ability to manufacture cellular phones. More manufacturers means more phones, resulting in lower prices, which mean lower profits. Ollila hopes the lure of the Nokia brand and its personalization of phones will outweigh the attraction of low-cost, mass-market clones.

Then there is the threat of new technology making the cell phone obsolete. Phone technology is due to move through GPRS to 3G broadband, promising the transmission of video and audio to a cell phone. But technology isn't always what it's cracked up to be—witness the hype of WAP and its subsequent washout. Competing wireless technologies threaten the supremacy of cellular phones, as do voice-enabled PDAs and mobile computers. Nokia counters that these are cellular phones by another name, and adds that it plans to participate in a selection of alternative devices.

Nokia has continued to innovate in its core business. In 1999, it introduced the first WAP Internet mobile phone and, in 2000, added the same capability to its professional mobile radio systems. In 2001, Nokia introduced the world's first multimedia messaging solution for mobile phones, giving users access to audio, video, images, photos, and text. And, in 2002, the company took its 3G capability a stage further by achieving the first commercial packet data call.

Network business offers some consolation for Ollila. A quarter of sales in 2000 came from this part of Nokia's operations, and the company is still well regarded. In INSEAD business school's 2001 report "Competitive Fitness," a study of 67 multinationals, Nokia was ranked number one. But Ollila can't afford to rest on the company's reputation for long. Difficult challenges lie ahead. Only time will tell if Ollila is able to deal with them successfully.

Context and Conclusions

Jorma Ollila took a cumbersome, unfocused company called Nokia and dragged it into the 21st century. He stripped out the unnecessary operations, ditched the distinctly low-tech businesses, and remodeled the company as a high-tech cellular telephone manufacturer. The transformation, accomplished by a mixture of clever brand development, radical organizational restructuring, and astute strategic thinking, made him one of the most talked about managers in Europe and his company a stock market favorite. Ollila's job at Nokia is far from over. His reputation as a great businessman will rest partly on what happens over the next few years. He has made some big judgment calls, and only time will tell if he is right. But so far, regardless of Nokia's dip in fortunes, he remains one of the best C.E.O.s in the world.

CLOSE BUT NO CIGAR
MARJORIE SCARDINO

Marjorie M. Scardino became chief executive of the international media group Pearson (owner of the *Financial Times*) in 1997. Before that she was chief executive of The Economist Group, in which Pearson has a 50% stake. In 1985, Scardino became managing Director of the North American division of *The Economist*, where she increased circulation and profits. Since taking over, Scardino has focused Pearson as a media company, selling a number of unrelated businesses such as Madame Tussaud's Waxworks, and purchasing various educational and publishing concerns. Scardino is the first woman to head a top 100 firm on the London Stock Exchange.

Despite a sparkling start, Pearson's recent results have disappointed, leaving Scardino searching for ways to leverage more value out of her media empire.

For More Information

Books:

Merriden, Trevor. *Business the Nokia Way: Secrets of the World's Fastest Moving Company*. New York: John Wiley, 2000.

Steinbock, Dan. *The Nokia Revolution: The Story of an Extraordinary Company That Transformed an Industry*. New York: AMACOM, 2001.

Pierre Omidyar

1967	Born.
1988	Graduates from Tufts University.
1991	Cofounds Ink Development Corporation in 1991.
1995	Starts eBay as homepage hosted by the local ISP.
1996	Ink Development, renamed eShop, sold to Microsoft.
1996	eBay profitable by February.
1997	Three million items sold. Recruits Meg Whitman as C.E.O.
1998	Completes 10 millionth auction in May. Over one million registered users. I.P.O in September.
2001	Over 29.7 million registered users. Net income totals $64.5 million to September.
2001	eBay Stores launched.
2001	Named as second richest young American.
2002	Joint venture with Sotheby's.
2003	Business-to-business site launched.

Summary

From an idea sparked by a casual conversation, Pierre Omidyar built one of the world's most successful Internet companies, eBay. Started in 1995, eBay is the online equivalent of Aladdin's cave, a treasure trove stuffed to the rafters with everything from Beanie Babies to grand masters. With millions of items up for auction and 600,000 new ones added every day, it is a collector's paradise. Profitable almost from the beginning, Omidyar's handling of his idea has been masterful. He started the business as a hobby but was astute enough to recognize the tremendous commercial possibilities. He hired the right people—including Jeff Skoll and Meg Whitman—to manage the company through rapid expansion, to I.P.O. and beyond. But Omidyar was always on hand to make sure the business stayed true to his original vision. By 2001, eBay had nearly 30 million registered users and was still turning a handsome profit.

Life and Career

Born in 1967, Pierre Omidyar moved to the United States from his native France at the age of six. The family settled in Maryland, where Omidyar's father took up a residency at the Johns Hopkins University Medical Center. At school Omidyar cut class so he could spend more time on his hobby—computing. For six dollars an hour, he hired himself out to the school library writing computer programs to print out catalog cards.

Omidyar studied computer science at Tufts University in Massachusetts. It was there he met his wife, Pamela, who was studying for a biology degree. Pamela was to have a major influence on Omidyar's career in a way he could never have suspected. When he left university, Omidyar went into the

For six dollars an hour, he hired himself out to the school library writing computer programs to print out catalog cards.

computer industry, first as a software developer at Claris and then at General Magic, Inc. His first attempt at starting his own company was Ink Development Corporation, set up with three friends. The company created software that allowed computers to interpret instructions entered using a pen, rather than a keyboard. Later renamed eShop, the firm was sold to Microsoft in 1996, making Omidyar a wealthy man.

Contribution

The question was what to do next? The idea for eBay emerged from a conversation with Pamela, his then fiancée, while Omidyar was still at General Magic. Pamela was a keen collector of Pez dispensers—the candy brick dispensers with a cartoon character head that tilts back. She hankered to meet other enthusiasts and trade dispensers. This gave Omidyar the idea for a Web site where collectors could meet to buy, sell and discuss their collections with fellow enthusiasts. The selling element would take the form of an online consumer-to-consumer auction. "What I wanted to do was create a marketplace where everyone had access to the same information," Omidyar later observed.

eBay started life as a humble homepage hosted by a local ISP (Internet service provider) in 1995. A clue to its "local" origins lies in the name eBay, which stands for "electronic Bay Area" after the Bay Area of San Francisco. But what began as a small-scale hobby soon blossomed into a business. "I didn't set out to create a huge business with eBay," Omidyar noted in an interview with the *New York Times*. "When it happened, I took advantage of it." By 1996 he had given up his day job to look after eBay.

Online auctions were perfectly suited to the medium of the Internet. It soon became apparent to Omidyar that the commercial potential for his new business was huge. But his motivation in creating eBay was not primarily to become a billionaire. Rather, he says, it came from a genuine philosophical desire to use the Internet to create a more efficient market. "I'd really given a lot of thought to the way efficient markets are supposed to work and how the financial markets work. What I realized is that individuals—ordinary people like you or me—usually can't participate in the most efficient markets because we don't get access to all the information the professionals do. The stock market is a great example of that. I wanted to create a place on the Web where—since everyone has access to the same medium—I could, in theory, create an efficient market."

Others were persuaded by Omidyar's vision. Venture capital firm Benchmark Capital put in $6.7 million for 22% of the new company. By April 1999 the value of the stake had increased to $5.1 billion. And, unlike other dot-com businesses, eBay turned a profit as early as February 1996. From then on, it was just a question of marking the mileposts: three million items sold by the end of 1997; ranked number one e-commerce site on time spent by users in May 1998; completed its 10 millionth auction in May 1998; over one million registered users by August 1998. The I.P.O was in September 1998. From $18, the share price shot up to $53.50. eBay staff celebrated by dancing a conga. Omidyar was worth $274.1 million on paper.

Through luck or judgment, Omidyar had hit on one of the best business models on the Net. Revenue comes from the seller's fee, plus a commission on the realized price. Commissions may only amount to a few dollars, but with more than half a million new items added daily, it mounts up.

Omidyar was also astute enough to realize when his company had outgrown his ability to manage it single-handedly. He brought the right people in at the right time. Early on Jeff Skoll, a Stanford MBA and friend, was brought in as a partner. And in 1997 he recruited former Disney marketing executive Meg Whitman from Hasbro to oversee the company's I.P.O.

By 2001 eBay was firmly established as one of the Internet's top brands, along with other virtual heavyweights such as Amazon.com and Yahoo! For the nine months ending September 30, 2001, revenues rose 78% to $529.4 million. Net income totaled $64.5 million, up from $24.4 million. There are over 29.7 million registered eBay users who buy and sell items in more than 4,500 categories. Millions of items are up for sale every day.

The company has remained one step ahead of the competition. It bought into traditional bricks-and-mortar auctioneers to add cachet, build brand and increase its user base. It has expanded aggressively into Europe, all but wiping out its competitors such as QXL. In 2001, the company established eBay Stores, a specialist site where groups of people selling similar goods could create the equivalent of an online store. In 2002, a joint venture with distinguished auction house Sotheby's took the company upmarket, capturing some of the premium auction business and richer clientele, by offering goods such as old master paintings. A year later, the company moved into the business sector by launching a business-to-business auction site.

In his self-declared drive to rid himself of 99% of his fortune during his lifetime, Omidyar has given birth to a new form of philanthropy—venture philanthropy.

Omidyar meanwhile is content to take a back seat. In 2001, he was named second richest young American. Like many wealthy businessmen before him, he has turned philanthropist. But he is approaching philanthropy with a new twist. In his self-declared drive to rid himself of 99% of his fortune during his lifetime, Omidyar has given birth to a new form of philanthropy—venture philanthropy. The theory is that he and his wife will seed a number of causes favoring those that present a solid business plan and meet key criteria on points such as earnings streams. Then, in a scenario that mirrors the savage world of dot-com business, the nonprofits that perform poorly are dropped and the ones that prosper go on to become national organizations.

Context and Conclusions

To date, eBay has been one of the most successful dot-com companies. Regardless of its eventual place in business history, Omidyar's achievements are significant. He was one of the first to show the business world that the promise of the Internet wasn't an illusion, that it does have the power to change markets. He has created the equivalent of the village market online. And it's a transparent market; the power of the specialist is eradicated in a click of the mouse. When it comes to collectibles such as rare books and manuscripts, the specialist book store can no longer claim that its third edition of Adam Smith's *An Inquiry into the Nature and Causes of the Wealth of Nations with Additions (3 vols.)* is worth $6,000. The would-be acquirer can now log onto eBay and discover it for sale for $1,500. Before eBay, the seller who lives in the United States and the purchaser who lives in Australia, would never have found each other. Omidyar has ripped the heart out of the vendor's local advantage, based on unequal knowledge and lack of choice. eBay offers the nearest thing to a perfect market that we are likely to see for some time.

CLOSE BUT NO CIGAR

JAY WALKER

Jay Walker founded Priceline, one of the most high-profile dot-com companies. Along with Omidyar and Amazon.com's Jeff Bezos, Walker became one of the most famous sons of the new economy. In 1998, Walker ran a $15 million radio blitz advertising campaign on Priceline.com, Inc. The ads invited consumers to log on and name their price for airline tickets. Priceline soon became a household name. In its first year, the company generated revenues of $35 million. Its I.P.O in March 1999 valued the company at $13 billion.

Walker went on to try to extend his price distribution system beyond transportation into hard goods such as groceries and gasoline. When the dot-com crash came, a collapse in Priceline's stock market valuation forced it to scale back its ambitions.

For More Information

Book:

Bunnell, David. *eBay Phenomenon*. New York: John Wiley, 2000.

Web site:

eBay: **www.ebay.com**

David Packard

1912	Born.
1934	Meets friend and future partner Bill Hewlett at Stanford University, Palo Alto.
1938	After a spell at General Electric, teams up with Bill Hewlett once more.
1939	Starts Hewlett-Packard in a garage in Palo Alto with just $538 of capital.
1942	HP turnover is $2 million.
1970	The company declines to make wholesale layoffs when the U.S. economy hits a recession.
1972	HP introduces the handheld scientific calculator, the model 35.
1980s	HP consistently in top five computer manufacturers.
1990s	Back-to-basics drive revitalizes company fortunes.
1996	Dies.

Summary

From a rented garage in Palo Alto, California, David Packard and Bill Hewlett founded one of Silicon Valley's most enduring IT companies—Hewlett-Packard. When Packard met Hewlett at Stanford University in the 1930s, Palo Alto was best known for its prunes. By the time he died, it had established itself as the epicenter of the most famous high-tech cluster in the world, and Hewlett-Packard had become one of the pillar companies of Silicon Valley.

Packard graduated from Stanford in 1934 and, after a stint at General Electric, teamed up with Hewlett to start a rent-an-inventor company in a garage in Palo Alto. First-year profits were $1,539. By 1942, sales were $2 million. In the 1970s the company made a tactical switch to computing, and throughout the 1980s it was consistently among the top five IT companies. In the 1990s Packard revitalized it with a back-to-basics move.

Life and Career

Born into a middle-class family on September 7, 1912, David Packard grew up in Pueblo, Colorado. At an early age he decided that he wanted to be an engineer. Unlike the millions of children whose ambitions to become an astronaut, firefighter, doctor, or nurse come to nothing, he was not be shaken from his goal.

Packard studied at Stanford University. It was there that he met his friend and partner-to-be, Bill Hewlett. When he graduated in 1934 America was still recovering from the Great Depression. Packard took one of the few jobs available to an electrical engineering student, working at General Electric. He also studied for a master's degree at the Massachusetts Institute of Technology. In 1938 Packard returned to Palo Alto and teamed up with Bill Hewlett. They decided to start their own company.

Contribution

The company was founded in 1939 with just $538 of capital. The original location, a Palo Alto garage, was to become part of Silicon Valley folklore. It sent a message to all future entrepreneurs that great businesses could grow from small beginnings. A number of corporate giants were later to be hatched in the humble garage.

The original plan was for Packard to become a kind of rent-an-inventor. But his creativity soon ran riot, and he and Hewlett began developing their own gadgets together. The inventions were many and varied. Early designs included an electric shock machine to help people lose weight and an optical device to trigger automatic urinal flushing. But the first invention that made money was a piece of equipment designed to help sound engineers make better recordings. By the end of the first year of business, Hewlett and Packard had amassed a profit of $1,539. The garage was replaced with more substantial premises in 1940. The company, by now named Hewlett-Packard, prospered during World War II, even though Hewlett joined the Signal Corps and left Packard to run the business. By 1942 sales were $2 million. In the immediate post-war period, however, business dropped off alarmingly. Nevertheless, when Hewlett returned from the military, a number of talented staff were hired, and the business began to improve again.

In a division of duties, Packard assumed the managerial role, with Hewlett in charge of engineering and R&D. Although Packard had little theoretical knowledge of management—his only experience was growing the company—he proved a natural. He introduced a system of management that involved walking among the employees and maintaining a visible presence. This was in contrast to the idea, prevalent among companies at the time, that the management and the workforce were breeds apart and should have little to do with each other. That philosophy was perpetuated by corporate institutions such as the management dining room, where the great and the good tucked into a three-course culinary extravaganza while the workers huddled around their workstations eating baloney sandwiches.

> *That philosophy was perpetuated by corporate institutions such as the management dining room, where the great and the good tucked into a three-course culinary extravaganza while the workers huddled around their workstations eating baloney sandwiches.*

Packard, however, spurned the trappings of executive status. He maintained a policy of openness, making himself available to speak to employees. His accessibility and the practice of management by walking about (MBWA for short) endeared him to the staff. Packard repaid their respect by empowering them in their daily work. "We figured that people will accomplish more," Packard said, "if they are given an opportunity to use their talents and abilities in the way they work best." While many managers have paid lip service to worker empowerment and enlightened management practice, these are often the first casualties in times of difficulty and economic downturn. Not in the case of Hewlett-Packard, however. In 1970, when the U.S. economy slipped into recession, Packard did not make wholesale layoffs. Instead, he agreed a new working pattern with the staff. Employees worked nine days in every two weeks instead of ten. In addition, management and workforce alike took a 10% pay cut.

Within a year, the U.S. economy was staging a recovery. Packard had avoided the unnecessary expense of layoffs followed by rehiring. Besides following forward-looking human resource policies, he took an innovative approach to organizational structure. "I've often thought that after you get organized you ought to throw the chart away," he stated. It wasn't that Packard didn't believe in organization, it was just that he believed in small agile units operating within the company. So, whenever a division grew cumbersome and unwieldy, Packard would break it up into small units.

"We figured that people will accomplish more," Packard said, "if they are given an opportunity to use their talents and abilities in the way they work best."

In 1972 Hewlett-Packard introduced a handheld scientific calculator, the model 35, and during the 1970s and 1980s the company moved into the computer business.

Throughout the 1980s, HP was one of the top five computer manufacturers in the United States. In the 1990s, however, it struggled as competitors began to out-innovate it. Packard's solution was a return to basics, back to management by walking about. Although both Packard and Hewlett were approaching 80, they took action to reinvigorate the company. The HP hierarchy had grown unwieldy, they decided, so they took a scalpel to the organization, cutting out unnecessary layers. The philosophy of small teams and less management was restored, as was Hewlett-Packard's competitiveness, and the company reclaimed its place among America's leading IT corporations.

David Packard died in 1996, knowing that his company was once more in shape to compete with the best. Today, HP's future looks less certain, but many of Packard's enlightened management principles remain etched in the company's culture.

Context and Conclusions

From a small engineering company founded in a garage, Dave Packard, with the help of his friend and fellow student Bill Hewlett, built a multinational technology company with over 100,000 employees and annual revenues in excess of $40 billion.

Packard's key contribution to Hewlett-Packard and business, according to Bill Hewlett, his lifelong business partner and buddy, was "the HP Way," a set of values and management principles put together by Packard in 1957. In his book of the same name, he explains that one of the objectives of the company was "to maintain an organizational environment that fosters individual motivation, initiative, and creativity, and a wide latitude of freedom in working toward established objectives and goals." It is for this enlightened attitude to worker empowerment and the other forward-looking practices enshrined in *The HP Way* that Packard will probably be best remembered.

CLOSE BUT NO CIGAR
JOSEPH C. WILSON

Wilson staked his small company, Haloid Corporation, on a new, commercially untried technology developed by a physicist called Chester Carlson. The technology was xerography. The first copier, the 914, was shipped in March 1960. It was one of the most successful single products ever. In 1959 Haloid revenue was $2 million; in 1960 it was $4 million; in 1963 it was a staggering $422 million. The company went on to become the Xerox Corporation.

For More Information

Book:

Packard, David. *The HP Way: How Bill Hewlett and I Built Our Company* New York: HarperBusiness, 1995.

Web site:

Hewlett-Packard: **www.hp.com**

John H. Patterson

1844	Born.
1867	Graduates from Dartmouth College.
1884	Purchases National Manufacturing Company and renames it National Cash Register.
1887	Company holds first annual sales convention.
1893	New, modern factory building constructed.
1911	Over one million cash registers sold.
1913	Dayton floods.
1915	Court of Appeals overturns Patterson's conviction on antitrust charges.
1922	Dies.

Summary

The seeds of John H. Patterson's (1844–1922) rise to fame were sown on his family's farm. If his father hadn't constantly asked him how much he charged customers for the farm produce, he might not have been interested in the invention of a local trader. Patterson took that invention, the automatic cash register, and turned it into a multimillion dollar business, National Cash Register. On his way to a personal fortune, Patterson redefined the art of salesmanship, introduced the idea of the corporate classroom, and saved a town from drowning. He was a pioneer in linking productivity to better working conditions.

Life and Career

Born near Dayton, Ohio, in 1844, John Henry Patterson spent his childhood working on the 2,000-acre family farm. One of eight children, Patterson would help out when he was growing up by selling his father's farm goods. The amounts charged for the produce would frequently go unrecorded, and Patterson would be interrogated by his father, day or night, about whom he had charged and how much they paid.

Patterson attended local schools, followed by Miami University and Dartmouth College, graduating with a B.A. in 1867. In the meantime he fought in the Union army in the American Civil War.

When Patterson left college he was determined to go into business for himself. He saved money from a job collecting tolls on the Miami & Erie Canal and set up as a coal retailer back in his hometown. From selling coal he moved into coal and iron ore mining with his brother Frank; then, again with his brother, he established a mining supply store store. Here the stock sold well, but the profits failed to materialize. Since the brothers were applying a

> *On his way to a personal fortune, Patterson redefined the art of salesmanship, introduced the idea of the corporate classroom, and saved a town from drowning. He was a pioneer in linking productivity to better working conditions.*

healthy markup, something else was clearly wrong. Patterson determined to track down the discrepancy. Hearing of a machine invented by local merchant that automatically recorded sales, he bought two.

Contribution

Primitive though they were, when Patterson saw the machines he immediately appreciated the possibilities they offered. If he had a use for one, wouldn't every shopkeeper in the country? In 1884, moving swiftly, he bought out inventor Jacob Ritty's business for $6,500, changing the name from the National Manufacturing Company to National Cash Register. But when he looked over the books he discovered the business was losing money, and suffering a temporary loss of faith he offered $2,000 to get out of the contract. Luckily for him, the seller wasn't interested.

Patterson was forced to make a go of the cash register business. He acquired premises in a down-at-heel section of Dayton known as Slidertown, and began manufacturing cash registers on a commercial scale. He was by no means an enlightened employer; he saw his work force only in terms of production. In return his employees, uninspired by their work and their boss, took advantage whenever they could. The result was poor quality—$50,000 worth of faulty machinery in one year—and poor performance.

Eventually it dawned on Patterson that if he were to treat his workers a little better, he might improve the quality of his products. He started in a small way by buying a property opposite the factory where the workers could get coffee. It was the first time any provision had been made for refreshments for them. He began buying other property in the neighborhood and gradually improving conditions in the surrounding area, where most of the workforce lived.

Turning his attention to the factory premises, he hired architects to design a new building that would be as comfortable for the workforce as it was efficient for the work performed there. When the people of Dayton saw the new building—constructed predominantly from glass and steel—they laughed at Patterson, declaring that there wouldn't be an unbroken window in the building before a week was out. But Patterson had the last laugh. His modern building, with its built-in lecture rooms, air conditioning, showers, and movie theaters, instilled a sense of civic pride in Slidertown. Very few windows were broken. Patterson even opened up his private estate to the public, including his golf course and swimming pool.

Patterson's style of paternalistic leadership wasn't always successful. His insistence that workers use the baths provided by the company and attend various entertainments caused resentment. By the time he had backed down, it was too late to stop a threatened strike. But in a masterly outflanking maneuver he gathered his employees together, reassured them that he understood the reasons for their dissatisfaction, and proclaimed that everyone needed a rest. At which point he promptly shut down the factory and went traveling. The stunned workers were triumphant at first, but as the weeks passed triumph quickly turned to concern and then to despair. The workers telegraphed Patterson, imploring him to reopen the factory. After two months he returned to a hero's welcome. His pointed comments about there being several offers on the table to relocate his factory elsewhere did not fall on deaf ears.

When Patterson returned he didn't hold a grudge against his employees, and they in turn put in extra effort. Patterson's innovative ideas on sales were beginning to reap rewards. NCR was one of the first companies in the United States to train a professional salesforce. Sales agents had to memorize a 16-page, 4,500-word sales primer. Patterson would drop in on the agents and quiz them on the contents of the primer—anyone who failed was fired. By 1894 NCR was producing half a million copies of its sales newsletter, *Hustler*. Sales conventions were held annually after 1887. By 1911, over one million cash registers had been sold.

Brilliant at promoting sales of NCR cash registers, Patterson was equally effective at stifling the sales of competitors' products. In fact he was sometimes too effective. Patterson called in a promising executive from the Rochester office to coordinate the company's response to the competition. The executive was a former piano salesman, Thomas J. Watson (who was later to found IBM). With Watson's help Patterson eliminated the competition by means of acquisitions and the vigorous defense of his cash register patents. So successful was his campaign that he attracted the unwelcome attention of the U.S. government. Against a backdrop of public antitrust sentiment, he and 28 other NCR executives each received a year's jail sentence and a $5,000 fine.

Brilliant at promoting sales of NCR cash registers, Patterson was equally effective at stifling the sales of competitors' products.

Patterson's reputation might have been permanently stained by the judgment were it not for the great Dayton floods. On the night of March 25–26, 1913, Dayton was submerged under 17 feet of water following three days of heavy rain that had deposited an amount of water comparable to the monthly flow over Niagara Falls. Patterson personally took control of the situation. In the hours before the flood hit he organized safety and rescue plans and constructed hundreds of makeshift boats at the company's lumberyards, building rafts at the rate of one every seven minutes. For his role in the town's relief efforts he was dubbed "the Savior of Dayton." The townsfolk petitioned President Woodrow Wilson to pardon Patterson, a petition that would probably have been successful had the decision not been overturned in any case by the Court of Appeal in 1915.

During World War I Patterson committed his company's resources to the war effort. He insisted on carrying out contracts on a fixed-fee instead of a cost-plus basis, refusing to profit from the war. He died on May 14, 1922.

Context and Conclusions

Patterson is the perfect example of a man with the right product at the right time. National Cash Register replaced the pencil behind the ear of the grocery store clerk with on-the-counter, state-of-the-art technology. In addition—after an early conversion—he turned out to be a model employer. An early exponent of classroom learning in the corporation, Patterson was one of the first of the great entrepreneurs of his time to make the connection between improved productivity and better working conditions. And unlike many of his contemporaries, his heroism was not just corporate: he was a real-life hero, too, organizing the rescue and relief of his hometown from dramatic floods.

For More Information

Book:

Marcosson, Isaac F. *Wherever Men Trade: The Romance of the Cash Register*. Manchester, NH: Ayer, 1972.

Web site:

NCR: **www.ncr.com**

Arthur Rock

1926	Born.
1948	Graduates from Syracuse University.
1951	Finishes MBA at Harvard Business School. Joins Hayden Stone.
1957	"Traitorous eight" leave Shockley labs.
1959	Fairchild Semiconductors formed.
1961	Founds the firm of Davis and Rock.
1968	Davis and Rock dissolved after a seven-year life. Backs Gordon Moore and Bob Noyce, who found Intel.
1970	Forms Arthur Rock & Associates; sets up on his own as Arthur Rock & Co.
1980	Invests in Apple Computing. Joins board of Directors.
1993	Steps down from Apple board because of conflict of interests.
1994–1999	Director of Air Touch Communications.
1998	Appointed to board of governors of NASD.
2002	Named Business Leader of the Year.
2003	Donates $25 million to Harvard Business School.

Summary

Arthur Rock is the man credited with coining the term "venture capital." Without the venture capital industry, there probably would have been no new economy or information revolution. Without Rock, there might not be a venture capital industry. Rock was the first venture capitalist (VC) operating on the West Coast of the United States. He organized the funding that got the computer revolution under way when he helped eight researchers break out from William Shockley's laboratories to found Fairchild Semiconductors. Then, he rounded up financing for some of the biggest companies in Silicon Valley, including Intel and Apple. It wasn't just money that Rock supplied. He also provided sage advice from his seat on the board of Directors. He was still passing on the benefit of his considerable experience well into his seventies.

Life and Career

The son of a candy store owner, Arthur Rock was born in the United States in 1926. After graduating with an MBA from Harvard Business School in 1951, Rock went to work for Hayden Stone, a New York investment banking firm. Hayden Stone specialized in financing companies. At the time, the venture capital industry didn't exist in a formal sense: they tended to be private family organizations, such as the one run by the Rockefellers.

Rock's lucky break came when he was shown a letter sent to one of the firm's brokers by the son of a client. The writer of the letter was Eugene Kleiner, a scientist at William Shockley's laboratory in California. Shockley was a brilliant but erratic research scientist who pioneered research on the transistor. Unfortunately his man-management skills were negligible and he was verging on the paranoid, making the atmosphere at the labs extremely unpleasant. Revolution was in the air. Key employees decided that they could no longer work with Shockley, but, before the team was split up, Kleiner wrote a speculative letter to Hayden Stone asking if anyone knew of a place where they could continue to work together. Intrigued, Rock persuaded one of Hayden Stone's partners to fly out to the West Coast with him and meet Kleiner and his associates.

Contribution

Kleiner explained that the research team wanted to investigate the possibility of manufacturing transistors using silicon. If the process worked, it would revolutionize the computer industry. Rock was impressed with the young scientists and agreed that he would help Kleiner raise $1.5 million to establish a separate company. Rock contacted a long list of potential investors, but managed to raise nothing more than a few eyebrows. Luckily, at the last moment, he thought of Sherman Fairchild.

Sherman Fairchild was the largest stockholder in IBM; he had financed Tom Watson, Sr. when he founded the predecessor company to IBM. He was also an inventor. Fairchild thought Rock's proposal was a good one and agreed to invest $1.5 million through Fairchild Camera and Instrument. Kleiner and his associates were given an option to buy all the stock for $3 million.

The world's largest producer of microprocessors started with a modest $5.5 million of private funding, raised on the strength of a business plan written on one and a half pages.

The new company was named Fairchild Semiconductors. It was the technology gene pool from which, eventually, the Silicon Valley high-tech phenomenon evolved. Rock's success with the Fairchild deal spurred him on to investigate other investment opportunities on the West Coast. He made friends with Tommy Davis. Davis was working for Kern County Land Company, advising the firm on using surplus cash to finance other companies. Davis left Kern County Land in 1961 to join up with Rock, and together they formed the investment partnership Rock & Davis.

Investment in Rock's first partnership fund came largely from private individuals on the East Coast who were his contacts. Institutional investors showed little enthusiasm. From an investment of roughly $3 million of the fund's capital, over $70 million was returned to the limited partners. Unlike some later VCs, Rock's approach was about much more than just investing money. He also sat on the boards of companies he invested in, working closely with them to increase their chances of success. In the case of Teledyne, one of the fund's first investments, Rock was on the board for 33 years. Another early investment was in Scientific Data Systems. The company was sold to Xerox in 1969 for some $990 million—in Rock's words, "a humongous deal in those days."

In 1970 Rock formed a new partnership, Arthur Rock & Associates. Fairchild Semiconductors was in a state of flux. Sherman Fairchild was dead and a new C.E.O., John Carter, was in charge of the Fairchild Group. Carter's ideas about business conflicted with the ideas of Bob Noyce and Gordon Moore, two of the key researchers at Fairchild. Disenchanted with life at Fairchild, Moore and Noyce approached Rock and explained that they wanted to start their own company to research and produce semiconductor memory. Rock raised $2.5 million from 25 investors to invest in the new company, including $300,000 of his own money. It took him two days. The new company was called Intel. The world's largest producer of microprocessors started with a modest $5.5 million of private funding, raised on the strength of a business plan written on one and a half pages. Rock remained on Intel's board for over 30 years.

The financing of two of the most important companies in the history of computing would have been enough to ensure Rock's place in the pantheon of venture capitalists, but Rock followed Intel with another seminal computing company, Apple Computers. Mike Markkula, ex-vice President of Intel, tipped Rock off about a small fledgling computer company called Apple. Rock was not immediately persuaded and decided to pay a visit to the San José Homebrew Computer Show to see for himself. When he arrived he was unable to get anywhere near the Apple stand because of the assembled crowds, desperate to get a glimpse of the mock-up computer the two young entrepreneurs, Steve Jobs and Steve Wozniak, were demonstrating. But despite the obvious interest, Rock invested only $57,000. As usual he assumed his position on the board, a position he relinquished years later only because of a conflict of interest.

> *Rock lit the VC match that ignited the technology industry in Silicon Valley.*

His contribution to technology business was recognized in 1998 when he was appointed to the board of governors of NASD, the technology investment governing body. In 2002, he was nominated Business Leader of the Year and, the following year, he set out to encourage others by donating $25 million to Harvard Business School to fund the Arthur Rock Center for Entrepreneurship.

A lot has changed in Rock's time as a venture capitalist. As Rock says, "It's just a different world. It's an order of magnitude different. The pace of venture capital has changed. You don't get much time to look at the company. Sometimes you have to make up your mind that day."

One of the questions Rock is asked most often is, "What makes a good VC?" Is it luck, or perhaps a technology background? Rock says neither. According to him, being a good VC is about the ability to listen, about having a diverse variety of interests and, above all, about being able to read people. It's a talent that takes years to develop, and Rock has it in spades. In his seventies, Rock works in the industry he helped to create. Based in San Francisco, he is a Director on a number of boards, both profit and nonprofit. And he still recalls the words of his Harvard professor: "If you're interested in building a business to make money, forget it. You won't. If you're interested in building a business to make a contribution to society, then let's talk."

Context and Conclusions

Arthur Rock is an important figure in postwar economic history. Rock lit the VC match that ignited the technology industry in Silicon Valley. Through his efforts, eight of the brightest researchers in their field were able to form Fairchild Semiconductors. Without him, the best research team in its field would have scattered across California, the United States, or even the world. Instead they worked together to give the world the silicon chip and then to found Intel, the powerhouse of the personal computer revolution. Rock also helped shape the nature of the PC by investing in Apple Computers. The fact that Eugene Kleiner, one of the original "Fairchildren," later went on to found the VC firm Kleiner Perkins means that Rock can also lay claim to having helped create the modern VC industry.

CLOSE BUT NO CIGAR

TOM PERKINS

After a stellar career with tech companies like Spectra-Physics and Hewlett-Packard, Tom Perkins founded the venture capital firm Kleiner Perkins in 1972. Perkins's partner in the firm was Eugene Kleiner, the man who brought Arthur Rock out to the West Coast. Kleiner Perkins and its later partnership incarnation (Kleiner Perkins Caulfield & Byers) were at the heart of the IT revolution on Sand Hill Road in Menlo Park. The firm pioneered the concept of incubators and hatched companies such as Genentech, Tandem Computers, America Online, and Amazon.

For More Information
Web site:
Intel: **www.intel.com**

John D. Rockefeller

1839	Born.
1855	Starts work at Hewitt & Tuttle.
1869	Rockefeller, Andrews, & Flagler becomes the Standard Oil Company of Ohio.
1882	Standard Oil businesses brought under control of the Standard Oil Company.
1890	Nationwide distribution system reaches most towns in the United States.
1892	Trust dissolved by Ohio government. Reconstitutes as Standard Oil Trust (New Jersey).
1900	Standard Oil controls over three-quarters of the U.S. petroleum industry.
1904	80% of U.S. towns served by Standard Oil carts.
1911	Resigns as President. Standard Oil Trust dissolved.
1913	Establishes Rockefeller Foundation.
1937	Dies.

Summary

In the course of his long life, U.S. industrialist John D. Rockefeller (1839–1937), the son of a farmer, progressed from being an office boy earning $25 a month to being an oil tycoon worth over $900 million. Starting work aged 16, Rockefeller had his own firm within three years and by 1862 had moved into the oil business. After buying out most of the local competition, Rockefeller set his sights on building a national oil company with a national delivery network. He accomplished his vision with Standard Oil, which by 1879 controlled 90% of the oil refining in the United States. Rockefeller withdrew from active management of the company in 1897, remaining President until 1911, when the Standard Oil trust was finally dissolved by the U.S. government. Rockefeller's final years were devoted to giving away the bulk of his huge fortune.

Even at this tender age, the young Rockefeller displayed a keen business mind. He raised turkeys, sold them for a profit, and then lent the proceeds at 7%.

Life and Career

John D. Rockefeller was born in 1839 in Richford, Tioga County, New York, the eldest son and second of six children. His parents were farmers, and Rockefeller, along with his brothers and sisters, was expected to help out on the farm. Even at this tender age, the young Rockefeller displayed a keen business mind. He raised turkeys, sold them for a profit, and then lent the proceeds at 7%.

By the time Rockefeller was 14, his family had moved to Cleveland, Ohio. Here, in 1855, after a year at high school and a stint at Folsom Mercantile College, Rockefeller was offered employment as an office boy and assistant bookkeeper at the firm of Hewitt & Tuttle, produce commission merchants. No salary was agreed at the outset, and Rockefeller received no payment for 14 weeks, at which point he was handed $50 and put on $25 per month.

Rockefeller stayed at Hewitt & Tuttle for three years, leaving when the firm declined to meet his wage demands of $800 a year. Having spent the previous three years paying particular attention to how a business is run, Rockefeller decided to start his own.

Contribution

With his partner, Morris B. Clark, and $1,000 borrowed from his father at 10%, Rockefeller started a produce business. He visited all the local farmers, charmed them, and left his card. The response was so good that, in its first year of business in 1859, the company's revenues were $500,000.

About this time oil was just beginning to make an impact in Ohio. Several refineries had been opened near Cleveland. Rockefeller, sensing the potential of the new fuel, wasted no time forming Andrews, Clark, and Co., oil refiners, in 1862. Later he sold his produce commission interests to Clark and bought out Clark's interest in Andrews, Clark, and Co., to form Rockefeller & Andrews.

During his lifetime Rockefeller came in for much criticism, as well as some odd mythologizing. It was claimed, for example, that he would eat only bread and milk.

By 1869 Rockefeller's firm had acquired a number of other similar small firms and was now called Rockefeller, Andrews, & Flagler. But the oil business generally was going through a tough time. With the proliferation of firms all trying to get in on the action, the price of oil became so severely depressed that many companies went bankrupt. Undeterred, Rockefeller chose to merge Rockefeller, Andrews, & Flagler into the Standard Oil Company of Ohio in 1869, with $1 million capital and himself as President.

He then proceeded to apply to Standard Oil's business the "combination" strategy that J. P. Morgan had so successfully applied to the steel industry. The best way to ensure survival, he figured, was to spread the risk of operating in such a volatile and risky industry. The obvious way to achieve this was to buy up competitors, both locally and elsewhere in the United States. By 1872 Standard Oil had acquired all the refining firms in Cleveland. In 1882, after a prosperous decade, all the businesses belonging to Standard Oil were brought under the single umbrella of the Standard Oil Trust.

The dominance of the Standard Oil Trust soon gave rise to a barrage of criticism. In 1892 the Attorney General of Ohio won a suit to dissolve the Trust. During the court case, brought in 1890, Rockefeller was put under severe stress; he lost all his hair, including his eyebrows, and was reputed to have suffered a nervous breakdown. The effects of the court case on Standard Oil were less dramatic. The company simply reformed as the Standard Oil Company (New Jersey), because the laws of New Jersey permitted a parent company to own the stock of other companies. The Standard Oil Company (New Jersey) controlled three-quarters of the U.S. petroleum business.

Rockefeller remained President of Standard Oil until 1911. That was the year in which the U.S. Supreme Court finally ordered its dissolution, declaring the company to be in contravention of the country's antitrust laws. The 38 companies that made up the oil giant were split into separate entities.

During his lifetime Rockefeller came in for much criticism, as well as some odd mythologizing. It was claimed, for example, that he would eat only bread and milk. Another persistent story was of his phenomenal capacity for hard work and long hours, something that Rockefeller denied all knowledge of. "People persist in thinking that I was a tremendous worker, always at it, early and late, winter and summer," he said. "The real truth is that I was what would now be called a 'slacker' after I reached my middle thirties...I never, from the time I first entered an office, let business engross all my time and attention."

The latter years of Rockefeller's life were spent carrying out philanthropic work. He gave over $35 million to the University of Chicago, founded the Rockefeller Institute for Medical Research, the Rockefeller Foundation, and the Rockefeller Sanitary Commission, which eradicated hookworm in the southern areas of the United States. At its height Rockefeller's wealth was $900 million. When he died, aged 97, on May 23, 1937, at his home in Ormond Beach, he had given away all but $26,410,837.

Context and Conclusions

John D. Rockefeller created the modern oil industry. The impact of Rockefeller's business on the United States may have been less immediate than that of Edison's electric light or Ford's Model T automobile, but without the cheap gasoline that Standard Oil produced, it is unlikely that either the widescale electrification of the country or the mass-marketing of the car would have happened when they did.

One of Rockefeller's greatest attributes was his understanding of the importance of hiring brilliant people. "Men, not machinery or plant, make up an organization," was one of his sayings. He assembled a team of the brightest men in business and harnessed their collective abilities to drive Standard Oil's expansion. In later years he was vilified as the head of one of the hated "trusts" dominating industry in the United States. It should be remembered, however, that, despite its controlling influence, the establishment of the Standard Oil Trust saw the oil industry through some difficult times, and ensured its strength in the United States for the following decades.

For More Information

Book:

Chernow, Ron. *Titan: The Life of John D. Rockefeller, Sr.* New York: Random House, 1998.

Anita Roddick

1942	Born.
1960	Attends Newton Park College of Education in Bath.
1962	Travels to Israel on a study scholarship.
1971	Opens bed and breakfast business in Littlehampton.
1976	The Body Shop opens in Brighton selling environmentally friendly cosmetics.
1976	Ian McGlinn's investment enables second store to be opened.
1978	First informal franchises open. First franchise outside the United Kingdom opens in Brussels.
1984	The Body Shop goes public.
1988	The Body Shop opens in the United States.
1989	Roddick commissions environmental audit of all company's practices.
1998	Steps down as C.E.O.
2000	Sets up Anitaroddick.com to communicate environmental issues.
2000	Publication of *Business As Unusual*.
2001	Publication of *Take It Personally*.

Summary

Anita Roddick (1942–), the British businesswoman and head of the cosmetics phenomenon The Body Shop, might never have started her business at all. It was an unusual combination of factors that led her to open her first store in 1976. But The Body Shop concept—based on environmentally friendly cosmetics and begun as a cottage industry—soon outgrew her small store in Brighton. If the company had expanded in the traditional manner, it might well have lost the small-business charm that made it so successful. Instead, Roddick expanded through franchises, a relatively new concept in the United Kingdom at the time, guaranteeing that the vibrancy and enthusiasm of the concept was maintained. By the year 2000 there were over 1,500 stores worldwide, and Roddick, who had stepped down as C.E.O. two years earlier, was spending much of her time and energy championing ethical causes close to her heart.

Life and Career

Born in Sussex, England, in 1942, Roddick was the third of four children. Her parents ran an North American-style diner in the sleepy English coastal town of Littlehampton. After secondary school, despite being offered a place at the prestigious Guildhall School of Music and Drama, Roddick attended the Newton Park College of Education in Bath.

After college Roddick flitted from one job to another. In Paris she worked for the *International Herald Tribune*; she taught in England; then she worked for the United Nations in Geneva. After the UN, Roddick followed what became known as the hippy trail to Africa, the Far East, and Australia, making her way around the globe. Her stay in South Africa was cut short when she was ejected for breaking the apartheid laws by attending a jazz club on "nonwhites" night. Her rebellious spirit may have earned her an early ticket out of Africa, but it was to stand her in good stead when she later launched The Body Shop.

Returning to Littlehampton, Roddick settled down, married, had children, and with her husband, Gordon, opened a hotel and then a restaurant. Running both businesses eventually became too demanding on family life. The restaurant was sold, and Roddick's husband declared that he was planning an ambitious expedition of his own—intending to ride a horse from South America to New York City.

Contribution

Unable to curb her entrepreneurial instincts, Roddick looked for another enterprise on which to concentrate, one that would also earn some money in her husband's absence. After some thought she came up with the idea of a cosmetics business with a difference: the use of natural ingredients. Her husband helped arrange a bank loan using the hotel as collateral, and Roddick bought premises next to a funeral parlor in the nearby town of Brighton.

On March 27, 1976, with her husband about to leave on his travels, Roddick opened for business, selling environmentally friendly cosmetics. The idea was not just to sell socially responsible products using natural ingredients, but to sell them in convenient small sizes that would tempt customers to try them out. Thus, many of The Body Shop's defining characteristics were decided upon at this early stage, though the decisions were often based on cost effectiveness rather than any grand strategic plan. The walls were painted green, not in anticipation of the Green movement, but to hide the damp patches. Product packaging was minimal and recyclable, and Roddick wrote the labels out by hand.

The Brighton store prospered, and she was soon planning another in nearby Chichester. When the bank refused to finance her, she turned to a local businessman, Ian McGlinn, who agreed to put up £4,000 for a half share of the business. Roddick agreed. For McGlinn, it proved to be the investment opportunity of his life. By the time Roddick's husband returned in 1977, The Body Shop concept was unstoppable. Her friends and family ran the first few stores, but requests to establish branches elsewhere in the country were flooding in. To cater to the demand for stores, Roddick and her husband began franchising the concept. Potential franchisees would finance the business and agree to buy their stock from Roddick, and, in return, would be licensed to use The Body Shop name. She interviewed many of the early franchisees herself. A high proportion of them were women, and she can justifiably claim to have helped change the traditional male-dominated image of entrepreneurs in the United Kingdom.

> *Roddick had little time for the beauty industry, believing that it was in the business of selling unattainable dreams. The Body Shop was different.*

What she had started was not a conventional cosmetics business. Roddick had little time for the beauty industry, believing that it was in the business of selling unattainable dreams. The Body Shop was different. Roddick made no special claims for her products. In fact she didn't advertise, relying mainly on word of mouth to bring customers through the store doors.

"Making products that work—that aren't part of the cosmetic industry's lies to women—is all-important," Roddick has said. "Making sure we minimize our impact in our manufacturing processes, clean up our waste, put back into the community...we go where businesses never want to because they don't think it is the role of business to get involved."

Roddick espouses profits with principles. Through The Body Shop she has supported campaigns by Greenpeace, Friends of the Earth, and Amnesty International, among others. Messages on shopping bags and vehicles express The Body Shop's support for these causes.

In April 1984 the company became publicly listed. The share price shot up on the opening day, and Roddick, her husband, and Ian McGlinn all became paper millionaires overnight. From one small store next to a funeral parlor, The Body Shop network has expanded to over 1,800 stores worldwide, offering over 400 products. Roddick, now one of the richest women in England, has been showered with awards as a result of both her business endeavors and her social conscience. Besides the titles of London's Business Woman of the Year and Retailer of the Year, she has received the United Nations' "Global 500" environmental award and the Order of the British Empire.

In 1994 Roddick brought in external management help to refocus the business. Unsurprisingly she found the shift from her hands-on role difficult to adjust to. In 1998 she stepped down as C.E.O., and remained as co-Chair with her husband, Gordon, until 2002, when she adopted a new role as creative consultant to the company. The fact that she now spends less time with The Body Shop allows her more scope to champion the causes she so passionately believes in. One of her first actions was to establish AnitaRoddick.com, a Web site devoted to raising awareness of issues she cares about. She has also been busy writing books. *Business As Unusual* was published in 2000, followed a year later by *Take it Personally*, a book encouraging people to take action to change the world.

Context and Conclusions

Displayed on the side of The Body Shop vehicles is the following: "If you think you are too small to have an impact, try going to bed with a mosquito." The phrase is one of Roddick's favorite quotations—not surprisingly, considering her achievements. She has taken on the big cosmetic companies and captured a large share of the market with her ethically driven approach to business. She has built a global company from a one-woman cottage industry, changed the attitude toward businesswomen through her franchise operation, and, in addition, found time to make her voice heard championing the rights of minorities and unsung causes—often through her company.

For More Information

Books:

Older, Jules. *Anita!: The Woman behind The Body Shop*. Watertown, MA: Charlesbridge Publishing, 1998.

Roddick, Anita. *Business As Unusual*. New York: HarperCollins, 2000.

Roddick, Anita. *Take it Personally: How to Make Conscious Choices to Change the World*. London: HarperCollins, 2001.

Web site:

The Body Shop: **www.thebodyshop.com**

Julius Rosenwald

1862	Born.
1885	Moves to Chicago.
1885–1895	Manufactures men's summer clothing as Rosenwald & Weil.
1895	Takes share of Sears, Roebuck as sleeping partner.
1896	Becomes Vice-President of Sears.
1900–1906	Total sales increased from $11 million to over $50 million.
1908	Sears retires. Rosenwald becomes President.
1916	Over 40 million catalogs distributed.
1925	Opens first retail store. Becomes Chairman. Personal holdings worth $150 million.
1932	Dies.

Summary

Julius Rosenwald started in the retail business at the tender age of 21, with his own clothes store in New York. He then showed an excellent nose for an opportunity, first by ditching his retail business to manufacture men's summer clothing, and then abandoning manufacturing to join Sears, Roebuck as Vice-President. His big break was choosing Chicago as the base for his manufacturing business. There he met the entrepreneur R. W. Sears, who made his fortune with a mail-order business. Sears needed the right person to take his business into the 20th century—he chose Rosenwald. By the time Rosenwald died in 1932, the company had revitalized its mail-order business, expanded its product range, introduced innovative work practices, and opened hundreds of retail stores throughout the United States, leaving competitors like Montgomery Ward far behind.

Life and Career

Julius Rosenwald was born in Springfield, Illinois in 1862. As a child he would sell goods door to door in his hometown. He pumped the bellows on the church organ, peddled pamphlets, and sold chromolithographs, the latest consumer craze. During the summer vacation, he worked in a fancy goods store.

He pumped the bellows on the church organ, peddled pamphlets, and sold chromolithographs, the latest consumer craze.

At age 16, Rosenwald left school to work for his uncle's wholesale clothing business in New York. By living frugally, he saved enough money so that at the age of 21 he could afford to buy a small retail clothing store on 4th Avenue.

One day Rosenwald was in idle conversation with the owner of a nearby business. The man, who manufactured summer clothing for men, revealed that he was struggling to keep pace with orders. Rosenwald turned the statement over and over in his mind until, in the middle of the night, he dramatically resolved to abandon his retail store. Chicago was the city that Rosenwald chose to start his new business. There, with partner Julius E. Weil, he formed Rosenwald & Weil, manufacturers and wholesalers of summer clothing.

Contribution

One of Rosenwald's best customers was Richard Warren Sears of Sears, Roebuck & Company. Sears's one problem was that he needed more capital to expand. He asked if Rosenwald was interested in investing in the business. Rosenwald agreed, and took a quarter interest in Sears, Roebuck for $70,000.

To begin with, Rosenwald was a silent partner. However by 1896, Sears—who ran the company single-handed—asked Rosenwald to join him as Vice-President. Over the next 30 years, Rosenwald transformed Sears, Roebuck into one of the largest retailers in the United States.

Rosenwald first turned his attention to the Sears, Roebuck catalog. As Ingvar Kamprad of IKEA would find out over 50 years later, Rosenwald discovered that if mail-order companies were less than honest in the wording and illustration of their catalogs, it damaged the reputation of the entire industry. Even Sears, Roebuck was guilty of delivering products that didn't always correspond to the promises of the lavishly worded and sumptuously illustrated catalog.

Rosenwald insisted on a fastidiously precise correlation between the advertisements in the catalog and the goods supplied. First, he ensured that every illustration and description in the catalog was carefully compared with the relevant article. He established laboratories and employed scientists to examine merchandise received from suppliers. Any defective goods were immediately rejected and returned. To increase consumer confidence, he introduced a novel concept—a "money back if not satisfied" guarantee—supported by an advertising campaign. In this way Rosenwald removed the burden of risk from the consumer and placed it squarely on the shoulders of Sears, Roebuck.

Once consumer confidence was secure, Rosenwald set about broadening the range of products offered in a mail-order catalog. Soon everything from buttons to bungalows was sold by mail order. Other innovations were introduced. To secure quality supplies, Rosenwald constructed factories employing over 20,000 workers. Technological innovations such as the conveyor belt were introduced (it was said that Henry Ford "borrowed" Rosenwald's idea for his assembly lines). The catalog was expanded, and special editions were introduced for seasonal goods and special events. New goods like shoes and books were featured in the catalog. Shoes, an unlikely candidate for mail order, earned revenues of $1 million a month. The sale of *Encyclopedia Britannicas* alone added an incredible $5 million in revenues to the annual balance sheet. Between 1900 and 1906, total sales increased from $11 million to over $50 million. By 1914 they had reached $100 million.

He spurned the trappings of status, preferring to be seen as one of the workers.

Rosenwald was also making changes to the way the company's employees were treated.

He spurned the trappings of status, preferring to be seen as one of the workers. Asked what it felt like to have so many people working for him he replied, "I always think of them as just working with me." When he was presented with an oriental rug to cover the floor of his executive office, it remained rolled up in the corner. Rosenwald figured if linoleum was good enough for everybody else, it was good enough for him. "I have played only a very small part in the building up of Sears, Roebuck and Company," he modestly told his admirers. To improve the lot of his workers, Rosenwald introduced recreation facilities, as well as an innovative "employee savings and profit-sharing scheme." True, his management style was a little paternalistic. He was overprotective of his female employees, for example—familiarity between men and women was forbidden at social functions, and the sexes were segregated in the cafeteria.

Eternally cost-conscious in business, Rosenwald encouraged his workers to be equally parsimonious. Employees who earned below $1,500 received a bonus on the anniversary of their joining the company. The bonus was a percentage of the annual salary, equal to the number of years an employee had worked for the company. Starting in the fifth year, it rose to 10% in the tenth year, and remained at 10% thereafter. His employees, Rosenwald suggested, should save the bonus.

On Sears' retirement in 1908, Rosenwald became President and, in 1925, Chairman. In the 1920s he took the company in a new direction. The mail-order catalog was still an essential element of the Sears, Roebuck retail strategy, but now Rosenwald expanded into retail stores. In 1925 Sears opened its first retail store in Chicago. By 1929 there were 324 stores with the name Sears, Roebuck above the doors.

In his final years, Rosenwald focused his attention on philanthropy. He established the Julius Rosenwald Fund, a charity for the economic, medical, and cultural advancement of African Americans, with an endowment of $30 million. He gave money to aid the Jews in the Middle East and to help German children after World War I. He also endowed the University of Chicago and helped to establish the Museum of Science and Industry in Chicago. He died in 1932.

Context and Conclusions

Julius Rosenwald took a promising business and turned it into a great one. Without his intervention, it is arguable whether Sears, Roebuck would have become the retailing giant it did. At the time Rosenwald joined, the reputation of the mail-order industry was under a cloud because of the less-than-scrupulous practices of many of the companies involved. Through a variety of innovations, Rosenwald breathed new life into a tired format. Greater choice, better quality, and a money-back guarantee were among the features that won the customers back. Internally, Rosenwald concentrated on ensuring a quality supply of merchandise and keeping the workforce happy. Finally, he moved to secure the future of the company by extending the brand and opening a chain of retail stores.

CLOSE BUT NO CIGAR
AARON MONTGOMERY WARD
Montgomery Ward is said to have founded the first dry goods mail-order business in 1872. He also coined the phrase "satisfaction guaranteed or your money back." But by 1900, after Julius

Rosenwald had injected new life into Sears, Roebuck, Montgomery Ward's eponymous company began to trail its main rival. Montgomery Ward died in 1913, 13 years before his company opened its first retail store. Had he been alive in 1930, he might have sanctioned a merger with Sears—proposed but declined by Ward's Directors. Instead his company's fortunes subsided until, in 2001, it pulled down its shutters for the last time.

For More Information

Books:

Harris, Leon. *Merchant Princes*. New York: Harper & Row Publishers, 1979.

Sorenson, Lorin. *Sears, Roebuck and Co.: 100th Anniversary 1886–1996*. St. Helena, CA: Silverado Publishing Co., 1985.

Werner, M. R. *Julius Rosenwald: The Life of a Practical Humanitarian*. New York: Harper & Brothers, 1939.

David Sarnoff

1891	Born.
1916	Sarnoff states his vision for radio.
1919	Radio Corporation of America (RCA) incorporated.
1920	Cuts a deal with Armstrong to secure the latter's radio technology patents.
1921	RCA begins radio broadcasting.
1930	Aged 39, Sarnoff becomes President of RCA.
1933	Has new headquarters constructed for RCA. Armstrong invents FM.
1939	Introduces television to the United States just before World War II at the World's Fair.
1954	Introduces color television.
1965	His son Robert becomes President of the company; Sarnoff becomes Chairman.
1970	Dies.

Summary

David Sarnoff (1891–1970) was a media pioneer. He was responsible for the introduction of radio and television in the United States as forms of mass media. Born in Russia, Sarnoff emigrated to the United States in 1900; by 1930 he was President of the Radio Corporation of America (RCA). He went on to develop FM radio on a commercial basis and bring color television to the American people. Behind Sarnoff's public success story with RCA, however, lay the personal saga of his long-running relationship with the inventor Edwin H. Armstrong. Originally based on friendship, the relationship descended into animosity and ended with Armstrong's suicide in 1954. Sarnoff was succeeded at RCA by his son, Robert, in 1965. The remaining years of his life were spent bitterly watching his son modernize the company that he had spent his life building.

Life and Career

David Sarnoff was born in Uzlian in Russia. His father, Abraham, was a Jewish painter who traveled to the United States in 1896, determined to earn enough money to bring the rest of his family across the Atlantic to join him. It took him four years.

When Sarnoff arrived in Manhattan on July 2, 1900, his father was renting a squalid apartment on the lower East Side. In the four years since Abraham had arrived in the sprawling metropolis, he had been struggling to make a living. Not only was he reduced to doing menial work for little pay, but his health had deteriorated to the point where he was unable to provide for his family. At the tender age of nine, therefore, Sarnoff became the family breadwinner.

He started by selling Yiddish newspapers on street corners, earning a quarter for every 50 papers sold. To supplement his income he delivered another paper in the morning and sang at the local synagogue for a small fee. Despite the long hours—he rose at 4:00 a.m. for the morning round—Sarnoff still managed to find time to study at a local school, the Educational Alliance. Within a year he could read the English newspapers. At 14 he opened his own newspaper stand, employing his father and brothers.

Like several other great business leaders of his generation, Sarnoff started out on the path to success in the employ of a telegraph company—in this case, American Marconi Wireless

Telegraph. At that time Marconi's U.S. operation was a loss-making company, unlike its English parent. Sarnoff started at Marconi as an office boy, little realizing that he would spend the next 60 years at the company and its successor, the Radio Corporation of America, rising to become President before the age of 40.

Contribution

Brashly, Sarnoff introduced himself in person to Marconi as the newest employee of the company. His impudence paid off, and he was promoted to junior wireless operator, and not long after to chief inspector.

It was as chief inspector that Sarnoff met the man who was to change his life. Edwin H. Armstrong was an inventor who had been working on an improved wireless receiver. At a demonstration of his invention in front of Sarnoff and three other Marconi engineers, Armstrong received radio signals from Clifden, Ireland, and a radio station in San Francisco. Sarnoff, immediately aware of the commercial potential of the machine, advised his bosses to explore the possibility of developing a similar device.

Unfortunately for Sarnoff, his superiors were not as impressed, preferring to stick with the existing point-to-point system that had served Marconi so well. In 1916 Sarnoff, with considerable foresight, wrote a memo to the board: "I have in mind a plan of development which would make radio a household utility in the same sense as the piano or the phonograph."

During World War I the U.S. Navy made significant technical advances in radio engineering. At the end of the war companies stood in line to purchase the new technology. The U.S. government was reluctant to hand over its know-how to a British company like Marconi, so a new company, Radio Corporation of America (RCA), was incorporated in 1919. The new company held the patents of GE and Marconi; its commercial manager and second-in-command was Sarnoff. Now in a better position to lobby for his vision of ubiquitous radio, Sarnoff sent a 28-page "blueprint for success" to the Chairman. Sarnoff got his way, and RCA began to churn out radio sets. The ensuing radio craze assured RCA's success, despite competition from companies like Westinghouse.

Armstrong, meanwhile, was continuing to develop radio technology. In 1920, hearing that Armstrong had come up with yet another breakthrough, Sarnoff cut out the middlemen and went straight to him to secure the technology patents. After some tough bargaining, he got the technology and Armstrong received enough stock in RCA to make him the leading shareholder—plus some cash. Armstrong also agreed to give RCA first refusal on future innovations.

The Wall Street Crash of 1929 and ensuing financial chaos hit RCA badly. This was despite the company's domination of its market, the increasing popularity of radio as a form of entertainment, and the creation of the National Broadcasting Company. In January 1930 after a boardroom shuffle, Sarnoff, aged 39, became President of RCA.

In December 1933 Armstrong surfaced once more with yet another invention: Frequency Modulation (FM). This time, however, Sarnoff was less interested; his focus was directed toward television rather than radio. He introduced television to the United States just before the outbreak of World War II at the 1939 World's Fair.

After the war a private conflict broke out between Armstrong and Sarnoff over FM.

Eventually, after years of banging his head against the giant RCA, Armstrong was forced to agree a settlement in the courts. In 1954, embittered by the outcome, Armstrong jumped to his death from a 13th-story window. Sarnoff's only comment on learning of the death of his one-time friend was, "I didn't kill Armstrong."

Sarnoff carried on business as usual. He introduced color television in 1954. To avoid damaging litigation, he placed all RCA's color television patents in the public domain and at the same time tripled spending on color programming. Any manufacturer could produce a color television set, but RCA had first mover advantage in color broadcasting.

Color television was Sarnoff's last throw of the dice. The protracted litigation with Armstrong may have taken more of a toll on him than he realized at the time. In 1965 his son, Robert, was made President of the company and Sarnoff became Chairman.

A change of name and logo for RCA, pushed through by his son, roused Sarnoff one last time, and he fought successfully to reinstate the old name. In reality it was a hollow victory. The RCA that Sarnoff had created metamorphosed into a conglomerate containing a disparate collection of companies, including Hertz car rentals and Random House Publishing. After a lengthy illness David Sarnoff died in December 1970.

Context and Conclusions

Sarnoff was more than just a forerunner of modern media magnates such as Rupert Murdoch and Ted Turner. He pioneered the mass-market entertainment industry of radio and television. Edwin Armstrong played a large part in creating the technology of commercial radio, but it was Sarnoff who had the vision to recognize the commercial potential of Armstrong's scientific inventions when others did not. Moreover, Sarnoff had the sense to tie up the technology patents in the case of radio and, more remarkably, to place all RCA's color television patents in the public domain. This last act alone is testimony to Sarnoff's genius and was a forerunner of the approach taken by Linus Torvalds when developing the computer operating system Linux.

For More Information
Books:
Bilby, Kenneth M. *The General: David Sarnoff and the Rise of the Communications Industry.* New York: Harper & Row, 1986.
Lyons, Eugene. *David Sarnoff: A Biography.* New York: Harper & Row, 1966.
Myers, Elisabeth P. *David Sarnoff: Radio and TV Boy.* Indianapolis, IN: Bobbs-Merrill Co., 1972.
Sobel, Robert. *RCA.* New York: Stein and Day, 1986.

Web site:
RCA: **www.rca.com**

Alfred P. Sloan, Jr.

1875	Born.
1899	Buys a controlling interest in Hyatt Roller Bearing Company.
1903	Hyatt makes profits of $60 million.
1916	Sloan becomes President of the United Motors Corporation.
1918	United Motors becomes part of General Motors.
1923	Sloan becomes President of General Motors.
1937	Steps down as President, but remains Chairman and C.E.O.
1946	Steps down as C.E.O.
1956	Relinquishes position as Chairman.
1966	Dies.

Summary

Alfred P. Sloan, Jr. (1875–1966) was both a brilliant engineer and a forward-thinking manager. After transforming the fortunes of Hyatt Roller Bearing Company, Sloan became President of United Motors Corporation, which soon merged with General Motors. Sloan succeeded Pierre du Pont as President of General Motors in 1923.

From this position Sloan created one of the most influential organizational designs of the 20th century. He restructured the company along divisional lines, with an executive committee sitting above the divisions. Sloan's design became the organizational blueprint for corporations for the next 50 years. Six years after Sloan took over the GM presidency, net sales were $1.5 billion and the stock price was up by 480%. During his tenure he consistently out-thought his main competitor, Ford, turning GM into the world's greatest automobile manufacturer.

Life and Career

Alfred Pritchard Sloan, Jr. was born in New Haven, Connecticut, on May 23, 1875, the first of five children in a prosperous family. His father, an engineer by training, was an importer of coffee and tea who later became a wholesale grocer.

At age ten Sloan moved with his family to Brooklyn, New York, where he attended public school and then Brooklyn Polytechnic Institute. Sloan wanted to go on to MIT. Told he was too young, he persisted with his application and eventually took his place there to study electrical engineering. The youngest member of his class, he graduated in 1895 after just three years.

Having displayed a talent for engineering, Sloan went to work at Hyatt Roller Bearing Company in Harrison, New Jersey. To his disappointment he was employed as a draftsman, salesperson, and general gofer. Sloan could see no future at the company, so he left to join a household refrigerator business. But he was not there long before he changed his mind and in 1899 returned to Hyatt. The firm was in financial difficulties and, with help from his father, Sloan bought a controlling interest.

The ambitious young man soon brought his influence to bear on his new company. Aged 24, Sloan became President of Hyatt and proposed that the company manufacture a new antifriction bearing for automobiles. With this move to manufacturing products for the rapidly growing automobile market, Sloan forged a connection with the industry that would propel him to greatness.

Contribution

Until Hyatt's production of the antifriction bearing, the automobile industry had been using a well-greased axle. Immediately the Olds Motors Company, followed by Ford and the other automobile manufacturers, turned to Sloan and signed contracts for the new bearing. By 1903 Hyatt was making profits of $60 million.

As part of the drive to keep Hyatt's customers happy, Sloan organized a big party once a year. Known as "frictionless feasts" in reference to the company's auto bearings, these events drew the greatest names in the automobile industry. Sloan would mingle with luminaries such as Henry Ford and the Dodge brothers as guests drank cocktails pumped from a 50-gallon container made to resemble a service station oil drum.

> *Sloan forged excellent contacts in the industry, particularly with Henry Leland, who became his mentor.*

Sloan forged excellent contacts in the industry, particularly with Henry Leland, who became his mentor. Leland, one of the architects of manufacturing using interchangeable parts, had worked for Olds, Cadillac, and General Motors, and created the Lincoln. Leland's watchword was quality—a mantra that rubbed off on Sloan.

Despite Sloan's apparent success at Hyatt (people would comment on the constant emergence of new buildings as they passed the plant on the Pennsylvania Railroad), he was still concerned about the company's future prospects. Its two largest customers were Ford and GM, and either of these giants, Sloan knew, could easily build a plant to manufacture bearings.

In 1916 Sloan sealed his own and Hyatt's future by securing a deal in which William Crapo Durant, who had just regained control of GM, took a financial interest in Hyatt. Hyatt merged with several other companies to become United Motors Corporation and Sloan became President of the new company. United Motors was in turn subsumed into GM in 1918, with Sloan becoming Vice-President in charge of accessories and a member of GM's executive committee.

At GM Sloan worked closely with its founder, Durant. He admired Durant's tenacity while frequently disagreeing with his methods. By 1920 Sloan had risen to the position of Vice-President. In the same year Durant was forced by his bankers to relinquish his position in the company and was succeeded as President by Pierre S. du Pont. In 1923 du Pont was succeeded by Sloan.

As company President Sloan set about reorganizing GM. The architecture he developed secured his place in business history. He structured the company into separate divisions. Under Durant's management GM cars had competed with each other in the market; Sloan ensured that each car and truck division had its own price and style categories. Each GM model was updated annually, offering greater choice to the consumer than Ford's mass-market Model T (famously available in any color—"as long as it's black").

Soon companies under the GM umbrella, such as Buick, Cadillac, and Pontiac, were semiautonomous, responsible for almost every aspect of their business. This mix of decentralization and coordinated policy control left Sloan and the senior executives free to worry about GM corporate strategy while the divisional managers ran their divisions as they saw fit—providing, of course, they made a profit.

And make a profit they did. When Sloan took over GM's presidency, net sales were $698 million. Just six years later, net sales were $1.5 billion and the stock price was up by 480%. With Sloan's new organizational structure came a new type of employee, the professional manager. Sloan took management—until then conducted largely in an amateurish, entrepreneurial way—and turned it into a serious professional discipline focusing on decision making based on facts, particularly financial facts.

Sloan remained President of GM for 14 years, from 1923 until 1937, continuing as Chairman until 1956. He ran the company quietly from behind the scenes, known by his workers as "Silent Sloan" and preferring to trust in the ability of his managers. He also liked to get out of the office and visit his clients—he traveled the breadth of the country regularly.

Later in life Sloan made considerable philanthropic donations. He established the Alfred P. Sloan Foundation, to which he and his wife gave $305 million during his lifetime. Gifts from the foundation have benefited, among other institutions, the Sloan-Kettering Institute for Cancer Research in New York and Sloan's alma mater, MIT. Sloan died of a heart attack in 1966, aged 90.

Context and Conclusions

Alfred Sloan made his name by revolutionizing the structure of the corporation and, in doing so, making General Motors the greatest automobile company in the world. Unlike his contemporaries Henry Ford and William Crapo Durant, Sloan was as comfortable with his management role as he was in the workshop. A prudent man who took measured risks, Sloan restructured GM along divisional lines and introduced rigorous financial controls. At the same time he created a new type of business executive—the professional manager. Sloan may justifiably be remembered for his contribution to the U.S. automobile industry because of his work at General Motors. He should be remembered equally for his role in the evolution of management and corporate structure.

For More Information

Book:

Sloan, Alfred P., Jr. *My Years with General Motors*. Reissue. New York: Doubleday, 1996.

Web site:

General Motors: **www.gm.com**

Martha Stewart

1941	Born.
1964	Graduates from Barnard College.
1965	Gives up modeling.
1967	Obtains job as a stockbroker.
1973	Moves to Westport, Connecticut, and starts a catering business.
1982	Publishes her first book, *Entertaining*.
1987	Stewart signs up to a $5 million, five-year contract with Kmart.
1988	*Time* magazine refers to her as "the guru of good taste."
1990	Divorces Andy Stewart.
1991	Launches *Martha Stewart Living* magazine.
1997	Forms Martha Stewart Living Omnimedia. Becomes chair and C.E.O.
1999	*Fortune* magazine names her as one of America's "50 Most Powerful Women."
2000	Ranked in the Forbes Four Hundred list of billionaires.
2001	Sells shares in ImClone Systems.
2002	Resigns from board of New York Stock Exchange.
2003	Charged with securities fraud.

Summary

A U.S. icon, Martha Stewart has fashioned a fortune from her lifestyle. She studied architectural history at college, and put the learning to good use renovating the country home that became the hub of her business empire. After careers in modeling and stockbroking, she turned to cooking, first in a small way, then in a multimillion-dollar way. Her catering business was lucrative, but it was her books that really launched her to stardom. Her first, *Entertaining*, was published in 1982. It was followed by TV shows, magazines, product endorsement, consultancy, and public speaking. In the 1990s everyone in the United States wanted a piece of Stewart's life. And she was only too happy to sell them her version. Her reign as the Queen of Homemaking has made her a billionaire.

Life and Career

Martha Stewart was born Martha Kostyra in Jersey City, New Jersey, on August 3, 1941. When she was three, she moved with her family to Nutley, a New Jersey suburb of New York City. Stewart owes much of her later business success to her childhood. As a girl she would cook, bake, and sew with her mother, who was a schoolteacher by profession but stayed home to bring up six children. Her father, who was a pharmaceutical salesman, was a keen gardener and taught her about planting, garden design, and flower arranging.

There was no clue to Stewart's eventual career, however, in her choice of subjects at college. She studied history and architectural history at Barnard College, Columbia University, on a partial scholarship. To pay for her tuition, she relied on modeling fees; she had modeled part time from the age of 13. While at college she married Yale law student Andy Stewart. She was 19.

It was to modeling that Stewart turned for full-time work when she left Barnard College in 1964. But she was forced to give it up in 1965 when she gave birth to her daughter. A complete change of direction followed when, in 1967, with the help of her father-in-law, she got a job as a stockbroker.

Stewart excelled at her new career, her salary soon reaching $100,000 plus. However, the timing was unfortunate. In the early 1970s the oil crisis brought about an economic slowdown in the United States. In 1973, with Wall Street in the grip of a recession, Stewart and her husband packed their bags and moved to Westport, Connecticut.

Contribution

Stewart readily adjusted to rural life. With her husband she set about restoring the farmhouse they had purchased, known locally as "the Westport Horror." While her husband commuted to New York City, Stewart redecorated the house and began to overhaul the garden. Soon the house was completely renovated and the grounds boasted an orchard, vegetable garden, beehives, and a variety of livestock. Stewart still lives in the house today, with her chow chow dogs and Himalayan cats. She uses it as a base for her business.

By 1976, with the house fixed up, Stewart had turned her attention to cooking. She gave herself a crash course in cookery and swiftly moved on to teach, first children and then adults, in her own home. She opened a small gourmet food business in Westport called Market Basket. When the business began to grow, she moved out of her shared premises and into her home. When requests for her services became too great for her to manage alone, she went into partnership with a friend, Norma Collier. But within a year the partnership was over. Collier said later that she didn't want to work a "128-hour week."

Soon the house was completely renovated and the grounds boasted an orchard, vegetable garden, beehives, and a variety of livestock.

Stewart had no such qualms. She continued the business on her own, catering for celebrated Connecticut neighbors such as Paul Newman. She called her company Martha Stewart, Inc., and slowly raised her profile through teaching, catering, and writing articles for publications such as the *New York Times* and *Family Circle* magazine.

What started as cottage industry soon grew into a large business, and by 1986 was worth $1 million. She had, by this time, outgrown her house's kitchen and moved into a separate building next to the house. On the way to her first million, Stewart wrote one of America's most successful books of its type, *Entertaining*, published in 1982. A small library of books followed, each accompanied by promotional book signing tours and each garnering plaudits and more fans, so much so that by 1988 *Time* magazine was referring to her as "the guru of good taste (and taste buds) in American entertaining, looked to by millions of American women for guidance about everything from weddings to weeding."

Stewart was not without her detractors. After the publication of *Entertaining*, there were accusations of plagiarism. *Newsweek* reported similarities between her recipes for orange almond cake and cherry pound cake with raisins and recipes in *Mastering the Art of French Cooking, Vol III* by Simone Beck and Julia Child. But the allegations were never proved, and the controversy subsided. In her later books Stewart ensured that recipes were credited if necessary. But while her business life blossomed, her personal life suffered: she was divorced from her husband.

Business continued to grow at a phenomenal rate. In 1987 Stewart signed a $5 million, five-year contract as a consultant to Kmart department stores. She had her own lines of paint and linen, produced a series of commercials, and gave up the catering business to concentrate on writing.

The *Martha Stewart Living* magazine and television programs followed, as did lecturing, personal appearances, and a host of accolades. She was named among the "50 Most Powerful Women" by *Fortune* magazine in 1998, and received Emmy awards for her television shows. In 2000 she made the *Forbes* Four Hundred list of billionaires—a prime example of "the American dream" come true.

The dream turned into a nightmare in June 2003, however. That month saw the culmination of over two years' speculation about Stewart's financial affairs. In December 2001, she sold shares in a company called ImClone Systems, which at one time had been run by an acquaintance. While Stewart has consistently denied accusations of insider dealings, probes into the sale set off a chain of brand-damaging events. As a result, in October 2002 she resigned from the board of the New York Stock Exchange and by the end of December 2002, Martha Stewart Living

Underneath the glossy veneer of well-lit cuisine and perfectly painted interiors, beneath the public persona of the immaculately turned out, finely groomed ex-model, is a relentlessly driven, extremely hardworking, acutely savvy businesswoman.

Omnimedia had lost $2 million. Worse was to come. In June 2003, Stewart was charged with securities fraud and the obstruction of justice in relation to the ImClone shares and was committed to face trial in January 2004.

Context and Conclusions

Martha Stewart is a symbol of modern culture. She turned her life into a business and transmuted cookies into cash. Underneath the glossy veneer of well-lit cuisine and perfectly painted interiors, beneath the public persona of the immaculately turned out, finely groomed ex-model, is a relentlessly driven, extremely hardworking, acutely savvy businesswoman. Whether she will safely navigate 2004's stormy waters remains to be seen.

CLOSE BUT NO CIGAR
DELIA SMITH

The U.K. Martha Stewart equivalent, Smith has capitalized on her mildly mumsy image to cook up a small fortune. However, Smith will never quite make it to Stewart's exalted standing. Not that Smith lacks pep; she's always on the go, managing to combine her culinary empire with her

Directorship of Norwich City Football Club. But Smith has a different approach to the public/private mix. Her private persona is kept firmly under wraps; no holiday snaps or interior decor shots on *her* Web site! And, if the public don't have an admission ticket into her life, they're unlikely ever to aspire to be Delia Smith, or to connect with her as the U.S. public do with Martha Stewart.

For More Information

Books:

Byron, Christopher. *Martha Inc.: The Incredible Story of Martha Stewart Living Omnimedia.* New York: John Wiley, 2002.

Oppenheimer, Jerry. *Just Desserts: Martha Stewart, the Unauthorized Biography.* New York: William Morrow & Co., 1997.

Web site:

Martha Stewart Living Omnimedia: **www.marthastewart.com**

Levi Strauss

1829	Born.
1847	Sails to join half-brothers in the United States with sisters and mother.
1853	Becomes U.S. citizen, and sails to San Francisco.
1866	Levi Strauss makes its headquarters at 14–16 Battery Street.
1872	Jacob Davis writes to Levi Strauss, tells him about riveting process.
1873	Levi Strauss and Jacob Davis awarded patent for rivets on men's pants; they begin manufacturing of copper-riveted "waist overalls."
1890	Levi Strauss & Co. incorporated. Number 501 used for identification.
1902	Dies.

Summary

Born in Bavaria, Germany, Levi Strauss emigrated to the United States in 1847. He stopped long enough in New York to study his brother's dry goods business and learn to speak English. Then he joined the crowds heading west to the California gold rush. Strauss didn't do any digging though. Opening a dry goods wholesalers, he got his customers to dig into their pockets to buy his newfangled riveted "waist overalls," the toughest pants in the West. So popular was the new style of jeans that Strauss was known as the "cowboys' tailor." By the time of his death in 1902, jeans had made Strauss $6 million, a considerable amount more than most prospectors ever achieved.

Life and Career

Levi Strauss was not born in Nimes, France (from which denim—"of Nimes"—derives its name) but in Buttenheim, Bavaria, on February 26, 1829, one of seven siblings. Strauss's father died of tuberculosis in 1845, and two years later the Strauss family were in New York. Two of Levi's brothers, Jonas and Louis, had already made the journey and established J. Strauss Brothers & Co., a dry goods business where Levi worked. (Levi was christened Loeb, but in the 1850 census he is listed as Levy.)

In 1853 Strauss, now a U.S. citizen, headed for the West Coast to share in the prosperity generated by the California gold rush. He planned to make his fortune not from panning gold, but from selling provisions to the prospectors. He took the boat around the Cape of Good Hope. When he set out he carried cloth, silk, some luxury goods, and a roll of canvas, all donated by his brothers. When he arrived in San Francisco, he had sold them all except the canvas.

He planned to make his fortune not from panning gold, but from selling provisions to the prospectors.

Contribution

When Strauss arrived in San Francisco, so the story goes, a disheveled miner approached him demanding to know if he had any pants to sell. The rough terrain of the mines wore hard on the miners' pants; they were a valuable commodity. Strauss, spotting an opportunity, replied that although he hadn't brought any pants to sell, he could make a pair from the left over canvas. He did, the miner was happy, and so Strauss started in the pants business. It's a nice story but, although often recounted, probably not true.

What is known is that, more mundanely, Strauss established a San Francisco branch of the family dry goods business, opening first at 90 Sacramento Street under the name "Levi Strauss." The waterfront location was convenient for receiving goods delivered by boat from his brothers' business in New York.

Through the 1850s and 1860s Strauss expanded his business and moved addresses several times, each time to larger premises, finally coming to rest at 14–16 Battery Street. During this period the company was renamed Levi Strauss & Co. (1863). The premises at Battery Street were a grand affair, complete with an elevator and gas chandeliers, still a relative rarity at that time. As the dry-goods business expanded, Strauss slowly became a recognized and respected figure. He played an active role in the city's Jewish community and belonged to the San Francisco's first synagogue, the Temple Emanu-El.

When the riveted "waist overalls" first appeared on the market, Strauss was convinced that these new garments would be very successful. He was right. They became so popular through the Southwest that he was known as the "cowboys' tailor."

Enter Alkali Ike, a rough, tough prospector who worked the Comstock Lode mines in Nevada. The Comstock Lode was one of the greatest single mineral strikes in history, containing predominately silver deposits rather than gold. The citizens of the West swarmed to mine in the Washoe region of Nevada, hoping to get rich, and mining towns sprang up everywhere. The new metropolis of Virginia City, with 20,000 inhabitants, became the second largest city in the West. There, among the teeming transient population digging out their claims, sweated Alkali Ike, a man who suffered from pocket trouble.

Ike was sick of his pockets giving way under the weight of the valuable nuggets he carried in them. It was a common problem. "Nothing looks more slouchy in a workman than to see his pockets ripped open and hanging down, and no other part of the clothing is so apt to be torn and ripped as the pockets," commented the *Pacific Rural Press* of June 28, 1873. Ike complained bitterly to his local tailor, Jacob W. Davis, and insisted he find a solution. Davis, with a flash of inspiration, thought of riveting the material together with copper wire. A few weeks later Ike was back, this time not to complain but to thank his tailor for solving the problem.

Davis, who regularly bought material in bulk from Strauss in San Francisco, wrote to Strauss telling him of the popularity of this new design feature. Davis couldn't afford the patent fee of $68. He suggested that Strauss should help him safeguard his new discovery. Together they filed for a patent, which was granted on May 20, 1873. The day is now considered the birthday of the firm Levi Strauss & Co.. The new Strauss jeans sold for 22 cents a pair.

When the riveted "waist overalls" first appeared on the market, Strauss was convinced that these new garments would be very successful. He was right. They became so popular through the Southwest that he was known as the "cowboys' tailor." He brought Davis to San Francisco from Nevada to supervise the cutting production. As demand increased, production was scaled up and factories on Fremont and Market Streets were opened. Encouraged by the popularity of the waist overalls and denim, Strauss expanded his product line to include blanket-lined trousers and coats. To maintain the quality of the product, Strauss purchased the Mission and Pacific Woollen Mills in 1875.

Levi Strauss & Co. was incorporated in 1890, the same year that the number 501 was used to identify the denim waist overalls. Strauss by then had handed over the day-to-day running of his business to his nephews, Jacob, Sigmund, Louis, and Abraham. Much of Strauss's later life was dominated by philanthropic and other work in the community. He was a member of various organizations, including the San

Continually refining his "waist overalls," he produced a clothing item that became a national icon—19th-century Levi jeans can be worth up to $100,000.

Francisco Board of Trade, the Hebrew Board of Relief, the San Francisco Gas and Electric Company, and the Liverpool, London and Globe Insurance Company. He died in 1902, leaving close to $6 million in his estate.

Context and Conclusions

Levi Strauss was a clever man. Instead of risking anguish and heartbreak by joining the masses on the gold and silver strikes of the West, he found a more certain route to riches. Miners wore pants; miners worked over rough terrain; miners' pants wore out quickly; ergo miners needed stronger pants. The problem was how to make them stronger. Luck was with Strauss when Davis offered him the solution. But luck had little to do with Strauss's thorough exploitation of the new clothing technology. Continually refining his "waist overalls," he produced a clothing item that became a national icon—19th-century Levi jeans can be worth up to $100,000. Like Hershey bars and Coca-Cola, Levis are synonymous with American style and culture, and the word "jeans" is synonymous with Levis.

CLOSE BUT NO CIGAR
JOHN BARBOUR

In many ways the British equivalent of Levi Strauss, John Barbour left his family farm in Galloway, southwest Scotland, for South Shields, at the age of 20. There, from 1870, he worked as a traveling draper. He started his own firm, J. Barbour and Sons, supplying oilskins and other waterproofs to the sailors, fishermen, rivermen, and dockers who worked in the unpredictable North Sea weather. Before long his business had become an international one, supplying countries across the world via his mail-order catalog. He died in 1918. Today the Barbour raincoat has taken on an iconic status in the United Kingdom.

For More Information

Book:

Finlayson, Iain. *Denim. An American Legend.* New York: Simon and Schuster, 1990.

Eiji Toyoda

1913	Born.
1933	Cousin starts automobile production.
1936	Toyoda joins the firm, which is renamed Toyota.
1950	Toyoda visits Ford River Rouge plant in Dearborn, Michigan.
1955	Crown model successful in Japan but not in United States.
1967	Becomes President of Toyota.
1968	Successfully launches Corolla in United States.
1975	Toyota replaces Volkswagen as number one imported car in United States.
1989	Launches luxury Lexus model.
1994	Resigns.

Summary

If Eiji Toyoda hadn't joined his family business, the Toyota name might have been associated with the textile industry instead of automobiles.

Toyoda helped to grow a thriving automobile business from a loom manufacturing company. He joined the company in 1936 and was responsible for recruiting the best research engineers and organizing production. Toyota's breakthrough came when Toyoda visited Ford's Rouge automobile plant in the 1950s. It was a revelation to him. He returned to Japan determined to combine the best of U.S. manufacturing processes with his own innovative approach to production. The result was the Toyota Production System. Successful models—from the Corolla to the introduction of the Lexus—paved the way for the company's global success.

Life and Career

It is no surprise that Eiji Toyoda grew up to be an industrialist. Born on September 12, 1913, Toyoda spent much of his childhood in and around his father's textile mill near Nagoya. From his earliest years he was surrounded by both business and heavy machinery.

The driving force behind the textile business was Toyoda's uncle, Rashomon Sakichi Toyoda. Sakichi was a carpenter by trade and an inventor by nature. In 1929 the British company Platt Brothers paid Sakichi £100,000 for the rights to a textile loom he had invented. Sakichi put the money to one side to invest in automobile production.

Given the nature of the family business, Eiji Toyoda's choice of an engineering degree was a natural one. He started his studies at Tokyo Imperial University in 1933. While Toyoda was taking his degree his cousin Kiichiro, Sakichi's eldest son, was setting up an automobile plant at the Toyoda

The driving force behind the textile business was Toyoda's uncle, Rashomon Sakichi Toyoda. Sakichi was a carpenter by trade and an inventor by nature.

Automatic Loom Works. In 1936, his degree completed, Toyoda joined his cousin at the plant. In that year the company changed its name from Toyoda Automatic Loom Works to Toyota.

Contribution

Toyoda's first assignment was to organize the company's research facility, hiring talented scientists and engineers to work on research and development. Next he worked on the shop floor in production planning.

At that time Toyota was producing a car designed to be built with Chevrolet parts. Toyota's first cars rolled off the production line in 1936. The timing was unfortunate: the advent of World War II and Japan's entry into the war in December 1941 meant that Toyota's production expertise had to be redirected toward the manufacture of trucks for the war effort.

After the war Eiji Toyoda made plans to establish a chinaware business. Kiichiro Toyoda was diversifying the company, expecting the occupying forces to place limitations on the automobile business. Instead, as Japan underwent a period of reconstruction, the Toyota car plant was called upon to build vehicles to help get the country moving again.

Despite the boost in production, trading conditions were still extremely tough; Toyota was driven to the brink of bankruptcy. The company was saved only by dramatic cuts in the work force, which Toyoda had the painful task of enforcing. He also created a new company, Toyota Motor Sales, to help ease cash flow problems and satisfy his bankers' concerns.

It wasn't until the 1950s that Toyota firmly established itself as a major car manufacturer. The breakthrough came when Toyoda visited Ford's immense River Rouge plant in Dearborn, Michigan. Toyota had by then been in the car business for 13 years and had produced just over 2,500 automobiles. The River Rouge plant turned out a staggering 8,000 vehicles a day. Impressed with the scale of U.S. automobile production, Toyoda realized that if he could combine the best of U.S. and Japanese production methods, Toyota could be a world-beater.

With the help of his production guru Taichi Ohno, Toyoda established the Toyota Production System (TPS), also known as "lean production." It was a revolutionary approach to manufacturing comprising three main elements. The first is just-in-time production. There is no point in producing cars simply hoping that customers will buy them. Waste (Japanese *muda*) is bad; therefore production must be linked to the market's requirements. Second, responsibility for quality rests with everyone, and any quality defect needs to be rectified as soon as it is identified. The third element is the "value stream": instead of seeing the company as a series of unrelated products and processes, it should be seen as a continuous and uniform whole—a stream that includes suppliers as well as customers.

Toyota's first full scale production car, the Crown, proved a somewhat shaky start. Driven off the production line by Eiji Toyoda—dressed in a tuxedo—on New Year's Day, 1955, the Crown was a success in Japan, but it failed to make any impression on the U.S. market when it was introduced in 1957. Designed for Japanese roads, it was slow and prone to overheating—problems that made it ill-suited to U.S. highways.

Persistence eventually paid off and by the 1960s Toyota cars were a hit, with the Corona and Corolla both selling well. The success of the Corolla in 1968 enabled the company to make a big leap forward, and by 1975 Toyota had replaced Volkswagen as the number one imported car in the United States. In 1984 the company entered a joint venture with General Motors to build Toyota vehicles in the United States. Along the way Toyota established an unrivaled reputation for build quality. But it was the Toyota Lexus that finally secured the company's reputation in the United States.

The Lexus was a personal triumph for Toyoda. In August 1983 he had convened a top-secret meeting inside the company, asking those present, "Can we create a luxury car to challenge the very best?" The answer was a resounding yes.

In the luxury car market Toyota faced competition from a variety of established brands, including Mercedes and BMW. Undaunted by the scale of the task, Toyota created a new brand—the Lexus—to create psychological distance from the other Toyota value-for-money models. Toyoda neutralized any concerns over the reliability and quality of the Lexus by insisting that the company should out-engineer Mercedes and BMW. The eventual result was the Lexus LS400. It took seven years, $2 billion, 1,400 engineers, 2,300 technicians, and 450 prototypes—and generated 200 patents. The Lexus was tested in Japan on miles of carefully built highways that exactly imitated roads in the United States, Germany, and the United Kingdom. Toyota even reproduced foreign road signs.

Toyota is now the dominant car manufacturer in Japan and the third biggest carmaker in the world (behind General Motors and Ford). It now sells nearly 1.5 million cars in the United States every year. Toyoda stepped down as President in 1994.

Context and Conclusions

Eiji Toyoda didn't found the Toyota Motor Corporation, but he did help make it a world-beater.

After an inauspicious attempt to crack the U.S. market with the Crown, Toyoda was quick to admit that Toyota would need an extra competitive edge to compete with the likes of Ford and General Motors. It was no good trying to compete on price alone; instead Toyoda concentrated on efficiency and quality.

He employed the inventive Taichi Ohno to help develop a new production system that came to be known as the Toyota Production System. Through quality and reliability, Toyota took on the great U.S. automobile manufacturers and emerged victorious. And if imitation is the sincerest form of flattery, the modest Toyoda must be embarrassed by the number of U.S. firms that have tried to adopt Toyota's production methods.

For More Information

Books:

Braddon, Russell. *The Other 100 Years War: Japan's Bid for Supremacy 1941–2041*. London: Collins, 1983.

Toyoda, Eiji. *Toyota: Fifty Years in Motion*. Tokyo: Kodansha International, 1987.

Web site:

Toyota: **www.toyota.com**

Robert Edward Turner III

1938	Born.
1970	Acquires the UHF station, WTCG.
1976	WTCG becomes WTBS and goes nationwide. Transmits across the United States via satellite. Buys the major-league baseball team, the Atlanta Braves.
1977	Wins America's Cup with his yacht *Courageous*.
1980	Cable News Network launched.
1986	Acquires MGM Entertainment Company.
1991	*Time Magazine's* "Man of the Year."
1994	Turner Broadcasting Systems merges with New Line Cinema.
1996	Turner Broadcasting Systems merges with Time Warner.
2001	Time Warner merger with AOL approved.
2001	Loses control of Turner Broadcasting.
2002	AOL Time-Warner posts $100 million loss.
2003	Turner Foundation loses value and declines current fund requests.
2003	Resigns Chairmanship of AOL Time-Warner.

Summary

Robert Edward (Ted) Turner III (1938–) started in business in unfortunate circumstances after his father's suicide. Showing considerable resilience, he went on to improve on his father's business and, ultimately, to help create the biggest entertainment and media company in the world—AOL Time Warner. Turner became President and chief operating officer of the Turner Advertising Company in 1963 and set out on a trail of acquisitions and channel launches. A UHF station, professional sports teams, Headline News, TNT, The Cartoon Network, Turner Classic Movies, New Line Cinema: all these and many more came under Turner's control as he built his company—the Turner Broadcasting System—into a media giant. Turner is probably best known for the creation of the news station Cable News Network, CNN, in June 1980, and the part he played in the formation of AOL Time Warner in 2000/2001.

Life and Career

Robert Edward Turner III was born in Cincinnati, Ohio, in 1938. His checkered school career was notable for eccentric and unconventional behavior rather than academic excellence. At McCallie, an exclusive school for boys in Chattanooga, Tennessee, he was an unruly pupil who showed a peculiar penchant for taxidermy and for catching squirrels in pillowcases. McCallie's method of punishing offenders was to issue demerits. Each demerit required the recipient to walk a quarter of a mile. Turner earned over 1,000 demerits in his first year, farther than any pupil could walk in the time available. The school was forced to reinvent its disciplinary methods especially for him.

At Brown University Turner continued to challenge authority. Eventually, having been caught with a woman in his room, he was asked to leave but not before he had made a name for himself on the university sailing team. Sailing was to remain an abiding passion and he later won the America's Cup in 1977 with his yacht *Courageous*.

After college Turner returned home to work in his father's advertising billboard business. His father made him manager of the firm's operation in Macon, Georgia. Turner married and settled down to a tough schedule, working 15 hours per day for six and a half days each week. Like his father, he was a natural salesman making fast progress in the business.

Turner's often difficult relationship with his father came to a shocking end in March 1963 when he was just 24. His father, under severe pressure at work, took a silver .38 revolver and shot himself in the head. In these terrible circumstances Turner became President and C.O.O. of the Turner Advertising Company.

Contribution

Turner expanded the company into television with an audacious move to acquire the UHF station WTCG in 1970. At the time WTCG was the worst placed of the major television channels in Atlanta. Turner engineered a deal that involved taking Turner Advertising public, acquiring the assets of WTCG, and forming a new company, Turner Communications. Determined to lift the station's fortunes, he changed the programming schedule and fed the viewers a diet of reruns—classic shows and black and white movies. It worked. Bemused critics could only watch as the viewing figures shot up and the advertising revenue flooded in. In 1976 the station went nationwide as WTBS, transmitting to cable systems across the United States via satellite—it was the start of the "superstation concept."

Turner continued to diversify and expand, and not always into obvious areas. In 1976 he bought a major league baseball team, the Atlanta Braves, and in 1977 the Atlanta Hawks of the National Basketball Association. Once again he was ahead of the game. His instincts told him that televised sports would attract a big audience.

In 1980 Turner used the profits from Turner Broadcasting System to launch CNN (Cable News Network). The critics were scathing, predicting inevitable failure for the 24/7 all-news network. But once again Turner proved that, despite his often dogmatic approach, when it came to business he knew best. "I am the right man in the right place at the right time," he said. "Not me alone, but all the people who think the world can be brought together by telecommunications."

CNN was a hit. It brought news, like the Reagan assassination attempt, to viewers as events unfurled. It revolutionized the news industry. CNN cemented its reputation with its coverage of the Gulf War when, for the first time, a TV audience could watch a war in real time, from the comfort of their armchairs.

Turner continued to collect television stations: Headline News (1982), CNN International (1985), TNT (1988), SportsSouth (1990), The Cartoon Network (1992), Turner Classic Movies (1994), CNNfn (1995), and CNN SI (1997) were all added to the network. Shortly after Castle Rock Entertainment joined Turner Broadcasting in 1993, Turner merged TBS with New Line Cinema.

Not everything Turner touched turned to gold. Eager to purchase a film studio, he made a bid for CBS. The hostile takeover bid failed. Another Turner idea, the "Checkout Channel," providing in-store news and information, proved a disappointment. Turner also paid $1.6 billion for the MGM film library, a sum many commentators considered too generous.

In 1996 he completed the biggest deal of his career to date, when he merged TBS with Time Warner. Holding 10% of Time Warner, Turner had the largest single shareholding. It was an astute move, leaving him well positioned to profit from the development of a new communication phenomenon—the Internet. He assumed the role of Vice-Chairman in the new organization, taking responsibility for Time Warner's Cable Networks division, which included the assets of Turner Broadcasting System, Inc. (TBS, Inc.), Home Box Office, Cinemax, and Time Warner's interests in Comedy Central and Court TV. He was also responsible for New Line Cinema and the company's professional sports teams.

In 2001 Turner was involved in one of the biggest mergers of the postwar period when AOL merged with Time Warner to create the largest entertainment conglomerate in the world. Time Warner's shareholders received 45% of the new company to AOL's 55%. Turner became Vice-Chairman and senior adviser of AOL Time Warner.

It proved an ill-fated move. Almost immediately Turner found himself side-lined and he lost control of Turner Broadcasting, the company he had built. In a bad year, he was involved in a divorce with Jane Fonda and lost his World Wrestling Championship, along with its star Hulk Hogan, to long-time rival World Wrestling Federation. Worse was to follow in 2002 as AOL Time-Warner posted a record loss of $100 billion. In 2003, he resigned his Chairmanship. The loss also hit the Turner Foundation badly since much of its value derived from AOL Time-Warner investments. In 1997, the Foundation hit the headlines when it made a $1 billion donation to the UN for humanitarian projects. In sharp contrast, 2003 saw the Foundation unable to meet any funding requests.

Context and Conclusions

Turner's career is distinguished by relentless drive, an uncanny ability to predict consumer demand, and a supreme confidence in his own vision. Competitiveness and drive are evident in his sailing achievements, too. He could have made a good living as an international yachtsman. Probably the best illustration of Turner's qualities, though, is the founding of CNN. Critics derided the idea of a nonstop news network. Turner thought differently and pursued his vision doggedly. He was right, the critics were wrong, and CNN's coverage of the Gulf War has become part of media folklore. Turner may make an occasional bad call, but more often than not his instincts have proved successful. It is this quality of vision, and having the guts to execute it, that has made him one of the world's great media magnates.

For More Information

Book:
Bibb, Porter. *It Ain't As Easy As It Looks: Ted Turner's Amazing Story*. New York: Crown Publishers, 1993.

Web site:
CNN.com: **www.cnn.com**

Cornelius Vanderbilt

1794	Born.
1810	Mother gives him $100 to clear and plant eight-acre field. He buys a boat with the proceeds.
1812	U.S. war with England.
1817	Robert Fulton and Robert R. Livingston introduce steamboats.
1829	Uses savings to start a steamboat business.
1851	Forms the Accessory Transit Company.
1863	Has amassed a fortune of $40 million. Switches focus to railroads.
1869	Merges the Hudson River Railroad with the New York Central system.
1877	Dies.

Summary

Cornelius "Commodore" Vanderbilt is one of America's greatest-ever businessmen. Applying the principles of economy, competition, and innovation, Vanderbilt expanded from a small-time ferry operator to a shipping and railroad magnate. In his lifetime Vanderbilt amassed fabulous wealth—some $105 million. Yet he did so by genuinely improving the lot of people. Wherever Vanderbilt opened for business, the prices came down and the services improved. He risked arrest to bust state-subsidized monopolies by running competing services illegally. By eradicating state monopolies, Vanderbilt increased the incentive to invest in improving technology to provide a competitive advantage. It was a classic case of how capitalism and competition can deliver a better deal for the consumer, and benefit a nation's economy.

Life and Career

Cornelius Vanderbilt was born on May 27, 1794 on Staten Island, New York. His father was a farmer who sold produce in the markets of New York, sailing across the harbor to get there.

Vanderbilt paid little attention to school, preferring the outdoor life. As a child he could barely read and write. He did, however, take a keen interest in business. In 1810, when he was 16, Vanderbilt's mother gave him $100 to clear and plant an eight-acre field. Instead of frittering the money away, the enterprising Vanderbilt used it to buy a small flat-bottom sailing boat. He then started a ferry business, taking passengers between Staten Island and New York City. The business was almost sunk in the first few weeks when the boat hit an obstacle, but both boat and business survived.

The ferry business taught Vanderbilt some important commercial lessons. Known locally as "Cornele, the boatman," he discovered that by taking any fare, no matter how rough the weather, he obtained a reputation for both reliability and a willingness to please the customer. This in turn brought him repeat business. He also learned the simple economics of low costs, high turnover, consistently undercutting his rivals, and filling his boat.

Contribution

Like many other entrepreneurs, when war with England came in 1812 Vanderbilt saw the conflict as an opportunity to improve his business. As well as continuing to ply his normal routes, he was awarded an army contract and also made extra money ferrying food along the Hudson River to a blockaded New York City. With the profits, he bought an interest in two more boats.

By the age of 24, Vanderbilt had saved $9,000, expanded his business to ply the coastal routes between Chesapeake Bay and New York, and developed a retail business selling provisions to ships in the harbor. In addition, he owned interests in a number of boats. Things were going well for Vanderbilt when, in 1817, the steamboats arrived. Entrepreneurs Robert Fulton and Robert R. Livingston had brought their new technology to New York and were granted a monopoly on all steamboat traffic for a period of 30 years.

Realizing that sailboats were about to become obsolete, Vanderbilt sold up rather than persist with outdated technology. He went to work for a small steamboat operator, Thomas Gibbons, a wealthy attorney and plantation owner, and learned how to sail the steamboat. As soon as he was able, he began ferrying passengers from New Jersey to Manhattan in direct contravention of the monopoly. He persuaded passengers to use the service by undercutting Fulton and Livingston's $4 ticket price, charging only $1. The loss was made up on food and drink prices.

In 1824, the United States Supreme Court declared the Fulton and Livingston monopoly illegal. Now Vanderbilt could operate openly. With the monopoly broken, things changed quickly in the steamboat business. Prices came down, competitors entered the market and boat technology improved. In a competitive environment where innovation was rewarded, Vanderbilt thrived. In 1829 he used his savings to start his own steamboat business. He put together a connected service—steamboat, stagecoach, steamboat—from New York City to Philadelphia. And, in what became a classic Vanderbilt business strategy, he immediately slashed prices. The competition, fearing a price war, gathered enough money together to pay him to go away.

Vanderbilt had discovered a new way to make money. Keen to protect the market and unwilling to cut their profits to provide real value to the customer, the lazy established operators would rather pay Vanderbilt to stop operating. It was the same story in the Hudson River. Up against the Hudson River Steamboat Association, Vanderbilt cut fares savagely until he was carrying passengers for free and, as before, making the losses up on the food. It wasn't long before the Steamboat Association caved in. They gave Vanderbilt $100,000, as well as ten annual payments of $5,000, in return for him leaving the area.

Before long, Vanderbilt—now Commodore Vanderbilt—owned over 100 steamboats and was worth many millions of dollars. His next move was inspired by the discovery of gold in California in 1848. The ensuing gold rush created a demand for transport from East Coast to West. Initially clipper boats took passengers around Cape Horn—a journey that took 90 days. Next, an alternative route was organized that involved land travel across the Isthmus of Panama. It was at this point that the ever-innovative Vanderbilt entered the fray. Studying the maps he discovered a new route, which involved sailing inland along the San Juan River, on across Lake Nicaragua, and finally across the shortest 12-mile land gap to the Pacific Ocean.

Vanderbilt formed the Accessory Transit Company, struck a deal with the Nicaraguan government, constructed a port on the Pacific Coast and, in 1851, started sailing the new route. As usual his fares were cheaper—$400 compared to the competition's $600. And as usual, after some political wrangling and maneuvering, the competition offered Vanderbilt $672,000 not to operate a route to California. His first foray into the transatlantic and shipping routes was no less successful. Used to competing with government subsidized business by now, Vanderbilt cut fares, built volume, and used the latest technology in shipping so that, when government subsidy was finally withdrawn from the competition, he was best-placed to take advantage.

By 1863 Vanderbilt, in his sixties, had amassed a fortune of $40 million. For most people this would have been enough. Not for him. Over the next 13 years, abandoning water for land, Vanderbilt switched from old technology—steamboats, to new technology—the railroads.

By 1869, Vanderbilt had taken control of the Hudson River Railroad and the New York Central system. He merged the two companies, gained control of railroad lines from New York to Chicago, and created a consolidated railroad system between the two cities. Toward the end of his career, Vanderbilt continued to apply the principles of competitiveness, low costs, and innovation to the business. He upgraded iron rails with steel imported from England, doubled tracks, and built the Grand Central Depot in New York, the largest railroad terminal in the world.

By the time of his death on January 4, 1877, Vanderbilt commanded a railroad empire that extended over 740 miles of track and included 486 locomotives and 9,000 freight cars. Every year thousands of passengers were transported courtesy of Vanderbilt. When he died, he left a fortune of $105 million in his will.

Context and Conclusions

Cornelius Vanderbilt was simply the most brilliant businessman of his generation. He combined an innate understanding of the principles of economics with a consummate grasp of business strategy. Everything that Vanderbilt touched turned to gold. Only once was he ever bested. When he tried to corner the stock in the New York and Erie Railroad Company, notorious financiers Jay Gould and Jim Fisk merely kept on issuing new shares until finally Vanderbilt had to give up. But no one ever beat him fairly. Why? Because Vanderbilt understood that delivering a reasonable service, at a low cost, would always win out over a government-subsidized monopoly. Rather than fleece consumers by providing a substandard, outdated, expensive service, Vanderbilt gave his customers innovation and value for money. In doing so he helped drive economic growth on both the East and West Coast, and to fast-track technological innovation in transport. And, in the process, he became fabulously wealthy.

For More Information
Books:

Metzman, Gustav. *Commodore Vanderbilt (1794–1877): Forefather of the New York Central.* New York: The Newcomen Society of England, 1946.

Smith, Arthur D. Howden. *Commodore Vanderbilt: An Epic of American Achievement.* New York: Robert McBride, 1927.

Samuel Walton

1918	Born.
1945	Gets franchise for Ben Franklin store in Newport, Arkansas.
1953	Obtains pilot's license.
1962	Opens first Wal-Mart discount store in Rogers, Arkansas.
1964	Second Wal-Mart store in the town of Harrison, Arkansas.
1970	Raises $5 million on the stock market through a public offering of Wal-Mart stock.
1970s	Builds 452 new stores.
1974	Retires for two years.
1980s	Builds 1,237 new stores.
1985	Wal-Mart stock makes him wealthiest man in America.
1987	1,000th store opens.
1991	Wal-Mart overtakes Sears to become biggest retailer in the United States.
1992	Dies.

Summary

Samuel Moore Walton created a retail empire after the fashion of the great Frank Woolworth. A hard upbringing in the depression-ridden Midwest was followed by college and then commerce. Having sampled the retail business courtesy of JCPenney, Walton opened a Ben Franklin store with $25,000 borrowed from his father-in-law. When he lost the lease on his first store he simply opened another, and then another. Soon he had a small collection of retail outlets. To keep tight control of them, he would fly himself from one to the other. Walton opened the first Wal-Mart in 1962 and the second in 1964. By 1987 there were over 1,000. At the time of his death in 1992, Walton had made millions from his retail business, and so had many of his shareholders. One hundred shares bought in 1970 for a mere $1,650 were, by 1992, worth a staggering $2.6 million.

Life and Career

Samuel Moore Walton was born in Oklahoma on March 29, 1918. His father was employed variously as a farm loan appraiser, a real estate salesman, and an insurance salesman. Walton and his family moved from small town to small town in Missouri as his father pursued work. When they finally settled in Columbia, Missouri in 1933, Walton helped bolster the family income by taking on several jobs.

His work commitments did not prevent Walton from attending school. He was bright enough and hardworking enough to gain a place at the University of Missouri at Columbia, where he studied for a business degree, graduating in 1940. After college he decided to take a position as a management trainee in Des Moines, Iowa, at the retail store JCPenney. It was here that he learned many of the management techniques that he was to apply later—these included fostering a sense of inclusion by calling his employees "associates" and managing by walking about or, in Walton's case, by flying about.

Walton enlisted to fight in World War II. Unfit for full service because of a heart irregularity, he spent the war in the United States serving in the military police. He also married during the war, in 1943. It was a fortunate marriage. When Walton returned to civilian life at the end of the war, he decided to set up in business himself rather than return to JCPenney. He borrowed $20,000 from his father-in-law and bought a Ben Franklin store in Newport, Arkansas. It was September 1945, Walton was 27, and he was in the retail business.

Contribution

Walton proved tough competition for the nearby better established businesses. One such was the Sterling Variety store, where Bud Hewitt, who would become a great friend of his, worked. In 1947, however, they were in competition, and when Hewitt had a run on rayon underwear for women (he was cleaned out of stock), Walton was determined to outdo him. Rather than place an order, Walton went to Little Rock and bought the distributor. At a stroke, he cut the competition out of the market and secured his own store's supply of lingerie.

In 1950, despite his success, Walton was unable to renew the lease on his Newport store and was forced to sell out. He didn't quit though; he merely moved to nearby Bentonville where he bought another Ben Franklin store, calling it "Walton's Five and Dime." Before long he had added to his burgeoning retail empire by acquiring a number of other stores in the region. They were spread out over a wide area and potentially difficult to keep in touch with and manage satisfactorily. He solved the problem imaginatively; he gained his pilot's license in 1953 and acquired a decrepit prewar airplane, in which he simply flew from one store to the next.

Walton then cast his eye further afield. He began by visiting a couple of Ben Franklin "self-service" stores in Minnesota. The idea of self-service was then a new one, and the fact that it enabled the owner to pass on cheaper prices to the customer appealed to him. Back in Bentonville he opened his own self-service store. One of Walton's greatest strengths was that he was always willing to embrace innovation, whether it was self-service or, as in the early 1960s, the discount store concept.

The first Wal-Mart opened in 1962. It owed a great deal to the Kmart store in Chicago, a shop that Walton had visited to observe its operations at first hand. It was tough going initially. It wasn't easy to stock a full range of goods, since suppliers were reluctant to be associated with mass merchandising. Walton spent much of his time over the next few years experimenting with different layouts and different mixes of stock to create the perfect discount store. All this time he continued to earn the bulk of his income from his chain of Ben Franklin stores. The second Wal-Mart opened in 1964 in Harrison, Arkansas. The first day was a disaster, primarily because of the inhospitable temperature of 115 degrees. The manure from the donkeys providing rides was trodden through the store. The watermelons outside popped in the heat. Local businessman David Glass uttered the legendary observation: "It was the worst retail store I've ever seen." Glass went on to become President of the Wal-Mart Corporation.

In 1970 Walton raised $5 million on the stock market through a public offering of Wal-Mart stock. The 1970 financing enabled Walton to construct six more stores as well as a distribution center. In fact, from the 1970s onward, the rate of construction of new Wal-Mart stores increased phenomenally; 452 were built during the 1970s and 1,237 in the 1980s.

As the Wal-Mart empire blossomed, Walton spent more and more time keeping his employees happy and up to scratch. He would still travel from store to store by plane and, where he found a store that didn't meet his high standards, he would close it on the spot and not reopen it until it was ready. Somehow Walton managed to keep in touch with his thousands of employees. He wrote a monthly column in the company newspaper, *Wal-Mart World*, he personally replied to letters from staff raising questions or suggesting ideas, and he insisted on attending the opening of new stores whenever possible. His commitment to the staff in his business was illustrated in 1983 when he promised to dance down Wall Street in a grass skirt if the company posted profit targets. It did, and Wall Street was graced with the sight of Walton dancing the hula.

By 1987 Wal-Mart had opened its 1,000th store and was an early adopter of network technology linking all the stores through a satellite system, something that, sadly, obviated the need for Walton's airborne excursions, much to the relief of the shareholders. They profited greatly from his canny business sense. One hundred shares bought in 1970 for a mere $1,650 were, by the time of Walton's death, worth a staggering $2.6 million.

In 1968 Walton was diagnosed with bone marrow cancer. He died on April 6, 1992.

Context and Conclusions

Frank Woolworth pioneered the concept of the five and dime store. He was also one of the first mass-market retailers with thousands of stores across the world. Sam Walton was a retailer out of the same mold, the Frank Woolworth of his generation who steadily built up a network of mass-merchandise discount stores under the Wal-Mart name. Always keen to embrace innovation, he pioneered the self-service concept, was one of the first retailers to adopt network technology via satellite to link stores, and championed hypermarts. A stickler for high standards, he also was known to close down stores immediately if he felt they failed to come up to scratch. One of the greatest retailers of his generation, he died one of the richest men in the world, having built an empire of over 1,000 stores.

CLOSE BUT NO CIGAR

SEBASTIAN SPERING KRESGE

Kresge was a traveling tinware salesman who founded a chain of S.S. Kresge discount retail stores in 1912. All the goods were priced at less than a dime. World War I inflation pushed the price limit up to a dollar. Kresge opened his first Kmart store in 1962. He died in 1966, the same year company sales topped $1 billion.

RICHARD WARREN SEARS

Sears was station agent for the Minnesota and St. Louis Railroad in North Redwood when he became the beneficiary of an unwanted consignment of watches. He sold them to other station agents and started the R. W. Sears Watch Company in 1886. This became Sears, Roebuck, & Co. in 1893 with the addition of Alvah C. Roebuck, a watchmaker. Sears went on to build the biggest retail business in the United States through the use of the mail-order catalog.

For More Information
Web site:
Wal-Mart: **www.walmart.com**

Paul Warburg

1868	Born.
1893	Embarks on around-the-world trip.
1895	Marries Nina Loeb in the United States.
1907	Publicly criticizes U.S. banking system.
1910	Outlines plan for U.S. Federal Reserve Bank at a secret meeting with Senator Nelson Aldrich and others.
1911	Naturalized as U.S. citizen.
1913	Federal Reserve Act passed. Warburg is appointed to the Federal Reserve Board.
1918	Forced to resign from the Federal Reserve.
1921	Launches International Acceptance Bank.
1932	Dies.

Summary

Paul Warburg (1868–1932) was born to be a banker in the German family firm M. M. Warburg and Company. Instead he followed his heart, marrying the U.S.-born Nina Loeb in 1895, moving to the United States, and becoming a partner in the prestigious Wall Street bank Kuhn, Loeb, and Company.

Shocked by the primitive financial systems in place, the scholarly Warburg became a prominent figure on the strength of his published papers on banking and finance. His ideas drew the attention of the powerful Rhode Island senator, Nelson Aldrich. In 1910 Aldrich invited Warburg to a secret conference at Jekyll Island, Georgia. On that trip Warburg was instrumental in laying down the foundations for the U.S. Federal Reserve Bank. A friend to both Republicans and Democrats in power, Warburg was eventually appointed to the board of the central bank he did so much to design.

Life and Career

Paul Moritz Warburg was born in 1868 into a wealthy banking family in Hamburg, Germany. In each generation, the sons were groomed to take their place at the head of the family bank, M. M. Warburg and Company, founded in the 1700s. Warburg accordingly received the finest education money could buy—with the emphasis on banking and finance.

Leaving school at 16, Warburg went to college and then gained hands-on work experience in Europe's major cities. He worked for two years in London, most of the time being spent in a banking and discount firm, with a stint as a stockbroker. He later went to France, where he worked for a Russian bank, before returning to Hamburg. In 1893 he was sent on a trip around the world, taking in India, China, Japan, and the United States.

Upon his return to Hamburg Warburg was deemed fit to become a partner in the family's banking firm. A leading role in the family business was his birthright. Yet Warburg passed up a comfortable life in Hamburg for love. Returning to the United States in 1895, he married Nina Loeb. Fortunately for him, Nina's father was Solomon Loeb, one of the most powerful men on Wall Street and a partner in the international banking house Kuhn, Loeb, and Company.

Contribution

Initially the couple settled in Germany. But when his wife's parents fell ill and wanted their daughter nearby, Warburg accepted the offer of a partnership in Kuhn, Loeb in New York City.

In a foreign country and unable to speak English well, Warburg kept his head down and worked hard. He was involved in a number of multimillion dollar deals, including the financing of the Pennsylvania Railroad's development of the railroad in New York, which involved tunneling underneath Manhattan.

Away from the commercial realities of banking Warburg was a scholarly man who cast a critical eye over the U.S. banking system. In his view, U.S. banking and finance was a shambles compared with the sophisticated banking system in Europe. But as an outsider Warburg was reluctant to comment, although he recorded his thoughts in an essay that he locked away in a drawer. By 1907, with a severe financial crisis impending, Warburg found it too much to bear, and urged on by his colleagues and acquaintances he went on record with his opinions about the shortcomings of the U.S. financial system.

"The United States is at about the same point that had been reached by Europe at the time of the Medicis," Warburg wrote. "We have been shown bricks of the time of Hammurabi, the Babylonian monarch, evidencing the sale of a crop and similar transactions, and I am inclined to believe that it was as easy to transfer ownership of these bricks from one person to another as it is today for an American bank to realize upon its discounted paper, if indeed it was not easier." The Americans didn't take kindly to being compared to the Babylonians, but the normally unassuming Warburg had a point and they knew it.

Warburg worked on a solution to the banking deficiencies, writing a number of technical papers on the subject and becoming known as a strong proponent of a central bank. These papers, including "A Plan for a Modified Central Bank," attracted the interest of Senator Nelson Aldrich, the head of the National Monetary Commission. This body had been convened to investigate a central bank and other ways to reform the country's monetary and banking systems. In November 1910 Aldrich organized a secret conference on Jekyll Island, an exclusive resort for millionaires off the coast of Georgia.

Aldrich took a select few men with him: Frank Vanderlip, President of National City Bank; Harry P. Davison, a partner at J. P. Morgan; A. Piatt Andrew, assistant secretary of the treasury; Benjamin Strong, Vice-President of Banker's Trust; and Paul Warburg. They were some of the most intelligent, experienced, and powerful men in U.S. financial circles. The trip was proposed under the cover of a duck hunt; its true purpose had nothing to do with ducks, although to complete the deception the men were required to wear duck-hunting clothes—and Warburg had to borrow a rifle. Because of the secrecy of their mission the men were to be referred to throughout the operation by their first names only. Their real mission was to develop a plan for banking and currency reform to put before Congress. Working day and night, the group thrashed out the basis for a new banking system founded on a central bank.

After about ten days they had drafted a proposal that called for a central bank based in

Washington and supported by regional branches throughout the United States. The proposal, known as the Aldrich Plan, was a team effort, but Warburg is credited with the most significant contributions to its formulation before, during, and after the Jekyll Island meeting. The plan was presented to the public in January 1911 and endorsed by the National Monetary Commission in January 1912.

After the Jekyll Island outing Warburg went on a crusade to educate the business community and the public. A persuasive advocate for the new banking system, he was appointed head of the National Citizens League for the Promotion of Sound Banking. Warburg resisted political partisanship, working with both Republicans and Democrats. When Democrat Woodrow Wilson took office before the Aldrich Plan could be passed into law, the new President agreed to use the plan as the foundation for reform.

Despite some antibanker sentiment, Wilson appointed Warburg to the Federal Reserve Board after the Federal Reserve Act was passed in December 1913. Warburg accepted, and, resigning from his partnerships at Kuhn, Loeb and M. M. Warburg, he happily traded a salary of $500,000 for one of $12,000.

But it was bad timing for Warburg. The war against Germany was looming and the Federal Reserve was no place for a man many still regarded as a German. Woodrow Wilson refused to renew Warburg's term on the Federal Reserve Board; Warburg was forced to resign. He subsequently went on to found the International Acceptance Bank but never recovered from what he felt was his betrayal at the hands of the politicians. He died on January 24, 1932.

Context and Conclusions

Paul Warburg was an exceptional man. Somehow he shrugged off the handicap of being a foreign national living in the United States and having a poor grasp of English (his children had to edit his prose). Overcoming this burden through an understated persistence and intellectual brilliance, he rose to the attention of the men in power. Commonly described as shy or mild-mannered, Warburg might easily have kept his head down and settled for a quiet life. Instead he opened himself to criticism by publicly addressing the deficiencies in America's banking and finance systems. He may not have founded a famous company, or even restored the fortunes of a well-known brand, but in playing an instrumental role in creating and structuring the U.S. Federal Reserve Bank, Warburg deserves his place as one of the great business leaders of the 20th century.

For More Information

Book:

Chernow, Ron. *The Warburgs: The Twentieth-century Odyssey of a Remarkable Jewish Family.* New York: Vintage, 1994.

Thomas J. Watson, Sr.

1874	Born.
1893	Sells musical instruments.
1898	Joins the National Cash Register Company.
1914	Joins Computing-Tabulating-Recording Co. Revenues $4 million.
1924	Company's name changed to International Business Machines Corp.
1944	IBM builds world's first large-scale computer.
1946	IBM revenues $115 million.
1952	IBM manufactures world's first commercially available computer, the 701.
1956	Dies.

Summary

Thomas J. Watson, Sr. is reported to have made the unfortunately inaccurate prediction, "I think that there may be a world market for possibly five computers." But his misjudgement didn't prevent him from building the industrial and technological titan IBM. Watson graduated from hawking pianos to selling the cash register. He learned his trade under John Patterson, who taught him about commerce and social responsibility. When Watson was sacked by Patterson after an argument, he took with him progressive ideas about corporate culture and the working environment, and a small sign that said "THINK!" At Computing-Tabulating-Recording Co., the company that eventually became IBM, he engineered a corporate transformation, pumping money into research and development, nurturing exciting new technologies, and galvanizing the sales force.

Life and Career

Thomas J. Watson, Sr. was born in Campbell, New York, on February 17, 1874. Son of an upstate New York farmer, Watson's upbringing was a traditional, rural 19th-century one. Life was shaped by a strong moral code. Dignity, respect for others, self-respect, conscientious work, optimism, and loyalty were values ingrained in Watson throughout his childhood. Unlike many of his peers, he carried the values throughout his public and private life.

His first real job was as a bookkeeper at Clarence Risley's Market in Painted Post, NY. Later, when he was 18, Watson drove a horse and buggy across northern New York State, hawking an unlikely combination of pianos and sewing machines to farmers. As farmers were often short of cash, he took all manner of goods in trade. Animals, farm equipment, and produce were all exchanged and then sold again by Watson. It was invaluable training. It taught him the value of goods and that if he kept his customers happy, more people would buy his goods on recommendation.

Contribution

In 1898, Watson went to work for the National Cash Register Company, known universally as "the cash." NCR was run by John Patterson, an eccentric, charismatic businessman and a remarkable business pioneer, who introduced many enlightened liberal working practices. Watson joined as a salesman. His first few weeks were spent calling on various prospects, without success. His manager, after giving the dispirited Watson a talking to, promised to accompany him and show him how it should be done. He was true to his word; they traveled together, and Watson finally made a number of sales. The attitude of his manager made a great impression on Watson. Later at IBM, he made sure all managers were able to work with their staff and provide them with adequate training.

With his first few sales in the bag, Watson made swift progress. In 1899 he was promoted to manager of the company's Rochester branch and then to general sales manager—Patterson's right-hand man. While at NCR he came up with the slogan that would later become firmly associated with IBM—"THINK!" Not many people know that the motto was originally conceived, and used to good effect, to pep up a dispirited NCR salesforce.

After a number of disagreements with Patterson, Watson was fired from NCR. In 1914 he moved on to the Computing-Tabulating-Recording Company (CTR), an alliance of three small companies, as general manager. When he arrived, CTR was in poor shape. Worse still, as a newcomer brought into shake things up, Watson was resented by the staff who naturally feared for their jobs. But Watson did not fire a single member of staff. Instead he determined to make the existing workforce better at their jobs. This was the foundation of IBM's famous policy of job security. This policy was even adhered to during the great depression. Despite one quarter of the United States labor force being unemployed, IBM carried on expanding, producing excess inventory and stockpiling it, a gamble which ultimately paid off.

At CTR, Watson also took a lead from Patterson's liberal working practices and theories. He didn't have the resources to build a modern, forward-looking factory like NCR's in Dayton, but he did do

> *At IBM, Watson always went out of his way to keep his employees happy. In 1939, he took 10,000 people to IBM Day at the World's Fair, at the company's expense.*

everything in his power to create an enthusiastic atmosphere at the company. This included staging concerts, picnics, and other entertainment, as well as giving rousing speeches. This close and almost paternalistic relationship with his employees led to the "open door" policy, where Watson made himself available in person to see his employees whenever they wished and actively encouraged their visits. This policy was another key element of Watson's management strategy at IBM and only lapsed after his death, when the size of the company made it impracticable.

At IBM, Watson always went out of his way to keep his employees happy. In 1939, he took 10,000 people to IBM Day at the World's Fair, at the company's expense. The sales conventions became increasingly extravagant affairs. Waking delegates were greeted with newspapers recounting the previous day's events, and overseas visitors were provided with headphones through which they heard a translation of the proceedings. A visit by General Eisenhower in July 1948 was extended, after some persuasion by Watson, to allow Eisenhower to address workers at the IBM plant, who were all given time off work to attend.

Watson's obsession with excellent customer service is illustrated by an incident that occurred during World War II. On Good Friday in 1942, an official from the War Production

Board telephoned Watson late in the afternoon. He placed an order for 150 machines and challenged Watson to deliver the equipment to Washington D.C. by the following Monday. Watson agreed. Saturday morning saw him, with his staff, phoning IBM offices across the country to organize the dispatch of 150 machines over the Easter holiday. To emphasize the effort he was making, he instructed his staff to let the War Production Board people know the minute each truck began its journey to Washington, no matter what time of day or night. Police and army officials were rounded up to escort trucks, which were driven through the night. A makeshift factory was also established in Georgetown to deal with the reception and installation of the equipment. It was a remarkable effort, typical of Watson's attitude.

Between 1914 and 1946, IBM's profits grew 38 times, giving great weight to Watson's management strategy. And even though this growth was a magnificent achievement, it was nothing compared to what happened in the postwar period, as IBM grew its revenues from $115 million in 1946 to $1.7 billion by 1961, with employee numbers growing from 17,000 in the United States to 80,000 during the same period. One hundred shares bought in 1914 would have cost $2,740. By 1962, shortly after Watson's death, they were worth $5.45 million.

Much of this was due to the success of a new breed of computer. The Mach 1 was the world's first large-scale computer, built by IBM in collaboration with Dr. Howard Aiken and presented to Harvard University in 1944. This was followed with the first commercially available IBM computer, the 701, in 1952.

Thomas J. Watson, Sr. died on June 19, 1956. A month earlier, he passed over his control in the company to his eldest son, Thomas J. Watson, Jr.

Context and Conclusions

Thomas J. Watson, Sr. achieved great things at IBM. He managed the growth of a small company with a promising technology into a billion-dollar company with a technology that changed the world. The history of computing is not just about the scientists and inventors. It is also about the men who manage creativity and innovation, and who help turn the fantastic dreams of scientists into commercial reality. Watson was one such man. He cajoled, he improved, he inspired. Many of his methods he owed to his inspirational mentor, John Patterson at NCR. Watson took Patterson's ideals forward into the 20th century and, in doing so, created one of America's most enduring companies.

For More Information

Books:

Rodgers, William. *THINK. A Biography of the Watsons and IBM*. New York: Stein and Day, 1969.

Watson, Thomas J., Jr, and Peter Petre. *Father Son & Co. My Life at IBM and Beyond*. Rev. ed. New York: Bantam, 2000.

Jack Welch

1935	Born.
1960	Starts at General Electric.
1961	Almost quits General Electric.
1963	Put in charge of chemical development.
1968	Becomes General Electric's youngest ever general manager.
1981	Becomes C.E.O.
1986	Buys RCA.
1995	Introduces Six Sigma
2000	Postpones retirement to oversee Honeywell Bull deal.
2000	Receives $7 million book advance.
2001	Steps down as C.E.O..
2002	Public criticism of retirement settlement.

Summary

One of the most renowned corporate leaders of the 20th century, Jack Welch maintained General Electric's reputation as a world-beater throughout his 20-year reign as C.E.O. Under Welch the company moved into new business areas and reached new heights.

Jack Welch, named in 1999 as *Fortune*'s "manager of the century," started at General Electric as a trainee in 1960. At the age of 33 he became the youngest general manager in the company's history, and in 1981 became C.E.O. Over a 20-year period he oversaw revolution, reorganization, Six Sigma, tough targets, and a blaze of corporate acquisitions. The results were a 600% increase in profits, 100 consecutive quarters of increased earnings, and a status as one of the most profitable companies in the world. Welch stepped down as C.E.O. in September 2001.

Life and Career

Jack Francis Welch, Jr., one of most celebrated managers and leaders of the 20th century, was born on November 19, 1935 in Peabody, Massachusetts. He grew up in Salem, where his father worked as a railroad conductor. As a boy he suffered from a stutter that might have badly affected his confidence, had it not been for his mother's imaginative explanation. "She told me [it was] just that my brain worked too fast," Welch said.

At school he was a keen sportsman; he also was described by classmates as the "most talkative and noisiest boy" they knew. After high school he set off for the University of Massachusetts, where he studied chemistry. Then came the University of Illinois, where he obtained a Ph.D. in chemical engineering. From there he moved to Pittsfield, Massachusetts, to start his first real job at General Electric.

Contribution

Welch's meteoric career at General Electric (GE) almost didn't happen. In 1961, sick of the cumbersome bureaucratic systems, Welch quit. Fortunately for GE, his boss at the time persuaded him to stay. In 1963 Welch was put in charge of chemical development, and in 1968, aged 33, he became GE's youngest general manager ever. By 1972 he had risen to the

343

position of divisional Vice-President and set his sights on rising even higher. On his employee evaluation form Welch was asked to state his long-term ambitions—to become C.E.O., he wrote. By 1979 he was Vice-Chairman and Executive Officer.

Along the way he built plastics into a formidable $2 billion business, turned around the medical diagnostics business, and began the development of GE Capital. In December 1980 Welch was announced as the new C.E.O. and Chairman of GE, at 45 the youngest chief the company had ever appointed and only the eighth C.E.O. in 92 years.

> *On his employee evaluation form Welch was asked to state his long-term ambitions—to become C.E.O., he wrote. By 1979 he was Vice-Chairman and Executive Officer.*

At the time, GE was in reasonable shape. That year *Fortune* magazine voted it the best-managed company in America, and Reg Jones, the C.E.O. who Welch had replaced, was ranked number one among C.E.O.s. Yet GE's stock was performing poorly. Against the backdrop of a faltering world economy, the Japanese were posing a real threat to U.S. manufacturers with new production systems such as "lean manufacturing."

During the 1980s, recognizing that GE would have to change in order to compete successfully on the world stage, Welch declared that it was going become the world's most valuable company. This meant getting rid of all unprofitable areas. The focus was shifted to service industries, creating over 1000 new businesses, and resulting in the disposal of 70 existing businesses.

But that was only a start. Next Welch turned his attention to the organizational structure. He pared down the organization, devolving power to the individual business units in a massive push for decentralization. An elaborate management hierarchy was tossed onto the scrap heap. "Fight it. Hate it. Kick it. Break it," railed Welch in an antibureaucracy exhortation to the troops.

Nearly 200,000 GE employees left the company and over $6 billion was saved. The media dubbed Welch "Neutron Jack." But by the end of the 1980s, having proved that he could tear the company apart, Welch moved on to stage two: rebuilding a company fit for the 21st century. To encourage innovation and the communication of ideas, he vowed to create what he called a "boundaryless" organization. "Knock down the walls that separate us from each other on the inside and from our key constituents on the outside," was the way he put it. In the pre-Welch era, employees with a good idea would squirrel it away. Now they would be willing to share their ideas and would be encouraged to do so, and the culture would make sure that they received the praise they deserved.

To make sure that all employees were pulling in the same direction, Welch used corporate values as a reference to guide behavior. He famously carried a copy of them printed on a card.

In the mid-1990s, in a drive for quality, Welch adopted the concept of Six Sigma, developed by Motorola in 1985. A statistical term, Six Sigma refers to products with a 99.9998% perfection rate. Implementation relies on rigorous measurement and testing to deliver results. Welch made sure that the adoption of Six Sigma had 100% management backing, and attributed a 3% increase in profit margins between 1995 and 1999 to the roll out of Six Sigma at GE.

A stack of figures attest to the success of Jack Welch's reign: between March 31, 1981 and November 1999, for example, the GE stock price rose from just over $4 to $133 (allowing for four stock splits), an increase of 3,200%. From 1980 onward, the average total return on GE shares was about 27%, and the company has returned 100 consecutive quarters of increased earnings from continuing operations. To put the company's performance in context: if you had bought $10,000 worth of General Electric shares in March 1981 and reinvested the dividends, by the end of 1999 they would have been worth $640,000. Over the same period GE sales rose from $27.2 billion to $173.2 billion, while profits rose from $1.6 billion to $10.7 billion. By 1999 General Electric was the second most profitable company in the world.

The only slight tarnishing of Welch's luster came in 2001. Due to retire, Welch postponed his departure for one last hurrah: a mega deal with Honeywell Bull, snatched from under the noses of intended purchasers, United Technologies. Despite Welch's best efforts, however, this deal was scuppered by European Union regulators. In some ways it was an unfortunate end to a majestic career. Commenting on the affair, Welch was his characteristic self: "GE was a great company before I took a swing at it. It's a great company after. It would have been better if we had gotten it. But as far as regrets for doing it? No way. I'd do the same thing again tomorrow." He finally handed over the baton to his successor, Jeff Immelt, on September 7, 2001. His next job—to promote his autobiography, *Jack: Straight from the Gut.*

Retirement started with promise, a $7 million advance from his publishers, and an extremely generous retirement package, but personal matters changed public attitudes. In 2002, he admitted to an affair with an editor of the *Harvard Business Review* and, during the subsequent divorce proceedings, there was public outrage when the scale of his retirement package was revealed.

Context and Conclusions

The failed Honeywell takeover and the personal revelations dominated press coverage of the end of Welch's rule at GE. The actions of the E.U. regulators briefly blotted out the achievements of an exceptional leader. But the three stages of development under Welch—destruction, creation, and quality—have reshaped GE and made Welch the C.E.O. role model of his generation. Inevitably, he also has his critics. They point to the size of corporate pay packets, GE's ecological record, high levels of layoffs, and the lack of loyalty throughout the organization. But there can be little disagreement that Welch has made a

> *A stack of figures attest to the success of Jack Welch's reign: between March 31, 1981 and November 1999, for example, the GE stock price rose from just over $4 to $133 (allowing for four stock splits), an increase of 3,200%.*

difference where it matters, from the investors' perspective at least. History will remember Welch as one of the most important corporate leaders of the 20th century.

CLOSE BUT NO CIGAR
JOHN MAROUS

Concentrating on investor value worked for Welch, but it didn't work for Marous. A Westinghouse Electrical Company executive man and boy, Marous had been at the company for 40 years before he became C.E.O. in 1988. The similarities between Welch and Marous are many: both excelled at sports, were tough negotiators, and were results-driven in the extreme. "Don't just bring me bad news, bring me solutions," was a Marous motto. Under his leadership, some of Westinghouse's core businesses were sold off and Westinghouse Credit was given a free rein to lend, lend, lend. In 1990, the year Marous stepped down, the stock price was at its highest ever. But from there it was all downhill. After his departure the once great company drowned in the sea of bad debts left by its subsidiary Westinghouse Credit.

For More Information
Books:

Crainer, Stuart. *Business the Jack Welch Way*. New York: AMACOM, 1999.

Slater, Jack. *New GE: How Jack Welch Revived an American Institution* Chicago: Irwin, 1993.

Tichy, Noel M., and Sherman Stratford. *Control Your Destiny or Someone Else Will: How Jack Welch Is Making General Electric the World's Most Competitive Corporation*. New York: Currency Doubleday, 1993.

Welch, Jack, and John A. Byrne. *Jack: Straight from the Gut*. London: HarperCollins, 2001.

Web site:

General Electric: **www.ge.com**

Frederick Weyerhaeuser

1834	Born.
1852	Aged 18, emigrates to the United States.
1856	Starts in the timber industry at Mead, Smith, and Marsh sawmill.
1857	Put in charge of Coal Valley operation.
1858	Mead, Smith, and Marsh is bankrupted.
1860	Buys Mead, Smith, and Marsh sawmill. Renames it Weyerhaeuser & Denkmann.
1871	Forms Mississippi River Logging Company with 17 charter members.
1899	Moves into 266 Summit Avenue, St. Paul, Minneapolis.
1900	Founds the Weyerhaeuser Timber Company and becomes President.
1902	Buys the Everett sawmill for $243,000.
1905	Has amassed 1.5 million acres of timber.
1914	Dies.

Summary

One of the unsung heroes of U.S. economic history, Frederick Weyerhaeuser's story is a classic tale of rags to riches. Born in Germany, he emigrated to the United States at the age of 18 in 1852. Settling in Rock Island, Illinois, he joined a local sawmill and worked his way up. He took advantage of the owner's misfortune, buying the business when his boss went bankrupt. By the 1880s, through a series of astute maneuvers and shrewd investment, he was in charge of several companies involved in the timber industry and owned vast tracts of pine forest. He moved to St. Paul, Minneapolis in 1899 and, over dinner with a neighbor one evening, did a deal to acquire 900,000 acres of railway-owned land for the bargain price of $6 an acre. Founding the Weyerhaeuser Timber Company in 1900 to exploit the land, Weyerhaeuser remained President until his death in 1914, head of the largest timber company in the world.

Life and Career

Frederick Weyerhaeuser was born in 1834 in Niedersaulheim, Rhein Hessen, Germany. Like many other young men of his generation, Weyerhaeuser left Europe for the United States to seek his fortune. He arrived there in 1852, aged 18. He had no money, no skills to speak of and no valuable possessions to sell. All he had were his strength and a willingness to work hard.

Weyerhaeuser's first job was as a laborer in Erie, Pennsylvania. There he met and married his wife Elisabeth. The couple then moved to Rock Island, Illinois, where he worked on the railroad. In 1856, when he was 22, Weyerhaeuser obtained work at the local sawmill, Mead, Smith, and Marsh. It was dirty, difficult work but Weyerhaeuser applied himself assiduously, and impressed the mill owner enough to earn a promotion. He was put in charge of lumber sales. Shortly after, in 1857, he was chosen to head an offshoot operation of Mead, Smith, and Marsh's in Coal Valley, Illinois. It was the start of a lifelong career in the timber industry, in which he would rise from laborer to multi-millionaire.

Later Weyerhaeuser attributed his tremendous success to honest endeavor. "The secret-...lay simply in my readiness to work. I never counted the hours or knocked off until I had finished what I had in mind," he said.

Contribution

In 1858, the Mead, Smith, and Marsh mill went bankrupt. Weyerhaeuser was out of a job. But like all good entrepreneurs, instead of crumbling at the first sight of adversity, he turned a setback into an opportunity. Two years later he bought the sawmill for $3,500 with his brother-in-law, Frederick Denkmann. The new venture was called Weyerhaeuser & Denkmann. Weyerhaeuser went out to build up the business, and Denkmann ran the sawmill. It took all of Weyerhaeuser's capacity for hard work to keep the debt-riddled company going.

"I went around among the farmers, exchanging lumber for horses, oxen, hogs, eggs, anything they had, which I then traded to the raftsmen for logs," Weyerhaeuser said. In at the deep end, he learned his trade quickly. He traveled upriver to meet the rivermen, visited the loggers in their camps and learned how to fell trees and scale logs.

At the time, hardwood was logged from close to the river's banks in the local area, and pine was logged to the north and floated down the Mississippi River. The traditional method for getting the pine downriver was with giant log rafts, crewed by up to 35 rivermen using oars to steer the cumbersome vessels. This all changed when a boatyard owner invented a steamboat specifically designed to tow the logs. The steamboat's first run towed a Weyerhaeuser & Denkmann raft down the Mississippi to the Rock Island sawmill. Sensing a commercial opportunity, in 1871 Weyerhaeuser formed a coalition of sawmill owners under the auspices of the Mississippi River Logging Company. Weyerhaeuser became President. During its busiest time of year, the Mississippi River Logging Company had 75 steamboats towing logs on the upper Mississippi and employed some 1,500 men. Other sawmills were acquired by Weyerhaeuser and, in 1878, he and Denkmann founded the Rock Island Lumber and Manufacturing Co. As business began to flourish, Weyerhaeuser purchased tracts of pine forest in Wisconsin. Through the 1870s and 1880s, he bought over 200,000 acres in Wisconsin from Cornell University.

As the end of the 19th century approached, Weyerhaeuser was in charge of the largest lumbering enterprise in the United States. The business, located in the Midwest, had logged much of the old forest of the Great Lakes region. Weyerhaeuser needed more land and turned his attention to other states; he decided to move. He packed his bags and, leaving his daughter Apollonia in their family house on Rock Island, moved to St. Paul, Minneapolis. It was probably the best decision he ever made.

In 1899, Weyerhaeuser moved into 266 Summit Avenue. Formerly owned by newspaper magnate Frederick Driscoll, the substantial town house, with its marble floors and majestic hardwood staircase, was a measure of Weyerhaeuser's business success. But there was better to come. One of his new neighbors was James J. Hill, a long-time St. Paul resident and President of the Great Northern railway, then in the process of completing the rail link from St. Paul to Seattle. Weyerhaeuser became firm friends with Hill and frequently dined at his house. By 1900, Hill had acquired a controlling interest in the Northern Pacific railway, Great Northern's principal competitor. Along with ownership of the company and all its railroad interests, came the possession of vast swathes of land—originally donated in the 1880s by the federal government for the construction of the transcontinental railroad. The land was portion of the original allocation of 44 million acres, equivalent to 68,750 square miles.

At dinner one evening, Weyerhaeuse inquired how much he would have to pay for the 900,000 acres of Northern Pacific land in Washington. He suggested five dollars an acre, Hill suggested seven, and they settled on six. It was one of the best land deals ever. For $3 million up front and eight payments of $300,000, plus interest, Weyerhaeuser acquired 900,000 acres of prime forestry land. "There is a great lot of it, in every conceivable direction," he said, commenting on the quantity of timber. As part of the deal, he negotiated shipping rates with Hill for transporting the timber that were far below commercial rates.

The deal, speculative as it was, was too big for Weyerhaeuser alone—so he turned to other timbermen for help. It took nearly all the timbermen of the upper Mississippi River to raise the down payment. Together with the other investors, in 1900 Weyerhaeuser founded the Weyerhaeuser Timber Company, with himself as President. In 1902, the company bought the Everett sawmill for $243,000. The renovated mill turned out 50 million feet of lumber a year. By 1905, Weyerhaeuser owned 1.5 million acres of timber. He died in 1914, having built the largest timber company in the world. His son John succeeded him.

Context and Conclusions

Many of the great business leaders in history are people who have invented a product and then exploited it commercially. Frederick Weyerhaeuser belongs to a different class of businessmen, no less great, who exploited natural resources to help build a nation. Through hard work, entrepreneurial endeavor and brilliant management, Weyerhaeuser brought together the rivermen, the loggers, the millers and the other diverse trades involved in the timber industry, and built the biggest timber company in the world. Today, in an environmentally sensitive age, his rapacious plundering of the forests of the United States might raise an outcry. The Weyerhaeuser Company, still trading today and employing over 45,000 people in 17 countries, no doubt takes a more considered approach to its activities in this regard than did its founder. But it should not be forgotten that Frederick Weyerhaeuser was in the engine room, driving a rapidly expanding economy. He was one of the unsung heroes that helped make the United States the economic powerhouse it is today.

CLOSE BUT NO CIGAR
CAPTAIN ROBERT DOLLAR
Lumberman and shipping owner, friend of emperors and Presidents, Captain Robert Dollar rose from his humble Scottish origins to become one of the biggest producers of lumber in the United States in the early 20th century. From cook's boy to international ambassador, Dollar—through his Dollar Steamship Company—laid the foundations for American-Asian import-export.

For More Information

Books:

Hidy, Ralph, et al. *Timber and Men (The Weyerhaeuser Story)*. New York: Macmillan, 1963.

Sensel, Joni. *Traditions Through the Trees: Weyerhaeuser's First 100 Years*. Seattle: Documentary Book Publishers Corporation, 1999.

Oprah Winfrey

1954	Born.
1963	Moves to live with mother.
1972	Wins Miss Black Tennessee pageant.
1976	Moves to Baltimore and lands job with WJZ-TV.
1984	Achieves first major television success with AM Chicago.
1985	Plays Sofia in movie *The Color Purple*.
1986	Goes nationwide with *The Oprah Winfrey Show*.
1987	Wins first daytime Emmy for *The Oprah Winfrey Show*.
1994	Repositions her show as "change your life television."
1996	Establishes book club.
1998	Named second most admired woman in the United States.
1998	Lifetime achievement award at Emmys.
1999	Launches Oxygen cable TV network.
2000	Diversifies into publishing, brings out new magazine called *O*.
2003	First African-American woman billionaire.

Summary

The child of separated parents, the victim of childhood sexual abuse, poverty, and juvenile delinquency, Oprah Winfrey (1954–) overcame a difficult start to become an American icon.

Her career in broadcasting began as a teenager reading the news on the radio. By the age of 30 she had become the talk-show queen of the United States, hosting the nation's number one talk show. In 1988 she became the third woman ever to own her own film studio, Harpo Productions. At a time when talk shows seemed to be descending into the gutter, she pulled them back out again with a move to "change your life" television. Winfrey's future seems assured: she has secured her talk-show contract until 2004, she publishes a number of magazines and produces other television programs, and she's becoming more involved with social issues in the United States.

Life and Career

Oprah Winfrey had a tough start in life. Born to unmarried teenagers on July 29, 1954, she grew up in poverty on her grandmother's farm in Mississippi. The first Winfrey's father knew of her existence was when he received an instruction to send some clothes for her. Brought up initially by her grandmother, at four she moved to Milwaukee to live with her mother. After a brief but happy interlude with her father, Vernon Winfrey, a businessman in Nashville, Tennessee, she again ended up with her mother in Milwaukee in 1963. During her time there she was raped, at the age of nine.

Her mother attempted to send her to a home for juvenile delinquents, but she was unable to wait two weeks for a place to become available. Winfrey was despatched back to live with her father. Had it not been for her father, Winfrey's life might easily have been a tale of loss and waste. Luckily for her, her father was a strict disciplinarian, and with his help Winfrey began to turn her life around.

At 16 she got her first lucky break. As the first African American girl to win a national beauty contest, she was invited on a tour of a local radio station to pick up her prize. Her talent was spotted there and she was asked to read the radio news after school. She had her next big break at 19, landing a job as a reporter for the Nashville radio station WVOL. At the same time she enrolled at Tennessee State University to study performing arts.

When she was initially offered a TV job, she turned it down until one of her professors persuaded her to change her mind. Winfrey became a news anchor on WTVF-TV in Nashville, the first African American to do so. Her star quality was evident from the moment she was put in front of the camera. On television she was a natural. Her personality lit up the screen.

Contribution

In 1976 Winfrey moved to Baltimore, Maryland, and landed herself a job with WJZ-TV as a news coanchor. The management wasn't impressed, criticizing her appearance and eventually demoting her to a morning spot. Luckily a station executive, Phil Baker, offered her an opportunity to cohost a chat show on the station. Reluctant at first, she accepted. It was a risk for the station to put an African American woman on as host of its principal talk show. And it was a risk for Winfrey, who thought her future lay in news. The show was called *People Are Talking*, and viewers were soon talking about Winfrey. They liked her down-to-earth style, and her Nielsen ratings began to rise. In 1984 she moved to Chicago to host WLS TV's morning talk show, *AM Chicago*, going head-to-head with Phil Donahue, America's top-rated talk-show host. Her show ranked number one within a month. Winfrey was just 30 years old.

Winfrey continued in her own inimitable style, being open and honest about her past and her emotions. It struck a chord with her audience. Viewers empathized with her. Her high profile began to pay dividends as she was asked to audition for the part of Sofia in Steven Spielberg's 1985 movie adaptation of Alice Walker's novel, *The Color Purple*. When she received a call telling her Steven Spielberg wanted her in his office in California the next day, she was at a health spa on one of her frequent attempts to lose weight. She was warned that if she lost as much as a pound it might jeopardize her chances of getting the part—she later joked that she stopped off at a Dairy Queen on the way to California. She got the part and was nominated for an Oscar for Best Supporting Actress.

The timing couldn't have been better for Winfrey. She was about to launch her nationally syndicated chat show, *The Oprah Winfrey Show*. It was 1986 and, despite one viewer in Iowa calling in to say he could get better ratings with a potato, Winfrey had hit the big time. Her style remained unaffected, and she soon racked up ten million viewers across the United States.

Astutely Winfrey took control of her own destiny in 1988 by forming Harpo Productions—her name spelled backward—acquiring the rights to her show from Capital Cities/ABC. She also spent $20 million on a production facility in Chicago, a step on the way to becoming only the third woman to own a major studio (following in the footsteps of Mary Pickford and Lucille Ball).

Winfrey's professional life was blooming, but her personal life was plagued by her struggle with her weight. Her repeated and very public attempts to reduce her weight varied from exercise to a radical, four-month-long liquid diet. Eventually she managed to come to terms with herself and her weight, an achievement that helped her self-esteem and her bank balance: her 1994 book *In the Kitchen with Rosie* (Rosie was her chef) became the fastest selling book in the country.

Winfrey's immense success spawned a host of imitators. Talk shows sprang up on every station, delving into the private lives of individuals, exposing the underbelly of human existence. Appealing to the lowest common denominator, such programs can at times seem little more than a license to televise sleaze. In 1994 Winfrey decided to distance herself from the excesses of the genre by repositioning herself in the marketplace. She vowed to concentrate on more uplifting and more highbrow issues, calling her concept "change your life" TV. She has succeeded in both redefining herself and differentiating her show in the talk-show marketplace. The shift of emphasis has secured another series run until 2004. The "Oprah Factor" has also begun to move beyond television in recent years. The appearance of "Oprah's Book Club" on U.S. screens in 1996 had a dramatic effect on book sales in the United States, and any title recommended by Winfrey in the on-air book discussion group went on to massive success.

In 1999, she launched the Oxygen cable TV network. 2000 saw her using her influence to encourage others. She made a series of $100,000 "Use your Life" awards to people who improve the lives of others. Her contribution to broadcasting has not gone unrewarded. In 1998, she was voted second most admired woman in the United States behind Hillary Clinton, followed by a lifetime achievement award at the 1998 Emmys. The material rewards were there too when, in 2003, she became the first African-American woman to become a billionaire

Context and Conclusions

Oprah Winfrey's story is one of triumph over adversity. It offers a message of hope to those from disadvantaged backgrounds: that it is possible to achieve success through talent, hard work, and a little good fortune. Winfrey has become an American icon, an African American woman who has conquered television and found a place in the hearts of the American public. She has succeeded by being herself and today Winfrey is one of the most influential people in the United States. With no sign of Winfrey's star fading, who knows what she will turn her hand to next? A growing interest in social issues suggests that her career could take on a more political direction.

For More Information

Book:

Mair, George. *Oprah Winfrey: The Real Story*. Rev. ed. Secaucus, NJ: Carol Publishing Group, 1998.

Web site:

Oprah©.com: **www.oprah.com**

Robert Winship Woodruff

1889	Born.
1919	Father's syndicate buys Coca-Cola Company.
1923	Becomes President of Coca-Cola.
1926	Creates Coca-Cola's Foreign Department.
1928	Coca-Cola supplies beverages for Amsterdam Olympics.
1930	Foreign Department becomes Coca-Cola Export Corporation.
1933	Automatic Coca-Cola dispensers introduced at Chicago World's Fair.
1939	Steps down as President.
1965	Officially retires.
1985	Dies.

Summary

Robert Woodruff was the natural heir to the Coca-Cola empire. His father was behind the $25 million buyout of the Candler family interests in Coca-Cola in 1919. Yet to begin with his familial advantage did Woodruff no good at all. When he sought a job outside the family's beverage interests, his father attempted to restrict his career at every turn. Woodruff succeeded on his own terms as a sales representative for White Motor Company before bowing to the inevitable and joining Coca-Cola in 1923. For the next four decades until his official retirement in 1965, he ruled the company. He presided over a period of momentous growth that transformed Coca-Cola into a global corporation. By the time of his death in 1985 he had helped create one of the world's most valuable brands.

Life and Career

Woodruff was born on December 6, 1889, in Columbus, Georgia. His father, Ernest Woodruff, was President of the Trust Company of Georgia, which was part of a syndicate that bought control of the Coca-Cola company. Ernest Woodruff became the company's President.

For the first stage of his education Woodruff was sent to the Georgia Military Academy. He proved a poor student. The school may have overlooked his disappointing grades, however, as the young Woodruff saved the academy from bankruptcy. Discovering that the Atlanta National Bank was about to foreclose on the school's mortgage, Woodruff paid a visit to the bank's Vice-President, and through a combination of bluffing and name-dropping he persuaded him to hold off.

Woodruff completed his education at Emory College, where he paid other students to complete his homework. When asked later in life about his tips for a being a successful manager, he replied, "If you can get someone to do something better than you can, it is always a good idea." Despite delegating his college work, he still failed to complete his degree.

Woodruff's working life also got off to an inauspicious start. He was dismissed from a series of jobs for no obvious reason. In fact he was not responsible for his appalling employment record: his father was. Ernest Woodruff had arranged for his son to be fired on each occasion to teach the young man that having a rich father was no guarantee of an easy life. Once, when Woodruff was refused a raise, he discovered that his father was interfering in his career and swore that he would never work for him again.

Instead he went to work as a truck sales representative at White Motor Company, but was swiftly promoted through the company, becoming Vice-President and then general manager.

Contribution

While Woodruff was climbing the corporate ladder at White Motor Company, his father had been putting together an investment group that in 1919 paid $25 million for the Candler family's interest in the Coca-Cola Company. As part of the deal 500,000 shares of Coca-Cola common stock were sold on the stock market for $40 a share. Asked by his father if he wished to participate in the syndicate, Woodruff agreed—picking up a large holding of the company's stock at $5 a share.

In 1923, aged 33, Woodruff achieved a business reconciliation with his father by accepting the presidency of Coca-Cola. He must have wanted the position badly because he took a substantial pay cut and turned down an offer to be President of Standard Oil at a salary of $250,000. Woodruff later said that the reason he took the job was that it was the only way he could boost the value of his stock in the company.

Over the next six decades Woodruff oversaw the transformation of Coca-Cola from a promising U.S. soft-drink manufacturer into a global giant. His influence extended into every aspect of the company's operations and began with changing the company's marketing strategy. Only positive images were to be associated with the product: all negative connotations were banished, and Coca-Cola's medicinal roots were severed.

In production and distribution Woodruff set in motion a drive for quality. In 1928 soda fountains exceeded bottled sales, and Woodruff made sure the employees who serviced the fountains were highly trained and could pass their knowledge on to the storekeepers operating the fountains. A Fountain Training School was established where sales representatives could learn how to mix Coca-Cola properly. Woodruff also introduced a standard procedure manual. At the same time, realizing that the bottled drink was the future of the company, he introduced quality standards in the bottling plants. All employees were to wear uniforms, and hygiene and quality checks were introduced.

While all these changes were an essential part of Coca-Cola's success, Woodruff's most important contribution to the company was probably his move to open up international markets. As early as 1900 the Coca-Cola drink had been taken abroad by Asa Candler—the first international order was from England. Through the early 1900s the company built bottling plants in a number of countries from Cuba to the Philippines. But the expansion was disorganized, with no coordinated management of international product rollout.

In 1926 Woodruff changed that by creating the Foreign Department, which four years later became a full blown subsidiary, the Coca-Cola Export Corporation. Coca-Cola's march to global domination was inexorable under Woodruff. The company cleverly brokered a deal with the Olympics movement, with Coca-Cola being exported to Holland for sale at the 1928 Amsterdam Olympics. Woodruff secured Coca-Cola's beachheads abroad by investing in local economies, building bottling plants, and employing locals for the distribution. In this way the brand acquired goodwill in its export markets.

Although Woodruff resigned as President in 1939 he continued to play an active role in the company. As World War II approached he promised, "We'll see that every man in uniform gets a bottle of Coca-Cola for five cents, wherever he is and whatever it costs our company." The war helped proliferate Coca-Cola throughout the world.

In the postwar period Woodruff's efforts were increasingly concentrated on battling rival Pepsi-Cola. His influence at Coca-Cola persisted right up until and beyond his retirement in 1965. He remained a kingmaker, grooming potential C.E.O.s, including Roberto Goizueta, from behind the scenes. He died on March 7, 1985, aged 95.

Context and Conclusions

Robert Woodruff the private man was an enigma. He was not a cultured man: he didn't read, nor, unlike many other wealthy executives, was he interested in collecting art or antiques. He had a fear of being alone and would often call friends and colleagues to his home in the small hours to keep him company. Yet he was also an intensely private person who installed a private elevator to his office.

Woodruff "the Boss," however, was a different story. The force behind one of the biggest corporate success stories of the last century, he was a restless, driven, controlling figurehead. Unlike many entrepreneurs, Woodruff didn't invent the product his company sold. But he was responsible for aggressively marketing Coca-Cola to a thirsty world—and for taking a caramel-based soda drink and turning it into an American icon. Woodruff's personal creed was, "There is no limit to what a man can do or where he can go if he doesn't mind who gets the credit." Much of the credit for creating one of the world's most enduring products must go to him.

For More Information

Book:

Pendergrast, Mark. *For God, Country, and Coca-Cola: The Definitive History of the Great American Soft Drink and the Company That Makes It*. 2nd ed. New York: Basic Books, 2000.

Web site:

Coca-Cola: **www.cocacola.com**

Frank Winfield Woolworth

1852	Born.
1858	Family move to 108-acre farm near Great Bend, New York.
1873	Woolworth goes to work at Augsbury & Moore's store.
1878	The five-cent table causes a stir in U.S. retailing.
1879	First Woolworth store opens in Utica, New York.
1895	28 stores and revenues of over $1 million.
1905	F. W. Woolworth & Co. incorporated.
1913	Company moves into the tallest skyscraper of its time, in New York City.
1918	In January the 1000th store opens on Fifth Avenue, New York City.
1919	Dies.

Summary

Frank Winfield Woolworth (1852–1919) was a pioneer of the chain store. He came from a humble background, and became one of the richest men in America, despite many early setbacks in his career. Emerging from a small town in New York State, the farmer's boy rolled out his "five and ten cents" concept first across America and then around the world. From a single store in 1879 to a thousand in 1918, the growth of F. W. Woolworth & Co. was phenomenal, changing the nature of retailing and bringing its founder riches and fame. Woolworths was the original price-driven retail chain. The secret of his success he put down to delegating well.

Life and Career

Woolworth was born in Rodman, the eldest son of the family. In late 1858, when Woolworth was seven, the family moved to a 108-acre farm near Great Bend, New York. In a town with a population of only 125, Woolworth's opportunities for education were limited; there was only a one-room schoolhouse, which he attended along with his brother. Much of Woolworth's time, in fact, was taken up helping his father with the family's eight-cow dairy herd rather than studying.

When he was 16 Woolworth attended commercial college for a brief period before offering his services first to the stationmaster's small store, and then to Dan McNeil's general store in Great Bend as a clerk. On both occasions Woolworth worked for free. In return, Dan McNeil recommended Woolworth to William Moore, the owner of a leading dry-goods store in Watertown, New York. In 1873 Moore agreed to take Woolworth on.

At Augsbury & Moore Woolworth started at the bottom of the ladder. He swept floors, created win-

At Augsbury & Moore Woolworth started at the bottom of the ladder. He swept floors, created window displays, delivered goods, and generally made himself useful.

dow displays, delivered goods, and generally made himself useful. The hours were long—six days a week, 7:00 a.m. to 9:00 p.m.—and the pay offered little compensation. The owners initially wanted Woolworth to work for a year with no salary, but after some discussion Woolworth persuaded them to let him work for three months for nothing, rising to $3.50 for the following three months.

Two years later Woolworth moved on to another store, Bushnall's Department Store, as a senior clerk. In 1876 he married Jennie Creighton, a Canadian, and purchased a four-acre farm. Unfortunately, the tough conditions and lack of support at work meant Woolworth suffered from fever and stress-related illness, which forced him to give up his position at Bushnall's and kept him at home for a year unable to work. As he was recovering, his old employer William Moore came knocking at his door requesting him to return to work at the now renamed Moore & Smith's. Woolworth accepted on a salary of $10 a week.

Contribution

In 1878 Woolworth's daughter was born and his mother died. But it was also a year of radical change in the world of retailing. In stores in the Midwest a new tactic had made its debut—the five-cent table. Surplus merchandise was marked down to a nickel by retailers and displayed on a five-cent table. Customers snapped up the bargains and were then drawn into buying other goods at full price. Moore traveled to New York City and came home with $100 worth of five-cent goods for Moore & Smith. Woolworth arranged the counter, and they were sold out in a day.

With goods supplied by Moore, Woolworth opened his own store in Utica, New York, selling only on the five-cent principle. "The Great Five Cent Store" opened for business on a Saturday evening in February 1879 with $321 worth of five-cent goods. The first ever item sold was a fire shovel. However, the store was a failure and soon closed. Undaunted, Woolworth opened another in June of the same year in Lancaster, Pennsylvania. Now he sold goods for five and ten cents. The Lancaster store was a success. In November 1880 he opened a second store in Scranton, Pennsylvania. This too was a success, and Woolworth never looked back.

In 1916 the F. W. Woolworth stores served over 700 million customers and had revenues of over $87 million.

Woolworth brought in family members to help expand his empire. By 1895 he had 28 stores, including that of his ex-boss William Moore, and revenues of over $1 million. The growth continued at break-neck speed. In 1900 there were 35 stores; by 1908, 189; and by 1911, 600. In January 1918 the thousandth store opened on Fifth Avenue in New York City.

Woolworth's one-man retail business had burgeoned into a global enterprise. In 1905, bowing to commercial pressures, he incorporated F. W. Woolworth & Co. issuing 50,000 shares to executives and employees. Corporate offices were first located in the Stewart Building overlooking City Hall Park in New York City. Then, in April 1913, the company moved into the Woolworth Building, the tallest skyscraper of its time. Woolworth's office was situated on the 24th floor. Thirty feet square, its design was based on Napoleon's famous Empire Room and contained the clock and other articles from the original room.

In 1916 the F. W. Woolworth stores served over 700 million customers and had revenues of over $87 million. Every town in the United States with a population of over 8,000 had a Woolworth's.

By the time Woolworth was installed in the Woolworth Building he was approaching the end of his career. With his health failing, he began taking periods of rest in Europe. His wife, Jennie, was suffering from premature senility. Woolworth's own health continued to decline steadily, partly due to a refusal to care for his teeth. On April 4, 1919 he fell desperately ill, dying four days later.

Context and Conclusions

F. W. Woolworth & Co. was the pioneer of price-driven retail. Laying down a tradition of value for money that was later followed by companies such as Wal-Mart, Woolworth was one of the first merchants to build a retail empire founded on chain stores and volume retailing.

Working for very little or no money, enduring long periods of ill-health, and with three out of his first five stores failing, no one would have blamed Woolworth for giving up his business dreams. Instead, his extraordinary persistence saw off all his five-and-ten-cents competitors and made him the most successful retailer of his time.

Woolworth's concept of a business based on bargain goods survived until the 1990s. In 1997, however, the Woolworth corporation announced that it was to close its last 400 F. W. Woolworth five-and-dime stores in the United States, finally retreating from the low-priced general merchandise business that had shaped its identity for 117 years.

What was Woolworth's secret? Delegation apparently: "So long as I was obsessed with the idea that I must attend personally to everything, large-scale success was impossible. A man must select able lieutenants and/or associates and give them power and responsibility."

For More Information
Books:

Baker, Nina Brown. *Nickels and Dimes: The Story of F. W. Woolworth*. New York: Harcourt, Brace & World, 1954.

Nichols, John P. *Skyline Queen and the Merchant Prince: The Woolworth Story*. London: Trident Press, 1973.

Plunkett-Powell, Karen. *Remembering Woolworth's: A Nostalgic History of the World's Most Famous Five-and-Dime*. New York: St. Martin's Press, 1999.

Winkler, John Kennedy. *Five and Ten: The Fabulous Life of F. W. Woolworth*. Freeport, NY: Books for Libraries Press, 1970.

Index

THE
ULTIMATE BUSINESS
LIBRARY

[Essential resources for anyone and everyone in business]

BUSINESS: THE ULTIMATE RESOURCE
Introduction by Daniel Goleman

"The closest we have to a business bible" *(USA Today)*, *Business: The Ultimate Resource* includes over 100 original best-practice essays from the world's leading thinkers and practitioners, over 300 practical checklists, a world almanac, listings of over 3,000 information resources, and much more. **HARDCOVER ISBN 0-7382-0242-8**

BEST PRACTICE
Ideas and Insights from the World's
Foremost Business Thinkers
Introduction by Rosabeth Moss Kanter

Featuring 100 essays and interviews, *Best Practice* captures the state of the art in management thinking and practice today. **PAPERBACK ISBN 0-7382-0822-1**

THE ULTIMATE BUSINESS DICTIONARY
Defining the World of Work

Over 6,000 entries. Features a multi-lingual glossary; abbreviations, acronyms, and business slang; world economic data; listings of international stock exchanges and trade organizations; and worked examples of finance and accounting terms. **PAPERBACK ISBN 0-7382-0821-3**

THE BIG BOOK OF BUSINESS QUOTATIONS
More than 5,000 Indispensable Observations on
Commerce, Work, Finance and Management

A compendium of the most memorable, insightful, and amusing quotes on business, leadership, and the economy. **PAPERBACK ISBN 0-7382-0848-5**

THE BEST BUSINESS BOOKS EVER
The 100 Most Influential Management Books
You'll Never Have Time to Read

From *The Art of War* to *Being Digital*—the 100 books that have shaped management thinking and practice. **PAPERBACK ISBN 0-7382-0849-3**

[AVAILABLE WHEREVER BOOKS ARE SOLD]